# CAMPUS MINISTRY

RESTORING THE NEW TESTAMENT CHURCH ON THE UNIVERSITY CAMPUS

## DOUGLAS A. DICKEY

Copyright © 1994
College Press Publishing Company

Printed and Bound in the
United States of America
All Rights Reserved

Library of Congress Catalog Card Number: 92-75786
International Standard Book Number: 0-89900-686-8

# TABLE OF CONTENTS

# Foreword

Anyone who undertakes the writing of history soon becomes aware of two serious limitations. One is the fact that all history is colored by the subjective preferences of the historian, and the other is the physical impossibility of ever gathering together all the facts.

I make no apologies for the first of these limitations since I agree with Paul Ricoeur who has said, "History is written because of certain subjective interests of the historian."[1] I have been deeply and enthusiastically involved in campus ministry for more than twenty years, and I am unashamedly prejudiced in favor of this exciting ministry. If someone questions this point of view, may I point out that the university, which is the context of campus ministry, is riddled with people who are motivated primarily by other subjective interests — private ambition, "New Age," and secular religions of various types. I am completely willing to enter this arena since I am convinced that campus ministry, and the deeper faith which it represents, that is, that the only ultimate meaning for human existence is found in Jesus Christ as the revelation of God, can more than hold its own.

The second of the limitations all historians face is more frustrating — even embarrassing. Every campus ministry whose history is recorded here has been inadequately and in some cases inaccurately, portrayed. I have tried my best to keep these weaknesses to a minimum, and I deeply regret my failure to eliminate them entirely.

What has amazed me increasingly during the writing of this book is the fact that this story, like the story of the gospel itself, has a way of transcending the inadequacies of any historian and getting itself told.

My deepest thanks to all those who have helped me gather material for the book — students, campus ministers, board members of campus ministries, and especially for the patience of all those who have heard me promise to write this book at every campus minister's retreat for the past ten years! I am also grateful beyond expression to my wife, Marilyn, for the patience she has shown me during the long periods when I was preoccupied with the writing of this book. It is no exaggeration to say that without the skilled typing and computer work of Mrs. Kathi Bonham, Assistant to the Dean at Pacific Christian College, this project would never have been completed. I have given it my best effort, and I pray that God will use it to advance the Kingdom.

## NOTE

1. Quoted by William H. Willamore in *Interpretation: A Biblical Commentary on Acts* (Atlanta: John Knox Press, 1988), p. 7.

# Introduction

"Campus ministry is the best kept secret at this university." These are the words of the manager of a large residential hall at Purdue University in the mid-eighties who, in searching for resources to serve his students outside of regular university channels, discovered campus ministry.

The purpose of this book is to tell the exciting story of thirty-plus years of campus ministry among some of the churches of the Restoration Movement, where it is still "the best kept secret." It is always saddening for those who love this Movement for Christian unity to admit that it is now fragmented into three separate groups. Nomenclature is always a problem for us, so to simplify matters I will be referring to the Christian Church (Disciples of Christ) as the *Disciples*, the "Independent" Christian Churches/Churches of Christ as the *Christian Church* and to the *a cappella* churches as the *Church of Christ*. My experience as a campus minister is almost exclusively among the Christian Churches, and if the campus ministries among other branches of the Movement are neglected, there is no ill intent. Others have told their story elsewhere.[1]

A campus minister with 27 years of experience has recently written, speaking of campus ministry:

> It is a very important story in the history of the church, but one which has not been told often enough or well enough. Campus ministers themselves may not know fully the legacy they have inherited; very few courses in seminaries highlight the church's ministry in higher education. Worse, the contemporary mission of campus ministry is not often described in the persuasive and compelling terms it deserves. If the story is ever going to be told in language which the churches understand and appreciate, now is the time.[2]

## The Strategic Importance of Campus Ministry

It is crucial as we begin to tell this story that we cite several compelling reasons for the vital importance of campus ministry, and why it must be a part of the strategy of the church as it seeks to fulfill its mission to the world in the 21st century.

## 1) The University Has Its Place and Power

Charles Malik, former president of the General Assembly of the United Nations, recently has written, "The university is a clear-cut fulcrum with which to move the world." He goes on to say that the university is a microcosm of our society; it is the most powerful institution in the modern world.[3] This claim may seem exaggerated until one considers how the tentacles of the university reach out into every segment of modern society: education, the media, medicine, law, the arts, politics, business, science and technology, and even the church.

The missionary strategy of the Apostle Paul was clearly to attack the centers of power in the ancient world with the power of the gospel: Athens, Rome, Corinth, Ephesus, and others. We are surely in the sound tradition of the great apostle when we seek to penetrate the university community with the gospel of Christ. In the Restoration Movement, for reasons I intend to suggest later, we have had a very ambivalent, if not adversarial, relationship to the university. We have therefore forfeited an incredible opportunity to bring to bear the influence of the gospel in this crucially important part of the modern world. Campus ministry has been, for thirty years, a significant movement in helping change this situation, as I intend to demonstrate.

## 2) The People Are There

There are more than thirteen million students in the secular colleges and universities of America.[4] Many perceptive critics are saying that there is a growing spiritual hunger among these students and faculty which may portend a modern great spiritual awakening. My twenty years of experience on the college campus leads me, along with many of my fellow campus ministers, to agree with this assessment.[5]

Among the millions attending the universities and colleges, there are thousands of "our" young people, that is, people from Restoration congregations, who chose to go to the university, often for very good reasons, rather than to the Bible or Christian College. Conservatively estimated, for every student who goes to a Christian college from our churches, there are at least *ten* who go to other campuses. This being the case, since there are at this writing 8,377 students in our Bible and Christian Colleges, there are now more than *80,000* young people from our Christian Churches and Churches of Christ on other campuses.[6] (This analysis is in no way meant to be pejorative of our Bible colleges and Christian colleges, but rather to point out an alarming fact with which we must come to terms if we are to be responsible stewards of the lives and faith of our young people.) Until very recently we have left these young people to shift for themselves in the often hostile environment of the college campus — in spite of the considerable investment we have in them through the local church, Bible schools, and Christian service camps, not to mention our personal concerns as parents, preachers, and friends. Therefore, one of the major missions of campus ministry is to minister to these students.

I do not intend to suggest that campus ministry is *only* a salvage operation to save the faith of these students, although it has been that in numerous cases. It is not so much a case of helping a Christian student to save his or her faith, as it is a matter of helping him or her to discover a *genuine* faith for the first time.

Nor is it intended to suggest that the churches have failed to teach these young people. Rather, it is in the nature of the college experience to re-evaluate *all* one's beliefs and relationships, to seek authentic personal identity and make life-changing choices. The Christian faith a young person brings to college is usually an undeveloped faith, carried over from preachers, parents, and peers — a faith that has not been fully "owned" or internalized by the individual.[7] Campus ministry serves as a kind of mid-wife which aids this sometimes painful process of achieving maturity — intellectual, social and spiritual — while the student is in the challenging environment of the university. One of the deep joys of campus ministry is to see this growth take place in the lives of these young adults.

However, as I have suggested, campus ministry is not just a salvage operation; it also challenges Christian students to live among and witness to people who are not like themselves. Donald Shockley says that the experience of "otherness" is one of the most valuable aspects of campus life, particularly for the Christian. He compares this experience to that of the apostle Paul in Corinth:

> Paul's experience in Corinth provides an interesting image for campus ministry. Like the modern campus, the city was an astonishing mixture of people, cultures, ideas and values . . . Paul lived among these people, sharing their weekday world and trying to figure out how to communicate the gospel to folks who did not seem to have the background necessary to understand it and who lived in an environment teeming with alternative ways of thinking and acting . . . the theological vitality of Paul's letters arises from his constant engagement, in very practical ways, with the phenomenon of otherness.[8]

The writer of Proverbs says, "Iron sharpens iron, and one man sharpens another" (27:17, RSV). So, Christians on the university campus can be incredibly strengthened by the experience of "otherness," both as Christians, and as witnesses to the "others." Yes, the people are there, and strong campus ministries must be there with them.

## 3) The Leaders Are There
Most of the people who will be the leaders and decision makers in all

strata of our society in ten to fifteen years are now students at the universities. There is a crisis in leadership in our world, and the kind of strong Christian leaders who are being developed by campus ministry can make a powerful difference in the growth of the Kingdom of God. Ward Patterson, veteran campus minister at Indiana University, has recently published a list of 29 different careers and professions that graduates of the IU campus ministry have entered during the past twenty years, taking their Christian faith with them to leaven the larger world.[9]

It has come as a pleasant surprise to many of us in campus ministry that the ministry is not only producing strong leaders for the world, but is also producing leaders for the specialized ministries in the church. A recent survey discloses that fifteen hundred to two thousand people have moved from campus ministries into the preaching ministry, the mission field, and into other specialized, full-time leadership roles in the church.[10] Here campus ministry is complementing the Bible colleges and Christian colleges which have been the main source of church leaders throughout most of the history of the Restoration Movement.

Every church needs capable, committed ministerial leadership, which our Bible and Christian colleges are producing, but it also needs strong "lay" leadership. No preacher, as I can testify from 30 years of ministering in a local church, can possibly do the job without strong "lay" persons to strengthen the Body of Christ with their manifold gifts. Campus ministry has been the source of thousands of such leaders during its relatively brief history.

When we are talking about leaders on the campus, we must mention the international students, thousands of whom are in our universities and colleges in America. Many of them are leaders in their own countries. They have brought the "foreign mission field" to us, and they are, in many cases, uncommonly curious and open-minded about Christianity. They also are being evangelized in large numbers, and many of them will take the gospel with them to countries where missionaries are not able to go.

*THE LEADERS ARE THERE, AND CAMPUS MINISTRY MUST BE THERE TO RECRUIT AND TRAIN THEM!*

## 4) Campus Ministry Provides a Caring Community

University students are surrounded by a non-caring community. It is a terrible irony that in the modern university students have come to be seen by faculty as a liability to the purpose of the institution. A dear friend of mine at Purdue University was awarded the "Teacher of the Year" award for several successive years. His Dean called him on the carpet for "spending too much time with students," and informed him that if he didn't begin to publish more scholarly papers and do more research, he would be denied academic tenure. Robert S. Clark, active campus minister at the University of Minnesota, in his recently completed thesis on campus ministry, writes:

> In the typical research university students are perceived as an obstacle inherent within the structure. In fact, professors confess that some of their peers often quip that "students are to the university as pigeons are to the cathedral." This type of attitude is bound to be at least non-verbally communicated to students. They are merely a necessary inconvenience to the greater mission of research and development.[11]

If I were asked, "What is the greatest value of campus ministry?" I would unhesitatingly reply, as I often have during my twenty years as a campus minister; "To provide a caring community." This, more than anything else, has made campus ministry such a life-changing force on the university campus for more than thirty years. My fellow campus ministers agree, as I show below.

## My Qualifications and Point of View

Allow me to suggest some of my qualifications for writing this book. I spent twenty-eight years as the minister of a local congregation in Indiana, going there directly out of college. In 1966, at the height of the student revolts and the counter-culture movement on the campuses, I began a full-time campus ministry at Purdue University in Indiana. I was there for sixteen years, and then moved to Southern California where I worked in a campus ministry at two state universities for another four years.

I love the church, and I love campus ministry, and in no way do I see them as incompatible. Although campus ministry does not take the same shape or use the same methods as the local church, it has proven both its desire and its ability to strengthen the church in many ways, as outlined above. It has been my privilege to have been intimately involved for twenty years of the thirty-year growth of campus ministry among our churches, on both the local and national level, and I am eager to tell the story.

## The Plan of This Book

Now for a word about this book . . . in the first two chapters I intend to sketch briefly the educational background of campus ministry. In chapter one, after a summary of the rise of the university from Plat's Academy through Medieval University, we will look at the Colonial Colleges in America, followed by the rise of state-supported universities after the Morrill Land Grant Act of 1862. This chapter will conclude with a closer look at the modern secular university, some of its strengths and weaknesses, and some suggestions as to how campus ministry can minister in that setting.

Chapter two will consider the colleges of the Restoration Movement, beginning with Alexander Campbell's Bethany College. I will suggest that there were "two roads from Bethany." One road was taken by the colleges which continued Campbell's emphasis on the importance of *liberal arts*. The other road was that taken by the colleges which followed Campbell in his insistence on the *Bible* as the center of education. This chapter will close with the claim that campus ministry is an excellent way to heal this breach and to pull these two "roads" back together.

Chapter three will trace early student movements in the history of the church in general, and will acknowledge the pioneering movement toward the universities taken by the Disciples in their unique "Bible Chair" Movement. The chapter will conclude with a review of the early campus ministries among Christian churches before 1960, beginning with the vigorous college ministry begun in 1923 by W. R. Walker and the Indianola Church in Columbus, Ohio.

Chapter four will cover, in some detail, the exciting story of the "explosion" of campus ministries that took place among Christian churches in the decade of the 60s, ironically enough during the very period when there was so much turbulence and unrest on the university campuses across the nation.

Chapters five, six, and seven will detail the founding of twenty-one campus ministries in fifteen states and on forty-two campuses during the decade of the 70s.

Chapter eight will chronicle the continued spread of campus ministries among Christian churches during the 80s and 90s on twenty-three campuses as well as three specialized ministries to college-career people.

Chapter nine will review in summary the history of more than thirty years of campus ministry among Christian churches and will raise some cogent questions about the future of campus ministries. Donald Shockley's words express my feelings exactly:

> In the hope that it is never too late, I am eager now to talk about my life in campus ministry, to be an interpreter and advocate of the work to which I have devoted so much of my life. I am motivated to write by concern for the welfare of the church as a whole and not merely for that part of it which is closest to me. Based upon what I see and hear as I move among students and faculty today, I have high hopes for the mission and ministry of the church tomorrow. That, above all else, is what moves me to write.[12]

# NOTES

1. Campus ministry among the Disciples has been given excellent coverage by Thomas R. McCormick, *Campus Ministry in the Coming Age* (St. Louis: CPB Press, 1987). Rick Rowland, Professor at Pepperdine University, has done a careful and comprehensive job of telling the story of campus ministry among the Churches of Christ in *Campus Ministries: A Historical Study of Churches of Christ Campus Ministries and Selected College Ministries from 1706 to 1990* (Ft. Worth: Star Bible Publishers, 1991).

2. Donald G. Shockley, *Campus Ministry: The Church Beyond Itself* (Louisville: The Westminster/John Knox Press, 1989), p. 2. I will be referring to this excellent book often. Shockley writes lucidly and persuasively out of his twenty-five year experience as a campus minister.

3. Charles Habib Malik, *A Christian Critique of the University* (Downers Grove, IL: InterVarsity Press, 1982), p. 20. Malik writes: "The universities, then, directly and indirectly, dominate the world; their influence is so pervasive and total that whatever problem afflicts them is bound to have far reaching repercussions throughout the entire fabric of Western civilization. No task is more crucial and urgent today than to examine the state of mind and spirit in the Western university."

4. Shockley, *Campus Ministry*, p. 52. A word about my use of the word "secular." I do not at all mean to use this word in a derogatory sense, nor do I want to suggest that a secular university or society is wholly "Godless." It is my conviction that there are "pockets" of faith and belief where God is at work in even the most secular society or university. I agree with Donald Shockley when he writes: "The world of higher education today represents a frontier which both intrigues and intimidates the church. It is in many respects a microcosm of the world, and as such, it is a rich smorgasbord of belief, unbelief, and indifference. But the church makes a serious mistake when it sees the campus as alien territory, a land by nature hostile to its presence."

5. See *The Coming Great Awakening* by David L. McKenna (Downers Grove, IL: InterVarsity Press, 1990), in which he claims the college campus is the probable locale of a coming great spiritual awakening. See also "The University Campus is White for Harvest" by Rich Nischan in *Christian Standard*, August 24, 1986, pp. 1-5.

6. *Christian Standard*, 1993-1994 College Issue, February 20, 1994.

7. John Scazoni wrote an article entitled "No Faith to Lose" in *Eternity*, December 1965, pp. 19-21. He claims that many college students, in spite of the best effort of their home churches, enter college with "no faith to lose" because of the superficiality of their participation in their home churches.

8. Shockley, *Campus Ministry*, pp. 54-55.

9. Letter to author from Ward Patterson, campus minister, Indiana University.

10. Source: Several questionnaires completed by full-time campus ministers between 1985 and 1994.

11. Robert Stanley Clark, M.A.R. Thesis, Emmanuel School of Religion, 1990, pp. 61-62.

12. Shockley, *Campus Ministry*, p. 7.

# CHAPTER ONE

# The Rise of the University

In order to understand the modern university — the theater in which campus ministry takes place — it is necessary to understand the forces which have combined to create it.

Christianity, by its very nature, has had a profound stake in education from the beginning. Not only did Jesus teach and Paul instruct, but the spread of the church itself was an educational process, informing men and women of the nature of God's world and their place within it. One historian said:

> Since the earliest encounter with the Greco-Roman civilization, Christianity found twin enemies in illiteracy and ignorance; it was a religion serving an intelligent deity in an intelligible world and on the basis of an intellectual revelation.[1]

Conversely, education has been heavily dependent upon Christianity throughout history. The university arose out of the Christian faith, and continued dependent upon it until the 18th century Enlightenment which finally cut the ties, resulting in the complete secularization of higher education which we now face. Campus ministry is interested in healing this breach, and has demonstrated its ability to do so, in limited but specific ways.[2]

## The Greek Roots

Although the main forces which created the modern university were Christian, it must also be admitted that there were Greek influences at work as well. The only schools available to the early Christians were the grammar and rhetoric schools of the Greco-Roman, non-Christian culture, which had their roots in Plato's Academy and the Lyceum of Aristotle.[3] The early church Fathers, particularly Origin and Clement of Alexandria, argued vigorously that Christianity is the culmination of Greek philosophy. They, for example, set up catechetical schools at Alexandria to teach young Christians, and to train them in relating to Greek philosophy and the pagan world. Thus, early Christian education was influenced by Greek thought, and this influence remains as a part of the modern university in various ways.

# The Monastic Schools

During the "Dark Ages," the years between AD 500 and 950, when barbarian invaders dominated the life of Europe, ". . . the only schools were the ones maintained in the monasteries, those islands of orderly living in a time when civilization was at a low ebb."[4] These monastic schools were a forerunner of the university in a more profound and lasting way than most of us realize. Kenneth Scott Latourette, a renowned church historian, says of this period:

> To the northern peoples who had invaded Western Europe and to whom the world about them had neither order nor meaning, the Christian faith brought the conception of a universe created by One whose august purpose is shot through and through with love and who governs the world by uniform law. . . . History, so Christianity teaches, is not sound and fury, signifying nothing, as the barbarians had believed, nor is it a weary repetition of cycles as the Greeks had regarded it. It had a beginning in the creative act of God and moves towards a culmination determined by Him. It is not strange, therefore, that the beginnings of the science and machines of Western Europe are found in this period and among those whose spirits and minds had been gripped by the Christian faith. . . . Whether or not this is true, it was to those who were moved by the Christian faith that the beginnings of the scientific outlook and method in Western Europe must be traced.[5]

# The Cathedral Schools

The next period in the rise of the university began about AD 950 when order began to appear in Western Europe after centuries of invasion and cultural decay. Communities of scholars began to form around the cathedrals, many of them organized by bishops. They were an expansion of the renewed interest in intellectual pursuits, especially theology, which had become "the queen of sciences."[6] Out of these schools in the 12th and 13th centuries arose the universities. Among many of these were the University of Oxford, England and the University of Paris, France. At first these schools were primarily for the education of clergy. Most of the great names in Medieval theology were associated with these universities: Anselm, Abelard, Peter Lombard and, especially, Thomas Aquinas.

Thomas Aquinas provides a particularly dramatic illustration not only of the intimate relationship between theology and the universities of this period, but also of a kind of medieval "campus ministry." The Crusades had introduced Aristotle's Metaphysics to Western Europe. Muslim philosophers had used their interpretation of Aristotle to insist that reason and philosophy should be free from any constraints imposed by faith and theology. Returning Crusaders brought this brand of Aristotelianism home with them, and it created a crisis in the universities by setting up a conflict between faith and reason. Between those who rejected this "destructive philosophy" outright, and those who embraced it enthusiastically, Thomas Aquinas "explored the possibilities that the new philosophy offered for a better understanding of the Christian faith."[7]

Thomas Aquinas left the Abbey of Monte Cassino, where he had been placed by his parents at five years of age, to become a Dominican monk at the age of 20. As a Dominican he studied under his teacher, Albert Magnus, who made him aware of the problem created by the Aristotelianism in the universities. He went to the University of Paris in 1252 and spent the rest of his life teaching and working to reconcile Christian theology and Aristotelian thought. One church historian has said, "Thomas' significance is . . . in his ability to turn a philosophy that many considered a threat into an instrument in the hands of faith."[8] Here is an inspiring example, not only of the power of Christian faith to overcome strong intellectual opposition, but also a kind of Medieval prototype of "campus ministry" meeting the challenge of the university head on.

## The Renaissance and the Universities

The next critical juncture in the rise of the university came with the Renaissance in the late 13th and early 14th centuries. The shift in interest from theology to humanity has been described as follows:

> Toward the end of the Middle Ages there was a renewed interest in those studies that stressed the importance of man, his faculties, affairs, worldly aspirations and well-being. The primacy of theology and other worldliness was over; reducing everything to theological argument was rejected, since it no longer expressed the reality of the new situation.

The "new situation" had begun when secular studies were introduced into the cathedral schools in the middle of the 12th century. Non-theological subjects such as grammar, rhetoric, logic, navigation, agriculture and medicine, or, in our terms, liberal arts and sciences came into the universities. By the time of the Renaissance, this trickle of humanism raged into a flood. There was a radical shift in the perception of reality on the part of scholars and people in general. From long centuries of preoccupation with God and heaven, a passionate interest arose in man and nature. This highly significant intellectual and cultural transition is most graphically illustrated in Renaissance art.

> Therefore art, until recently devoted almost exclusively to religious instruction and to the glory of God turned its attention to human splendor. . . . The Adam that Michelangelo painted in the Sistine Chapel, receiving God's finger the power to rule over creation, is very different from the frail Adam of Medieval manuscripts. He embodies the Renaissance view of what it means to be fully human, born to create, to leave one's imprint on the world.[9]

This is a crucial move in terms of the rise of the university, as well as the rise of the Western culture in general. It is difficult, from our perspective, to fault this move toward the secular. After Thomas Aquinas, there had been an increasing preoccupation in the universities with theological minutia and irrelevant doctrinal trivia. The universities also were coming under increasingly oppressive ecclesiastical authority. The Renaissance freed them from these threats and brought a healthy "new birth" to Western Europe, and, eventually, to all of the Western world. However, the Renaissance also marks the beginning of a tide of secularism and humanism which, considering the turn it took, had its down side as well, for both the university and the culture in general.

## The Reformation and the Universities

Another factor which pushed the universities toward secularism and humanism, ironically enough, was the Protestant Reformation. Two strains came together in the Reformation: the humanism which had arisen in the late Middle Ages, and the need of the Reformers to educate people so they could read the Bible. Luther was much concerned about improved education, both for children and adults. This interest of Luther influenced the spread of schools in Germany, and eventually throughout Europe.

The humanistic element in the Reformation was represented by Erasmus, a one time respected friend and colleague of Luther. It was Erasmus' desire to emphasize the humanistic element of the Reformation that caused Luther to turn away from him.

The Reformation, along with the Renaissance, also freed the universities from increasing ecclesiastical control, and opened them up to the fresh breezes that were beginning to blow through all of Europe.

## The Enlightenment and the Universities

By far the most decisive of all movements that prepared the way for the modern university, and the whole Western culture of which it is a microcosm, was the 18th century Enlightenment. Lesslie Newbigin says that Enlightenment is a "conversion word," not of individual experience as in Buddhism, but of whole cultures. "If we want to grasp the essential element in what we call modern Western Culture the best place to begin is with the exhilarating feeling that light has come into the world and banished darkness . . . ."[10]

The radical paradigm shift in human consciousness which began in the Renaissance became all-pervasive in Western Europe by the middle of the 18th century. Two main streams of thought converged in Enlightenment thinking — the empirical and the rational.

The rise of science, which Diogenes Allen says was more significant than the Renaissance and the Reformation combined in shaping modern thought,[11] reached a crescendo during the Enlightenment. Copernicus (1473-1543) had, through his pioneering work in astronomy, removed the earth from the center of the solar system, thereby creating what Pascal called "cosmic intimidation" in the human psyche. Francis Bacon (1561-1626) introduced the inductive, empirical study of nature against the deductive generalizations and dogma of Medieval thought. Bacon demanded that the schools be scientific workplaces in the service of life and that they should put the exact sciences before logic and rhetoric. Huston Smith says that Bacon was motivated by more than the desire to find a more practical way of knowing; he was also eager to find power over nature.[12] (Here is the beginning of the scientific and technological power which has been so immensely successful, and so potentially destructive, in our modern world — these words are being written on the 47th anniversary of the atomic bombing of Hiroshima — and this power comes out of universities!)

Isaac Newton gave us a mechanistic, impersonal and purposeless universe of cause and effect with no place for or need of God, (although Newton himself was a Christian and an accomplished Bible scholar of his day.)

Empiricism, then, the scientific method in which reality is conceived of as "nothing but" naturalistic elements, is one of the major contributions of the Enlightenment to the modern university and Western culture.

There is, as well, a rationalistic element in Enlightenment thinking. E.F. Schumacher reminds us that Descartes (1596-1650), the father of modern rationalism, made his contribution to the Enlightenment by insisting that reality must be reduced to "knowledge and ideas that are precise and certain beyond any possibility of doubt because his primary interest is that we should become 'masters and possessors of nature.'"[13] Lesslie Newbigin summarizes the effects of Enlightenment as follows:

The thinkers of the Enlightenment spoke of their age as the age of reason, and by reason they meant essentially those analytical and mathematical powers by which human beings could attain (at least in principle) to a complete understanding of, and thus a full mastery of nature — of reality in all its forms. Reason, so understood, is sovereign in this enterprise. It cannot bow before any authority other than what it calls the facts. No alleged divine revelation, no tradition however ancient, and no dogma however hallowed has the right to veto its exercise.[14]

Newbigin's incisive description is precisely that of the modern university.

# The Colonial Colleges

The various elements which constituted the Enlightenment were slow in coming together and its influence was not immediately felt in all areas of Western Culture. One notable example of a continuing strong relationship between Christianity and education is in the colleges in the New World. Eight colleges were established in the Colonies before 1776. They were Harvard College in 1636; College of William and Mary in 1693; Yale in 1701; Princeton in 1754; University of Pennsylvania in 1753; Brown in 1765; Rutgers in 1766; and Dartmouth in 1769. The prime motive for the founding of each of these colleges was to educate ministers for the various Protestant denominations that settled Colonies.[15]

One leading historian of Colonial America has said that these colleges do not represent "A disinterested dedication to the pursuit of learning in the abstract," but were founded to defend and disseminate the Christian faith as understood by each of their different Protestant viewpoints.[16] For example, the motto on the Harvard seal, which is displayed in all its schools and departments to this day, is *Christo et Ecclesiae* (For Christ and for the Church) surrounding the word *Veritas* (Truth). In 1754, the president of Yale said that "Colleges are societies of ministers, for training up of persons for the work of the ministry. . . . The great design of founding this school was the educate ministers in our *own* way."[17]

There are three major influences which brought about the change from the Christian (Protestant) orientation of these schools at their founding in America to their present state of complete secularization. The first is the general decline in Christianity in the Colonies after the Revolutionary War. Lyman Beecher, a student at Yale College during these years, speaks of the "ungodliness, skepticism, rowdyism, intemperance, profanity and licentiousness among the student body." By 1799 there were left only a handful of ministerial students in all of these colleges and very few in the entire student bodies who claimed to be Christian.[18]

The second cause of decline was the influence of the Enlightenment which finally reached the Colleges in the New World. This process has been described by one historian as follows:

> By 1700 Harvard, swayed by the breezes of Europe's Enlightenment, ventured some earnest renovations. Its texts, cobwebbed with Aristotelianism, were replaced with newer ones by Locke and Newton. In 1718 it added mathematics and science to its offerings, and 20 years later it enriched itself with a professorship of mathematics and natural philosophy.

The third cause of the transformation of education in America to secularization was the rise of the state-supported universities.

## The Rise of the State-Supported Universities

Thomas Jefferson, strongly influenced by John Locke and the Enlightenment, founded the University of Virginia in 1819, an institution which has been characterized as, "The first frankly secular university in America and closest to the modern day conception of a state university."

There is a fascinating sidelight here, of special interest to campus ministers. Jefferson, himself a Deist who had re-written the New Testament to eliminate all reference to the supernatural, nevertheless proposed the establishment of religious schools "on the confines of the University, so as to give their students ready and convenient access and attendance on the scientific lectures of the University . . . always understanding that these schools shall be independent of the University and each other."[19] His stated reasons for making this proposal were to make up for the omission of a chair of divinity at the University, and because:

> The relations which exist between man and his Maker, and the duties resulting from these relations, are the most interesting and important to every human being, and the most incumbent on his study and investigation. The want of instruction in the various creeds of religious faith existing among our citizens presents, therefore, a chasm in a general institution of the useful sciences.[20]

The tragedy here is that the churches to whom Jefferson made this offer were so jealous and suspicious of each other that they never accepted the challenge! It is saddening to realize that Thomas Jefferson, Deist and strong advocate of the separation of church and state, had a clearer vision of the need for religious and moral influence in the university than did the clergy of his day![21]

Jefferson was ahead of his time with his concept of state-supported universities. The Colonial Colleges had been partially supported by the Colonies and later the states until the Supreme Court ruled in 1819 that Dartmouth College was a *private* institution and was therefore not eligible to receive state funds.[22]

In 1862 the Morrill Land Grant Act provided federal support in the form of land and money to the individual states for the establishment of public institutions of education. Shockley says, "This was a major turning point for American higher education since it not only provided federal government support of the universities, but also established a trend toward the equality of practical studies with the liberal arts."[23]

The church colleges reacted to the spread of these public institutions in two different ways. Some of them saw the need for campus ministries of some kind, and moved to establish them, as we shall see. However others, perhaps the majority, saw them as "godless universities" and rejected all relationships with them.

> This claim was based not only on the fact religion was not taught, but because the classical form of education was now being replaced by a practical, vocational, and technical style of education. It was difficult for church leaders to conceive of how this idea of education could nurture the moral character and spiritual nature of students.[24]

This attitude was wrong on two counts. The universities were not then, and are not now, as "godless" as some believed them to be. Thomas R. McCormick says: "In actuality, the pagan nature of the universities was exaggerated by critics. Many of the faculty were churchmen, and many of the students were church members as well."[25] The churches also erred in that they failed to see that the conditions they feared were precisely the conditions which created, not only the opportunity for, but the crucial need for campus ministry.

## Strengths and Weaknesses of the Secular University

The long path we have followed here has led us from Plato's Academy to the massive tax-supported universities which, along with great private institutions like Harvard, now dominate higher education in America and the world.[26]

There are some unquestioned positive aspects to the universities. They have made higher education more widely available to all economic classes than ever before in world history. (Unfortunately, rapidly rising tuition costs are now changing this situation.) Science and technology which are the very heart of the university have brought innumerable benefits and have enriched the quality of life in the modern world. The doctrine of the separation of church and state has freed education from authoritative and oppressive ecclesiastical control.

There is, however, a *secular* dogmatism which has replaced *ecclesiastical* dogmatism in higher education. Science, which was made possible by a biblical worldview which presupposes the reality of matter and the orderliness and basic goodness of the universe,[27] has now become *scientism* which is as rigidly dogmatic as theology ever was. A recent editorial in *The New York Times* agrees with this judgment:

> In a new book, *Killing the Spirit*, the historian Page Smith assails the smothering domination of an "academic fundamentalism" that regards scientific rationalism as the sole means to knowledge. Mr. Smith, the founding provost of the University of Santa Cruz, argues that this fundamentalism has distorted values and killed the humanistic spirit that ought to animate education.[28]

A dangerous corollary to this dogmatism, as Huston Smith suggests, is a loss of moral values in the university. Naturalistic presuppositions which see all reality as "nothing but" matter in motion (the core of the modern university's worldview) eliminates, not only moral values, but all purposes, qualities, meanings, and love.[29]

In fact, not only is there no moral center to the university, but there is no center whatsoever. For years, knowledgeable critics have pointed out that the university has become a "multiversity," that is, a loose collection of separate, autonomous disciplines with no central, unifying set of values. Once critic says: "The vast intellectual and moral chaos of our time has been brought about largely by the transformation of the university into a cafeteria or a smorgasbord, a "multiversity."[30]

Alexander Campbell, in founding Bethany College, insisted that the essential ingredient in a college is a core of moral integrity, in both the individuals and in the institution.[31] Modern support for Campbell's view comes from a surprising source. Norman Lear, producer of controversial television shows like *All in the Family*, and a man who has been accused of being an immoral influence on society through his work, spoke in July 1990 to the National Education Association meeting in Kansas City. There were 8,000 educators in the audience. A brief quote will indicate the major theses of Mr. Lear's speech to that group: "In addition to instilling knowledge, public education must feed the heart and soul . . . . Teachers in the classroom must start teaching about values, morals, and the role religion has played in the American society." His thirty-five minute speech was interrupted by applause eighteen times, and with two standing ovations.[32]

The current cry for "politically correct" thinking, and the emphasis on the need for cultural, racial, and sexual diversity in the universities is an attempt to bring some values, radical and secular though they may be, into an essentially fragmented and confused institution.[33] What William Butler Yeats said in his poem, "The Second Coming" about the modern world, "Things fall apart, the centre cannot hold; Mere anarchy is loosed upon the world . . ." may be said with equal conviction about the modern university.[34]

It is perhaps too large a claim to suggest that campus ministry can help to bring some cohesive meaning into the university, but for more than thirty years this ministry has brought the healing of the gospel to literally thousands of students caught in a maddening maelstrom. Perhaps it is not too much to hope that campus ministry may at least provide a platform from which a healing process may be brought to the university as a whole.

## NOTES

1. William A. Clebsch, *From Sacred to Profane in America: The Role of Religion in American History.* (New York: Harper & Row, 1968), p. 105.

2. Not all campus ministers would agree that this is the goal of campus ministry. Charles Malik says that it is not enough to evangelize and nurture individual students and faculty members. He says the university itself must be radically brought under the Lordship of Christ. I agree. Malik, *A Christian Critique*, pp. 101-102.

3. Malik, *A Christian Critique*, p. 15.

4. Kenneth Scott Latourette, *A History of Christianity.* (New York: Harper & Brothers, 1953), p. 552.

5. *Ibid.*, pp. 552-553.

6. *Ibid.*, p. 495.

7. Justo L. Gonzales, *The Story of Christianity. Vol. 1.* (San Francisco: Harper & Row, 1984), p. 316.

8. *Ibid.*, pp. 316-318.

9. *Ibid.*, pp. 368-369. Another Renaissance giant who embodies this same transition is of course, Leonardo da Vinci.

10. Lesslie Newbigin, *Foolishness to the Greeks: The Gospel and Western Cultures.* (Grand Rapids: Eerdmans, 1986), p. 23.

11. Diogenes Allen, *Christian Belief in a Postmodern World.* (Louisville: Westminster/John Knox Press, 1989), p. 23.

12. Huston Smith, *Beyond the Post-Modern Mind.* (New York: Crossroads, 1982), p. 102. Famous quotes attributed to Bacon are: "Knowledge is power" and "We must put nature to the rack."

13. E.F. Schumacher, *A Guide to the Perplexed.* (New York: Harper & Row, 1977), p. 9.

14. Newbigin, *Foolishness to the Greeks*, p. 25.

15. Gary Weedman, *Higher Education and the Restoration Movement.* (Lincoln, IL: Lincoln Christian College Press, 1983), p. 3.

16. *Ibid.*, p. 3.

17. *Ibid.*, p. 4. Also Malik, *A Christian Critique*, p. 357.

18. Weedman, *Higher Education*, p. 5.

19. Richard Butler, *God on the Secular Campus*. (Garden City, NY: Doubleday & Company, 1963), pp. 21-22. Butler's quotations from Jefferson are from *Notes on the University of Virginia*. October 7, 1822, p. 957.

20. *Ibid.*, pp. 21-22.

21. *Ibid.*, p. 27.

22. Weedman, *Higher Education*, p. 5.

23. Shockley, *Campus Ministry*, p. 32.

24. Thomas R. McCormick, *Campus Ministry in the Coming Age*. (St. Louis: CPB Press, 1987), p. 4. Also Clebesch, *From Sacred to Profane*, p. 115.

25. *Ibid.*, p. 5.

26. Malik, *A Christian Critique*, p. 16.

27. Allen, *Christian Belief*, p. 23 ff.

28. "Education" Section of the *New York Times*. September 12, 1990.

29. Huston Smith, *Beyond the Post-Modern Mind*, pp. 66-68.

30. Michael D. Aeschliman, *The Restitution of Man: C.S. Lewis and the Case Against Scientism*. (Grand Rapids: Eerdmans, 1983), p. 35.

31. Campbell says: "On the subject of moral culture, it is uniformly agreed, among all persons of superior or even common education, that, without it, more intellectual improvement but furnishes the individual with means and facilities not only of being more eminently wicked, but more extensively mischievous to society." Essay on "Education" in the *Millennial Harbinger*. (1837), p. 258.

32. From an article by Knofel Staton in "Christian Colleges — Which Kind?" *Christian Standard*. June 30, 1991, p. 9.

33. See cover story in *Newsweek*. December 24, 1990. Also an editorial by George Will "Curdled Politics on Campus," *Newsweek*. May 6, 1991, p. 72. and "Illiberal Education" by Dineah D'Souza in *The Atlantic Monthly*. March 1991, pp. 51-79. Also see "The Danger of Being Politically Correct" by Gerald C. Tiffin, *Christian Standard*, May 16, 1993, pp. 10-11.

34. *Selected Poems and Two Plays of William Butler Yeats*. Ed. M.L. Rosenthal, (MacMillan Paperbacks, 1962), p. 91.

# CHAPTER TWO

# Alexander Campbell
# and Bethany College

Having traced the rise of the university in order to point out the need for campus ministry, we now need to look at the origin and nature of colleges of the Restoration Movement as part of the background for campus ministry.

The key to these colleges is the prophetic educational vision of Alexander Campbell as embodied in Bethany College. Campbell insisted that a college must combine the liberal arts and sciences with the centrality of the Bible in its curriculum. He wrote:

> Bethany College is the only college known to us in the civilized world, founded upon the Bible. It is not a theological school, founded upon human theology, nor a school of divinity founded upon the Bible, but a literary and scientific institution, founded upon the Bible as the basis of all true science and true learning.[1]

## Alexander Campbell's Philosophy of Education

People who are familiar with the Restoration Movement know quite well that Alexander Campbell insisted that the Bible must be the foundation of the curriculum in Bethany College, which he founded at Bethany, Virginia, in 1841. Not so well-known is Campbell's insistence upon the necessity of the liberal arts and sciences as *equally* crucial to the curriculum. He held this conviction with great tenacity. Perry Epler Gresham, one-time President of Bethany College, has said of him, "He was critical of his contemporaries in church colleges who claimed to teach 'sacred knowledge'. He defended the scientific and literary studies as part of man's intellectual love of God."[2] We can trace some of the early influences on Campbell which led him to take this position.

Alexander Campbell was born in Ireland in 1788. Until he left for the new world at the age of nineteen, the bulk of his schooling was under the direction of his father, Thomas Campbell. "My father, though I say it, was the best educator of young men I ever knew. He caused me, when a boy, to memorize largely many selected passages from the most celebrated English poets, amongst whom were Milton, Young, Cowper and

Shakespeare. . . ."[3] Here are the roots of his interest in literature. His interest in science can also be traced to his father's influence, because ". . . He personally conducted his son through John Locke's *Letters Concerning Toleration* and *Essay on Human Understanding*, and did it so persuasively that Alexander ever afterward considered the 'Christian Philosopher' as another name for Locke."[4] The empirical method of learning, prominent in Locke's philosophy, impressed Alexander Campbell so deeply that it became an integral part of his educational philosophy. As a result, liberal arts and sciences, so central to the modern university with which campus ministry has to deal, were a part of the colleges of the Restoration Movement from the beginning.

The next formative experience in Alexander Campbell's life and thought came during a year he spent studying at Glasgow University. Thomas Campbell, unhappy with the growing sectarian spirit displayed by the Presbyterians among whom he ministered in Ireland, and in need of a sea voyage for his health, sailed for America in 1807. He left son Alexander, then only nineteen years of age, in charge of the family — his mother and six younger children. A little more than a year later, Thomas Campbell sent word to his family to join him in America. They set sail from Londonderry on October 1, 1808, but their ship ran aground on the coast of Isley, one of the Hebrides.[5] The family survived and made their way to Glasgow, where they stayed for nearly a year before sailing again for America.

There were at least four powerful currents that washed over Alexander Campbell's consciousness in Glasgow which were to stay with him for the rest of his life. One of these was the year of study at the university itself, which was also the *alma mater* of his father. He experienced what all of us campus ministers so love — the stimulation and excitement of being part of a great university. At this time, 114,000 people lived in the city of Glasgow, and the university enrolled 1,500 students.[6] This year "Gave him the opportunity to carry on his general education . . . as well as to widen his acquaintance with the main currents of British thought and culture."[7]

There were two brothers, Robert and James Haldane, who had set up a training school for lay preachers in Glasgow. The man in charge of this training school was Greville Ewing. Alexander had brought with him a letter of recommendation for Mr. Ewing, given to him by a man he had met in Isley after the shipwreck.

> Mr. Ewing showed every hospitable attention to the serious minded young Irishman and his mother and brothers and sisters, helping them to find accommodations, and performed many friendly offices suggested by his own generous nature and the obvious needs of a shipwrecked family. He became Alexander's closest and most helpful friend during that year in Glasgow.[8]

It was this experience with Ewing and the school for lay preachers that began to shake Alexander's faith in the clergy-dominated Seceder Presbyterian Church from which he had come. He insisted later, during the entire life of Bethany College, that it was not a school for clergy. In a Baccalaureate address at Bethany in 1852, he said:

> But young men, we do not contemplate you as disposed or designed to engage in the Christian ministry, or in any one of the learned professions. We want educated minds, moral dignity, and Christian integrity in all the walks and callings of social and civilized life. And whether we guide the plough or the helms of church or state, we may be useful, honorable, and happy men.[9]

Campus ministry has picked up on this aspect of Campbell's educational philosophy, and, as we have seen above, has been producing thousands of educated and dedicated "lay" leaders for the church during the past thirty years.

There is a sidelight here that is of special interest to campus ministers. Greville Ewing, in addition to being a warm and caring friend to Alexander Campbell, also "delighted in gathering university students at his home for what he would call 'discussion groups,' and who preached regularly (in a building constructed for a circus and big enough for that purpose) to the great audiences which his eloquence attracted."[10] Campus ministers can identify, not only with the discussion groups, but also with the large crowds of students who have gathered at great conferences and retreats to be addressed by eloquent preachers during the past thirty years.

In addition to the stimulation of the university, the influence of the lay training schools, and the warmth and caring ministry of Greville Ewing, Alexander Campbell also began his turning away from sectarian creeds toward the Bible while in Glasgow. The creedalism and Calvinism of the Seceder Presbyterian Church, which his father had begun to question before his voyage to America, became more and more of a problem to Alexander during his year in Glasgow. Garrison and DeGroot describe his crucial decision:

> Near the end of his stay in Glasgow the strain reached the breaking point. The occasion was a communion season. He had attended the preparatory service, passed his tests, and received the metal token which was his certificate of fitness to commune. At the communion service itself, he delayed until the last group, then went forward and deposited his token on the table and walked out. In doing so he virtually walked out of the Presbyterian Church.[11]

The several strands of these early influences came together in Alexander Campbell's educational philosophy. The evidence presented to account for Campbell's insistence on the importance of the liberal arts and sciences should not be taken to mean that he did not see the Bible as important. On the contrary, he not only saw the Bible as the way to unify the other studies, he saw it as the *only* means to bring unity to the college curriculum. His father not only taught him the English classics and the philosophy of John Locke back in Ireland, but he had also taught him the Bible so that he could say often that Bethany was, ". . . the only college in the New World, or in the Old World, known to me, founded upon the Holy Bible and our common humanity."[12]

(It may seem "naive to the extreme" to suggest that the modern university might be brought to meaningful unity by a return to the Bible, and that campus ministry can be an instrument to help accomplish this goal, but that is the precise claim I mean to make in this book.)

## Campbell and the Colonial Colleges and Seminaries

The particular way in which Alexander Campbell wanted to incorporate the Bible into the central core of Bethany College must be seen in contrast to the conditions in the Colonial colleges and seminaries at the time of Bethany's founding.

When the Colonial colleges began to abandon their religious orientation after the Revolutionary War, several denominations in the Colonies responded by establishing seminaries. Nearly twenty of these institutions were established between 1784 and 1836. Their purpose, in reaction to the secularism of the Colonial colleges, was twofold: 1) to supply an educated ministry for the churches, and 2) to become the center for articulation of sectarian theological positions.[13] The result was that choices available in higher education in America from 1784 to 1836 were either the secular colonial college or the sectarian denominational seminary. Campbell offered Bethany College as an alternative, where the Bible was intended to permeate all of learning.

> In so proposing Campbell was offering a different model of education than was available. It was certainly different than the Colonial colleges with their abandonment of the Bible and Christian world view. It was different than the religious seminaries (which Campbell called "cemeteries") with their speculative, divisive and truncated curriculums.[14]

Campbell approached the Bible, not as a collection of proof texts for the support of specialized theological positions, nor as a source of allegorical interpretations which could be wrapped around some pre-conceived creed or doctrine. Rather, following Bacon and Locke before him, he saw it as a book to be studied the same as any other book, ". . . devoid of doctrine and presented as history, ethics, literature, etc. Biblical matters like all others, must commend themselves to active human reason for acceptance."[15]

Perry Epler Gresham said that Campbell . . .

had it written into the character of Bethany that systematic theology should never be taught in that institution. His feelings were deep on the matter because of bitter personal experience. His own childhood had been clouded by intellectual difficulties precipitated by Calvinistic doctrine, total depravity, and election. Locke had been his liberator.[16]

It is interesting to those of us committed to campus ministry at secular universities that Campbell did not oppose the secular knowledge of the Colonial colleges. "He held that secular knowledge was not contrary to religion."[17] He further said,

secular knowledge, so far from inimical to religion, is, in reality, its most powerful auxiliary. The direct tendency of mental culture is to prepare the mind for reception of truth, and is, therefore, a most efficient agent in paving the way for the ultimate triumph of Christianity.[18]

Great ideas are often the result of holding together in creative tension different aspects of the truth. Alexander Campbell's philosophy of education held together, in creative tension, the liberal arts and sciences on the one hand, and the centrality of the Bible on the other. Creative tension is difficult to maintain in either institutions or individuals; unfortunately, the colleges of the Restoration Movement gave up the tension in two different ways. To speak metaphorically, one of the "roads" from Bethany was taken by those colleges which emphasized the Bible. This distinction is not uniformly applicable to all the colleges of the Movement, but it is accurate enough to be useful as we try to understand those colleges. Let us now look at the two "roads from Bethany."

# Alexander Campbell and the
# Two Roads from Bethany

## *The Liberal Arts Road From Bethany*

There were two other colleges started early in the Movement, one of which preceded the founding of Bethany by five years. Bacon College, founded in 1836 in Georgetown, Kentucky, was named after Francis Bacon, and it incorporated Campbell's educational philosophy. Walter Scott, a stalwart of the Movement, was its first president. The history of Bacon College is an illustration of the commitment to liberal arts in some of the colleges of the Restoration Movement.

In 1858 Bacon College merged with Kentucky University, which in turn merged with Transylvania University in 1865. The name of Transylvania College was assumed in 1915, *because only the liberal arts colleges remained from the former university establishment* (emphasis added).[19]

Another example of a college founded on Campbellian principles which finally became primarily a liberal arts college is Butler University in Indianapolis, Indiana. It began as Fairview Academy in Rush County, Indiana in 1849. "Fairview became the nucleus of Butler University, first called Northwestern Christian University, chartered in 1850 at Indianapolis, with classes beginning in 1855."[20] Since Butler is my *alma mater*, I can speak from experience. When I was an undergraduate in the 1930s, the University had become primarily a liberal arts institution. I received an excellent education at Butler University, taking classes in both the School of Religion and in the liberal arts department toward an undergraduate degree.

Transylvania and Butler were not the only colleges of the Movement which finally became primarily liberal arts institutions. Thomas R. McCormick, in his excellent study of Disciples campus ministries, includes seven case studies of campus ministry at Disciples-related colleges. The seven are Transylvania, Atlantic Christian College, Drake University, Midway College, Chapman College, Culver-Stockton College, and Eureka College.[21]

Each of these colleges had been founded, to one extent or another, on Campbellian principles of education, but by the time Mr. McCormick wrote in 1987, each of them had become so exclusively a liberal arts institution that it became necessary, in order to bring a Bible emphasis back into these colleges, to institute some form of chaplaincy or campus ministry.

It is fair to conclude that the majority of Restoration Movement colleges now affiliated in some way with the Disciples have become primarily liberal arts institutions. Perry Epler Gresham, writing in 1971 when he was still President of Bethany College, said:

This fear (that colleges might lose affiliation with the churches) proved to be justified, for many of the institutions have moved away from their churches . . . the percentage of Christian Church young people in some of the colleges is very low and many faculty members are not even aware of any church affiliation. . . . These institutions tend to be alike in that their priorities are on the side of the arts and sciences rather than toward other aspects of college life that might have more appeal to members of the churches.[22]

Earl C Hargrove, Chancellor of Lincoln Christian College in Illinois, made the same case more strongly, in 1960, when he said:

Great institutions which had been started by Bible-centered people turned their attention to educational endeavors which, to quote, were "Christian in atmosphere." Texas Christian, Butler, Eureka, Transylvania, Bethany, and many others turned their main attention to secular education.[23]

Some people of the Restoration Movement often mistakenly equate "liberal arts" with "liberalism." The importance of this distinction may be seen in the history of another early college founded upon Campbell's educational philosophy. Franklin College was founded in Nashville, Tennessee, by Tolbert Fanning in 1844. It was staunchly based on Campbellian principles. "Fanning brought to his native South and to the Church of Christ the Campbellian view of education . . . in Fanning's Franklin College, while the Scriptures were taught at all age levels, it was a liberal arts program rather than a Bible College."[24] The interesting development here is that the colleges which came out of Franklin College, and which are today supported by the Churches of Christ, have been generally successful in holding together strong Bible teaching and liberal arts. They have been able to teach liberal arts and sciences without liberalism. (The story of these colleges is told by M. Norvel Young in his very competent book *A History of Colleges Established and Controlled by Members of the Church of Christ*.)[25]

The liberal arts "road from Bethany" is not bad in itself. I do not see it that way, and I am confident that Alexander Campbell would not have seen it in that way. In fact, it has some definite advantages. Dr. Gary Tiffin, now Dean at Pacific Christian College, writing in his 1968 Stanford University Ph.D. dissertation stated:

> Normally Disciple ministers studied in an atmosphere of general education at such colleges as Bethany, Hiram, Cotner, Culver-Stockton, Transylvania, Drake, and Eureka. . . . Therefore Disciple ministerial education was not so isolated from the rest of American higher education as independent Disciples ministerial training eventually developed, but was closely allied with general stream American education.[26]

The problem is not the teaching of liberal arts and sciences, which are a necessary part of a sound education, but doing so apart from the meaning-giving and integrating power of the Bible. It is not the *liberal arts* component of a college curriculum that is dangerous, but rather it is the *liberalism*, and liberalism has become almost universal in Disciples colleges. There is an irony here. Campbell's view of how the Bible should be studied was a much needed emphasis in his day. Dr. Richard Phillips of Milligan College has said:

> There are some real positive contributions which the Enlightenment has made in American Christianity, and more specifically in our own movement. The "inductive" reasoning which betrayed an obvious debt to Lord

Francis Bacon was a refreshing switch from the blind creedalism and confessionalism of Protestant orthodoxy. This fresh "scientific" approach put our people at the cutting edge of developing Biblical scholarship for a time.[27]

The Enlightenment presuppositions, so refreshing in Campbell's day, have now become a rationalistic and naturalistic dogmatism which, instead of seeing human reason in the critical light of biblical revelation, sees biblical revelation in the critical light of human reason.[28] This is what we mean by "liberalism," and it has become the dead-end of the liberal arts "road from Bethany" among many, if not most, of the colleges and churches in the Disciples branch of the Movement.

This situation was recently recognized, and deplored, by Dr. Ronald Osborn, a prominent leader among Disciple churches for more than forty years. Writing in *Mid-Stream* in 1989, Dr. Osborn calls for a return to biblical education and scriptural preaching among Disciples. He charges that the neglect of biblical preaching has created a situation in which "the prevalent theology in our congregations is a shapeless, ethereal vapor with the odor of moralism and the smudge of secularity . . . ." "Now, if ever," he says, "we must come to terms with the need for serious, honest, theological reflection on the rich and diverse witness of the Scripture."[29]

If campus ministry can indeed become a factor in challenging the modern, secular university to find a unifying force in the Bible, and thus in contemporary culture, it must be done from the base of biblically-centered churches and colleges. If the churches and colleges of the Movement have abandoned the Bible as central, how can campus ministry hope to do its work on that weakened foundation? There is another "road from Bethany," the Bible road, which we will now consider.

## The Bible College Road From Bethany

There were three major movements among the colleges of the Restoration Movement that, in one way or another, took the "Bible Road From Bethany." The first is that of those colleges which followed what Gary Weedman calls the "separatist approach."[30] The most notable of these was the College of the Bible in Lexington, Kentucky. We have seen that Transylvania University in Lexington had become primarily a liberal arts college. In 1865, a separate but adjacent school was established at Transylvania. Enough of the Campbell influence was still alive so that this new institution was not called a seminary, but rather "The College of the Bible."

In its early years, it was conservative and orthodox. Robert Milligan, who had previously taught at Bethany, was its first president. In 1895, John W. McGarvey, a Bethany graduate, became president, and continued in that capacity for sixteen years. McGarvey was highly regarded in the Movement and was a gifted teacher. Upon his death in 1911, liberal forces gained control of the school, and this particular "Bible road" became the center of a bitter controversy as we shall see.

Several other colleges adopted the "Lexington" model. "Colleges of the Bible" were established at Drake University in Des Moines, Oklahoma Christian University and at Texas Christian University. The effect of these schools was to separate Bible teaching and ministerial training from general education. "The liberal arts integrated with a Biblical understanding had been a crucial part of the educational scene from the beginning. It would not be recaptured for some years to come."[31] (Except in campus ministry and in other ways we shall consider later.)

Another "Bible Road from Bethany" was taken in the establishment of "Bible Chairs" at state universities. The first of these was established by the Disciples at the University of Michigan at Ann Arbor in 1893. Thomas McCormick describes the concept:

> The concept of the Bible chair was imaginative. It was an arrangement in which a "Chair," or teaching position, at a state university was either endowed or funded on an annual basis by a religious group. The instructor was usually chosen by the church, and was recognized by the university. The arrangement allowed students to take courses in religion at the Bible Chair, for which they might (or might not) be granted credit on their degree program.[32]

The Bible Chair movement was the first attempt by any of the churches of the Restoration Movement to take the gospel and the Bible to the state university. The Disciples are to be commended for this movement which, Garrison and DeGroot say, "is the Disciples' most distinctive contribution to American education."[33] No figures are available to me on the number of Bible Chairs established by the Disciples, but there was a substantial number. At the height of this movement, Tri-State College at Angola, Indiana, reported that over 200 young people went into full-time Christian service as a result of the Bible Chair at that College.[34]

It is fascinating to realize, as we have noted earlier, that the basic idea of the Bible Chair movement was first suggested by Thomas Jefferson at the University of Virginia. This movement was the nearest thing to campus ministry, and to Campbell's philosophy of education, to be attempted in connection with the state universities by churches of the Restoration Movement up to that time.

Unfortunately, the Bible Chairs eventually died out or were absorbed into the religious studies departments of the state universities.[35] One might think, at first glance, that religious studies departments in state universities would be a move toward Campbell's educational philosophy. Sadly, according to Robert McAfee Brown (who taught for 14 years at

Stanford and who is now on the faculty at Pacific School of Religion in Berkeley, California) most of these departments at state and private universities have given up any commitment to Bible teaching.

> In an almost frenetic rush for academic respectability, it was assumed that teachers of religion should either (ideally) have no religious commitments of their own, or (second best) promise to keep such commitments carefully and totally hidden. It was a disadvantage to believe and an advantage to disbelieve.[36]

The third, and most enduring "Bible Road from Bethany" is that taken by the Bible colleges begun and supported by the Christian Churches of the Restoration Movement. Dr. Marshall Leggett, President of Milligan College, has written that the rise of these colleges took place in three stages: the early evangelistic Bible college, the Bible college that arose in protest to liberalism, and the later, evangelistic Bible college.[37]

The first of the "early evangelistic" Bible colleges was founded by Ashley Johnson, and was located on his own farm near Kimberlin Heights, Tennessee. It was first called "The School of the Evangelists," and the name was later changed to Johnson Bible College in 1909.[38] Ashley Johnson intended to found a college based specifically on the model of Bethany College. Mr. Johnson wrote:

> We propose to give our boys a good English and classical education, but all these things are tributary and subservient to the one great end . . . a goodly, indeed the best, Bible education . . . we are training men to do in this generation what Alexander Campbell trained men to do in his best days at Bethany College.[39]

Johnson Bible College is alive and well today, and has kept the Campbellian dream alive for one hundred years. In the 1993–94 school year, Johnson enrolled 483 students and graduated 79.[40]

Kentucky Christian College, another of the early evangelistic Bible colleges, did not begin as a Bible college, but as a teacher training school for public school teachers. It was founded by J.W. Lusby and J.O. Snodgrass in 1919 in Grayson, Kentucky. The name was changed to Kentucky Christian College in 1944, since its purpose had changed to that of educating ministers and church leaders. This college also has remained strong in its life and witness, having enrolled 476 students in the 1993–94 school year, and having graduated 87 in that same year.[41]

Johnson Bible College and Kentucky Christian College were, and still are, viable and effective colleges in the Campbellian mold, but they are both located in rural areas and do not have direct impact on the state universities which are so powerful a part of the modern educational scene.

The other two early evangelistic Bible colleges were founded by a man whose dream it was to locate Bible colleges on or near the campuses of state universities. Eugene C. Sanderson picked up on the idea that was first advanced, as we have seen, by Thomas Jefferson. In the Washington State Convention of 1889, Sanderson read a paper entitled "Our Educational Interests" which stirred interest in establishing a Bible college in the Northwest. In 1892, the Convention appointed trustees for Northwest Christian University, and Sanderson was selected to head the project. Feeling the need for more education, Sanderson returned to school. In 1893, he received the Bachelor of Divinity degree from Drake University, and the following year a Bachelor of Sacred Literature degree from the University of Chicago.[42] In October 1895, Eugene Divinity School opened her doors, near the campus of the University of Oregon.[43] Sanderson stated the reason for this location: "The institution, adjacent to the University of Oregon campus, was so located that students might make use of the extensive resources of the state-supported institution."[44] In 1930, Spokane University merged into what was then called Eugene Bible College. In 1933, the name was again changed to Northwest Christian College. This school is still very much alive and it has produced some of the strongest leaders in the Movement, both for the Disciples and the Christian Churches. (In recent years, however, there has been more emphasis on liberal arts than on biblical studies at NCC.)[45]

Sanderson's dream was realized in three other locations before his death in 1939. He and a graduate of Eugene Bible University, David Eugene Olson, established International Christian Bible College near the campus of the University of Minnesota in 1913. "It was modeled after Eugene Divinity School, with the exception that its primary concern was the reaching of the immigrants with the gospel message."[46] After some serious financial problems in 1924, Sanderson was able to save the school, which became Minnesota Bible College, and he served as its president until 1932.

In 1927, Sanderson purchased property adjacent to Kansas State Agricultural College in Manhattan, Kansas, and Kansas Bible College was opened. This was the forerunner of Manhattan Bible College, now Manhattan Christian College.[47] Just before his death in 1939, Sanderson attempted to start a school near San Jose State University in California. In 1939, he asked William L. Jessup to take over the school, which became San Jose Bible College, now San Jose Christian College.[48]

All of these early evangelistic Bible colleges are alive and well; they are an important part of the Bible college movement, the most enduring of the various "Bible Roads from Bethany." Among them, the vision of Eugene Sanderson comes nearest to Campbell's philosophy of education, and one that makes the heart of any campus minister beat faster. Modern campus ministries are attempts, in various ways, to revive the Sanderson dream on 90 campuses across the United States as these words are being written.[49]

The second wave of Bible colleges, according to Marshall Leggett's scheme, are those that were established to protest liberalism. The "flagship" of these schools is Cincinnati Bible Seminary (now College) founded in 1924. Leggett writes:

> The founding of Cincinnati Bible Seminary in 1924 was the dividing line in the history of the Restoration Movement Bible Colleges. Bible Colleges are either "before C.B.S." or "after C.B.S." The inception of those founded before Cincinnati Bible Seminary involved no great theological issue within the Movement. They were begun solely for evangelistic purposes. The subsequent schools were founded by conservative brethren within the Movement both to evangelize and propagate the ideals of the Restoration Movement as they understood them within the context of the threat of modernism.[50]

When J.W. McGarvey died in 1911, men of liberal views slowly assumed leadership of the College of the Bible in Lexington, Kentucky. Finally, in 1923 a committee of conservative leaders (some from College of the Bible) founded McGarvey Bible College in Louisville, Kentucky. In the same year, another group of conservative leaders founded Cincinnati Bible Institute in Cincinnati, Ohio. These two schools merged in 1924 to form Cincinnati Bible Seminary.[51] This school is the clearest example of a Bible college founded to protest liberalism, but it has also been a strong evangelistic influence since its founding.

Between 1924 and 1944, five Bible colleges came into existence, four in the United States and one in Canada. We have mentioned Manhattan Bible College, founded in 1927, and San Jose Bible College, founded in 1939, both of which came out of the Sanderson movement. In 1928, Pacific Bible Seminary (now Pacific Christian College) was organized, first in Los Angeles, and then in Long Beach, California. (Now located in Fullerton, P.C.C., like some of the other Bible Colleges, has incorporated a strong liberal arts component in its curriculum.) Ozark Bible College (now Ozark Christian College) was founded 1942 in Bentonville, Arkansas, with F.W. Strong as president and Seth Wilson, Academic Dean. Alberta Bible College was founded in Alberta, Canada, in 1932. Each of these colleges was partly a response to liberalism, and partly a move to evangelize.

The third wave of Bible colleges founded in the Movement are those which Marshall Leggett calls "the later evangelistic Bible colleges."[52] These colleges are conservative defenders of the faith, but they are also aggressively evangelistic. Lincoln Christian College in Lincoln, Illinois, is the first, and in many other ways the model, of these colleges. Earl C Hargrove became the minister of the First Christian Church in Lincoln in

1937. He soon realized that the churches of the Movement were dying in great numbers in the state of Illinois, largely for lack of ministerial leadership. From 1914 to 1944, 175 churches had closed their doors in the state of Illinois. Of the 625 churches still alive in Illinois in 1944, only 278 had full-time preaching.[53]

With superb energy and enthusiasm, Mr. Hargrove called some men around him and established Lincoln Bible Institute in 1944. Now Lincoln Christian College and Seminary, this school was the first of a wave of scores of evangelistic Bible colleges started after World War II. When Gary Weedman wrote in 1983, there were thirty-eight Bible colleges, one liberal arts school, and four graduate schools.[54] In February 1993 thirty-one Bible colleges responded to a survey by *Christian Standard*.[55] In addition to these Bible colleges, there was one liberal arts school, Milligan College in East Tennessee. Milligan has held firmly to the Bethany model since 1886, and it stands out as a unique institution among the colleges of the Restoration Movement.

In addition to these undergraduate Bible colleges, there are now, in 1993, five graduate institutions which have grown out of the Bible college movement. Cincinnati Bible Seminary and Lincoln Christian Seminary are two of them. The Graduate School of Church Dynamics in connection with Pacific Christian College, Emmanuel School of Religion in Johnson City, Tennessee, and the graduate program at Northwest Christian College are the others.

The Bible colleges have unquestionably kept alive Alexander Campbell's emphasis on the crucial importance of the Bible in education, and have thus "saved the Movement," in the opinion of many. Gary Tiffin writes: "These Bible colleges represent an attempt to reunify that intimate relationship between higher education and religion which was once the character of most of American higher education."[56]

Their importance to the cause of the Christian faith goes beyond their influence within the Movement, however. One writer claims that in the broader world of evangelical churches, Bible colleges ". . . have maintained a defense against rationalism, naturalism, and skepticism that was greatly needed in the Christian Church."[57] In a strong statement reminiscent of Alexander Campbell, another evangelical leader says:

> The central feature of the Bible college is well worth looking at, because it carries implications far beyond this one kind of institution. This is a kind of education that solved for itself the perennial problem of educational philosophy, the identification of an integrating principle for the entire curriculum. For it, the Bible is, to use Lewis Mumford's brilliant figure, "a magnetic field at the center which will continually polarize each fragment that enters the field."[58]

For the most part, the Bible colleges have understood themselves as a positive protest against perceived destructive forces, and not reactionary and defensive. Tiffin says: "As in other Protestant rebellions, these independent Disciples thought of their revolt as basically affirmative rather than negative in nature, as they sought to conserve the truth, the values and the dogmas of the past centuries."[59]

Unfortunately, the positive contribution made by the Bible colleges to the Movement and to education in general has a negative side as well. In the process of defending and conserving Biblical truth, there has often developed an adversial attitude toward the culture and higher education that has proved costly. Tiffin notes, "Independent Disciples, traditional and conservative, were faced with the narrow choice of either modifying their Biblical message and theology to relate to a new culture or maintaining their Biblical message and theology at the possible expense of cultural relevance."[60]

The attitude of fear and suspicion toward secular higher education, state universities in particular, developed early on. William Clebsch deplores this situation:

> Thus the apparent paradox, that the self-same Christian churches which founded and fostered higher education in colonial America became jealous foes of the eventually dominant university. Broadly speaking, religious groups nurtured and managed our academies and colleges down to the Civil War; afterward, they restrained and often opposed the development of our leading universities.[61]

(Interestingly, Alexander Campbell never took this attitude toward secular colleges — perhaps because of his positive experience at Glasgow University in his youth.) Even within the Movement, J.W. McGarvey, as wise and revered a man as he was, opposed the founding of the Bible Chair at the University of Michigan in 1893, ". . . on the theory that the atmosphere of the state university was not conducive to the proper preparation of Christian workers."[62] On the contrary, it has been the experience of scores of campus ministers that the atmosphere of the state university can become a fertile field for the recruitment of committed Christian workers. (I will document this in upcoming chapters.) Charles Garrison, pioneer campus minister at the University of Kentucky, says of the university students in a sometimes hostile and anti-Christian environment: "The struggle to come to grips with his faith can become the most important adventures of college life and he/she can emerge from it with a dynamic faith that seeks to express itself."[63]

If the Bible colleges have, in defending the faith, paid a huge price in neglecting or opposing the state university, that situation is changing. Twenty of the Bible colleges out of the thirty-one now in existence have some kind of working academic relationship with state universities or other secular schools. (The Sanderson dream lives!)

Campus ministries have inadvertently helped to strengthen the relationship between the Bible colleges and the universities in at least two ways. On the one hand, the large part of presently active campus ministers on 90 campuses are Bible college graduates. On the other hand, large numbers of university students converted through campus ministries (statistics presented later), are going to Bible colleges and seminaries to prepare for the formal ministry, the mission field, and other types of ministry.

In summary, the general trend among the colleges of the Restoration Movement, with some notable exceptions as we have seen above, has been to travel either the "road from Bethany" to liberal arts and sciences and lose the Bible, or to go the "Bible road" and lose the liberal arts and sciences. Campus ministry has already, during the past thirty years, helped to heal that breach, and it offers the hope that it will continue to do so to an even greater degree in the future.

## NOTES

1. Alexander Campbell, *Millennial Harbinger* (hereafter *M.H.*), 1850, p. 291.

2. Perry Epler Gresham, *Campbell and the Colleges*, (Nashville: Disciples of Christ Historical Society, 1973), p. 27.

3. Alexander Campbell, "Preface," *M.H.*, 1862, p. 3.

4. Garrison and DeGroot, pp. 125-126. (Hereafter referred to as "Garrison and DeGroot.") These same authors point out Francis Bacon's influence on John Locke, and through him, on Campbell, p. 54.

5. *Ibid.*, p. 141.

6. M.M. Davis, *How Disciples Began and Grew*, (Cincinnati: The Standard Publishing Company, 1915, Revised, 1947), p. 37.

7. Garrison and DeGroot, pp. 141-142.

8. *Ibid.*, p. 142.

9. Alexander Campbell, "Baccalaureate Address," 1852, p. 362.

10. Garrison and DeGroot, p. 143.

11. *Ibid.*, pp. 143-144.

12. Alexander Campbell, "Notes on a Tour to Illinois," *M.H.*, 1854, p. 44.

13. Weedman, *Higher Education*, pp. 5-6.

14. *Ibid.*, p. 8.

15. Gresham, *Campbell and the Colleges*, p. 50.

16. *Ibid.*, p. 50.

17. *Ibid.*, p. 49.

18. Alexander Campbell, "Knowledge Indispensable to Religion," *M.H.*, 1841, p. 208.

19. Garrison and DeGroot, p. 249.

20. *Ibid.*, p. 252.

21. Thomas B. McCormick, *Campus Ministry in the Coming Age*, (St. Louis: CBP Press, 1987). pp. 95-102.

22. Gresham, *Campbell and the Colleges*, pp. 77-78.

23. Earl C Hargrove, "Bible-Centered Education A Must," in an address before the 14th Annual meeting of the Accrediting Association of Bible Colleges, Chicago, October 27, 1960, p. 3.

24. Leroy Garrett, *The Stone Campbell Movement*, (Joplin, MO: College Press, 1985), p. 310.

25. M. Norvel Young, *A History of Colleges Established and Controlled by Members of the Churches of Christ*, (Kansas City, MO: The Old Paths Book Club, 1949).

26. Gerald C. Tiffin, Ph.D. Dissertation, "The Interaction of the Bible College Movement and the Independent Disciples of Christ Denomination," (Stanford University, 1969), p. 66.

27. Dr. Richard Phillips, from the manuscript of an address, "Enlightenment Impacts on the Nature of the Church and Ministerial Education: A Mixed Blessing," given at Pepperdine University, Malibu, CA, July 21, 1989, p. 7.

28. Lesslie Newbigin. *The Gospel in a Pluralist Society*, (Grand Rapids: Eerdmans, 1989), pp. 1-13.

29. Ronald E. Osborn, "The Irony of the Twentieth-Century Christian Churches (Disciples of Christ): Making it to the Mainline Just at the Time of its Disestablishment," *Mid-Stream*, Vol. 28, No. 3, July 1989, p. 308.

30. Weedman, *Higher Education*, p. 10.

31. *Ibid.*, p. 12.

32. McCormick, *Campus Ministry*, pp. 6-7.

33. Garrison and DeGroot, p. 416.

34. McCormick, *Campus Ministry*, p. 15. There was also an extensive Bible Chair Movement among the Churches of Christ. That story is told in detail by Rick Rowland, Professor at Pepperdine University in his book, *Campus Ministries: A Historical Study of Churches of Christ Campus Ministries and Selected College Ministries from 1706 to 1990*, (Fort Worth: Star Publications, 1991).

35. McCormick, *Campus Ministry*, p. 16.

36. Robert McAfee Brown, "The Boundary Area Between Biblical Perspectives and Religious Studies," *NICM Journal*, (Summer 1981), p. 74. In this same connection, William F. Buckley Jr., in his caustic critique of the Department of Religion at Yale University, his *alma mater*, *God and Man at Yale*, (Chicago: Henry Regnery Company, 1951), p. 7 & 9, says that "A Bible course no more bespeaks an influence on behalf of Christianity than a course on *Das Kapital* would necessarily indicate an influence on behalf of Marxism." He also tells of one professor in the department who "has classified himself, before his students, as eighty percent atheist and twenty percent agnostic."

37. Marshall J. Leggett, "A Study of the Historical Factors in the Rise of the Bible College in the Restoration Movement." M.A. thesis, Butler University, 1961, p. 11.

38. *Ibid.*, p. 14.

39. *Ibid.*, p. 15.

40. *Christian Standard*, February 20, 1994, p. 4.

41. *Ibid.*, p. 4.

42. Leggett, "Study of the Historical Factors," p. 19.

43. Harry R. Baird, "The Life of E.C. Sanderson," M.A. thesis, Butler University, 1957, p. 24. Mr. Baird has done a superb job of telling the exciting story of the life and work of this unusual man.

44. Leggett, "Study of the Historical Factors," p. 20.

45. Letter to the author from William Richardson, long time professor at NCC, May 6, 1993.

46. Leggett, "Study of the Historical Factors," p. 22.

47. *Ibid.*, p. 24.

48. *Ibid.*, p. 26.

49. Report of the *National Association of Christian Student Foundations.* Dave Rockey, Secretary-Treasurer, (Stillwater, OK, February 1994) Also, *Christian Standard*, August 23, 1992, pp. 5-7.

50. Leggett, "Study of the Historical Factors," p. 30.

51. Marshall Leggett gives a detailed and graphic account of the "Lexington Controversy" and its aftermath in his thesis, "Study of the Historical Factors," pp. 61-65.

52. *Ibid.*, p. 37.

53. Weedman, *Higher Education*, p. 24.

54. *Ibid.*, p. 30.

55. *Christian Standard*, February 21, 1993, pp. 4-7.

56. Tiffin, "Interaction of the Bible College Movement," pp. 146-147.

57. Merrill C. Tenney, in the "Preface" to *The Bible College Story: Education with Dimension*, by S.A. Witmer (Manhasset, NY: Channel Press, 1959), pp. 11-12.

58. A statement by Frank E. Gaebelein, quoted by Witmer, *ibid.*, p. 19.

59. Tiffin, "Interaction of the Bible College Movement," p. 141.

60. *Ibid.*, p. 140.

61. William A. Clebsch, *From Sacred to Profane America: The Role of Religion in American History*, (New York: Harper & Row, 1968), p. 115.

62. Garrison and DeGroot, p. 379.

63. Charles Garrison, *Forgotten Christians: A Guidebook for College-Career Work*, (Joplin, MO: 1967), p. 58.

# CHAPTER THREE

# College Ministries Before 1960

Long before churches or individuals of the Restoration Movement took an interest in any kind of campus ministry, there were many significant Christian student movements which formed a rich and colorful backdrop for modern campus ministry.

The Disciples were the first Restoration people to see the importance of reaching the colleges with the gospel. The first Bible Chair program in America was founded by the Disciples at the University of Michigan at Ann Arbor in 1893.[1] After that beginning, the Disciples were aggressive in their efforts to establish campus ministries and various kinds of student works, especially in the years after World War II.

The Christian Church branch of the Restoration Movement was a latecomer to this important ministry. The first active efforts by Christian Churches to minister to college students began, with one exception, in the late 1950s, but they made up for their slow start in the decades to follow.[2]

## Early Christian Student Movements

In 1706, more than 250 years before Christian Churches began to take an interest in campus ministry, a Christian student society was formed at Harvard.[3] In that year, Cotton Mather preached a funeral sermon for a young man named Recompense Wadsworth. Mather told how this young man, before his death, had banded together with a small group of friends to form a committed fellowship of Christian students at the college. Donald Shockley says, "While this is the earliest existing reference to a student Christian organization in America, it is reasonable to suppose that there were others like it."[4]

The first "Great Awakening" in the Colonies also had roots in a Christian student group. It was Jonathan Edwards who sparked that significant movement with his sermon, "Sinners in the Hands of an Angry God." The Awakening spread, however, under the preaching of an itinerant evangelist from England named George Whitefield. Whitefield's preaching was so powerful that it influenced Benjamin Franklin, a confirmed Deist, to build a "preaching house" for Whitefield in

Philadelphia. This "house" later became the first building of the University of Pennsylvania. Not only did Whitefield contribute to the eventual establishment of a university, but he had also been a member of the "Holy Club" at Oxford University in England, along with John and Charles Wesley, in the early 1730s. The Great Awakening, partly fueled by a Christian student group, was a powerful influence, creating a hunger for political freedom which eventually led to the American Revolution.[5]

Following the Revolution, there was a sharp decline in morality and religion in the colleges, and in the Colonies in general.[6] In 1796 Timothy Dwight, grandson of Jonathan Edwards and president of Yale, attacked this corruption in a sermon at the college which led to the conversion to Christ of more than half of the student body within a year.[7] This movement spread slowly to many other colleges and campuses, helping to reverse the post-Revolution moral and religious decline.

The most famous of all the early Christian student movements began in the "Haystack Prayer Meeting" at Williams College in 1806.[8] Five students at Williams had begun to meet secretly for prayer in order to avoid public ridicule. They met outdoors on the edge of the campus. One day a sudden thunderstorm drove them to seek cover under a nearby haystack, where they continued to pray. David McKenna, president of Asbury Theological Seminary, describes that incredible event as follows:

> Williams College, however, remained a hard-core center for heresy, blasphemy and ridicule until the five students prayed under a haystack in 1806. With the mystery of the wind, the spirit of God swept over the campus bringing repentance and redemption to scores of students who, in turn, took the witness of revival from campus to campus, church to church and city to city until "Awakening" became the watchword for the struggling nation.[9]

The spontaneity and divine influence which is so often apparent in Christian student movements was not only clearly present in the "Haystack" incident, but it was also a part of the next major movement among Christian students. In 1844, twelve young clerks in a London dry goods store came together to find a way to relate their Christian faith to work in a large city. They decided to call their group a "Young Men's Christian Association," or YMCA. Their ideas soon spread to other cities in Great Britain, and by 1851, the "Y" had crossed the Atlantic and the first YMCA was organized in Boston. The movement spread from the cities to the campus in 1858, when chapters of the "Y" were formed both at the University of Michigan and the University of Virginia. Donald Shockley, Chaplain at Emory University, says:

> In less than twenty years Associations were started on more than forty campuses in the U.S. even though there was no apparent, organized devel-

opmental effort under way. In fact, leaders of the city-based movement, which was also growing rapidly, were puzzled by what was happening on the campuses.[10]

Three significant factors in the "Y" movement need to be pointed out. First, it was not, in the beginning, a social and physical fitness movement as it has become in our day, but it was an evangelical outreach to young men working in the cities. Later, it became an evangelical outreach to the campuses. Secondly, the movement was not exclusively for young men. Almost from its inception, women participated in the group at the University of Michigan. However, the first formal campus YWCA was established at Illinois State University in Normal in 1873. By 1889, there were YWCA chapters on 142 campuses across the country.[11] Thirdly, whereas the early Christian student movements were committed to personal devotions and prayer, along with theological and intellectual stimulation, the campus "Y's" added concern about Christian vocation, or ". . . the carrying of religion into the sphere of daily occupation."[12] Each of these three emphases of student "Y's" — evangelism, participation by women, and Christian vocation — are vigorously carried on by modern campus ministries.

Another consequence of the "Y" movement on campuses, combined with other streams of student activity, was a powerful emphasis upon the evangelization of the world in the latter part of the 19th century. In 1886, Dwight L. Moody came back to the States from a long and successful crusade in Great Britain, during which he had preached at the universities of Oxford, Cambridge, and Edinburgh.[13] Encouraged by the response of students there, Moody and other Christian students organized a month-long conference for "Y" leaders and other Christian students at Mt. Herman, Massachusetts. During that conference a wave of missionary enthusiasm arose which resulted in the formation of the "Student Volunteer Movement for Foreign Missions." During the next thirty years, this movement inspired more than 11,000 students to go overseas as missionaries.[14] This emphasis upon missions has also been revived among the campus ministries of the Restoration Movement.

# The Disciples Move Toward the Campuses

Although the first organized effort to minister to the college campuses by any of the churches of the Restoration Movement was the founding of the Bible Chair at the University of Michigan by the Disciples in 1893, there were, no doubt, individuals and churches which were active in the "Y" and other early campus ministries before that time.

The Bible Chair movement, which was considered by Disciple historians to be "the Disciples' most distinctive contribution to American education," spearheaded other campus ministries by the Disciples.[15] When the influence of the Bible Chair movement began to wane, visionary leaders among the Disciples, including Joseph C. Todd and others, insisted that the Disciples needed to have strong ministries on the college campuses. This they did, especially in the 1940s and 1950s.

My first encounter with campus ministry of any kind was with the work of Joe Wick in the Disciples Student Foundation at Purdue University during the 1940s. Joe planted seeds in my mind which took twenty-five years to bear fruit, but they were good seeds. The Disciples supported many Student Foundations like the one at Purdue, and there were many campus ministers like Joe Wick. (It is not my purpose, as I have said, to tell the story of the Disciples campus ministries here. That story has been very adequately told by Thomas R. McCormick.)[16]

The kind of vision which provides the rationale for all campus ministry was cogently stated by John McCaw, National Student Director for the Disciples, writing in the World Call in 1946:

> No longer can the whole task of student work be left to the earnest efforts of local churches and devoted individuals. The church in the university or college town, no matter how strong it is, can hardly absorb the responsibility of ministering to a concentrated and specialized university constituency which ebbs and flows with each academic year. Nor can such a church undergird with its local resources a ministry to several hundred — sometimes a thousand — new members to the congregation. In reality these student members are charges from congregations all over the brotherhood. Well-trained and full-time staff members are desperately needed for the important task of serving students.[17]

In the late 1950s Christian Churches began to realize the truth of John McCaw's words, and they began to establish working campus ministries on several university campuses.

## Early Campus Ministries Among Christian Churches

Although campus ministry among the Christian Churches eventually went beyond the work of individual churches, most of the early ones were the result of visionary leaders in local churches. The first of these, and among the most successful, was the college student ministry carried on for more than twenty years by W.R. Walker, minister of the Indianola Church of Christ in Columbus, Ohio.[18] The church building of that congregation was located a short walk from the campus of Ohio State University, and Mr. Walker and his people took full advantage of the happy circumstance to minister to O.S.U. students. During the whole twenty-eight years of Mr. Walker's ministry at Indianola, he taught a "student class." Steve Seevers, present Campus Minister at Ohio State says, "it became obvious that W.R. Walker had a charisma that attracted college students. The attendance in the Students' Class averaged more than one hundred the whole time he was there."[19]

Reviewing some of the highlights of that remarkable ministry will help to understand its vitality and its powerful influence on students. For example, in June of 1924, the graduating seniors of Ohio State University who were members of the Students' Class requested that Mr. Walker preach a special baccalaureate sermon for them. Listed among these graduates were students from the School of Arts, the College of Dentistry, the College of Education, the College of Engineering, and the College of Pharmacy.[20] A note in the Church Bulletin for April 11, 1926, indicates that the Students' Class, with 150 in attendance, was the largest class in the Sunday School for that day.[21] Like many present-day campus ministries, the work at Indianola not only reached students in a wide variety of vocations and careers, it also generated scores of Christian marriages among students.[22]

Frequent mention is made in the Indianola Church Bulletin during those years of special receptions which were held for incoming Freshmen each fall. This kind of special attention to college students is an essential part of the successful ministry to the students in any day and age. For example, the Indianola Bulletin for September 23, 1928, has the following note:

> A reception will be given for the Freshmen of O.S.U. Friday evening, September 28th. We hope all young folks will be on hand that evening to give greetings to these newcomers. We are planning on the largest Student Class in our history this year, and we need the help of all to realize it.[23]

An example of the cordial relationship between the Indianola students and the university as well as an early example of student interest in ecology, is seen in the visit of the Dean of the Agricultural Department of the University to lecture at the Church on "God and Nature," illustrated with 300 colored slides on April 24, 1931.[24]

After the retirement of W.R. Walker in 1948, the student work at Indianola declined somewhat, but never died out entirely. The Students' Class and the Christian Endeavor were combined into one organization called the "Student Christian Fellowship" in 1951. The new minister, Harold Scott, and his associate, Dean Jacoby, taught the class and led the group in activities, along with sponsors and student leaders.[25] Later, the college work of the congregation was formed into the "Student Christian Foundation," and it became a recognized student organization at Ohio State University.[26] There is a note in the church's annual report for 1962–63 that will resonate in the heart of any dedicated campus minister.

An anonymous writer says:

> Some 30,000 students grace the Ohio State campus in a year. As a church we are obligated to reach as many of these as possible. These young people will be our senators, governors, mayors, physicians, professors, etc. in just a few years. What they think matters. Their influence will be vital. Through the Foundation we seek to serve them.[27]

Later in the 1960s, the Indianola Church employed a part-time campus minister, and in 1975, they called a full-time campus minister. We will pick up the story of the later work at Indianola and Ohio State as we survey the decade of the 1970s. Before we move on to examine other early campus ministries among Christian Churches, let us pause here to acknowledge our gratitude to W.R. Walker and the Indianola Church for setting such high standards for campus ministry, and for implementing them in those early years in such an inspiring way.

The second serious effort among Christian Churches to establish campus ministry took place on the campus of the University of Minnesota. This ministry was not begun by a local church, but rather by a professor of a Bible college. We have already pointed out that Minnesota Bible College, which was founded in 1913 (originally as International Christian Bible College), was located on the campus of the University of Minnesota. Jerry Gibson and his wife were called to the faculty of Minnesota Bible College in the fall of 1955. He was assigned a classroom and an office from which he looked out directly over Fowlwell Hall and the campus of the university. Jerry was keenly aware of the traditions of Minnesota Bible College, founded by Eugene Sanderson and Davis Eugene Olson, for the purpose of reaching for Christ students at the University of Minnesota (primarily the Scandinavian students in the beginning). The old Sanderson-Olson dream began to stir in Jerry's heart, and he soon took measures to revive it. He enrolled as a graduate student at the university "to get the pulse of the campus." He converted an Indonesian student he met in class, and he became a member of the University Council of Religious Advisors, which was a part of the Staff of the Dean of Students. In 1960, because of the encouragement of Jerry Gibson, Rodney Vliet, a sophomore student at Minnesota Bible College, was able to get university recognition for the "Christian Bible Study Group," which later became a full-time campus ministry at the university.[28]

Jerry Gibson and Rodney Vliet, like W.R. Walker before them, were captivated by the tremendous opportunity for ministry on the university campus. They discovered some of the basic principles which have been followed by successful campus ministries since: geographical proximity to the university campus, cordial relationships with university faculty and staff, and, most importantly, provision of Christian community for students on campus.

Another of these early stirrings of interest in campus ministry among Christian Churches took place at Ball State University in Muncie, Indiana. Dean Hickerson, whose father had preached at the Webber Street Church in Urbana, Illinois, for fourteen years, first became aware of the possibilities of campus ministry while he was a student at the University of Illinois. After graduating from the University, he served in the Army in Korea, and then returned to get a degree from Lincoln Christian College. His first full-time ministry was with the University Christian Church in Muncie in 1957. The church building was located one block from the Student Union Building at Ball State. With moral and financial help from a couple in the congregation, Lance and Jean Van Tassel, Dean began a ministry to students. Dean describes that ministry as follows:

We utilized them in leadership roles, held studies in our front room (usually from fifteen to twenty) and in general attempted to give them a sense of community. During our nearly six years there, nine students elected to change to Christian majors. Five went to Cincinnati Bible Seminary and four went to Lincoln Christian College. Dr. Nelson Deutsch of Ontario, Canada was a product of that ministry. He is still one of the stalwarts of the faith after all these years.[29]

When Dean Hickerson left the ministry at Muncie, the work with students languished somewhat, but in 1966, it revived dramatically, and at this writing, it is one of the strongest campus ministries in the country.

The campus ministry at the University of Kentucky began in 1957 under the sponsorship of the Broadway Christian Church. Ard Hoven, minister of the Broadway Church, charged his newly-arrived youth minister, Ed Jones, to find a way to minister to the Christian Church students who were enrolled at the university. Ed describes the beginning of that ministry as follows:

In the fall of 1957 I went to Orientation Week and met with incoming freshmen students who were from Christian Churches. . . . At Orientation I was given time to tell what I had planned for the students. This helped me to formulate an outreach program. We were given a room in the Student Union Building where we could meet for two days a week. We met for a half hour of Bible Study followed by a half hour of lunch. . . . That year, the Broadway Church started a Sunday program called YAC (Youth After Church) for the college students. Ard Hoven, Broadway's minister, taught a Bible Study and then we would go to a church member's home or to a restaurant for a meal. In a short time the students started leading the discussions. Ard and I went to every YAC meeting. This was the beginning of what became the Christian Student Fellowship at the University of Kentucky.[30]

A significant move in the history of campus ministry among Christian Churches grew out of this ministry in Lexington in 1958. After a year during which the Broadway Church took full responsibility for the ministry, a group of nine Christian Churches, under the leadership of their ministers, formed a board of directors with the goal of establishing a full-time campus ministry at the University of Kentucky.[31] These nine men, along with several other ministers, had been meeting every week for years for fellowship and to plan a local TV program. The work of Ed Jones and the Broadway Church at the university came to their attention, and they organized the board and began looking for a full-time campus minister.

In May of 1958, this board called Richard Carpenter, who had just graduated from Southern Baptist Theological Seminary in Louisville, Kentucky, to this ministry. Richard was "full-time" in the sense that the bulk of his time during the week was given to work with students, but, in order to provide an adequate salary, the board members arranged for a weekend ministry in a local church for him. Under Richard's ministry, official recognition was obtained from the university for the Christian Student Fellowship, and this made it possible for the continued use of university facilities for meetings. Richard described his work with students as follows:

> The program consisted of locating students from Christian Churches . . . holding a devotional service in the YMCA Chapel (Student Union Building) Monday through Friday, after which we all ate together in the cafeteria. We also organized some evening programs (Bible Study and Social), as well as some service projects and "bull sessions" in the dorms.[32]

The support of campus ministry by several area churches first took place in this ministry at the University of Kentucky, but it has become a pattern followed by most campus ministries among the Christian Churches since. This grass roots kind of structure in support of parachurch organizations has become a widespread practice among Christian Churches, which are staunchly congregational in matters of church policy.

This group of Lexington area ministers, first under the chairmanship of Wayne Smith, Minister of Southland Christian Church, and later chaired by Ard Hoven of the Broadway Church, deserve a great deal of credit for their vision and pioneering spirit. There was, however, a difference of opinion between Richard Carpenter, the campus minister, and board of directors with regard to the purpose of the ministry. Richard describes the difference as follows:

> At this time the nine ministers were against programs that were in apparent competition with the local church. They wanted me to recruit students for their churches, and they basically judged my ministry on how well I met this criterion. I resisted this in favor of a direct ministry to the students although I encouraged their participation in a "real" church so that they wouldn't live in a "spiritual dreamworld."[33]

This kind of tension between campus ministers and their supporting churches was not uncommon in the early days of campus ministry. As the ministries spread and established an identity, it became clear that these ministries were not competing with the local churches, but indeed were, in the long run, helping to strengthen them. Even in Lexington in these early days, this was happening. Richard Carpenter lists with justifiable pride several strong leaders in the churches who came out of the Christian Student Fellowship during his relatively short ministry of two years.[34] With this strong beginning, it is not surprising that the campus ministry at the University of Kentucky has also become one of the most successful in the nation. There have been several other pioneering ventures which originated at Lexington to be mentioned later.

Another campus ministry began in these early years at East Tennessee State University in Johnson City, Tennessee. In the fall of 1956, several students from Christian Churches who were enrolled at the university met together and founded the Christian Youth Fellowship. The first student president of this group was Joe Mumpower of First Christian Church, Bristol, Virginia, during the school year of 1956-57. Dr. Kenneth Spaulding of the Economics Department at the university was faculty advisor, and he was assisted by Miss Velma Cloyd and Mrs. Joe McCormick, both in the Mathematics Department, and also members of First Christian Church.

When Jess Johnson became minister of the First Christian Church in Johnson City in 1959, he immediately gave strong support to the student group on campus. First Church had also called Jim and Mary Shields as youth ministers, and they began working with college students in the congregation. In addition to supervising the college-age class in the Sunday School, Jim and Mary organized a Sunday evening after-church fellowship for students which met in different homes each week. Dr. Spaulding and the Christian Youth Fellowship were meeting on Thursday nights on campus at this time. Jess Johnson and Jim Shields soon saw that Dr. Spaulding and the group were doing well, but could use some help.

Jess and the folks at First Christian enlisted the help of some students from nearby Milligan College, and they also called Bill Eaton, a student at Milligan to assist Dr. Spaulding and the students. Both the Sunday evening meetings at the church and the meetings on campus began to grow, so the next move was the inauguration of a Wednesday morning meeting in the Student Union Building of the university. Jess Johnson, Jim Shields, Bill Eaton, Dr. Spaulding and several student leaders combined forces to broaden the influence of the student group on campus. Jess, with some enthusiasm, describes this meeting and some of the results which came from it:

We started a meeting at E.T.S.U. Student Union Building on Wednesday mornings from 9 — 12 a.m. I would go to the campus with two ladies from the church. They would bring refreshments and serve them. I would spend my time talking to students who dropped in. Dr. Spaulding would be there when he could, as would Bill Eaton. Most of the students who came were from Baptist, Methodist, and Presbyterian Churches, since these groups had the largest representation on the campus. Most of them were in trouble with their faith since they had come from small, conservative churches which had not prepared them for the challenges they were encountering on campus. Our emphasis on the Lordship of Jesus Christ and the Living Word was a breath of fresh air for them. Eventually we began to reach some 300 Christian Church students at the university, most of whom were commuters. Jim Shields and I became convinced that a full-time campus ministry was needed at E.T.S.U. In 1962 we called Jim Saunders, a junior at Milligan College, to be the campus minister. At first, Jim was supported only by First Christian Church, but in time, he enlisted support from a large number of churches in East Tennessee, and he was able to work at the ministry on campus full-time.[35]

Again a strong foundation was carefully and prayerfully laid at E.T.S.U. which made possible a lasting and effective campus ministry still thriving on that campus at this writing.

Several of the recurring themes that have marked Christian Church campus ministries during their more than thirty year history were discovered and began their development in these campus ministries before 1960. Among these themes are the power of having genuine compassion for college students, the importance of close relationships with the university, good geographical location, attention to the needs of students (not only their spiritual needs, but their social and intellectual needs as well), and above all, a vision of the immense value to the mission of the church as a whole which is provided by campus ministry.

## NOTES

1. Garrison and DeGroot, p. 416.

2. As mentioned before, the excellent accounts of campus ministry among the Disciples (McCormick, *Campus Ministry*) and among the Churches of Christ (Rowland, *Campus Ministries*) need to be consulted in order to get a fuller picture of campus ministry among all the churches of the Restoration Movement.

3. Both Shockley (*Campus Ministry*, p. 13) and McCormick (*Campus Ministry*, p. 22) refer to this incident. Both of them are quoting from the classic work by Clarence P. Shedd, *Two Centuries of Student Christian Movements: Their Origin and Intercollegiate Life.* (New York: Association Press, 1934), pp. 1-2.

4. Shockley, *Campus Ministry*, p. 13.

5. David L. McKenna, *The Coming Great Awakening.* (Downers Grove, IL: InterVarsity Press, 1990), pp. 30-31.

6. See the previous section on Colonial Colleges in Chapter One.

7. McKenna, *Coming Great Awakening*, pp. 32-33.

8. *Ibid.*, pp. 29-30.

9. *Ibid.*, p. 33.

10. Shockley, *Campus Ministry*, pp. 16-17.

11. *Ibid.*, p. 18.

12. Clarence P. Shedd, *Two Centuries*, p. 102.

13. Shockley, *Campus Ministry*, p. 20.

14. Shedd, *Two Centuries*, p. 275.

15. Garrison and DeGroot, pp. 125-126.

16. McCormick, *Campus Ministry*, p. 102.

17. *Ibid.*, pp. 37-38.

18. From a letter to the author from Steve Seevers, present Campus Minister at Ohio State University, dated April 22, 1991.

19. *Ibid.*

20. *Indianola Bulletin*, Vol. I, No. 23, June 8, 1924, p. 2.

21. *Ibid.*, Vol. 3, No. 15, April 11, 1926, p. 2.

22. *Ibid.*, Vol. 4, No. 25, June 19, 1927, p. 2.

23. *Ibid.*, Vol. 5, No. 29, September 23, 1928, p. 2.

24. *Ibid.*, Vol. 8, No. 15, April 19, 1931, p. 2.

25. Indianola Church of Christ, *Annual Report*, 1951, p. 40.

26. *Ibid.*, 1958-59, p. 34.

27. *Ibid.*, 1962-63, p. 10.

28. From a letter to the author from Jerry Gibson, August 31, 1989.

29. From a letter to the author from Dean Hickerson, November 16, 1990.

30. From a letter to the author from Ed Jones, August 16, 1989.

31. A list of that original Board of Directors, along with Dr. Jonah W.D. Skiles, Faculty Advisor, is as follows: Royce Robey, Minister, Athena Christian Church; C. Russell Bowers, Minister, Berea Christian Church; Ard Hoven, Minister, Broadway Christian Church; Charles P. Hendon, Minister, First Christian Church; Early Ray Jones, Minister, Gardenside Christian Church; William E. Ransford, Minister, High Street Christian Church; William B. Cooper, Minister, Macedonia Christian Church; Jack Condor, Minister, Northern Heights Christian Church; Wayne B. Smith, Minister, Southland Christian Church.

32. From a letter to the author from Richard Carpenter, April 26, 1985.

33. *Ibid.*

34. Among those Richard mentions are: Brad and Barbara Walden, now ministering with the Tates Creek Christian Church in Lexington, KY; Emmery Emmert, Head of the Kentucky Christian Counseling Center, Lexington, KY; John Craycraft, U.S. Navy Chaplain; Margaret Cook Kim, missionary in Korea; and Omer Hamlin, Librarian for the University of Kentucky Medical Center Library. Every campus minister can add hundreds of names to this list.

35. From a letter to the author from Jess Johnson, December 12, 1990.

# CHAPTER FOUR

# Campus Ministries in the Decade of the Sixties

One of the paradoxes of campus ministry is that the first significant breakthrough in the spread of ministries on university campuses by Christian Churches took place in the turbulent decade of the sixties. All ministry is done within a specific cultural context, and if we are to understand the growth of campus ministries in the sixties it is necessary to have some understanding of the counter-cultural movements of that dynamic — some say destructive — decade.

It was an explosive period in American history, and the primary locale of the explosion was the university campus.[1] There was a population explosion during the decade as the post World War II baby boom created a huge demographic bulge in U.S. population. These "baby boomers" hit the campuses in the sixties, and the result was that the number of students enrolled in American colleges and universities doubled between 1963 and 1973.[2]

Not only were the large numbers of these students explosive, but also the kind of experiences they brought with them to college helped to create a revolutionary atmosphere. Growing up in the fifties, a period of unprecedented optimism and prosperity in America, they had been used to having their needs met with very little difficulty. When they arrived at college, however, they encountered rigid academic traditions, powerful faculty control, and administrative rules not at all to their liking. Because of their massive numbers they found that they could change the structure of the universities by resisting, if not by rebelling.[3]

In addition to the unstable mix on the campuses there were upheavals in society at large which had a profound effect upon this generation of students. One observer reminds us that the rise of the civil rights movement in the sixties created "a new sense of the reality of ethnic diversity in America (and it) became one of the key ingredients of the culture of the 1960s."[4] White, Anglo-Saxon Protestants (WASP's) were, for the first time in their lives, made aware of and challenged by other ethnic groups.

None of these factors alone or in combination were enough, however, to create the intensity which characterized the student rebellion in the sixties without the Vietnam War. For the first time in American history young men were drafted to fight in a war that was neither understood nor condoned by a large percentage of the young, nor indeed by much of the nation as a whole. Even those who were not drafted lived as much as eight years with the threat of the draft hanging over their heads.[5] Suddenly this massive generation of young people had to deal with unsympathetic academic institutions, a rapidly changing society, and the prospect of dying in an unknown, distant land for a cause they did not understand.

The fallout from these circumstances is well known, and is perhaps only now being understood. The student riots, protest music, hallucinogenic drugs, idealistic "communes," flight to Canada to escape the draft, general disillusionment with society as a whole, and widespread loss of hope are well known as the fruits of this chaotic decade. But there were other, more positive forces at work as well during this period. Donald Shockley, who was deeply involved in campus ministry in the sixties, says, "all other considerations aside, it was an era in which the spiritual dimension of human life was of great interest to the young."[6] Since I began to work as a full-time campus minister at Purdue University in the fall of 1966, I witnessed much of this spiritual hunger among students and can testify that it was a truly heady experience.[7]

This interest in spiritual things did take some non-traditional turns. Many "turned East" and experimented with various forms of Eastern religions. In the late sixties there was the phenomenon of the "Jesus People" — great numbers of college age young people were converted and became "turned on to Jesus" in large charismatic-type churches all over the country, especially in California.[8]

The irony of the decade of the sixties for Christian Churches is that in the midst of all this social and spiritual chaos campus ministry began to spread. During this ten year period, Christian Churches founded 19 full-time campus ministries and at least six influential retreat and area organizations for students on more than 21 college and university campuses in nine states. Those of us who had the privilege of participating in this movement were, and still are, convinced that no manipulative moves by human beings alone could have created this exciting phenomenon. Darrell Terry, charismatic leader of Project Challenge, a West coast college-career movement in the sixties, has said:

> A "Spiritual Explosion" is the only way I can describe the incredible expansion of college ministries throughout the brotherhood — I can see more imagination, enthusiasm, energy and manpower moving into these fledgling programs than any other area of evangelism — explosion is the only way I see it. It is an uncontrolled, out-of-hand, expansive and powerful God-ignited happening and it is thrilling to witness.[9]

# The Christian Student Fellowship
# at the University of Kentucky

One of the earliest and most influential full-time campus ministries among Christian Churches was the Christian Student Fellowship at the University of Kentucky. Building on the foundation laid by the Broadway Church, Dick Carpenter's ministry, and the support of area churches which began in 1957, Charles Garrison was called as full-time campus minister in 1960. During the eight years of Charlie's dynamic leadership at UK, many innovative concepts and practices were introduced that became role models for campus ministries across the country in subsequent years.

Charlie was one of the first to articulate a coherent and persuasive rationale for campus ministry among Christian Churches. Writing in the *Christian Standard* in 1963, he made an eloquent and impassioned plea for the churches of the Movement to take seriously the challenge of ministering to college students:

> We must decide whether the Restoration Movement is to participate in education or if it is to withdraw into isolation. To participate will require that we understand the spiritual needs which confront college students . . . and that we view the thousands of campus dwellers as persons for whom we have a great commission. . .We must not rationalize our failures. We lose more college students through our failure to provide adequate educational programs than through diabolical atheism on the campus.[10]

Charlie's book *Forgotten Christians*,[11] although written in 1967, is still one of the best books available on both the theoretical and practical aspects of campus ministry. Among the many merits of the book is the chapter on "The Restoration Movement and the College Mind," in which he shrewdly outlines how the biblical principles which have informed and animated the churches of the Movement are appealing to college students.[12] He cites, among other things, the nature of the Church as a fellowship rather than an organization, the concept of "No Creed but Christ," the freedom to study the Scriptures, and the non-authoritarian role of the campus minister.

Charlie also taught many of us how important it is for the campus minister to relate significantly to the life of the university. During all of his years at UK, Charlie was enrolled as a student in the University. In 1964 he earned a BA, in 1966 he earned an MA in counseling, and in 1968 he left the campus to work full-time on his PhD in Sociology, which he received in 1974. His role as a serious student not only enhanced his personal knowledge, but also gave him greater credibility with both students and faculty. This was a cross-cultural move not unlike that of a missionary learning the language of the people with whom she is ministering, and it opened the university community to the gospel in a truly effective way.

There is an old saying among real estate people that there are three important things to consider in buying real estate — they are "location, location and location." This has never been more true than it is in the case of campus ministry. Geographical proximity to the campus not only enhances the visibility of the ministry, but also increases its viability as a force in the university community. Charlie, along with his board and supporting churches (and students), were well aware of this fact, and in 1966 they dedicated a beautiful building which had been built immediately adjacent to the university campus. Previously the ministry operated from a house near the campus. The new building included a lovely worship room, an office for the campus minister, and a fellowship area.

Not only was this the first time a campus ministry among Christian Churches had built a building for the exclusive use of a ministry to students, it also marked the first time a special Sunday morning worship service was provided for students on or near campus. In 1966 the Christian Student Fellowship at the University of Kentucky set a precedent in this regard which was followed by many campus ministries in later years.

Charlie Garrison says that during his first few years at UK the expectations of the area ministers and churches were largely what they had been during Dick Carpenter's ministry — that is, that campus ministry was primarily a means of encouraging Christian young people to attend the local churches on Sundays.[13] As a result of strong support from the members of the board, and enthusiastic participation by students, this attitude slowly changed and the campus worship service at UK soon proved to be not only a means of nurturing the faith of Christian students, but also a surprisingly effective means of evangelizing non-Christian students. Because this is such an important issue, not only at UK in the sixties, but also on many campuses today, I quote at some length from Donald Shockley, who presents the following argument for on-campus worship services (in his case, at Emory University in Atlanta, Georgia):

> It has sometimes been suggested to me that worship should not be a prominent feature of campus ministry programs, at least not on Sunday mornings. I am aware of colleagues who have in fact been forbidden to hold such services by bishops, boards, or judicatories of one sort or another. While the reason for this is normally stated in terms of avoiding competition with local church programs, one might also infer that those who hold such views do not want students to have alternatives to the status quo in the near campus congregations. Some have even said, 'If they get used to the kinds of things you do in a campus chapel, they will never find a local church that suits them after they graduate.' By such comments, well-intentioned

persons betray their assumption that the mission of the church is to strengthen itself rather than to serve human need. Ironically, the self-interest of the church would probably be better served if it intentionally sought to foster a variety of opportunities for access to alternative worship experiences. The church would have more doors that way, and more people would find their way inside.[14]

During most of the history of campus ministries among Christian Churches, the gathering of students in "retreats" has been vital. This practice also was initiated serendipitously, by the Christian Student Fellowship at the University of Kentucky. In the spring of 1961, Charlie and about a dozen of his students gathered for a weekend retreat at Blue Grass Christian Assembly, south of Lexington. The students so enjoyed the experience they repeated it the next spring, this time meeting with students from other campuses. By 1963 students from six other campuses attended the annual event. Charlie describes the experience as follows:

> The students responded enthusiastically to the time of fellowship and to the sessions. By Saturday night everyone was tired, but it appeared that the session might last all night when at 10:30 p.m. questions were still being asked of the speaker and audience participation was lively.[15]

The "Blue Grass" retreat continued, growing in attendance each year, until the impressive French Lick Retreat, which drew an even larger number of students from all over the midwest, began in 1967. French Lick was not the only retreat which followed the example set by "Blue Grass." Gatherings of college students took place in Illinois, Missouri, Michigan, and other places. The retreat phenomenon begun at University of Kentucky became a dynamic part of the growth of campus ministries in the 1960s.

As campus ministries and work with college students began to increase in the early sixties, a need was felt for an organization beyond the local campuses to serve as an "umbrella" and a clearing house for exchange of information. Again, Charlie Garrison at the University of Kentucky was the initiator of meetings which led to such an organization.

The first meeting of interested parties was held in August of 1963 at the Southport Heights Christian Church near Indianapolis (Charles Garrison's home church), and nine campuses were represented.[16] The newly-formed organization was named the National Association of Christian Student Foundations (NACSF), and its purpose was stated as "an exchange of ideas for effective campus work." Those who were invited to participate were "all persons who have in the past or hope in the future to work with college students." Ed Bernard, teacher of the college-age Bible School class at the Indianola Church in Columbus, Ohio, was asked to become editor of a newsletter which was named *The*

*Exchange*. In 1966 By-laws of the NACSF were adopted and the organization took an active role in coordinating the French Lick retreat. The NACSF has been in continuous existence up to the time of this writing and has been of immeasurable support to campus ministry across the country. In 1991 the name was changed to the National Association of Christian Campus Ministers (NACCM), and in May 1994 at the annual retreat of the organization in Indiana, it was announced that there are now 90 active, full time campus ministries among Christian Churches. The University of Kentucky was one of the places where this remarkable movement of campus ministries began to grow during the sixties, but not the only place. For four years, from 1963 to 1966, Charlie Garrison compiled annually a list of campus ministries and work being done by churches and individuals among college students, which was published in the *Christian Standard*. The number grew from 20 in 1963 to 42 in 1965. (There was a decrease to 19 in 1966, no doubt due to fewer people reporting rather than fewer ministries.)[17] In a recent phone conversation, Charlie Garrison expressed amazement at the present growth and influence of campus ministries in view of what he considered small beginnings at the University of Kentucky in the early sixties. Many of the practices and programs which were first introduced by Charlie Garrison and the Christian Student Fellowship at the University of Kentucky have been incorporated into a large number of campus ministries since.

# The Christian Student Fellowship at East Tennessee State University

The campus ministry at East Tennessee State University became a full-time operation when James D. Saunders was called as campus minster in November of 1962. Jess Johnson and his congregation at First Christian Church in Johnson City had been working with the Christian Student Fellowship, organized in 1956 with Professor Kenneth Spaulding (Economics) as sponsor. Jim Saunders says,

> I continued until June 1964. I pretty much functioned as a youth minister. I met with the Fellowship on campus on Thursday nights, made calls on students, and helped them plan programs and activities. I also encouraged ETSU students to attend and place student memberships with First Christian Church.[18]

Jim Saunders left this ministry in 1964 to attend Southern Baptist Seminary in Louisville, Kentucky. Bill Eaton, the Milligan student who had worked with the Fellowship previously, was called as campus minister. Jim Saunders returned in September 1965, and some significant changes took place in this ministry. First Christian Church had taken full responsibility for the support of Jim Saunders and his work, but in 1966 Dr. Charles Gresham came to the area to join the faculty of the newly founded Emmanuel School of Religion. Dr. Gresham joined Jim Saunders in creating a wider base of support for the ministry at ETSU. In the Fall of 1967, there were "over 400 students enrolled at ETSU who indicated Christian Church — Church of Christ preference."[19] Saunders and Gresham argued that responsibility for these students should be shouldered by the churches in the area rather than by a single congregation.

In 1967 the Appalachian Christian Student Fellowship was formally organized, with Dr. Charles Gresham as chairman. At least 10 churches in the area participated in this broader support group for the campus ministry at ETSU. In 1968 the ACSF bought a house immediately adjacent to the campus. The house, which provided both a meeting place for the student groups and two rental apartments for married couples, was later purchased by ACSF and remains the center of a thriving campus ministry to this date.

Under Jim Saunders' leadership, and with the encouragement and support of Dr. Gresham and the area churches, this campus ministry became a strong force for Christ, as it remains today. Spring, winter, and fall retreats were initiated. Vigorous discussion groups covering a variety of topics of interest to collegians were held weekly, and a large number of exciting visiting speakers addressed the group. Jim Saunders continued as campus minister until 1970.

## The Christian Student Fellowship at The University of Illinois

In 1963 G. Stanley Smith, PhD, was a research associate in animal science at the University of Illinois, and an elder in the Webber Street Church of Christ in Urbana. He had been the teacher of the "Town and Campus" class at Webber Street since the fall of 1960. Work with college students in the church became so personally absorbing and challenging to Stan Smith that at the end of the spring semester in 1963, he resigned his full-time position as a professor in the university. and became first the part-time (with no pay, 1963–1966) and then the full-time (1966–1968) campus minister with the Christian Student Fellowship at the University of Illinois. At the time he said that he made this radical and sacrificial career change because "the main need of the world today is not just to produce food, but to relate men (and women) to the life found only in Jesus Christ."[20] God used many different people and varied sets of circumstances to launch the movement of campus ministry among Christian Churches, but one of the most powerful contributions to that movement was the example set by the ministry at the University of Illinois, and Stan Smith's leadership was a major part of that influence.

From the beginning, collegians from the Fellowship worshiped on Sunday mornings with the local churches, Webber Street in Urbana (John Pierce, Minister) and First Christian Church in Champaign (Orville Hubbart, Minister). Transportation to the churches was provided by the Fellowship, and Stan Smith reported in 1967 that student attendance in the two churches averaged 150 to 200, and at times recorded as high as 400.[21]

This ministry was sponsored from the beginning by a Board of Directors made up of ministers and elders from several Christian Churches in Central Illinois. A spacious ten room house was purchased by the Board in August of 1963, "located about five minutes walking distance from the campus [Location! Location! Location!] and also about five minutes walking distance from three of the university dormitory complexes."[22]

This house served as a residence for the Smith family for three years, and it serves to this day as the gathering place for the CSF. On Sunday evenings during Stan's ministry, 60 to 150 collegians gathered for "Supper Club" (a light meal prepared and paid for by the students) and a program emphasizing inspiration and fellowship. This big, old house on Oregon street in Urbana was another "Campus House," so prevalent now, patterned after the one at the University of Kentucky, and it was made sacred by the rowdy, riotous crowds of college students that gathered there regularly to laugh, pray, eat, sing, worship and love the Lord and each other.

During the school year of 1963–64, Stan Smith enrolled at Lincoln Christian College (Lincoln, Illinois) where he also taught an undergraduate course in biology. In the 1965–66 school year he again taught biology at Lincoln, and also led a seminar in "Science and Religion." Studying and teaching at Lincoln were a part of Stan's transition from university science professor to campus minister, which he continued along with his studies and teaching.

In 1966 Stan became the full-time campus minister at the University of Illinois (now on salary, but much reduced from his former salary as professor). During his ministry at the University, which lasted until 1968, several innovative programs were introduced. Among them was a remarkable ministry to international students, for which Stan had a special talent. He was greatly aided in this ministry by his wife, Eileen, whose warm gift for hospitality in their home, along with Stan's ability to relate to international students, resulted in the conversion of dozens of these students during their ministry. When Stan began his ministry at the University of Illinois there were 1,230 international students enrolled at the university from 81 foreign countries. He said, in 1967, "The college campuses in America have become the greatest field for 'foreign missions' in the world."[23] (Several campus ministries have followed Stan's lead, some of these with great success.)

The Christian Student Fellowship at the University of Illinois has been closely tied to local churches during all of its history. Stan taught the "Town and Campus" class at Webber Street during his entire ministry, and students were encouraged to worship in the local churches. In addition, a "Host Family" program tied students even closer to members of the local congregations, and to each other. "All students in the Fellowship were assigned 'host families' in the church who contacted collegians, invited them into their homes frequently, and worked toward helping the student to get to know others in the church."[24]

Marybelle Clark who, along with her husband, was one of the "host families" and a key person in organizing the program, describes the impact of the program on students and hosts alike:

> From the initial visit the friendships start and the "host family" becomes a "haven" away from the campus; if the plan succeeds the "host families" that are most successful are those who make a point of treating the student as a close friend, or one of the family, rather than a formal guest. We can be of real help to them when they are homesick, discouraged, and when they just need a friend (or an extra bed for an overnight guest on campus). Often I fix a pancake supper for a dozen or more of the collegians after evening worship. Someone, teasing me, said, 'Will pancakes keep a student faithful?' My answer: 'Maybe not, but served with a very generous portion of love and Christian fellowship, *it will help!*[25]

The practice of "Outreach Teams" probably originated at the University of Illinois. Since the students who were involved or potentially involved in the Fellowship were from towns and churches all over the state and beyond, teams of students were organized to visit as many of the churches as possible, usually on Sundays. The purpose of these visits was to keep in touch with the churches, to report on activities on campus, to solicit prayer and financial support for the ministry, and to recruit students for the university and the Fellowship. By this means the churches are informed, students develop leadership skills as they present their programs and the church and the campus ministry are mutually strengthened. This practice has become virtually a "staple" in most other campus ministries since.

Another means of keeping in touch was the *Christian Reminder*, better known as the "*newsy*-paper," a newsletter "mailed weekly to members of the CSF, prospective members, guests and visitors in the CSF sessions, CSF "alumni" and other interested persons as well as all supporting churches — in all about 600 copies weekly."[26]

The campus ministry at the University of Illinois was the first to inaugurate credit courses in religion. Recognizing that students indeed need fellowship and a "home away from home," but that they also need intellectual stimulation and biblical knowledge to integrate with their university studies, a program was begun which Stan Smith describes as follows:

> In the spring term of 1966, Lincoln Christian College initiated an Extension course program at the University of Illinois campus under the sponsorship of Christian Campus House. These courses carried two hours academic credit at Lincoln Christian College *and* the *credits are transferable* in most of the colleges comprising the University of Illinois. Five two hour credit courses in biblical studies, taught by professors from Lincoln, were offered in the school year of 1966–1967, and fifteen to twenty students took these coursed for credit.[27]

In this way the educational principles of Alexander Campbell and Bethany College, as well as the bold plan of Eugene Saunderson to unite Bible College and University studies, was revived. This type of academic program has been followed with great success by several other campus ministries.

The enthusiasm and Christian commitment which was so much a part of the Christian Student Fellowship at the University of Illinois began to spread from campus to campus in the decade of the sixties, as college students met with their peers in the area retreats and convocations. There was Blue Grass in Kentucky in the spring, Little Galilee in Illinois in the fall, and French Lick in Indiana in the winter. These dynamic gatherings are a story in themselves.

Stan Smith left the active campus ministry in 1968 to return to university research and teaching, but the momentum of his ministry was carried on by Jerry Gibson, who succeeded Stan at the University of Illinois, and who had been instrumental in starting the campus ministry at the University of Minnesota in 1956. Jerry also had a special talent for reaching international students for Christ, and I will give an account of his ministry, and later events at the University of Illinois as we look at the decade of the '70s.

If it is true, and we know it is, that "by their fruits you shall know them" (Matthew 7:20, KJV), the campus ministry at the University of Illinois passed the test admirably. Campus ministries at Purdue, Indiana University, University of Cincinnati, and Illinois State, among others, were inspired directly or indirectly by Stan Smith and his dynamic Christian students at Urbana. Students who were a part of the original group at the University of Illinois in 1963–1967 are, twenty-five years later, strong Christian leaders in many fields as a result of their intense experiences in this ministry.[28]

# Christians Unlimited and the Christian Campus Ministry at Southern Illinois University

The campus ministry at Southern Illinois University at Carbondale grew out of the ministry of the Western Heights Christian Church in that city. The church was established in 1959 and 1960 to minister to the Carbondale community and Southern Illinois University. From the very beginning, university students were part of the congregation; therefore, it was a natural step to provide a specialized ministry to university students.

Joseph Putman and his wife Lois came to minister with the Western Heights congregation in 1964. Joe's example of commitment to Jesus, his exceptional teaching ability, and his goal of equipping student leaders helped to build the campus ministry. Joe used his skill as an airplane pilot to enhance his ministry with students by flying teams to mission fields for short term periods of service.

In the fall of 1970 Don and Karen Wooters came to the Western Heights congregation and Don assumed the position of Director of the Campus Ministry, a position he still holds. The elders of the Western Heights congregation are the supervising Board for this campus ministry, but financial and prayer support come from churches and individuals throughout a wider area. Don Wooters has taught the college class at Western Heights since 1970, and students worship with the congregation; making up from one-fourth to one-third of the congregation on any given Sunday.

Don's office is in the church building, but through Christians Unlimited, a student group officially recognized by the university, regular meetings are held on campus in university facilities. The largest of these meetings is a gathering of forty to fifty students each Friday night in the SIU student center for fellowship, recreation and Bible study. A special emphasis of this group is a ministry to international students. For example, in the school year of 1988 students from Malaysia, China, Nigeria and Colombia participated in meetings, both on campus and with the Western Heights congregation.

Don Wooters has strengthened his ministry to the university community by continued study in and cooperation with the university. Don had two degrees from Southern Illinois University when he began the ministry — Bachelor of Music and Master of Music Education.

He has pursued studies toward a PhD in Philosophy and History of Education, and he received the degree in 1992. He also is on the university staff as a counselor, and in 1992 he was President of the Campus Ministry Association at SIU. In a survey of alumni from this campus ministry graduates listed the power of a loving fellowship as the main driving force of the ministry, but they also credited the strong biblical and apologetic teaching of Don Wooters with providing them staying power in the faith.

During the more than 20 years of Don and Karen Wooters' ministry at SIU, strong emphasis has been made upon the ministry of students to one another. The Lord has raised up an indigenous leadership from students involved in the ministry, and hundreds of strong Christian leaders have been recruited for Christ and the Kingdom because of, in Don's words, "Our special emphasis upon the ramifications of Jesus' Lordship for every area of work and study."[29]

# The Christian Campus Ministry at Northern Illinois University

The campus ministry at Northern Illinois University at De Kalb, Illinois has developed in three major stages.

The first stage began when Carl W. Morhaus became the first minister of the newly organized De Kalb Christian Church in 1963. From the beginning Carl was interested in a ministry to students at NIU, and in 1965 he and leaders from the De Kalb congregation organized "The Christian Church Student Association of Northern Illinois University" to work toward the following stated goals: 1.) to confront university students with the Lordship of Christ, 2.) to encourage the study of the word of God, 3.) to provide a Christian atmosphere of fellowship, 4.) to reinforce the faith of Christian students, and 5.) to maintain a dialogue with the religious community of NIU. The CCSA was officially recognized by the Student Activities Council of the University in October of 1966.[30]

The activities of this campus ministry centered in the local congregations. Gene Meyers, a faculty member at the university and an elder in the church, taught the college Bible study class. On the second and fourth Sunday evenings of each month "Chat and Chew" sessions were held at 5:30 p.m. at the church. Students assisted in planning other special gatherings for fellowship and recreation. Transportation was provided to and from the church building, and students participated in all phases of the life of the congregation under the leadership and ministry of Carl Morhaus.[31]

The second stage of this campus ministry began when Darrell Malcom became minister of the De Kalb Christian Church in 1970. Darrell intensified this ministry to students at NIU by giving about 30% of his time to it while the University was in session. He took advantage of the fact that there was no campus house near the university by drawing students to the local church. He organized "host families" in the congregation who met regularly with three or four students all year. Darrell also spent considerable time on campus with his "briefcase as his office," meeting students one-on-one and in groups in the cafeteria, dormitories, and the student union. Bible studies were organized in the dormitories and students continued to worship with the local congregation, one and a half miles from the campus, transported to and fro by car pools and vans.

In 1980 Darrell Malcom served as President of the Campus Ministries Association of NIU, with which he had been active since he arrived at De Kalb in 1970. Approximately 100 students were active in this ministry each year, and Darrell baptized many students into Christ during his 13 years at De Kalb.[32]

After Darrell left in 1983, the campus ministry at Northern Illinois University languished somewhat. It was briefly revived in 1988–89 when Rob Gray, a former student at NIU, became campus minister. The third and current stage of this ministry began in 1989 with the arrival of Scott Stocking as full-time campus minister, still sponsored and supported by the De Kalb Christian Church. Carl Morhaus, Darrell Malcom, and the De Kalb Christian Church demonstrated for several years that a viable campus ministry may be carried on without a campus house located near the university. However, during Scott Stocking's ministry at NIU a campus house was leased (in 1990) and the character of the ministry changed.

# The Christian Campus House at Eastern New Mexico University

Eastern New Mexico University at Portales is not a large university, either in terms of size or number of students, but the ministry on that campus has been a pace-setting leader among Christian church campus ministries.

Harold Starbuck was the minister of Central Christian Church in Portales in the middle of the sixties when he caught the vision of campus ministry. Beginning in 1965 Harold and the congregation at Central sponsored a series of part-time campus ministers who worked to reach the 3,000 students at ENMU for Christ.[33]

In 1967 Dean Overton was called as part-time campus minister by Central Christian Church while he was working on his Master's Degree in Religion at ENMU. Dean describes those early days of trial and error:

> Trying the traditional ministry approaches, I began to call on students on campus to invite them to our college class and worship service at Central. . . . When they saw me approaching, they took another route. I said to myself, "Overton, this isn't really my image of a campus minister — a religious truant officer hired by the church to get their rebellious young people to Bible School and church meeting. There has to be a better approach and more to campus ministry than this."
>
> Searching for answers and fellowship, I started visiting the two most active ministries on campus at that time — the Baptist Student Union and

the Church of Christ Bible Chair. The experience was invaluable. *It confirmed that the most effective ministry on this particular campus had to be on campus, not across town in a church building.*[34]

The result of Dean's experience was the selection of a committee by the Board of Central Christian Church, under the leadership of Harold Starbuck, the minister, to look into the situation. "Committee members traveled the state to interest other churches in the campus ministry at Eastern. Several individuals, and the congregation at Central Christian Church in Clovis, joined with Portales to form a corporation to secure personnel and a facility."[35] This Christian Campus House Board of Directors purchased a house across the street from university dorms sandwiched between a fraternity house and the Church of Christ Bible Chair building. The house included a living room, three bedrooms, two bathrooms, a kitchen, a recreational room, and a garage.

Dean's remarkable ministry, which continues to this day, was strengthened by the new facility, and even though he was still working part-time, it was enhanced even more by his deep conviction about the style of ministry that reaches college students:

> Use the same approach to ministry that Jesus used — a ministry of reconciliation. Be a peace maker and a friend. Treat them like you would like to be treated: as a person of dignity and worth. Alienated youth can be reached by a fellowship of deep love and acceptance that isn't an exclusive social, intellectual or spiritual club. A "half-way home" between the church and the campus could serve as a life-saving station.[36]

The first phase of the ministry at Portales began when Dean returned from a summer of farming in Oklahoma, and moved into the "dream house" in the fall of 1968. The heart of all successful campus ministry — building a loving fellowship among college-age students — began to take place. Much of the growth followed the familiar practices we have seen operating on other campuses. "Rap-sessions," a euphemism used during the 60s to refer to intense discussion groups, became popular. As the outer turmoil increased on the American campuses, the "rap-session" became an important way to tackle the difficult and explosive questions youth were asking and to throw the light of the Christian gospel on them.

Music, always a vital part of growing Christian fellowship, took on new dimensions. The traditional hymn book was put aside for the most part, and the piano was replaced by the guitar, but these innovations did not signal superficiality. On the contrary, students began to sing hymns taken from the Psalms and the Scriptures. Deep feelings were uncovered and expressed, and often music was the magnet that drew the seeking students to the group.

Dean finished his Master's Degree in Religion in the spring of 1969, and the Board asked him to return that fall on a full-time basis. Students were encouraged to attend worship service and Bible study at the church building of Central Christian Church on Sundays, where Ken Broad became the minister in 1969, but the center of weekly activity was the campus house. During Dean's first year as full-time campus minister, over 100 students were reached in a significant way on a campus of 5,000 students.

Up to this point the campus ministry at Portales was participating in the same "explosion" of growth which was taking place at other campuses, but in 1970 a development took place which has made the ENMS ministry unique. Dean writes:

> The building of our dream took a giant step forward when the university administrators authorized us to teach religion classes for credit. The Baptist, Methodist, and Church of Christ already had Bible chair programs. This giant step was actually accomplished in two half-steps. The first step came in the fall of 1970 when I was permitted to start offering religion classes at the campus house as a part-time instructor. The full step was completed in 1973 when Dr. John Eggleton joined us from the faculty of Manhattan Christian College to assume full-time teaching of undergraduate and graduate classes. John also served as the Director. I continued to serve as campus minister and part-time instructor.[37]

The importance of this academic program as an integrated part of the campus ministry at Portales can hardly be exaggerated. The early Bible chairs and the plan of Eugene Sanderson to locate Bible colleges near universities were at best programs that were "permitted" by the university. The program at Portales was, and still is 25 years later, an integral part of the Religion Department at Eastern New Mexico State University. Dean, like Charlie Garrison and Jerry Gibson before him, "paid his dues" and gained the respect of the university people by doing good, hard academic work. John Eggleton was able to build on that foundation. Campus ministry, to be successful, must deal seriously with the intellectual aspects of the life of students as well as the spiritual, physical, and emotional dimensions.

The campus house at Portales was next door to the Church of Christ Bible Chair building. The relationship between the Chrisitan Campus House and the Church of Christ Bible Chair became one of more than physical proximity. The Church of Christ Bible Chair had been founded in 1947. Stephen D. Eckstein, who was a 1950 MA graduate of ENMU, became Director of the Chair in 1952. He had earned his PhD by then, and was one of the first persons involved in Bible Chair work among the Churches of Christ.[38] When Dean Overton began teaching religion classes for credit in 1970, Dr. Eckstein was very encouraging, and the two men worked very closely together in a common cause until Dr. Eckstein left Portales in 1988. "During Eckstein's 33 years at ENMU, he had over 5,000 enrolled in his religion classes, with 167 Master's Degrees in Religion awarded while he served."[39]

In 1980, Dean Overton left Portales to pursue a Doctor of Ministry Degree at Fuller Theological Seminary in Pasadena, California. He was able to complete only one semester at Fuller, however, because of the sudden and unexpected death of John Eggleton in October. Dean returned to Portales to help "pick up the pieces" and resume his ministry. In the spring semester of 1983, Dr. Scott Caulley and his family were called to take over the academic part of the program which John Eggleton had led so admirably. Dean continued teaching the undergraduate courses. In July of 1988, Scott Caulley and his family left Portales to join the faculty at Manhattan Christian College. Dean Overton has been teaching in this remarkable program for 23 years, and he has tried to sum up its impact in various ways. During the "Eggleton years," for example, Dean says:

> The precise number of students that took credit courses from John during those seven years are not known, but it numbered in the hundreds. As a part-time instructor, I taught 28 classes with an average size of 22 students for a total of 610 students.[40]

The academic program at Portales continued to be very productive during the years of Scott Caulley's leadership, and beyond, under the continued leadership of Dean Overton. The other aspects of the programs for students were not neglected, but the academic program became Dean's first priority. Replying to a questionnaire I sent to him in 1992, Dean summed up this aspect of the ministry at Portales with the following statistics:

*Number of students in your ministry this year? — 110
*Total number of graduates from your ministry since its beginning? — 420
(Keep in mind many other transferred to other schools or never completed their degrees.)
*Number in "secular" professions and careers? — 350
*Number in church related ministries? — 70
*Number active in work of churches? — 220
*Number that married after having met on campus? — 132

In 1989 Ken Broad, who had been minister of the Central Christian Church at Portales, became part-time public relations and business manager of this campus ministry. Ken's experiences in many fields, and his love for campus ministry strengthened the program noticeably and freed Dean to do other things. This is a remakable campus ministry, and Dean Overton and his associates have done an outstanding job over the 26 year period of its existence. Dean wrote in 1987:

There is no way that we can give our readers the exact number of students who have come and gone from this "House by the Side of the Road." The most exact record I have to use are my grade books from 1970 to the present — the total is over 1,350 students. However, this figure does not include the students in the classes of John and Scott, and it does not include the hundred of students who participate in our fellowship without taking classes. So only God knows the exact number. We only know it has been "innumerable."[41]

## The Purdue Christian Campus House and Christian Student Fellowship at Purdue University

The campus ministry at Purdue University in West Lafayette, Indiana, began in the early 60s as a grass roots movement among Christian students. Several young people from Christian Churches who had elected to go the state university rather than Bible college, feeling the need of fellowship and support, banded together and formed the "Christian Student Fellowship," recognized officially by the University in 1962. Most of these students, while at college, had been attending one of the two Christian Churches in Lafayette and they were encouraged and supported by Les Parker, minister of the Linnwood Church of Christ, and Loren Hetrick (later Gary Edwards) of the Brady Lane Church of Christ.

The enthusiasm was high among these students — they told of study and worship sessions together in the South Tower Room of the Purdue Student Union Building. They reported intense times of fellowship, and visits to area churches to ask for support for a stronger campus ministry at Purdue University. (By the summer of 1966 these students had raised from interested churches and individuals $2,000 for this ministry). As a result of the persistence and prayer of this small band of students, their visits to churches, and their pestering of their parents, many of whom were leaders in their home churches, an open meeting was called for March 6, 1966, at the Linnwood Church of Christ, to consider launching a full-time campus ministry at Purdue. Stan Smith, dynamic campus minister at the University of Illinois, was the speaker. Representatives from 19 churches attended and a Board of Directors of 10 men was appointed to take the next steps.[42]

After an organizational meeting on March 12th, this Board met on April 16th to plan for the future. McCord Steele, Board Member from the Pine Village Christian Church, had already located two houses for possible purchase or lease for a campus house. At the third meeting of the Board on July 9, 1966, Doug Dickey, long time minister of the Williamsport, Indiana Christian Church, was called as full-time campus minister.[43] With the support of the new organization, now officially named "Purdue Christian Campus House," the Purdue ministry was underway. Shortly after the meeting, through the skillful work of McCord Steele, the house at 329 Russell Street, newly purchased by Purdue Research Foundation, was leased for a "campus house." The house was two blocks from the center of the Purdue campus.[44]

All through the history of this campus ministry there have been two complementary organizations and two specialized ministries. One level is the Board of Directors who acted as liaison between the supporting churches and the student ministry on campus. Officially, "Purdue Christian Campus House," this organization operated according to a set of bylaws as an incorporated body in the State of Indiana. On the other level is the student fellowship, recognized officially by Purdue University as "The Christian Campus House." I worked with both groups and I was overwhelmed from the beginning by the vision and vitality which operated in and between them. There was a deep conviction that God wanted something to happen at Purdue through these people.

The summer of 1966 was spent in preparing for the activities of the first semester on campus, and in contacting churches for support. I, the Board members, and the students worked together in this preparation. Linda Wolf, secretary for the student officers that first year, maintains that prayer was the most dynamic force operating in the origin and maturing of this ministry. Many students and others agree with Linda.

By the beginning of the fall semester of 1966 the campus house was cleaned and furnished, the campus minister was on board and the student leaders were eager for action. The first big event was the "Call Out" for freshman students on Sunday evening, September 11, 1966. More than 90 people attended, and a precedent was set for Sunday evening "Cost Suppers" when students would come for fellowship and special programs. There were no students living in the house the first semester, but it soon became the heart of the ministry. Worship, central to any ministry, was provided by the two churches, Linnwood and Brady Lane, on Sundays. Transportation was provided, and by the end of the first semester, more than 60 people were worshiping with these two congregations.

Bible study and education took two forms: special non-credit courses, and small group Bible studies. I taught a Wednesday night course on "The Relevance of the Bible" (averaging over 20 students), and Dr. Richard Phillips, recently resigned from the faculty at Lincoln Christian College, taught a non-credit course on "Christian Faith in the Scientific Age" (over 19 students attended). Several small group Bible studies were organized as well.[45]

An excellent relationship with supporting churches began the first year, and it has grown throughout the 28 years of this ministry. A strong Board of Directors and a "Minister's Advisory Committee" met every month to build this support, and to oversee and encourage the ministry of the students. The practice of "Outreach Teams" — groups of students who visited the church to present programs and build relationships — began early as an integral part of this ministry.

Evidence of the healthy relationship between the churches and the campus ministry came in the first annual meeting held at the Purdue Union Building on Saturday, June 10, 1967. Ninety-three people attended, representing 23 supporting churches. Business was transacted, reports presented, prayer and praise given for the first exciting year of the Purdue Christian Campus ministry and an inspiring address given by Dr. Dudley Dennison, a cardiologist from Indianapolis.[46] The student leaders, no doubt correctly, attributed much of the success of this first year to an intensive "Prayer and Planning Retreat" which had been held at Turkey Run State Park in January. In any case, after another summer of preparation, the second semester provided solid evidence, if any was needed, that this ministry was empowered by the purpose of God for the Purdue campus, and beyond.

The first "Call Out" for the second semester, September 1967, was attended by 137 people who came for chicken dinner, fellowship and to check out this new group on the Purdue campus. Even more surprising, and a little disturbing, was the fact that 97 people showed up on Sunday morning and tried to crowd into two rooms of the campus house for the first Sunday morning study class.[47] Several things became evident to all of us — we needed larger facilities and we had to think bigger about the future.

Since it is impossible to cover the 28 years of this ministry in detail, what I have done above is to sketch the events of the first year up to the beginning of the second year. Now, I will pick up on certain categories of this ministry which, beginning the first year, became "constants" throughout the 28 years, and through brief consideration of which we can get a view of the larger picture of this particular ministry, as well as some of the ways it related to campus ministries as they were developing across the country.

## Worship

Roger Callahan, long time campus minister at Purdue, wrote in 1988:

> Worship is the ultimate priority. We were made to worship God. For nothing is more important than worship — our ministry puts the most time, the most energy, the most planning, the most effort involving people in corporate worship. Every service has nearly 20 hours of preparation and involves 6 – 10 people.[48]

There are two issues regarding worship in campus ministry — one is the *place* and the other is *participation*. We have alluded before to the fact that campus ministry has often been criticized for providing worship on campus, away from the local church. Purdue made the decision in 1970 to begin worship services on campus. Before that time, as I have indicated, students were transported to the two local churches to worship with those congregations. There were two problems with this arrangement: 1) only Christian students will make the effort to go across town to worship — the non-Christian was left out. 2) students were deprived of *participation* in the planning and presenting of the worship service.

For these and other reasons, the Purdue ministry began worship services on campus in 1970. When the house became too small at the beginning of 1967, a portable building was purchased and erected in a vacant lot next to the campus house. Variously called "The Annex" or "The Outpost," this building served well until 1988 when, worn out, it was torn down. The rationale for this move was that if we were to reach the non-Christians on campus, we needed to have worship services available to him/her as close as possible. From the very first Sunday in the fall of 1970, the Annex was filled to capacity each Sunday for worship — 100 to 125 people.

When the "Purdue Christian Ministry Center" was completed in 1972 (story about this later) the worship service expanded into two on Sunday and reached even more students. These services served as a kind of "funnel" — visitors, seekers, non-Christians would come to the worship service and *then* become active in study, service and fellowship groups. The second advantage of the worship on campus was the opportunity for students to *plan* and *participate* significantly in the worship, which is superb training for their later leadership in the local church. At the time of the twentieth anniversary of the Purdue ministry in 1986, Roger Callahan reported, "Over 10,000 people have shared in our on campus worship services. Over 1,000 different people per year for the past ten years alone. The average weekly attendance is more than 300 people."[49]

## Study

Bible study is vital to ministry, and to any kind of personal Christian growth. The three categories of study which Purdue Campus Ministry offered over the years were: non-credit classes, small Bible study groups, and formal classes for academic credit. Among the non-credit classes offered to students were: "The Christian Use of Sex," taught by Wallace Denton of the Family Counseling Department at Purdue, and "Christ in Contemporary Culture," taught by Rondal Smith of the Faculty at Lincoln Christian College. Many special lecturers, both from the Purdue faculty and from specialized fields outside Purdue, were utilized over the years.

Small Bible study groups are a staple of campus ministry — not only at Purdue, but at campus ministries in general. One of my most satisfying experiences in this regard was a small group which studied Romans together during my second year at Purdue. Student participation is the key to these groups, and the learning is intensified through this method.

Beginning in 1973, through special arrangements with Purdue and Milligan College in Tennessee, an academic program in biblical studies was offered for Purdue students.[50] I, and others I recruited to teach in this program, were official instructors at Milligan College on the Purdue campus. Courses taken could be transferred for credit to the student's transcript towards graduation from Purdue. Seven different Bible courses, along with Apologetics, Greek and Christian Counseling, were offered from 1973 to 1981, and over 900 students took courses for credit in this program. When I left Purdue, Dr. Robert Ross was called to continue teaching in the Milligan program. In 1985, however, Purdue "changed rules" and the program had to be canceled. This did not end the educational offerings of the campus house, because Roger Callahan and others presented a rich variety of non-credit classes in place of the formal academic program.

The exciting thing about all three of the study programs offered during the history of the Purdue campus ministry, is that thousands of college students who had opted not to go to Bible college for whatever reasons were exposed to serious biblical study which, in many cases, was a life-changing experience.

## *Fellowship*

The word "fellowship" has a certain ambiguity, often suggesting superficiality in human relationships. A careful review of the history of the Purdue Campus Ministry suggests, however, a richer and wider connotation of the word. From the "fun," even silly, events on the one hand — hayrides, mid-winter beach parties, volleyball, pig roasts, barn dances, pot lucks, spontaneous cook-outs — to the deeply significant relationships of *koinonia*, this experience of belonging to a family, the family of God, where one is accepted and the love of God is experienced through relationships with persons is a life-changing experience.

It is difficult to define where the fellowship took place. Sometimes it was a cost supper; sometimes it was through living together in campus houses; almost always it was the product of the bus trip to Cookson Hills, where students worked together in the woods; and of large gatherings of college students from many campuses in "retreats," French Lick and Little Galilee and Blue Grass. Roger Callahan in his twenty year report put it this way, "Hundreds of parties, dinners, and social occasions were planned for the elimination of loneliness. Hundreds of people helping one another discover the fullness of Christ, to get through near failure, to change career goals, to get over discouragement, marked the twenty years of Purdue Campus Ministry."[51]

## Evangelism

The basic philosophy of evangelism at Purdue Campus Ministry has always been "Evangelism by Fellowship." By fellowship, but not exclusively. The regular worship service, Bible study groups, social events, service projects and day to day contacts of Christian students with fellow students and professors has been productive in winning students to Christ. (During one memorable trip to Cookson Hills Christian School in Oklahoma during the 70s, I baptized 25 Purdue students in one evening at the closing chapel service with the Cookson people. More than one-third of those who were baptized were students from the fraternities and sororities).

There were, however, specific evangelistic programs which were very effective. JC (Joy Celebration) Week began in 1972. It was an evangelistic meeting, held first in the Ministry Center and then in the large ballroom in the Purdue Union. Thousands have attended these meetings over the years to hear speakers like A. Dale Crain, Darrell Terry, Pete Gillquist, Mike Yaconneli, Larry Brandon, Logan Fox, Lewis Smedes, and others. One year, when Mike Yaconneli was the speaker, a fraternity dismissed their Friday night social event and came together to JC Week!

In the fall of 1990 the Christian Student Fellowship began the year with a specific evangelistic program. They described the program as follows:

> We decided to reach out to students who are unchurched — students who aren't sure about "organized religion," what they believe about God, or if they believe in God. We believe such students deserve to find a place where they can think seriously about God, Jesus, and the life patterned after eternal love. . . . It has been exciting to see students not accustomed to "going to church" attend and learn biblical truth, encounter students who are serious about their faith, and experience the power of Christian love in action. . . . The impact of this program is evident in this from a student: "where it was just a year ago when I was baptized. I have reflected many times during that year on the great role which you and others in the Campus House family played in making Jesus a new and very real force in my life."[52]

## Missions and Service

One of the surprises of campus ministry is the number of college students who have become interested in and committed to service projects and missions through their experience in campus fellowships. The Purdue Ministry began early to serve through mid-winter trips to Grundy Mountain Mission School in Grundy, Virginia, in 1966 and 1967, and beginning with the Christmas break in 1968 to Cookson Hills in Siloam Springs, Arkansas. By 1989 more than 1,000 Purdue students had taken a week out of their Christmas break, spent their own money, and had gone to Cookson Hills to cut wood, paint rooms, sew clothes, teach children, and generally experience the joy of service. In 1989 trips were also taken to two other Cookson locations, one in Florida and one in Haiti. The trip to Haiti is an example of college students' commitment to missions. In May of 1989, ten students went to the Cookson Orphanage in Haiti. Each person raised $600 for plane fare, food, and building supplies. CSF raised $3,000 to help these students take this trip, and when the 10 students left Haiti to return to Purdue they left $1,300 to help the mission. This trip was the subject of two feature stories in the Lafayette *Journal Courier.*

In addition to these trips Roger Callahan says an average of 100 students a year have been involved in at least one mission or service project in and around Lafayette. Also, an even broader vision of world mission has challenged the students in recent years.[53]

As we shall see later, the interest in missions has spread through other campuses through campus ministry until the University campus has again become one of the most fertile recruiting grounds for dedicated missionaries.

## *Relationship to the Churches*

One of the most persistent criticisms of campus ministry is that it tends to separate people from the local church. Not so at Purdue. The evidence of this is seen in several factors. From the beginning the Purdue Ministry has been strongly supported and overseen by a strong Board of Directors. These men and women, all outstanding leaders in their own congregations, and deeply committed to campus ministry, have made it a top priority to nourish the relationship between the ministry and the churches. Each year the annual meeting has had an increasing number of representatives of the local churches indicating strong support.[54]

Another evidence of the healthy relationship with the churches is the outreach teams — groups of students who visit churches and present programs nearly every Sunday of the year. Students are encouraged by the warmth of the reception they receive at the church, and church members are encouraged by the enthusiastic Christian young people from the university campus. Perhaps the most vivid symbol of the intimate relationship between the campus ministry and the supporting churches, however, is the annual "Century Club," which began in 1970. The idea is simple. Anyone who contributes $100 during the calendar year to the Purdue Campus Ministry is given two tickets to a free steak dinner which is held in the Ballroom of the Purdue Union, with entertainment provided by the world famous Purdue Varsity Glee Club. This event has become a true celebration of a mutual relationship in the Kingdom of God. In 1990, 305 individuals and couples contributed $49,000 to the Century Club, a powerful expression of support from the churches.[55]

There is a vital relationship between the campus ministry and the churches: the campus ministry depends upon the churches for support and encouragement, and the church depends upon the campus ministry for producing leaders for the future.

## Relationship to the University

If the campus ministry seeks only to serve its own students, ignoring the university community around it, it has failed. The Purdue Ministry has had a significant impact on the university during its 28 year history. Dr. Arthur Hansen, during over 10 years as President of Purdue, spoke for the campus house worship services several times, and taught the book of Job in the Milligan classes four different times. The Christian Ministry Center building would not have been possible without the strong support of Purdue Research Foundation (PRF), who sold the land to the campus ministry and encouraged the concept of construction from the beginning. There are now four campus houses, three of which are leased from Purdue Research Foundation, which means they approve of the presence of the campus ministry at Purdue.

During the 1974–1975 school year the musical *Godspell*, based on the Gospel of Matthew, was presented by the campus house students. Weeks of hard work and prayer went into rehearsals and the result was four performances with packed houses — three in the Fowler Hall on campus. Editors of *The Debris*, the Purdue annual, asked permission to do a picture story because, in their opinion, "this production was one of the most significant events on campus during the entire school year."[56] The Purdue campus ministry is no longer "one of the best kept secrets on campus."

## Leadership Personnel

Among others, there have been two practical principles that have been determinative in the life of the Purdue campus ministry. One is "people before property," and the other is "the importance of strong student leadership." From the beginning, those who have been in the position of full-time paid leaders have seen themselves, not in positions of power, but rather as catalysts to develop strong student leaders. The Reformation and Restoration principle of "the priesthood of all believers" has been taken seriously here from the beginning.

There have been nine people, with a variety of talents, who have served during various periods of time, "professional" leadership roles in the Purdue campus ministry. I was the first full-time campus minister, and I served in this capacity from 1966–1982. I came to Purdue from a 28 year ministry with the Williamsport, Indiana, Christian Church. I originated and taught in the Milligan academic program for nine years, in addition to my role as campus minister and administrator. I also earned a

Master's degree in Philosophy while at Purdue. I left in 1982 to go to California to teach at Pacific Christian College and to pursue campus ministry at California State University, Fullerton.

Shirley Felix, if she will forgive my saying so, is a beloved "institution" at Purdue, and among many other campus ministries. In these days when there is controversy about the role of women in the church, Shirley stands out as a true minister of Christ to students during her 26 years "and holding." She has been Secretary, Assistant, "Den Mother" to students, and general, all-around encourager to everyone. The history of Purdue campus ministry would have been much poorer without Shirley Felix.

Roger Callahan came to the Purdue campus ministry as my Associate in 1973. Roger brought a wealth of experience to Purdue. A graduate of Cincinnati Bible Seminary, and holding a graduate degree from Xavier University, Roger had been the Director of Challenged Unlimited, a pioneering College-Career ministry in Cincinnati, Ohio. While there, he developed a campus ministry at Miami University in Oxford, Ohio, and at the University of Cincinnati. He also planned and promoted the popular French Lick convocation each year, which was attended by 600 to 1,000 college/career people each spring.

In 1979, Roger left Purdue to serve as coordinator for Lafayette Urban Ministry, but he returned to Purdue in January of 1982. Roger continues at this writing as campus minister and he has been and continues to be one of the most creative and committed campus ministers in the country.

John Southwood served as Associate Campus Minister from 1975-1981. John had graduated from Purdue and had been active in the Purdue fellowship in all four years. After leaving Purdue, he received his graduate degree from Fuller Theological Seminary in Pasadena, California. He returned to Purdue as Associate Campus Minister in 1975 and left to go into business in 1981. John had a true gift for understanding students and for ministering to them. He left his mark on many lives during his years with Purdue Campus Ministry.

Peggy Clark was a Purdue graduate in English, and was also an alumnus of the Fellowship. She became an Associate Campus minister in 1980 and left in 1986 to be married. Peggy's warmth, laughter, and obvious commitment brightened all she did.

John Elliott was a graduate of Cincinnati Bible Seminary and a concert pianist when he came to Purdue in 1981. John was a blessing to the ministry through his musical talent, but also as a counselor and friend of students. He left in 1983 to pursue his musical career.

Rob Schrumpf grew up in Cookson Hills Christian School where his family served. For years he saw Purdue students come to Cookson and serve. He was so impressed by these students that he dreamed for years of becoming a part of the Purdue campus ministry, which he did in 1988 after graduating from Johnson Bible College. Rob is talented in music and drama and has a special touch with students which has proved to be an invaluable addition to the staff at Purdue. Nathan Charles, a native of Trinidad and a graduate student at Purdue, served on staff of the campus ministry in 1984 and 1985, and his insight into Scripture and his sensitive counseling were much appreciated while he served.

Professional leadership is important, but an outstanding characteristic of the Purdue ministry has been strong student leadership from the beginning.

## Property and Finance

Property — buildings — are essential to ministry. The "Guy's House" was leased from Purdue Research in 1966 and is still in use. The next acquisition was the portable annex bought in 1967 located next to the Guy's House. It served admirably until 1988 when, worn out by use, it was torn down.

The major acquisition of property, however, was the Christian Ministries Center. This interesting concept began in 1968 when we learned that Purdue would be willing to sell land *on campus* to religious groups who were willing to work together. We took the initiative, and called a meeting of the leaders of over 25 religious groups at Purdue in 1968. Four years later, after much prayer and many, many meetings, we dedicated the Christian Ministry Center, across the street from the large classroom complex on State Street. We shared it with four other religious groups, who had worked with us in the planning and financing, each group having its own office area and all of us sharing the large worship room upstairs. Fortunately, our group has had access to the large worship room all the years since the Christian Ministry Center was built.

The Girl's House, leased from Purdue in 1977, was the next move, and in 1991, Joshua House, a 15 room co-op was purchased by the campus house, and in 1992 another house was leased from Purdue. At this writing, the Purdue Campus Ministry is housed in the Christian Ministry Center, it has four houses which accomodate a total of 33 students, and it has made a tremendous impact on the campus at Purdue by these visible symbols of its ministry.

Finances are always vitally important. Budget of the Purdue Campus House was $17,000 in 1966 and 1967. The budget for 1990 was over $250,000. This money came from three sources: gifts from churches, gifts from individuals, and rental of property. Students carry their own program, contributing and increasing the amount each year until in 1990 they gave $29,436 to their own program, of which $1,500 was contributed to the larger budget of Purdue Christian Campus House.[57] Where there is commitment, the Lord will provide.

## The Product of the Ministry

There is no accurate measuring rod to determine the far flung results of the 28 years of this ministry. At the end of each school year, beginning in 1967, a "Sweatshirt Party" is held. Each graduating senior is given a sweatshirt emblazoned "CSF Has Been." At least 3,000 people are wearing these sweatshirts across the world. Many who did not receive sweatshirts are also products of this campus ministry, having participated in the worship or some other part of the ministry. Roger Callahan, in a questionnaire returned to me in 1992, indicated that at least 12,000 people have gone through this campus ministry in some significant way. 6,000 of these are in "secular professions," 50 are ministers or missionaries, and at least 300 are married couples.[58] The encouraging statistic, however, is that of a poll taken of graduates in 1992, which revealed that 98% of those who are active in the ministry on campus are still active in churches. They are in every imaginable profession, from farmers to teachers, from engineers to nurses, from space technologists to F.B.I. agents, and they are making a vital difference for Christ in the marketplace of the world.[59]

# The Bible Chair of the Southwest in Amarillo, Texas

It is to the everlasting credit of the Disciples that they had the vision to found the first Bible Chair at the University of Michigan in 1893. C.A. Young, the minister at the Disciple church in Ann Arbor, had apparently caught the vision of the Bible Chair from Thomas Jefferson who had proposed that different religious groups should be allowed to establish schools around the University of Virginia.[60] However, whereas Jefferson had believed that the religious schools around the university would benefit from their students taking liberal arts and science courses from the state schools, Young's purpose was the reverse — that the state university students would benefit from the religion instruction available from the Bible Chair.[61]

Following the latter purpose, several interested churches and individuals in Texas established the Bible Chair of the Southwest at Amarillo College in Amarillo, Texas. It was incorporated under the laws of Texas in 1966 after having been approved by the Board of Regents of Amarillo College. Excellent property was acquired across the street from the college for $25,000, and Grayson H. Ensign was called from the Presidency of Central Christian College in Moberly, Missouri, to be director.[62]

Offered at this Bible Chair are credit and non-credit courses, as well as a two-year Associate Degree with a major in religion. Trustees from each of three Christian Churches oversee the work and raise funds. Grayson Ensign served as Director until 1970; Frederick L. Black has taught and administered the program since 1970. Over 2,000 students have taken classes through this Bible Chair program, which also offers counseling and activities for Christian and non-Christian students.[63]

The Bible Chair at Amarillo is probably closer to the original model at the University of Michigan than any other campus ministry among the Christian Churches. Although the Bible Chair movement among the Disciples has virtually died out, the model has flourished among the Churches of Christ campus ministries.[64]

# Christian Student Foundation, Ball State University, Muncie, Indiana (Continued)

The campus ministry at Ball State University in Muncie, Indiana, progressed in four definite phases. During the years 1957–1962, Dean Hickerson laid the ground work for the ministry.[65] After Dean left the ministry at the University Church in Muncie, there was little activity until June of 1966 when John Brownlee became minister of the University Church. John and his wife Sandra picked up where Dean had left off, supported by Lance and Jean Van Tassel, sponsors of the college group at the church, which had been active in the intervening years.[66]

In the fall of 1966, after learning that there were 300 students at Ball State who had signed Religious Preference Cards indicating their membership in Christian Churches, John and the church held a "Know Your Church Night" at the University, and 50 freshmen attended the reception. The next such meeting was attended by 100 students, which caused John and Sandra to say, "Now we are really aware of the opportunity for campus ministry at Ball State."[67]

In September of 1966, John and Sandra began hosting a regular Tuesday night gathering of college students in their home which became, as John says, "The foundation of the campus ministry at Ball State." In that same month, John and Lance Van Tassel attended the Little Galilee conference in Illinois, which, as John says, "enlarged their visions" about the possibility of campus ministry at Ball State. On April 11, 1967, John was elected to the Religious Advisors Committee sponsored by the university, which confirmed the support of the ministry by the university.[68]

In June of 1967, I, having just finished the exciting first year of campus ministry at Purdue, and Gary Edwards, minister at the Brady Lane Church in Lafayette, met with John Brownlee at a dinner in his home to explore ways of strengthening the campus ministry at Ball State. Shortly after this meeting, John called together a Steering Committee, made up of several people from University Church and other interested churches. Through the work of this committee, in November of 1967, Gary Edwards became the full-time campus minister at Ball State, and by January 3, 1968, a campus house had been purchased, and the third phase of this ministry was under way under the leadership of Gary Edwards.

During the transition period between the work of John Brownlee and the ministry of Gary Edwards at Ball State, an exciting event took place which was symbolic of the 60s and which, in many ways, set the tone for the campus ministry under Gary Edwards' leadership.

Ball State University had a Council of Religious Groups made up of student representatives. This group planned a "Religious Emphasis Week" in the spring of 1968 which was to feature a speech by Anson Mount, religion editor of *Playboy* magazine. John Brownlee and Gary Edwards challenged this event as too one-sided, and they urged, rather, that a debate be held between Anson Mount and Bill Banowsky, then Executive Vice President at Pepperdine College in Los Angeles. This challenge was accepted by the students of the Religious Council, and the debate was set up for April 21, 1968, as an all-campus event. The proposition of the debate was to be "Is situation ethics consistent with Christian ethics?" — with Mount taking the affirmative position and Banowsky taking the negative.

By a strange turn of events, Anson Mount canceled this engagement, for whatever reason, and Dr. Joseph Fletcher, Professor at Episcopal Theological School, Cambridge, Massachusetts, and author of the book *Situation Ethics*, came in his place. More than 2,000 students appeared at the university auditorium for this event.[69] John Brownlee describes the paradoxical scene as these debaters appeared on the platform. Dr. Banowsky, who was young, tall, handsome and athletic, the students mistook for the spokesman for *Playboy*, and Joseph Fletcher, gray, middle-aged, and conservative appearing, they mistook for "the old preacher." As in most debates, there was probably not a clear winner, but what Bill Banowsky did was to make credible the case for Christian ethics in the eyes of hundreds of students at a time when Christianity was under intense fire from all sides. In any case, one university administrator was quoted as having said, "this is the greatest religious program to be presented at Ball State University."[70]

Gary Edwards' ministry at Ball State lasted from 1967–1972, and during that period a campus house was purchased at 101 N. Calvert Street, Muncie, Indiana, a few blocks from the campus. Even more importantly, Gary led in the construction of the Christian Student Foundation Campus House, a large, stone, A-frame structure adjacent to the university campus. In addition to a large room for worship, this building included a fellowship hall, offices, a kitchen and living quarters for students. This impressive building made possible student worship services on campus which, during Gary's ministry, were hugely attended. "60s" kind of music and Gary's exciting preaching made this building the center of some of the most vital campus ministry on this or on any other campus during that late, turbulent period of the 60s. Gary Edwards was a bold, innovative, "pied-piper" kind of campus minister whose influence spread outside of Ball State to campus ministries in many other parts of the country.

In addition to the worship services in the new building, Gary and his leaders planned the kind of program at Ball State which was particularly appealing to students of the sixties. Bible study groups, retreats, and work trips were the core of the program. In addition, several campus-wide concerts featuring well known musical groups playing sixties-style gospel music were sponsored by Gary and his students, and they were hugely successful. Gary left the ministry at Ball State in 1972 to become the campus minister at the University of Wisconsin in Madison, following the pioneering ministry of Sam and Bonnie Fox. Willard Walls succeeded Gary at Ball State, and the fourth phase of the campus ministry there began with Will's ministry.

## Campus Ministry at Illinois State University and Illinois Wesleyan University, Normal, Illinois

In 1967, Eastview Christian Church was a new and growing congregation on the outskirts of Normal and Bloomington, Illinois. Normal was the sight of two growing universities — Illinois State and Illinois Wesleyan. Because of the proximity of these two universities to the church, a forward looking and aggressive ministry to college students was being carried on by minister Bob Phillips, and the Eastview congregation. They were ministering to about 30 college students in 1967. These students met together on campus, and attended Eastview worship services by bus on Sunday mornings.[71]

Sensing the possibility of a more active campus ministry on these two campuses, Bob Phillips and Leon Appel, then President of Lincoln Christian College, met with J. David Lang in late 1967 to ask him if he was interested in becoming campus minister. Their choice of Dave Lang was an inspired one. He had not only become widely know among Christian Churches as a writer and editor at Standard Publishing Company in Cincinnati, but he also had been one of the prime movers in the organization of Challenge Unlimited, an "umbrella" organization that started several campus ministries in the Cincinnati area in the 1960s. Dave Lang and Challenge Unlimited had also organized the now famous "French Lick Convocation" which, in February of 1967, had been a powerful impetus to the whole campus ministry movement during the explosive 60s (more about Challenge Unlimited and French Lick later in this chapter). As Dave Lang left Standard Publishing Company in 1968 to become the full time campus minister at Illinois State and Illinois Wesleyan, he gave three reasons for his decision to Burris Butler, his boss at Standard: 1) Since he had attained some recognition for his editorial work at Standard, he believed he could be influential in campus ministry. 2) He felt that his background and experience as a minister in the local church could help him keep campus ministry on an even theological course. 3) He believed that the Lord's church was divine, but that it needed a new breath of fresh air from free-thinking collegians who could reform the church and bring about significant change.[72]

David Lang's five year ministry at Illinois State and Illinois Wesleyan was an important part of the explosion of campus ministry which began in the 60s. On November 17, 1968 open house was held in a newly acquired house near the campus of Illinois State. People from more than 30 Illinois communities visited the new facility on that day.[73]

The house provided a home for eight male students, including two international students and a decorated veteran of the Vietnam war.[74] David Lang offered college courses from Lincoln Christian College which could be transferred to ISU for credit. By 1970 more than 300 students were involved in a Christian student fellowship known as Christian Collegians. They purchased a school bus and provided transportation to the Eastview Christian Church on Sunday mornings where from 60 to 75 students attended special Bible school classes and worship services.[75] Thus David Lang's ideal of keeping a strong tie between campus ministry and the local Christian church was realized.

The passion which David Lang had for campus ministry is indicated in the following quotation from him which appeared in the *Lookout Magazine* in 1970:

I stand on the campus and observe the thousands of collegians who are crowding through the halls of learning in quest of tomorrow. They are vigorous, quick thinking, and devastatingly frank. They are sometimes gay, laughing, and care free; sometimes deeply troubled, frustrated, lonely, and guilt ridden. They have the daring energy to conquer the world, but may lack the maturity and patience to rule it. They are supremely confident but often secretly frightened to face the future. Can this reservoir of energy — physical, mental, spiritual — be released for Jesus Christ? Can the church recapture the imagination of these amazing young adults and challenge them to serve God through their chosen professions? I believe so! I know so![76]

The foundation was firmly laid for a strong campus ministry on these two campuses during the five years of David Lang's ministry. He resigned in 1973 and was succeeded by Jim Simkins. Jim was a graduate of Lincoln

Christian College and Seminary, and he has carried on a vigorous ministry on these two Illinois campuses for 20 years. A spacious and attractive building was built to house this ministry. This building is located on the campus of Illinois State University at 300 Normal Avenue, directly north of the Union/Auditorium Complex and across the street from the parking lot entrance. The building is central to the mainstream of university life, within walking distance of all Illinois State facilities, and only a short distance from Illinois Wesleyan University. It serves as the hub of fellowship, with activities occurring nearly every night of the week.

Jim Simkins and his student leaders offer a solid program of Sunday morning worship services, Sunday evening fellowship suppers, Wednesday night Bible study, and several discipleship groups for the training of leaders. They hold two retreats each year and they carry on a regular ministry in a local jail, as well as a Big Brother/Big Sister program for underprivileged children. Jim also teaches extension courses for Lincoln Christian College and does counseling with students along with his other duties. Social life, including athletic teams in basketball, volleyball, water volleyball, and other sports is an important part of the life of this ministry as well. More than 200 students are involved in this fellowship in any given year, and it is a worthy continuation of the campus ministry which was established by Dave Lang on these campuses in the sixties.[77]

# Campus Ministry at Indiana State University and Rose Hulman Institute

The Christian Campus Ministry of Terre Haute, Indiana, serving both Indiana State University and Rose Hulman Institute, began in 1968.[78] Students from both campuses had been attending Maplewood Christian Church in Terre Haute in rather large numbers for some time. Bob Reeves, minister of the Maplewood congregation, along with several leaders from that congregation and others from surrounding churches, took the lead in organizing the campus ministry. A Board of Directors was formed of people from several different churches in 1968.[79]

A. Dale Crain, minister of the Capitol City Christian Church in Lincoln, Nebraska, was called as campus minister in May of 1968. Dale, a graduate of Ozark Bible College (now Ozark Christian College), was eminently qualified for campus ministry since he had not only been working with college students in the congregation at Lincoln, but also had been doing graduate work at the University of Nebraska.

Under the direction of the newly formed Board of Directors, and with financial support from Maplewood and other congregations, Dale Crain began an exciting campus ministry in Terre Haute in the summer of

1968. One of the first things he did, along with his students, was to name the group SCAMPS. The name is an acrostic for "Serving Christ Alone Means Personal Satisfaction." This name, Dale reports, was originally suggested by an outstanding Chinese Christian named Lin Yutang.

The first property purchased by the campus ministry at Indiana State was a large abandoned hotel located very near the university campus. The hotel was never actually occupied by the SCAMPS, but due to Dale's shrewd business sense, it was sold at a profit of $7,000 and the money was used to buy an old grocery store, along with four adjacent houses and a garage near the campus. The grocery building was remodeled to provide office space, a kitchen, a worship room, and a study area. Three of the houses, which surrounded the building, were demolished to provide a large parking space. Dedication services for the "SCAMPS house" were held on Sunday, October 26, 1968, with a large attendance of interested people.

The program of the SCAMPS under Dale Crain's leadership consisted of Sunday worship services and Bible study for students, and Bible study classes for neighborhood children, led by students from the group. Outreach teams visited the churches regularly to solicit support, and special dinners were provided for international students on Christmas and Thanksgiving.

The SCAMPS, under Dale's leadership, and with strong student leaders and good support from the area churches, laid the foundation for an ongoing campus ministry in Terre Haute. Dale went on to work with a civil rights organization in Lynchburg, Virginia, in 1971, but the campus ministry at Terre Haute was continued under the leadership of Mr. and Mrs. Walter Puckett from 1971–1977. Mark and Sue Gallagher succeeded the Pucketts in 1978, and are serving this ministry at the present time.

## Campus Ministry at Missouri Southern State College, Joplin, Missouri

The campus ministry at Missouri Southern State College began in 1967 when Willard Black, then a faculty member at Ozark Bible College, began meeting regularly with a small group of students from the college. This group, which the students named Koinonia Student Fellowship, was given official recognition as a student group in the late 1960s.[79]

In 1969, B.A. Austin and the College Heights Christian Church to which he ministered took over sponsorship of the fellowship. Tom Marsh was called as the first part-time campus minister in 1972, and he worked with the group until 1974. Ron Jones was the second part-time campus minister, and he served until 1980 (Janice Jones, now Schlieker, was Ron's associate from 1977–1979. Janice served five years as the very efficient secretary of the NACCM). Bob Herbst served one year as minister with the fellowship until Ed Reynolds, the first full-time campus minister, came on board in 1981. The fellowship grew considerably during Ed's ministry and when he resigned in 1985, Matt Stafford became campus minister and served until 1989, assisted in his ministry by Brent Montgomery and Don Crockett. David Weaver, who had a degree in accounting from Missouri Southern, became the campus minister in 1989.

The College Heights Church building has provided space for this fellowship all during its 26 year history, although many meetings are held on the campus at Missouri Southern. In the mid-1970s the elders of the College Heights congregation decided that the ministry needed a more representative sponsorship, and a Board of Directors made up of men from several area churches was selected.

All the men and women who served as campus ministers of this group contributed in their own way to its well-being, but since David Weaver has become campus minister in 1989, the seeds that were sown during the previous years have begun to sprout and bear fruit. The program includes Tuesday night fellowship meetings, with music and Bible study. More than 200 attended this event each week in 1992. On Thursday noon, a free lunch is served in one of the dormitories, and a program of movies and Christian videos is presented. Weekend ministry trips, prison ministry, hospital ministry, nursing home ministry, and work trips to Mexico are all a regular part of this campus ministry.

The newsletters of 1991 and 1992 reflect the impressive growth and enthusiasm of this group. The number of students now reached in some way in a given school year is between 250 and 500. Phil Mehrens works with David Weaver in musical leadership, and his band assisted at an on-campus revival in November of 1991. There were three baptisms, fifteen recommitments, and numerous other decisions made during the four nights, with attendance averaging 100 people each night.[81]

A retreat was held in the fall of 1992 with several other campus ministries (Pittsburg State in Kansas and Southwest Missouri State in Springfield, Missouri, among others). "Over 300 students gathered at the Maranatha Retreat Center north of Mount Vernon, Missouri for what many students called 'one of the greatest weekends of their lives.'"[82]

Joplin, Missouri, has been well known as a center for many strong Christian organizations for many years, especially Ozark Christian College. Not so well known is the campus ministry at Missouri Southern College, which is ministering to college students while Ozark ministers to Bible college students. Both ministries are vital enterprises in the Kingdom of God.

# Campus Ministry at the University of Missouri, Stevens College, and Columbia College

The second campus ministry to be established in the state of Missouri, which now has more campus ministries than any other state, was begun at the University of Missouri in the fall of 1968. Many of the members of the Westside Christian Church, Columbia, were graduates or faculty members of the university. Because "they felt a strong need for a student center to give guidance and counsel to the Christian students, share Christ with the non-Christian students and professors, develop the leadership ability of the students for Christ, contact and evangelize the international student as one method of missions, and provide an oasis for spiritual refreshment to all who cared to share," they rented a house in September of 1968 and called Roy Weece from a successful twelve-year ministry at 9th Street Christian Church at Eldon, Missouri. Group sessions began with about 15 students participating in the fall of 1968.[83]

This ministry, under the leadership of Roy Weece, has become one of the strongest in the nation, not only through its influence in encouraging other campus ministries in the state of Missouri, but also by serving as a role model to campus ministers and campus ministries in other parts of the country. The fact that there are more campus ministries in the state of Missouri than any other state is largely due to Roy's encouragement and support of those who were interested in starting campus ministries on other Missouri campuses.

The two leased houses which were used by this campus ministry for the first three years were put up for sale in 1971. After a spectacular and prayerful fund raising drive in which $35,000 was raised in three months for the down-payment, the houses were purchased and used as headquarters and resident houses — one for male and the other for female students in 1971.[84]

There have been three main emphases in this campus ministry during the 26 years Roy Weece has been campus minister: 1) Evangelism 2) Training for ministry on many levels and 3) Ministry to International Students. More than 1,400 people have been baptized through this ministry, Roy Weece having set the example by his special gift for one-on-one evangelism. As a product of their emphasis on the equipping ministry (Ephesians 4:11-16), hundreds have been sent out from Columbia into both specialized ministry in the churches and various other professions. Students from Muslim, Buddhist, and Hindu backgrounds have been converted and baptized on this campus, which has had a full-time campus minister to the international students since 1981.[85]

In addition to these special emphases, the program at Columbia has been strong over the years in the more traditional areas — large

Wednesday night gatherings for fellowship and study, a Sunday worship service on campus, many small Bible study and prayer groups, short-term mission trips, participation in area retreats and convocations, and special non-credit classes taught in such subjects as: the Gospels, Apologetics, the Prophets, the Cults, New Testament Epistles, and Christian Unity.[86]

Roy Weece has had several talented and committed associates who have strengthened this ministry over the years. Jim Bilbro, a graduate of the University of Missouri in finance as well as a graduate of Ozark Bible College, has been Roy's associate since 1975. Others have been: Ross Duff, 1969–1974; Linda Adams 1975–1977; Dick Brzozowski 1981–1985; Randy Dolan, 1985–1988; and Craig Thompson, 1990–present.

All of these people have contributed to the success of this ministry in various ways, but Jim Bilbro has been especially influential during his eighteen years as Roy's associate. Recently the university chancellor ruled that all students were required to live in university dormitories, sororities, or fraternities during their first year on campus. Because Jim Bilbro had been Coordinator of the Campus Religious Advisors and had become known and respected by the university officials, he was able to get approval for the campus house housing (38 students) under this requirement. This is clearly an excellent example of the way campus ministers can support the university in its efforts to serve the students.

Typical also of the kind of power that campus ministry has had for Christ is the story of Rick Swindell. Rick came to the University of Missouri as a graduate student in 1971. He writes: "I had spent many years in agnosticism and atheism, but on the evening of September 4, 1971, I became a believer in Christ. Some of the students from the Christian campus house had prayed for me, and the Lord guided me to the campus house and that night I was baptized."

Rick concluded his graduate work at the university, and after spending some time overseas in agricultural work he decided that, "what poor countries needed most was not science, but Christian love and compassion." He returned to the States, entered Seminary, graduated and returned to the campus ministry at Columbia to work with international students during the 1986-87 school year. After that year he and his family (his wife Arlene had become a Christian while at Stevens College in Columbia) joined the campus ministry at Virginia Tech, where they now work full-time in a very productive ministry to international students.[87]

During his 25 years as campus minister at the University of Missouri, Roy Weece has been a kind of "ambassador at large" for campus ministry, speaking for revivals, rallies, workshops, and conventions all over the United States and in several foreign countries. Roy is certainly "Mr. Campus Ministry" in Missouri and God has used him in encouraging the organization of campus ministries in the state and across the country among Christian Churches.

# Campus Ministry at Indiana University

Beginning about 1962, a group of graduate students at Indiana University, most of them from Christian Churches, began meeting together regularly for discussion and prayer. They had been recognized by the university as an official religious club and their chosen name was CADRE. C.W. and Lois Callaway, missionaries to Thailand who were on furlough in the States, and doing graduate work at IU, were the first sponsors of the group. They had been instrumental in organizing it and they served as sponsors for several years.

In the late 1960s Gary Weedman, a graduate of Johnson Bible College who was doing graduate work at the university, became the sponsor of this group. Since the campus ministries at the University of Illinois and at Purdue had been so successful, Stan Smith (University of Illinois) and I (Purdue), along with several students were enthusiastic about helping to start other campus ministries. Indiana University looked like a fertile field because of the work that had been started there. Gary Weedman and I met in the summer of 1967 in the famous Gables Restaurant, on the IU campus. (The site was famous as the location of Hoagie Carmichael's composition of the well-known song Stardust). We met to discuss the possibility of a campus ministry at Indiana University, and out of that meeting came a dinner at the First Christian Church in Columbus, Indiana, held on March 12, 1966. Interested people from area churches were invited to this dinner to consider starting a campus ministry at Indiana University (Ard Hoven was the long-time minister of this outstanding congregation, and he added his prestige to the meeting and to the plans made there).

Several carloads of students from the University of Illinois and Purdue braved a severe snowstorm, as did the other people who attended the meeting, to attend the dinner and to give testimonies and show slides about their respective ministries. At this dinner a steering committee was appointed to take the next step toward a possible full-time campus ministry at Indiana University.

A permanent Board of Directors was soon formed, made up of representatives from several different congregations, and Gary Weedman was called as the campus minister. The parent organization was officially named *Indiana Campus Christian Ministry* and the student organization was officially named the *Christian Student Fellowship*. Gary began his ministry with the students in the summer of 1968. They began meeting regularly in the IU Student Union and later they rented a house near campus. This house was rented jointly with the Northside Church of Christ (*a cappella*) and Gary writes the following about that arrangement:

We rented it jointly with the Northside Church of Christ under the initiation of Doug Davis who was a colleague of mine at the University and also the minister of the Northside Church. When he suggested that we rent this building together, he said that I would be happy to know that there is even an organ in the building! While both the Northside Church and the I.U.C.C.M. carried on with our own programs, there were some sessions that we planned together and at any rate there was much crossover of "their students" and "our students" going to one another's meetings. It was always my regret that this nascent beginning of cooperation between the Non-instrumental churches and Christian Churches was never cultivated and it soon died out after I left.[88]

Gary Weedman continued as campus minister with this group until the summer of 1969 when he finished his work at the university and went to Johnson Bible College to teach. Jack Haun was called as full-time campus minister in 1969, and the program of the fellowship was expanded under his leadership.

In the late summer of 1969 a house was purchased close to the main campus of the university. This "campus house" provided housing for five male students, included a library and a bookstore, and became a gathering place for fellowship. Stanley K. McDaniel was Jack Haun's associate during his seven year ministry at Indiana University. In 1971, they inaugurated a Sunday worship service which was held in the Student Union building and began Sunday night cost suppers. Jack also taught several extension courses for Lincoln Christian College while at IU. Students in the fellowship taught Bible study classes for underpriveledged children, conducted programs in a convalescent home, and went on a service trip to Cookson Hills Christian School in Oklahoma each spring. One year they contributed seven hundred dollars to the school out of their own pockets. Another year they distributed 15,000 copies of the New Testament translation called *Good News for Modern Man* on the campus at IU.

Jack Haun's ministry provided a solid foundation for the next phase of the campus ministry at Indiana University, which began when Ward Patterson was called as associate campus minister in 1973.[89] When Jack left in 1976 Ward became campus minister and under his leadership this campus ministry grew into one of the strongest in the nation.

Gary Weedman tells about an incident which took place during his ministry with the fellowship at IU which gives some flavor of the mood which prevailed on the campuses in the 60s. Gary writes:

Another anecdote I remember from the early days of the CADRE Club was an attempt in October of 1967 to schedule a room in the Union for our meeting —normally a perfunctory task. This day, however, I was questioned intensely by the secretary and subsequently by the director of the Union himself. They were interested in the nature of the CADRE Club. I explained it was a church organization. They wanted to know with what church it was associated. I said it was just the Christian church. He wanted to know if it was associated with the First Christian Church. I explained no, it wasn't and gave him a history of the restoration movement. To make a long story shorter, we had reserved a room on the very day that there was to be on the campuses throughout the United States mass demonstrations against the draft. The IU administration had been warned to be on the lookout for an organization called the "Chicago Area Draft Resistance Enterprise — CADRE." We decided that the name might not reflect the true nature of this group![90]

## Campus Ministry at the University of Wisconsin

One of the hot spots of the counter cultural activity during the 60s was the campus of the University of Wisconsin at Madison. National attention was focused on this campus when in 1970, the mathematics research building was destroyed by a bomb planted by the radicals and an innocent student was killed.[91] The people who planted that bomb were not the only radicals on the campus of Madison — another revolutionary force entered there with the beginning of campus ministry in 1968.

God used a remarkable combination of dedicated people to launch that ministry. First were the Christian Churches of Madison. Their ministers and some of their members who saw the opportunity began to pray and plan for a way to reach the campus for Christ in the late 60s. Bruce Burdick, minister of First Christian Church; Howard Ganong Jr., Minister of Westwood Christian Church; along with John Mark Read, Minister of the Menomenie Church of Christ, took the leadership in this move. Howard Wakefield, Professor of Education at the University, was also an important person in this effort. From these interested parties came The Board of Directors of Madison Christian Student Foundations Inc., and in 1968 they called Sam and Bonnie Fox to be campus ministers.

Sam and Bonnie were both graduates of Nebraska Christian College, and they had been working with the Sixth Avenue Christian Church in Havre, Montana as youth ministers. There is a small college in Havre, the Northern Montana College of Education. Sam Fox was strongly attracted to this college, and he spent one night each week leading a study group there, and at least a half day each week "being available in the Student Union," as he put it.[92]

Sam's interest in campus ministry had been awakened by two men whom he had heard speak. One was Carl Ketcherside, one of the truly prophetic voices in the churches in the 60s and a minister at large for the churches of Christ. The other was Jerry Gibson, one of the originators of the campus ministry at the University of Minnesota.[93] Bonnie, Sam's wife, was also highly excited about the possibility of a campus ministry and had plans to enter the university as a pre-med student at Madison.

When the people in Madison approached Sam and Bonnie about

coming to Wisconsin as campus ministers, they had very little to offer except a challenge. In fact, Sam worked a forty hour week at a laboring job the first year and he and Bonnie used their apartment as the "campus house." The humble dedication and enthusiasm of these two people attracted both students and career people, and by the end of the first year a core group of about thirty students had been formed. The second year, Sam and Bonnie moved into an old house that was owned by First Christian Church. That house not only became their home, but the "campus house" and gathering place for the students.

The third key influence in launching the ministry at Madison came with the arrival of Dennis Helsabeck, Jr. on the Madison campus. Dennis came to the University of Wisconsin from Green Bay, Wisconsin, where he had been a high school guidance counselor. He had come to Madison to accept the position of High School Relations person in the office of the university. He was very talented in music and he formed the "Koinonia Singers" as a part of the campus ministry. They not only gathered a group of gifted students and career people together to sing "folk, Baroque, Renaissance, contemporary, gospel, and spiritual music,"[94] but they also became an influential public relations force among the churches as well as attracting considerable favorable attention on the campus at large. Dennis was a strong leader in the formation of this campus ministry until he left in 1970 to pursue graduate work at the University of Oregon , proving that it does not take "professional preachers" to do effective campus ministry.

The house where Sam and Bonnie Fox lived, beginning the second year of their ministry, also served as a campus house and was named the "Damascus Road House," alluding to the confrontation Paul the apostle had with Christ on the road to Damascus.[95]

Sam and Bonnie Fox left the campus ministry in Madison in May of 1972. The whole time they were there was a time of radical disruption by students on the campus of Madison, and Sam spent hours walking the streets talking to, confronting, and witnessing to all kinds of radical students during his ministry. The campus at Madison was a place of radical confrontation in the 1960s, not the least of which was the radical confrontation with Christ provided by the campus ministry under Sam and Bonnie Fox.

Gary Edwards came as the campus minister in 1972 to continue leadership in this significant campus ministry.

# The Beginnings of Campus Ministries in the State of Michigan

One of the outstanding characteristics of campus ministry among

Christian Churches is the variety of approaches that have been utilized in reaching the campus with the gospel. Since there are few, if any, established traditions to follow, there is considerable freedom in the strategies which have been adopted. Nowhere has this freedom been more evident than in the amazing growth of campus ministry in the state of Michigan over the past 25 years. The "Michigan Miracle" began in 1969 when Gary Hawes and his family were called from an associate ministry with the East 38th Street Christian Church in Indianapolis to become campus ministers at Michigan State University in East Lansing.

There had been some groundwork laid before his arrival. Don Stiffler, minister of the University Christian Church in East Lansing, Dr. Elwyn Miller, professor of animal husbandry at the university and a member of Stiffler's congregation, along with Gene Carter who was the minister of the Christian Church in Grand Rapids, Michigan, all had been interested in establishing a campus ministry at Michigan State for some time. They had been urged on by an eager group of Christian students from the University who had been influenced by attending the French Lick conference in Indiana in February 1967, and the Blue Grass conference in Kentucky in the spring of that same year. At these conferences the Michigan State students had met enthusiastic students from other campuses and had, as one of them said, "caught the disease of campus ministry."[96]

Other churches in the state became interested, and a corporation was formed in early 1969 under the name Michigan State University Student Christian Ministry, Inc.[97] This group called Gary Hawes, who began his unique ministry soon after. During the period when Gary was establishing the ministry at Michigan State, he and his leaders initiated certain principles of campus ministry which have been followed in the state of Michigan since. A house was soon purchased which was named "His House" and which became the center of a strong Christian community. Sunday worship services are not held on campus, but in congregations near the campuses. Intensive small group Bible studies with an emphasis upon accountability to Christ, to the church and to each other have been a regular part of the campus ministries in Michigan, as well.

The larger part of the "Michigan Story" took place in the 70s and 80s, and on into the 1990s, by which time seven full-time and several part-time campus ministries were established throughout the state and plans were under way to establish campus ministries overseas in the Philippines and other international locations. What makes the "Michigan Story" unique? First, of course, is the obvious working of the Holy Spirit through uniquely talented and dedicated people. The personality and distinctive gifts of Gary Hawes as an administrator and a pastoral minister — a rare combination — are a large part of the success of campus ministry in Michigan. After ten years of campus ministry on the Michigan State campus, during which time full-time campus ministries were founded on five other Michigan campuses, Gary became Executive Director of what by this time was named Michigan Christian Campus Ministries. Jeri Roesch, who was a new Christian when she arrived at Michigan State in 1972, and who became a strong student leader in that campus ministry, testifies to the special emphases on the campus ministry which we have mentioned above. Jeri was strengthened in her faith by the small group Bible studies which were, she says, "solid, biblically based, practical." Much of this Jeri Roesch contributes to Gary Hawes' strong leadership and role modeling.[98] The campus ministry of Michigan State remains the headquarters and heart of the campus ministries in the state of Michigan.

Gary's leadership, plus a strong Board of Directors, faithful supporting churches, and a growing number of enthusiastic and dedicated students has resulted in several unique features in Michigan. One is the centralized organization with several other campus ministries under a common board and Executive Director (There have been other campus ministries organized this way, but none as extensive or successful as this one). Second, an exceptionally dedicated Board of Directors, evidenced by the fact that several men who had served on this board resigned their jobs to become campus ministers.[99] Third, many students have come "up from the ranks" to become campus ministers, several of them having become Christians on the Michigan State campus.[100] Fourth, the vitality of these ministries is evidenced by the fact that Gary and his people are now looking for ways to found campus ministries overseas, especially in the Philippines.[101]

The "Michigan Miracle" began late in the 60s but its growth took place in the 70s and 80s and we shall tell the story of these campus ministries in the coming chapters.

## Project Challenge: A College—Career Ministry in Southern California

A significant part of the "explosion" of campus ministry in the 60s was, paradoxically, not strictly speaking a campus ministry at all. Project Challenge in California, although a definite influence in the rise of campus ministries in the Midwest, was a ministry that worked through local congregations to reach college and career young people rather than going to the campuses.

Darrell Terry, charismatic leader of this movement, gave two reasons for this approach, one practical and the other scriptural. The strategy is practical, Terry said, because there are so many colleges in Southern California, most of which are commuter schools, that it would be virtually impossible to establish campus ministries on each campus. Furthermore, since the churches are already distributed throughout the area, there is a natural network to work through, and the career adult who is not in college can be enlisted as well by working through the churches. The scriptural rationale is simply that because, as Darrell Terry said, "Christianity exists in the form of congregations, and unless and until the young adult is established in the local church, his faith has a small chance of survival. . . . a program that operates outside the congregation evades the real issue, besides the church is the greatest resource of love and help."[102]

Those who initiated Project Challenge were moved by the same conviction that had led Charles Garrison to write the book *Forgotten Christians.* That is the fact that there was a "horrible drain of college-age people from the churches."[103]

The Christian Churches of Southern California, along with a strong assist from Pacific Christian College, had sponsored a summer college gathering at Angeles Crest Camp in the San Bernadino Mountains beginning in 1955. It was at that college camp in 1962 that Darrell Terry, then minister of La Mirada Christian Church, began to discuss the possibility that other programs could be undertaken to reach college-age young people more effectively.[104] These influential people began to meet regularly to further these plans, and by the time of the 1963 camp they had formulated a three phase program consisting of: 1) Motivation; 2) Consultation; 3) Involvement.[105]

## Motivation

The heart of the Project Challenge approach was the gathering of college-age youth in area conferences, rallies, camps, and social events which were specially tailored to meet their needs. The first of these gatherings was a winter convocation held at the Arrowhead Springs Hotel in February of 1964. More than 200 young people came together in what was to become a precedent-setting event. Participants paid $25.00 each (a large amount in the 60s) to hear outstanding speakers and to experience intensive Christian fellowship in the atmosphere of a luxury hotel. This was a departure of the usual practice of holding college/career gatherings in cost-saving, rather primitive wilderness settings.

The featured speakers for this first convocation were Marshall Leggett, the minister of the Broadway Christian Church in Lexington, Kentucky, and Bill Bright, head of Campus Crusade for Christ. Leggett had been called on at the last minute to substitute for the scheduled main speaker, Dr. James Jauncy, who cancelled because of illness. One participant said of this weekend, which was climaxed by a communion service on Sunday morning, "the program was certainly one of the most spiritually uplifting experiences I have ever experienced."[106]

Other gatherings of college/career people were sponsored regularly by Project Challenge, including a Spring Banquet, a summer camp, a Labor Day weekend and social events during the year, but the winter convocation was the real heart of this program. Convocations were held each February from 1964 through 1969 in such places as the Hotel del Coronado in San Diego and the Miramar Hotel in Santa Barbara, with increasing attendance each year. Hundreds of college-age young people were influenced by these gatherings as described by Darrell Terry:

> They flocked together, as on cue, from congregations of Christian Churches and Churches of Christ throughout the area whenever Project Challenge sponsored a program for College/Career adults. — Dozens of groups have begun in churches after a few 'fired up' students and leaders returned home from a Project Challenge event. Indifferent faith often leaps to life in an intensive well-planned mass meeting.[107]

*Consultation*

The second phase of the Project Challenge plan was also in keeping with the congregation-based approach; they provided experienced help to local congregations in planning their college/career programs. This aspect of the Project Challenge program, Darrell Terry writes, is as follows:

> An association of college advisors has been formed in order to develop a solid network of people to teach and sponsor college/career groups in churches — finding willing and capable leadership in every church is difficult. This, however, is the keystone of the program. Professional leadership is the usual mark of present college programs. However, there are not now, and will never be enough "professional" leaders to do the task. Churchmen must be equipped to conduct their own programs in the church.[108]

Here, again, there is basic agreement with Charlie Garrison who wrote in his book that, "every congregation should be a college/career church."[109]

In spite of the importance of this aspect of Project Challenge's Ministry it was not as effective as Phase 1 and 3 of their program.[110]

*Involvement*

In 1967, when the Peace Corps and Vista were challenging young people to serve in needy areas of the world, the leaders of Project Challenge were pressured by college/career adults to launch a program of missions. Dick Wilson, minister of the La Habra First Christian Church, was chosen to direct this program, and in accepting this responsibility he said:

> The trouble with loving God is that it always demands a response — action. This love reminds us that the church is not an end in itself, but a means. It

was not the church that "God so loved," but the world and he loves the world *through* the church. Growing numbers of youth have heard the gospel of Christ, and have responded. The desire of thousands to serve in Vista and the Peace Corps is proof that young adults understand loving in terms of serving — Project Challenge in cooperation with our missionaries and our churches has come up with a bold new plan for a world-wide service.[111]

In the summer of 1968, teams of students went to Mexico to help build an orphanage in Ensenada, and to Alaska to do ten thousand dollar's worth of work for the Alaska Christian School in Homer.[112] In the summer of 1969, the Mexico-Alaska trips were repeated, and an additional team taught Vacation Bible School on an Indian reservation in Colorado.[113]

In 1969, Project Challenge began to phase out as a specific program, but its influence lives on, not only in the lives of hundreds of people, but also in identifiable ways in current campus ministry programs across the country. In April of 1992, I tape recorded a long session with Darrel Terry and Will Cooper, in which they tried to reflect upon and assess the strengths and weaknesses of this early college/career venture in the 1960s.

The attempt to work through the churches had both a positive and negative result. The plan to be congregation-based was scriptural and sound, but the peculiar circumstances created by the mood of the sixties caused serious problems. On the one hand, the students who were converted by Project Challenge programs often entered the churches with long hair, strange clothing, and a tendency to have a rebellious attitude. They were, even though Christians, children of the sixties, and it was difficult for many traditional congregations to accept them. In any case, however the blame should be assigned here, the tragedy is that a bold and imaginative plan to reach college/career people with the gospel succeeded amazingly well for several years, but is no longer a viable program in Southern California.

There are, however, solid and tangible results from Project Challenge. The gathering of college age students at rallies, retreats, and conferences, which originated in California, carried over into the Midwest, particularly in the organization of Challenge Unlimited and the French Lick Convocation. The desire for community and togetherness and the utopian dream for a better world was a powerful force among all of the college-age youth in the sixties, as evidence in the Free Speech Movement at Berkley in 1964, and the gathering of thousands at Woodstock in 1969. These movements died out because of drugs, violence, and lack of staying power, and they left thousands of disillusioned youth. However, the gathering of Christian young people which was begun by Project Challenge carried over into campus ministries in the Midwest *and is still alive as a truly revolutionary force in campus ministries all over the nation.* Not only has this element of Project Challenge survived and grown, but the mission programs begun by them in the late 60s have also been kept alive and have vastly increased throughout campus ministries all over the nation.

For example, the mission work which was begun by Project Challenge at the orphanage in Tijuana, Mexico, in the 60s provided the impetus for one of the most impressive mission programs among Christian Churches, the AMOR program (Aiding Mexican Orphans and Refugees). This outgrowth of the Project Challenge efforts has now become a vastly successful service project.[114] In the past twenty-five years, the people from AMOR have built fifteen thousand homes for the homeless in Mexico, using twenty thousand volunteers from all over the nation, and they now have a budget of 1.5 million dollars. Project Challenge was the inspiration for the beginning of this vastly impressive operation for Christ.

## Challenge Unlimited in Ohio

The success of Project Challenge in California sparked the interest of several people in Cincinnati, Ohio, and encouraged them to do something to minister to college career young people in that area.

In 1965 at the Chase Avenue Christian Church in Cincinnati, Dave Lang began teaching a college age Bible class which soon averaged more than 100 people in attendance each week. Roger Callahan was Youth Minister at the White Oak Christian Church in the same city at this time. Dave and Roger, along with several other interested people, met in early 1966 to discuss the possibility of an organization patterned after Project Challenge.[115] Dave Lang describes the motivation for this meeting as follows:

> Our thinking was that since Cincinnati was a hub for 15-20 large universities within 150 miles and in the heart of the Restoration Movement churches, we should be able to make an impact for Christ on these campuses and minister to students from Christian Churches who were virtually abandoned since they weren't going to a Bible College. This is to say nothing of the vast opportunities for evangelism and ministry to this critical age group.[116]

This group sponsored two rallies for college-age people in late 1966, one at the Chase Avenue Church which was attended by 150 people, and another in the Chapel at Miami University in Oxford, Ohio, which was attended by 65 people.[117] Encouraged by the response to these efforts, and following the lead of Project Challenge, an organization was formed called Challenge Unlimited in late 1966, and plans were begun to hold a convocation in some central location. The famous French Lick Sheraton Hotel, a luxury resort in French Lick, Indiana, was selected as the best location, and the date for the first French Lick Convocation was set for February 1967.

There is no doubt among those of us who were involved in this historic meeting that it was the "explosion" which gathered together people from all over the Midwest and launched the campus ministry movement in earnest. Dave Lang, writing in the *Lookout* in April 1967 described the gathering as follows:

> More than 150 Christian collegians, career youth, and advisers from Illinois, Indiana, Ohio, Kentucky, Michigan and Tennessee, converged on the plush resort facilities for a weekend of inspiration and fellowship. They came from more than twenty-five colleges and universities, from state colleges, Bible colleges, nursing colleges and business colleges. Some were teachers, some IBM operators, some secretaries. Their fields of interest included electronics, engineering, medicine, history, biology, music, English, education, economics and philosophy. They came because they had one thing in common: Jesus Christ. They carried no banners nor sang protest songs. The came to unite in a spiritual revolution. Intelligent, alive, determined, they came seeking to join their abilities in a mighty effort to turn the world upside down for Christ.[118]

Challenge Unlimited, which by now was formally organized and incorporated with a Board of Directors and with Dave Lang as Director, was not originally organized to start specific campus ministries, but rather to "hold one day college/career rallies within driving distance of Cincinnati, promote college/career groups in the local churches, and encourage Christian fellowship groups on college campuses."[119] Nevertheless, Challenge Unlimited did sponsor a campus ministry at Miami University in Oxford, Ohio, beginning in 1967.

The seeds of campus ministry at Miami University were planted by leaders in the Church of Christ. In 1964 George Huber, then minister with the Church of Christ in Oxford, Ohio, wrote a penetrating and prophetic article calling for campus ministries on the college campuses all across America. Huber wrote: "I believe this is one of the most important areas of Christian service today. The entire future of the Restoration Movement may well depend upon how we respond to this challenge of the long neglected campus ministry — this must be done *today* to provide our churches, our nation, our world, with the Christian leaders they need for tomorrow."[120]

Dr. Roy Ward, faculty member at Miami University and a member of George Huber's congregation, had sponsored a small group of Christian students on the Miami campus for several months until he became too busy to continue. Dave Lang took over the leadership of this group in 1967, and when Dave decided to become campus minister at Illinois State University in late 1967, Roger Callahan took responsibility for the Miami group and also became Director of Challenge Unlimited. By the end of the spring term in 1969 it became apparent that the Miami fellowship needed a definite location on campus (they had been meeting in the Chapel on the campus). With the help of his Board of Directors, his faithful students and support from several churches in the area in the spring of 1969, Roger purchased a house one-half block from the edge of the campus, and after spending the summer renovating it, he and six male students moved in the fall of 1969 (Roger had been commuting to Miami from his apartment in Cincinnati). Also in the fall of 1969 Roger obtained the religious preference cards from the University of Cincinnati, and since there were several Christian Church students on that campus, he began a Bible study there once a week. At the close of the 1969–1970 school year Roger Swango, a graduate student in psychology at the University of Cincinnati, took over the group in Cincinnati to free Roger Callahan to put in more time at Miami and as Director of Challenge Unlimited, which by now was sponsoring a yearly French Lick Convocation.

In the summer of 1970 Jim and Judy Cahoon arrived at the University of Cincinnati to begin graduate study. They had come from Madison, Wisconsin, where they had been "turned on" to the campus ministry by Sam and Bonnie Fox and the group at the University of Wisconsin. So committed were they to carrying on a ministry in Cincinnati, they gave $1,000 to help provide a down payment on a four-apartment building near the campus at the University of Cincinnati. The Swangos and the Cahoons occupied two of the four apartments and the others were given over to headquarters for the fellowship and became the campus house. This ministry grew so that by late 1971 a full-time campus minister was needed and the volunteer work by the Swangos was not sufficient to carry it on. In early 1972 Tom Smith, who was a product of the campus ministry at the University of Illinois, and a graduate of Lincoln Christian College, was called to be the full-time campus minister at the University of Cincinnati.

Challenge Unlimited went on, under Roger Callahan's leadership, to promote several more historic Convocations at French Lick.[121] This organization also sponsored a new campus ministry at University of Northern Kentucky just across the Ohio river from Cincinnati beginning in 1974.

Challenge Unlimited became a powerful force in the spread of campus ministries in the Midwest as Project Challenge had been in California. It is clear from this brief survey of campus ministries which "exploded" in the 1960s that this movement was not one manipulated by human ingenuity alone, but rather was a powerful force generated by the Holy Spirit to move the gospel onto the campuses of America.

# NACSF and Area Retreats

Before leaving the decade of the sixties, it is important to point out that two organizations which have been crucial in the life of campus ministries among Christian Churches originated in the sixties. Since Christian Churches pride themselves on their autonomy and freedom from hierarchical structure, other ways have been found to sustain inter-congregational communication and fellowship. For campus ministries, two nurturing bodies have been the National Association of Christian Student Foundations and the various area gatherings called "retreats." Both of these movements grew originally out of the leadership of Charlie Garrison and the campus ministry at the University of Kentucky in the early 1960s.[122]

The National Association of Christian Student Foundations was organized in August of 1963 during a meeting of campus leaders at the South Port Heights Christian Church in Indianapolis, Indiana.[123] This organization of campus ministries, membership in which is voluntary, has been in continuous existence since that date and has been invaluable in providing communication, fellowship, and continuity among campus ministries among Christian Churches. Annual meetings of this group have been held each year in various places in the country, for fellowship, exchange of ideas and experience, inspiration and mission support. In 1991, the name of the organization was changed to "The National Association of Christian Campus Ministries." (See Appendix A for a list of the officers of this organization from 1964–1994).

Two important "spin-offs" from the NACCM have been the annual gathering of campus ministers in retreats (see Appendix B for a list of these retreats). They have been held each year in the spring, at the close of the school year, in some central location. These gatherings have been in many ways the heart of the movement. Workshops, idea exchanges, recreation, inspirational speakers and general relaxation and spiritual renewal have made these annual gatherings mandatory for most working campus ministers.

Another by-product of the NACCM has been the sponsorship of annual "Leadership Conferences" for students and campus ministers. These began in 1976 and have provided weeks of intensive training and fellowship for student Christian leaders since then. More than 5,000 have been a part of these Leadership Conferences (see Appendix C for a list of the conferences).

Another vital part of the life of campus ministries has been the area gatherings of students and campus ministers from several campuses for retreats. These are now a staple of the program of most campus ministries meeting usually fall, winter or spring breaks. We have described the power generated by the Blue Grass Retreat in Kentucky, and the first French Lick Convocation in Indiana.[124] This torch has been picked up by the Little Galilee Conference in Illinois, retreats in Michigan, Missouri, Colorado, and elsewhere.[125]

# Conclusion

The turbulent decade of the sixties was a time of unprecedented movement of the gospel of Christ onto the college and university campuses. It was, as Donald Shockley notes, "An era in which the spiritual dimension of human life was of great interest to the young."[126] Among Christian Churches, it was an explosion; the breakthrough carried on the dream of Alexander Campbell to wed biblical and liberal arts education at Bethany College, the vision of the Bible Chair Movement at the University of Michigan in 1893, and the bold venture by Eugene Sanderson to bring Bible College and university education together. More importantly, this movement of campus ministries was a response to our Lord's command to "be my witnesses in Jerusalem, Judea, Samaria and to the end of the earth" (Acts 1:8).

This explosion was, however, no flash-in-the-pan. We turn now to the story of the spread of campus ministries among Christian Churches throughout the nation during the decade of the 1970s.

## NOTES

1. I use the word "explosive" metaphorically, but there were literal explosions on the campuses in the sixties. A university building was blown up at the University of Wisconsin, killing two people, and at Kent State in Ohio students were shot and killed by the Ohio National Guard.

2. Donald G. Shockley, *Campus Ministry*, p. 90.

3. For the power of students to change universities in the sixties, see the important book by Allan Bloom, *The Closing of the American Mind* (New York, Simon and Schuster, 1985). pp. 313-335.

4. Shockley, *Campus Ministry*, p. 93.

5. *Ibid.*

6. *Ibid.*, p. 90.

7. See the landmark article in *Christianity Today* (September 2, 1966, pp. 4-7), titled, "Crisis on the Campus: Why Does Spiritual Unrest Haunt the Universities?"

8. See *One Way: The Jesus Movement and Its Meaning*, by Robert S. Ellwood, Jr. (New Jersey, Prentice-Hall, 1973.) This is a brief but insightful study of this remarkable movement.

9. From "The Exchange," a publication of the National Association of Christian Student Foundations, August 1, 1968, p. 2.

10. *Christian Standard*, July 6, 1963. "The Church Goes to College," by Charles Garrison, pp. 7-8.

11. Charles Garrison, *Forgotten Christians: A Guidebook for College Career Work*. (Joplin, MO, College Press, 1967).

12. *Ibid.*, pp. 109-112.

13. Phone call to me, June 27, 1992.

14. Shockley, *Campus Ministry*, p. 70.

15. Christian Standard, July 6, 1963, p. 7.

16. Campuses represented at the first meeting according to the minutes of the NACSF were: The University of Kentucky, Miami University (Oxford, Ohio), East Tennessee State University, Cincinnati Bible Seminary, Ohio State University, Purdue University, Ball State University (Indiana), Southern Illinois University (Carbondale) and the University of Illinois.

17. The *Christian Standard* will resume the publication of this "Survey of Campus Ministries" in August of 1992.

18. From a letter to me, October 4, 1989.

19. "East Tennessee Christian," June 1967, p. 1.

20. *Christian Standard*, July 20, 1963, p. 12.

21. *Campus Ministry: A Summary of Statements Regarding the Christian Ministry at Secular Campuses.* (from a survey compiled by G. Stanley Smith, University of Illinois, Spring 1967, p. 1.) Hereafter referred to as "Smith Report."

22. *Ibid.*, p. 4.

23. *Ibid.*, p. 3.

24. *Ibid.*

25. "Will Pancakes Keep a Student Faithful?" *Christian Standard*, July 30, 1967, pp. 3,4.

26. Smith Report, p. 3.

27. *Ibid.*, p. 2.

28. Among those known to me are: Dr. John Cronkhite, Pediatrician; Dr. Robert Owen, Professor of Old Testament at Emmanuel School of Religion; Dave Lemons, Christian High School teacher; Tom Smith, leader in renewal churches; Jim Linder, Special Education teacher and "lay" minister — and many others, known to God.

29. Information about the campus ministry at Southern Illinois University was obtained from a telephone conversation with Karen Wooters along with brochures and news letters published over the years.

30. Smith Report, p. 7.

31. *Ibid.*

32. Information on the 13 years of Darrel Malcom ministry at NIU was obtained from questionnaires he completed and from a telephone conversation between Mrs. Malcom and the author in August of 1992.

33. These men were: Calvin Smith in 1965, John Hines in 1965–66, and Joe Wilson in 1966–67. (From a questionnaire returned to the author in 1985.)

34. From *A Time of Joy and Remembrance: A Short History of the Christian Campus House at ENMU*, p. 1.

35. "Share Christ on the State Campus," an article in the *Christian Standard* by Lewis Toland, January 23, 1977, p. 7.

36. *A Time of Joy and Remembrance*, p. 1.

37. *Ibid.*, p. 4.

38. Rick Rowland, *Campus Ministries: A Historical Study of Churches of Christ*

*Campus Ministries from 1706–1990.* p. 3.

39. *Ibid.*, p. 39.

40. *A Time of Joy and Remembrance*, p. 14.

41. *Ibid.*, p. 24.

42. This first Board of Directors consisted of:
> Coburn Marlatt, Williamsport
> Carl Yundt, Clark's Hill
> Phil Nine, Indianapolis
> Bob Pearson, Lafayette
> Max Brandt, Lucerne
> Keith Peters, Spartanburg
> McCord Steele, Pine Village
> George McKinney, Attica

From: "Campus Beacon," Brady Lane Church of Christ, March 9, 1966.

43. Minutes, Board of Directors, PCH, July 9, 1966. It is obvious that it will be difficult for me to be either objective or brief as I record the first 16 years of this ministry in which I was so deeply involved. I shall try!

44. This house, old at the time of the original house in 1966 is now — 28 years later — "The Girls' House" — an important part of this ongoing ministry.

45. Annual Report, 1966–67.

46. Annual Meeting Minutes, June 10, 1967.

47. Annual Report, 1967, 1968.

48. Annual Report, 1988–1989, p. 4.

49. "Twenty Years of Leadership in Campus Ministry," p. 2.

50. Milligan had approved this program in 1972, but approval from Purdue was not given until early in 1973. Dr. Robert Wetzel, Academic Dean at Milligan, and I met with the appropriate committee from Purdue. All the members of that committee were from the Philosophy Department, and since Bob had met two of them in National Philosophy Meetings, and since I knew all of them as my professors, and they knew me, approval was unanimous.

51. "Twenty Years of Leadership in Campus Ministry," p. 2.

52. Newsletter, Fall 1990, Century Club letter, December 1992.

53. Annual Report, 1988, 1989, pp. 9 and 20.

54. *Ibid.*, p. 9.

55. Annual Report, 1989, 1990, p. 18.

56. Annual Report, 1974–1975, p. 8.

57. Annual Report, 1989, 1990.

58. Questionnaire returned by Roger Callahan, 1992.

59. Annual Report, 1989–1990.

60. McCormick, Thomas R. *Campus Ministry in the Coming Age* (CBP Press, St. Louis, MO. 1987) p. 6.

61. *Ibid.*, p. 6.

62. *Christian Standard*, January 28, 1967, p. 8.

63. *Ibid.*

64. Rick Rolland, *Campus Ministries*. Rick gives no figures on the total Bible Chairs among the Churches of Christ but his book shows that the Bible Chair

model is followed much more often among Churches of Christ than among either of the other branches of the Restoration movement.

65. See Chapter 3, p. 57.

66. John Brownlee says Gene Crowcroft, the student who was President of the Church College Group, deserves a lot of credit for keeping the college ministry alive. (audio tape to author, 1992)

67. Information on the campus ministry at Ball State under the leadership of John and Sandra Brownlee came to me from an extensive audio tape John sent to me in 1992.

68. In March of 1967, John Brownlee planned a special dinner to which, in an effort to strengthen the witness of Restoration Movement churches on campus, he invited those who were working with Church of Christ campus ministries. However, the elders of the University Church resisted this move, and no more such efforts toward unity were made.

69. Article in the *Lookout*, sometime in 1968, pp. 13, 14. Exact date not available.

70. *Ibid.*, p. 13.

71. Letter to the author from J. David Lang, December 4, 1989.

72. *Ibid.*, p. 3.

73. *Christian Standard*, December 21, 1968, p. 13.

74. *The Lookout*, November 24, 1968, p. 9.

75. *Christian Standard*, April 11, 1970, p. 31.

76. *Christian Standard*, July 21, 1968, p. 8.

77. Publicity brochure (date unknown).

78. Information on the beginning of the campus ministry at Terre Haute was provided by a phone conversation between Dale Crain and myself in March 1993.

79. Among these Board Members were Dr. Donald Yates, Ophthalmologist, and a member of the Maplewood congregation, Carolyn Bartlett, a member of the faculty at Indiana State University, and Don Rush, a certified public accountant in Terre Haute.

80. Information about this campus ministry came from various questionnaires and a long phone conversation with David Weaver, campus minister with this group since 1989.

81. "Koinonia News," December, 1991.

82. *Ibid.*, Fall, 1992.

83. Roy Weece, *Christian Standard*, "If a House Could Talk," September 10, 1972, p. 7.

84. *Ibid.*, p. 10. In 1977 also the girls was torn down and a new one built, the two together provide housing for 34 students. Questionnaire from Roy Weece, 1985.

85. Questionnaire returned by Roy Weece in 1989, and an article in "Newsletter," June 1989. This same Newsletter announces that Randy Dolan and his wife, who had been ministers with international students on the Columbia campus since 1988 were going to Thailand as missionaries.

86. Questionnaire returned by Roy Weece in February 1992, and "Newsletter," November-December 1988.

87. "Newsletter," September-October, 1986 and Newsletter from Virginia Tech summer of 1992.

88. Letter from Gary Weedman to author, December 20, 1989.

89. Letter from Jack Haun to author, December 23, 1992.

90. Weedman letter.

91. Francis Schaeffer says this event was a turning point in the political activism of the radical students. Schaeffer says, "Before this (event) many of the students were really playing at revolution — thinking they could have a nice revolution without violence." Francis Schaeffer, *The New Super Spirituality* (Downers Grove, IL: InterVarsity Press, 1972), p. 8.

92. Newsletter, *On the Damascus Road*, December, 1968, pp. 7, 8.

93. *Ibid.*, p. 10. See pp. 56, 74 for previous references to Jerry Gibson.

94. Special NHCC Edition of *On the Damascus Road*, July, 1969, p. 1.

95. *Ibid.*, p. 2.

96. Among these students were Mary Carter (now Little), daughter of Gene Carter who was minister in Grand Rapids; Bruce Webster, a graduate student who is now engaged in new church evangelism in Indianapolis; and Doug Umbanahowar who became a missionary to Thailand. I met with these students and others in October of 1968 while I was attending a "Faith Promise Rally" at University Church. Don Stiffler and Elwyn Miller had arranged the meeting with the students who asked me to speak on "What's Happening at Purdue?". The enthusiasm of these students was remarkable, and was a powerful influence in the beginning of campus ministry in the state of Michigan.

97. The growing interest in campus ministry on the part of other Michigan ministers and churches was apparent during the Michigan State convention in April of 1969. I met with a group of interested people at that time to do a workshop on "Campus Evangelism," and to tell the "Purdue Story." Not long after this convention, the corporation and Board of Directors was organized.

98. From an audio tape of reminiscences sent to me by Jeri Roesch in 1992, in which she recounts much of her experience as a student in the Michigan State campus ministry.

99. These will be specified as we consider the individual campus ministries that were organized in the 70's and 80's.

100. These also will be pointed out in the coming chapters on the Michigan ministries, along with the remarkable number of students who have been baptized during the years of the Michigan Campus ministries.

101. Scott McKinney, son of Mr. and Mrs. Dennis McKinney, missionaries in the Philippines, and a graduate of Pacific Christian College, after spending a summer as an intern with the Michigan Campus ministries, had dedicated himself to campus ministry at Baguio City in the Philippines. He is assisted there by Steve Hong, also a graduate of Pacific Christian College.

102. Article in *Key Magazine*, Standard Publishing Co., Oct. issue 1967, pp. 47-48.

103. Charles Garrison, *Forgotten Christians* (Joplin: College Press, 1967), pp. 13-16. Also see the quote from the *Key Magazine* article on p. 47.

104. Among those who shared Darrel's enthusiasm at Angeles Crest in 1962, were: Gene Rogers and Frank Bixler, ministers; Paul Golightly, Executive with Pacific Telephone; Dr. Logan Fox, Prof. of Psychology at El Camino College; John Koekkoek, Prof. of Psychology at PCC, and others. One of the most enthusiastic

colleagues of Darrel Terry in organizing Project Challenge was Bill Cooper who was the minister of the Alvarado Church of Christ in California, 1962. Bill made a famous motivating speech to a large group of people in the Long Beach Christian Church on November 24, 1963, in which he outlined the tremendous possibilities for a college/career ministry in Southern California along the lines of Project Challenge. This meeting in Long Beach and Bill Cooper's speech were a very definite part of the motivation which resulted in the organization Project Challenge.

105. *Key Magazine* article, pp. 47-48.

106. David Root, Faculty member at Pacific Christian College, writing in the *Christian Standard*, May 16, 1964, p. 6.

107. *Key Magazine* article, pp. 47-48. It was my privilege to be the speaker and participant in several of these convocations — in 1965, 1967, 1968, 1969. These experiences were a strong influence on me as I made the decision to leave a settled ministry of twenty-eight years and go full-time into campus ministry in 1966.

108. *Key Magazine* article, p. 48.

109. Garrison, *Forgotten Christians*, p. 13.

110. This came out in a tape recorded interview I had with Darrel Terry and Bill Cooper in April of 1992 in which they reflected on the strength and weaknesses of the Project Challenge venture.

111. *Venture*, a Newsletter of Project Challenge, Oct. 1967, pp. 1-2.

112. *Ibid.*, Feb 1968, p. 2 and Oct 1968, p. 3.

113. *Ibid.*, April 1969, p. 3.

114. Scott and Gayla Congdon, Executive Directors of AMOR, were both powerfully influenced by the early mission trips of Project Challenge. Scott, as a university student, participated in one of the early mission trips, and decided to give his life to missions as a result. He and Gayla met on one of these mission trips and later were married and gave their lives together to the service of Christ in this amazing ministry in Mexico.

115. Some of the others in that meeting were: Jim Irby Jr., Youth Minister at a Christian Church in Hamilton, Ohio; Jim Carter (both of whom had been in California and had been involved in Project Challenge); Gary Coleman, Youth Minister at Clovernook Christian Church in Cincinnati; Bill Wade from Standard Publishing; Ken Wade from Standard Publishing; Ken Goble, Professor at Cincinnati Bible Seminary. Source: Letter from Dave Lang to me in December, 1989, and an audio tape from Roger Callahan in 1990.

116. Letter from Dave Lang, 1989.

117. Letter from Dave Lang, audio tape from Roger Callahan.

118. From an article entitled, "It Was Wow!", *Lookout*, April 30, 1967, p. 4. It was my privilege to be the speaker for this convocation, and one incident that took place on Saturday night confirmed our belief that God was at work in this in ways that none of us could have anticipated. I had forgotten my notes for the Saturday night banquet speech, and I went to my hotel room to get them. As I walked in the door the phone was ringing and it was Darrell Terry calling from California during the Project Challenge Convocation going on at Hotel Del Coronado at that very time. He had called to send greetings to our Convocation. When I went back to the banquet hall to report this "coincidence," the place erupted in cheers — and tears.

119. *Ibid.*, p. 15.

120. "Need for a Campus Ministry," by George Huber, *Christian Standard*, January 14, 1964, pp. 7-8.

121. The records of Challenge Unlimited are not completely available to me, but the French Lick Convocations sponsored by the organization in the 1960s, along with the main speakers for each, appear to be as follows: 1968, guest speaker Darrell Terry, Director of Project Challenge in California; 1969, guest speaker Gary Freeman, Church of Christ minister from California; 1970, guest speaker James Earl Ladd, President, Puget Sound Bible College, Seattle, Washington.

122. See above, pp. 69-70.

123. *Christian Standard*, September 21, 1963, p. 12.

124. See above, pp. 69, 111-112; see also Appendix B.

125. Retreats have been a dynamic part of campus ministries from the beginning. These gatherings of college students and campus ministers began in 1961 when Charles Garrison and about a dozen students from the University of Kentucky spent a weekend at the Blue Grass Christian Assembly south of Lexington, Kentucky. This retreat was the prototype for all those that followed. It was a remarkable center of spiritual dynamics, and it played an important part in the explosion of campus ministries that began in the early 1960s. The retreat was held every spring from 1961 to 1970, and it drew college students from all over the Midwest for eight or nine years.

A weekend gathering of college students and their leaders was held at Little Galilee Christian Assembly in Clinton, IL in the fall of 1963 and it continued yearly until 1973, attracting over 200 students from Midwest colleges each year.

The French Lick Convocation introduced a new concept in retreats. Blue Grass and Little Galilee had been held in campgrounds — French Lick was the first to be held in a luxury hotel. The first French Lick Convocation, held in the historic French Lick Sheraton Hotel, in February 1967, was sponsored by Challenge Unlimited. This Convocation attracted hundreds of college students and their leaders each spring from 1967 to 1979. In 1980 it was moved to Gatlinburg, TN, and was renamed "Fellowship Conference." In 1982 Bob Richards became director of Challenge Unlimited, and he planned the gatherings which were held in Asheville, NC in 1982, and Knoxville in 1983, the last to be planned by Challenge Unlimited.

There was no annual retreat in 1984, but in 1985, Tim Hudson, campus minister at the University of Georgia, along with other campus ministers from the South, organized the retreat at Gatlinburg, TN. This gathering has been held annually, attracting an average of 450 people from twelve campus ministries.

Roy Weece and his colleagues at the University of Missouri sponsored a retreat for campus ministries from Missouri and surrounding states beginning in April 1969. This gathering has attracted 200–350 people each year. When the facilities at Lake Ozark became too crowded, Tom Tucker and his staff at Tahlequah, OK organized another one for campus ministries in Oklahoma and Arkansas.

John and Janice Schlieker held a retreat in Colorado for their own campus ministries in January 1982. In 1983 this retreat attracted campus ministries from other states and it has annually attracted over one hundred people for an inspiring — and skiing — weekend!

126. Shockley, *Campus Ministry*, p. 90.

# CHAPTER FIVE

# Campus Ministries in
# the Decade of the Seventies

## Introduction

The decade of the 1970s on American campuses was both a cooling off period from the turbulent 1960s and a transition from that period of unrest to the conservative 1980s. It was also the period of the greatest growth of campus ministries among Christian Churches. When the 1960s came to a close, there were twenty-one full-time campus ministries in eleven states. During the 1970s, thirty-nine full-time campus ministries were begun on as many campuses in eleven more states. In a twenty year period, campus ministries among Christian Churches grew from virtually none to a total of sixty in twenty-two states.[1]

What were the conditions which contributed to this phenomenal growth? The social unrest and the revolutionary mood of students in the 1960s had focused the attention of the nation on the university campuses. While the nation as a whole was literally forced to pay attention to universities as a force to be reckoned with, the churches also began to realize that they had overlooked a crucially important mission field. It became painfully evident to many that, as Charles Malik had pointed out, "The university is the power that dominates the world; how can we then rest without seeking to ascertain where Christ stands with respect to this power?"[2]

On the one hand, some of the most violent acts that were the fruit of the rebellious 1960s took place on campuses in the 70s as students continued to oppose the Vietnam war and the society which they perceived as being the cause of it. As they watched the evening news on television, the whole nation saw student demonstrators at Kent State University in Ohio shot by National Guard troops on May 4, 1970. On the other hand, the "Jesus Movement" and the deep spiritual hunger among students which began to surface in the 1960s became even more evident in the 1970s so that, as Rick Rowland said of the Churches of Christ, the 1970s became "the golden age of campus ministries."[3]

There was a not-so-subtle shift of mood among students during the 1970s. At the beginning of the decade there was a carry over from the rebellious attitude of the 1960s which demanded change in the establishment, including the church. Slowly during the 70s it became evident that, as David Shockley says, "Students were more concerned about jobs than social change and more interested in money than in meaning."[4] By the end of the decade the "Me Generation" was in full swing. As Shockley further notes:

> As the wave of baby boomers hitting the job market began to crest, there were not enough jobs for all of them to do what they hoped to do, even with Ph.D.s in hand. So the word went to the back of the wave that only the fittest would survive, that the grade point average and resume would seal one's fate forever. The new conservatism among students was a rational response to economic reality on the part of young people who had become conditioned to want it all.[5]

As the attention of students shifted from concern about social action to inner anxiety about jobs, there was a surprising effect on traditional denominational campus ministers. The numbers of students who participated in these "mainline" campus ministries began to diminish, and as this happened budget-conscious denominations began to cut funds to campus ministry. Many of the campus ministers, especially those that were "ecumenically based," found themselves literally fighting for their lives.[6]

Ironically, this situation contributed to the growth of campus ministries among Christian Churches. One of the reasons for this is that our campus ministers, while not insensitive to social concerns (as will be seen in our examination of specific campus ministries in the 1970s) were much more responsive to the changing emotional and spiritual needs of students than many of the "mainline" denominational campus ministers.[7] For the above reasons, and no doubt many others which we have not noted here, especially the movement of the Spirit of God on the college campuses, there was a phenomenal growth of Christian Church campus ministries in the 1970s. If the 1960s were the time when the campus ministries were born among Christian Churches, the 1970s were the time of growth and maturity.

# LATER HISTORY OF THE CAMPUS MINISTRIES WHICH BEGAN IN THE 1960s

All of the campus ministries which came into existence during the 1960s grew and expanded in significant ways during the 1970s. The recent growth of some of the 1960s campus ministries illustrates this progress.

# University of Kentucky

Charles Garrison, after his pioneering work at the University of Kentucky (based on the previous ministry of Dick Carpenter and the Broadway Christian Church) resigned in 1968 to pursue full-time work on a PhD in Sociology.

Larry Brandon, a graduate of Milligan College and of Southern Baptist Theological Seminary was called to the campus ministry at the University of Kentucky in 1968. Larry came from a successful three year pastorate with the Christian Church of Converse, Indiana. During his seventeen years of ministry at Lexington, this campus ministry grew remarkably. One of the reasons for this was the Sunday worship services which were held in the building that had been built near the campus in 1966. This building was renovated and expanded in 1976 at a cost of $185,000 to accommodate the growth of the fellowship. In addition to the growth which came from the worship services, Larry says that "retreats produced the most fellowship and spiritual growth."[8]

One of the distinguishing marks of campus ministry, perhaps more apparent than in traditional ministries, is that they are often shaped around the special talents of the campus minister. This was certainly the case during Larry Brandon's ministry at the University of Kentucky. In 1975, "after seven years of planning, training, building and promotion," an accredited program in Clinical Pastoral Education for graduate students in seminaries of the Restoration Movement was inaugurated under Larry's leadership.[9] In ten years (1975–1985), forty-five ministers had completed this intensive program under Larry's supervision. This was the only program for training ministers in CPE in the Brotherhood, and actually the only one among the five hundred centers for such training in the nation that was located on a university campus. Not only were these forty-five people trained for whatever ministry they were to undertake, they also helped to increase the Kentucky campus ministry's outreach into almost every area and subculture of the university, as well as providing leadership for prayer groups, Bible studies, counseling and worship leadership while they were in training on the campus.

Larry Brandon also had talent in drama, which he put to use in producing five seasons of Broadway productions such as *Godspell* and *Fiddler on the Roof* during his ministry at University of Kentucky, using student talent. Through the interest generated by these productions, and the other aspects of the program at the University of Kentucky, new people were attracted to the fellowship and the size of the campus ministry doubled during Larry's tenure. Larry resigned as campus minister at the University of Kentucky in 1985 to become the head of the CPE program at Howard Community Hospital in Kokomo, Indiana. Dr. J. Robert Ross, who had been campus minister at Eastern Illinois University for ten years, became the interim campus minister until Warren K. Jones was called in June of 1986. Warren Jones' ministry was a fruitful one, but concluded after one year when he resigned "for personal reasons."

In August of 1987, Lynn Buckles and his wife Janene were called as campus ministers at the University of Kentucky. Lynn represents a trend which we shall see increasingly as we continue to survey campus ministries — he is a product of the strong campus ministry at the University of Tennessee where he worked for 13 years, first as a student and then as an associate under Sam Darden, the campus minister there. Lynn came to the ministry with undergraduate and graduate degrees in Physical Education and Special Education. He has used the physical education experience both to work with the Fellowship of Christian Athletes at the University of Kentucky, and to teach regular Bible study for University of Kentucky coaches.

Lynn says that the main feature of their program is still the Sunday morning worship service, but they also have Thursday night fellowship and praise gatherings and intensive small discipleship groups. They have recently developed a music/drama ensemble called *Day Star* involving 25-30 students. This group presented 10 programs to churches and other groups in 1992 in the Blue Grass area.

Another important aspect of campus ministry is the attitude of parents toward these ministries. The newsletter of the University of Kentucky Christian Student Fellowship in July of 1990 carried several testimonies from parents regarding their attitudes towards campus ministry. One set of parents wrote the following:

> You asked for four or five sentences on how we feel about CSF, but we could write you that many pages. We think it is the greatest thing UK has to offer. We feel that if our son stays with your group, he is in as good hands as any Christian College. We have nothing against a Christian College. I am sure they are great, and if our son wanted to attend we would send him. Having our son involved in your church has taken a tremendous burden off of us.[10]

These parents express an attitude which is duplicated, we are confident, among thousands of parents who are grateful for the ministry to their sons and daughters on these so-called "secular" campuses.

The University of Kentucky campus ministry has recently begun to emphasize a ministry to international students as well. Their annual Thanksgiving dinner for international students in 1992 attracted 60 students from 8 different countries. Retreats and working with the homeless on spring breaks are also special aspects of this growing ministry. Recently they have employed Rex Graham as associate campus minister. Rex was a student at the University of Kentucky and became deeply interested in campus ministry during those years. He has gone to Cincinnati

Bible Seminary part-time while he is serving as an associate with Lynn Buckles. This is another example of campus ministry producing its own leaders. The campus ministry at the University of Kentucky is continuing the tradition which Charles Garrison began in the early sixties of vigorous outreach to the university students and it is to be highly commended.

# University of Illinois

After Stan Smith resigned as campus minister at the University of Illinois in 1968 to return to research and teaching at the University of New Mexico at Las Cruces, Jerry Gibson succeeded him as campus minister. John Pierce was senior minister at the Webber Street Church of Christ in Urbana, Illinois, in 1968, and was also chairman of the Christian Campus Foundation, the supporting organization of the campus ministry. John and Stan Smith were particularly interested in Jerry Gibson as a potential campus minister at the University of Illinois because of his interest in International Students. Jerry had just returned from Ghana, West Africa, where he had helped to establish Ghana Christian College.[11] Jerry accepted the call, and during his 10 year ministry at the University of Illinois he specialized in working with International students. He describes his experience as follows:

> The key to our work with Internationals was when I recognized a shirt that a young black man was wearing while walking through Lincoln Square in Urbana. I chased him the length of the hall and asked him, 'Where did you get that shirt?' He said he was from Liberia, and was studying to get his PhD in Economics, and also said I was the first person to speak to him outside of some conversation about official business since he arrived in America. This meeting led to a fast growing friendship, and eventually the establishing of Liberia Christian College in Liberia, West Africa, where our first two teachers in that school were University of Illinois graduates, George Wacaser and Ron Ayers. Ron is still with the school in Liberia. From that time on, we continually made contacts and established relationships with Internationals from all over the world. Many of them are now back in their native lands as missionaries to their own people.[12]

Another unusual aspect of campus ministry which Jerry Gibson developed at the University of Illinois was his special work with athletes. He became chaplain of the University of Illinois football team and traveled with them often. He won several athletes to Christ during this experience.[13] Jerry also became an official counselor for the Dean of Students Office at the university, again pointing out the importance of campus ministry and campus ministers serving the university.

Ron Simkins, a graduate of Lincoln Christian College and Seminary, became associate campus minister with Jerry in 1970. Ron's main talent as a campus minister was in the academic area. He taught classes under the sponsorship of Lincoln Christian College which were accepted by the University of Illinois.[14] When Jerry Gibson left to become President of Mid-South Christian College in Mississippi in 1978, Ron became the full-time campus minister.

Don Follis, a graduate of Manhattan Christian College, was called as associate to Ron in 1978, and served in that capacity until Ron left to work with New Covenant Fellowship in Champaign/Urbana in 1982, when Don became full-time campus minister.

The main features of the ministry during Don Follis' years were: Friday evening fellowship, small group Bible studies, regular work and mission projects to Mexico as well as regular prison and nursing home ministries. During his years at University of Illinois, Don Follis earned a degree in Journalism from the university, and his regular newsletters from those years contain some real gems of insightful essays about Christianity and culture. Don was ably assisted during his ministry by Sue Ellen Butler from 1983–1987, David Sandel from 1989–1991, and David Blauw from 1991–1992.

There seems to be something about the campus of the University of Illinois that attracts people who are interested in working with international students. Stan Smith was gifted in this special ministry as was Jerry Gibson. After 10 years of fruitful ministry with undergraduates during which he had a growing interest in international students, Don Follis resigned in 1992 to work full-time with the 3,000 international students who are attending the University of Illinois. As this is being written, Don and his wife are carrying on the rich tradition which had been a distinguishing mark of the campus ministry at the University of Illinois since the beginning.

Dennis Durst became campus minister in 1992. He had been campus minister at the University of Nebraska for two years after his graduation from Nebraska Christian College and had then gone to Lincoln Christian Seminary where he earned a graduate degree. Dennis is carrying on the tradition of a strong and effective campus ministry on this campus which began with Stan Smith's pioneering work in 1963.

One of the unique by-products of the campus ministry at the University of Illinois was the founding of a new congregation. The New Covenant Fellowship, a renewal congregation, began in 1976. Ron Simkins became the minister when he left the campus ministry, and he is now assisted by Jim Linder, who is one of the students from Stan Smith's original group in the early 1960s. This strong evangelical congregation of 300 people has reached hundreds of students and university people during its history. The life of this congregation reinforces Donald Shockley's conviction, and the conviction of many of us, that there are large numbers of people in the university community who have a great interest in the spiritual dimension of life, but do not consider formal religious participation as a live option. Shockley says, "If the traditionally structured local church is all that is available, many of these persons, particularly the students, will remain at a distance."[15]

# East Tennessee State University

After Jim Saunders left this campus ministry in 1970 to go on to other areas of service, there was a succession of campus ministers until Dave Degler, present campus minister, arrive in 1987.

Steve and Annabelle Schertzinger served at ETSU from 1974–1979. They had come from four years at Indiana University where they had been active in campus ministry while Steve earned a pre-med degree there. Eighteen students attended the first meeting in the fall of 1974, and by 1976 there were forty students active in the group. Sunday morning worship services were begun, first in the campus house and later in the CULP Student Center on campus. These services were never well attended because of the tendency of students in the Appalachian area to go home on Sundays.

Other aspects of the program under the Schertzingers were Wednesday night Bible study, Friday morning prayer breakfast, and visiting churches in East Tennessee on Sunday evenings. Area retreats with the campus ministry at the University of Tennessee and attendance at the French Lick Convocation were also part of the program.

By 1978, due to some personal problems among the students in the group, the ministry was weakened and the Schertzingers moved on to other areas of service.

Those who served after the Schertzingers were: Tommy Oaks, 1978–1982; Dean Matthis, 1982–1986; Danny Slater, August 1986–March 1987. Each of these men contributed in his own way to the growth of this ministry.

Dave Degler came to East Tennessee State University in 1987, having spent a year studying Chemical Engineering at Michigan Technological University and having earned a degree in Christian Ministry at Great Lakes Bible College. The hub of activities for this ministry is the Wednesday night Praise and Prayer service which is planned by students and which attracts sixty to seventy people each week. The locale for this and other activities is the campus house which was purchased in 1968 and which, after years of wear and tear, was completely remodeled in 1991. The house is very close to campus and also serves as a residence for three male students or three female students in alternating years. The second most important aspect of this program, according to Dave Degler, is the discipleship groups which are intimate and intensive training groups to develop student leadership. These groups have developed a strong core of student leaders who plan and execute much of the ministry on the campus. Several students have decided to become preaching ministers and missionaries as a result of this program. Sunday worship services are not held on campus because there are so many Christian Churches in the immediate area which students may attend that it would not be feasible. However, a 9:00 p.m. Bible study is held on Sunday evenings which is attended by a regular group of about 12 students.

Mission trips involving many students are taken regularly to Mexico, Florida, and the Appalachian area surrounding Johnson City. Dave Degler spent four years as an Associate Minister at the Oakwood Forest Christian Church in Kingsport, Tennessee while also serving as campus minister. He testifies that this experience both strengthened his ministry on campus and kept him in close touch with an active local church. Not only did Dave serve in the local church, but at least 20 students are regularly involved in service in local churches in any given semester. This means that the motto for this campus ministry — "preparing the church for the Twenty-first Century" — is more than a motto. The growing tendency among campus ministries to develop their own leadership is evident at East Tennessee State University. Kay Heck, who was a student at ETSU, and became very active in the fellowship while she took a degree in English there, is now associate campus minister with Dave Degler. (Between her graduation from ETSU and her return there as associate campus minister, Kay taught at Pacific Christian College and was very helpful in the editing process during the writing of this book). Another evidence of the "networking" that takes place in campus ministry is the fact that John Derry, Dean of Students at Milligan College and campus minister at Western Illinois University for twelve years, served as Chairman of the Board of Directors for this campus ministry for seven years.

This is an active, vital campus ministry which is not only reaching students for Christ at ETSU, but also, in 1993, was instrumental in establishing a campus ministry at nearby Appalachian State in Boone, North Carolina, a college enrolling approximately 1,200 students. The leaders in this venture, in addition to Dave Degler, were a core of people who had graduated from ETSU and who had been active in the fellowship while there. Among them are Mr. and Mrs. Wade Dickison and Mr. and Mrs. Dean Stacy. Both of these couples met while active in the fellowship at ETSU and are obviously continuing a strong Christian witness in their present location. It is hoped that a full-time campus minister will be found for Appalachian State some time in 1993, and another campus ministry will have been established.

Dave Degler finished his work for the Master of Divinity degree from Emmanuel School of Religion in 1993. His thesis was entitled, "Shaping the Future of the Appalachian Christian Student Fellowship at East Tennessee State University." (This is one of the resources listed in the bibliography.)

The campus ministry at East Tennessee State University, one of the very first to be established among Christian Churches, is alive and well in 1993 and is a testimony to the stamina and staying power of campus ministry and campus ministers among Christian Churches.[16]

# Ball State University

Willard Walls became the campus minister at Ball State University in 1972, coming to this ministry from a successful pastorate in a local church. In 1992 this campus ministry celebrated its 25th anniversary and at the same time Will Walls completed 20 years at Ball State.

It would be difficult to find two men who differ more in personality and style of ministry than Gary Edwards and Willard Walls. Gary was spontaneous, charismatic, and a little flamboyant. The times required that kind of leadership to get a ministry started in the 1960s. Will Walls, by contrast, has led in this ministry over the years with quiet patience and stamina, and the two men have been used by the providence of God to establish an outstanding campus ministry at Ball State University, known and respected all over the campus, throughout the state and beyond.

The special distinguishing mark of Will's ministry has been his emphasis upon missions. The other aspects of the program have been strong as well — Sunday worship services, retreats, Friday morning prayer breakfast, fellowship suppers, Bible studies, peer counseling, and outreach teams to supporting churches. Will has been strong in emphasizing accountability to the supporting churches through the years.

More than 1,600 students have been touched by the Christian Campus House at Ball State in its 25 years of existence.[17]

The internship program carried on in this ministry for several years has emphasized missionary service especially — both short-term and long-term. It has produced 19 students who have served in short-term mission work, six in life-long mission work and dozens of students who have participated in mission workshops in other places. In addition to the emphasis on missions on campus, Will has also taken students to mission fields in Germany, England, and other sites to encourage students to consider missionary service. International students on campus are also given special attention at Ball State.

Will Walls has also been a faculty member at Ball State University for several years, specializing in courses in worldviews. This has not only provided an unprecedented opportunity to influence students that would not otherwise be reached by the campus ministry, but it has also given the Christian Student Foundation recognition and respect throughout the campus.

Will has been well supported in his ministry by talented associates. Lois Strouse has been a long time administrative assistant and there have been six associate campus ministers over the years. They are: Stan Sutton, 1971-1972; Greg Carter, 1974-1976; Dennis Steckley, 1977-1980; Jerry Telford, 1980-1985; Mark Pike, 1985-1992; and Mark Stafford, 1993-present.

During the campus minister's retreat at McCormick's Creek State Park in Indiana in May of 1993, Willard Walls announced his imminent resignation from the Ball State ministry. He and his wife Ruth will leave to do mission work in England with Christian Missionary Fellowship. It will be exciting to see whom God raises up to continue this remarkable ministry.

# Miami University in Oxford, Ohio

In the fall of 1969, Roger Callahan and six male students moved into the newly renovated house one-half block from the edge of the campus of Miami University. From 1969-1973 Roger was a very busy campus minister. In addition to supervising the growth of the Fellowship at Miami, he also directed Challenge Unlimited and was responsible for the oversight of the campus ministry at the University of Cincinnati. Roger also planned and promoted the French Lick Convocation which was becoming increasingly important as a gathering place for students and campus ministers throughout the Midwest.

Roger resigned from the ministry at Miami University and the supervision of Challenge Unlimited in 1973 to join the campus ministry at Purdue University. Mike Goldberg, who had been deeply involved in the campus ministry at Michigan State, succeeded Roger at Miami and continued until 1975. In 1976, Dave Walker, a graduate of Ball State University, took over at Miami and led the group until 1982. Dave had a fruitful ministry and was succeeded in 1983 by John Wineland, a graduate of Cincinnati Christian Seminary. John has previously attended Valparaiso University in Indiana, majoring in biology and chemistry. He continued the ministry at Miami until 1987 when he resigned to work on a PhD at Miami University.

In 1987 John Thybault, who had been campus minister at the University of Cincinnati since 1983, took over the campus ministry at Miami. John had become interested in campus ministry while he was a student at Central Michigan University where he earned a degree in social science and business in 1980. (Notice the increasing "networking" that is developing in campus ministry). When John left in 1988 to assume the campus ministry at Western Michigan in Kalamazoo, John Morfew and his wife became campus ministers at Miami (John Morfew had become interested in campus ministry while a student at Indiana State and his wife had been involved at the campus ministry at Purdue University).

John Wineland returned to Miami when the Morfews left in 1990, and he serves there at present. During the first year John returned they remodeled the campus house, and eight male students live there now. Students attend Sunday morning worship services in local churches. John leads a Sunday night Bible study for graduate students in the campus house and there is a weekly meeting for fellowship on Tuesday nights and a "Free Lunch" for students at the house on Monday, noon. Students lead Bible studies in the dormitories regularly.

This campus ministry celebrated its twenty-fifth anniversary in 1992, thus illustrating that campus ministries which began in the decade of the 60s have proven to have stamina and staying power.[18]

# Indiana State University and Rose Hulman Institute

The second phase of the campus ministry at Indiana State and Rose Hulman Institute began with the arrival of Walt and Pat Puckett as campus ministers in 1971. The Pucketts had left a successful dairy farming operation in Indiana several years before to attend Lincoln Christian College and Seminary. They brought with them to the campus ministry the advantage of experience and maturity, and their special gifts shaped the ministry at Terre Haute in unique ways.

The most distinctive contribution the Pucketts made to campus ministry was the creation of The Singing SCAMPS (SCAMPS = Serving Christ Alone Means Personal Satisfaction). Pat Puckett used her musical ability to put together a singing group of students of near-professional quality. Each year, the group put on impressive programs in churches, Bible colleges and other gatherings of Christian people. The effect on students who participated in this venture was considerable. It required discipline and self-sacrifice, and it gave them a concrete way to serve Christ during their college years. It also put them in touch with the people in the churches in very intimate ways. They performed at least twenty-five times during the school year, and often they were booked from six to eight months in advance.

Another distinguishing mark of Walt Puckett's ministry was his emphasis upon Biblical study and intellectual competence. He not only taught classes of near-seminary quality to these undergraduates, but he also brought a series of outstanding guest speakers to aid him in the educational aspects of his ministry.[19] Walt continually challenged his students to be both biblically competent and culturally aware as evidenced by the penetrating editorials in his newsletter, and the structure of his program on campus.

In addition to The Singing SCAMPS and the intensive Bible studies, plus a good dose of fellowship and recreation, the SCAMPS also continued the ministry to underprivileged children in the neighborhood which had been initiated by Dale Crain.[20]

In addition to the regular newsletter put out during the years of the Puckett's ministry the students also issued a campus newsletter entitled "SCAMP's House Son Shine News." Dr. James Ringer, Associate Dean for student administration, asked that several copies of each issue of this publication be brought to his office for distribution to students and Dean Ringer remarked that "some of the most mature and valuable articles written by university students that I have seen on campus are in this publication."[21]

Another innovation at the SCAMPS house during the Puckett years was the initiation of an internship program for Bible college and seminary students. Several of the young men who participated in this program went on to serve in campus ministries in other parts of the country.

Pat and Walt Puckett resigned from this ministry in 1977 to accept a ministry at the Oaklandon Christian Church in Indiana. Their six years of ministry at Terre Haute were productive and fruitful for Christ.

Mark and Sue Gallagher succeeded the Pucketts in 1978 and have been campus ministers at Terre Haute since that time. Sue, who is a product of the ministry under the Pucketts and was especially active in the Singing SCAMPS, has been a genuine co-minister with Mark during all of their fifteen years on the campus. Sue Gallagher became the director of the Singing SCAMPS begun by the Pucketts and has ministered through this group to hundreds of students and churches over the years.[22] Mark's motto for campus ministry is: "Worship, Work and Witness." Each of these elements is strongly represented in the program of the SCAMPS. Sunday worship services are held in the SCAMPS house each Sunday and weekly fellowship meetings and small group Bible studies are held regularly each semester. Retreats and mission trips are also emphasized. Several from this group have gone to Haiti in 1991 and to Honduras in 1992 were they obtained "hands-on missions experience and a heightened awareness of the world needs."[23]

There is a "down side" to campus ministry among Christian Churches which we have not mentioned up till now. Campus ministries across the country have found that it is especially difficult to enlist students from Christian Churches in ministry on campus. In 1984, Mark Gallagher wrote a thesis on the subject for his degree from Lincoln Christian Seminary. The thesis was titled, "Factors Contributing to Involvement of Christian Students in the Christian Campus Ministry of Terre Haute." The popular title which Mark gave to his summary of his thesis is, "Why Don't Our Kids Come to SCAMPS?" Mark pointed out that in one typical semester at Terre Haute (fall of 1983), out of one hundred students enrolled at Indiana State who were known to have come from Christian Churches, only nineteen became active with the SCAMPS ministry.[24]

Whatever the causes for this condition, it is clear that Christian Churches must take a hard look at how they prepare their students for entering college.

There have been three distinct phases of the campus ministry at Indiana State — Rose Hulman Institute: the Crain years, the Puckett years, and the Gallagher years. Each phase has been unique in emphases but each has contributed to a remarkable and productive twenty-five years of campus ministry. Mark Gallagher recently characterized this ministry using a metaphor from the world of creative artists: "work in progress — which God has not yet finished."[25]

# Indiana University

Jack Haun's ministry at Indiana University continued until 1976 when he accepted a call to serve as senior minister of the Englewood Christian Church in Indianapolis. Ward Patterson had been called as Jack's part-time associate in 1974, and when Jack left, Ward became full-time campus minister.

Ward Patterson, when asked what best prepared him for ministry to university students once said, "I think everything I have done has fit into my ministry in some way or another."[26] Ward had done an amazing variety of things before coming to Indiana University. He took a trip around the world on a motorcycle in the 1960s, sending regular reports back to be published in the *Christian Standard*. He had majored in religious studies and archeology at Cincinnati Bible Seminary, and had earned degrees from the state university in Fort Hays, Kansas in Speech, Drama, and English Literature. What Ward brought to the campus ministry was a wealth of experience and a calm, scholarly personality that God had prepared especially for the university setting.

Worship continued to be the heart of the ministry, the Sunday morning services growing until it was necessary to move to a larger room in the student union in 1978. Ward described this part of the ministry as an opportunity "to proclaim the Word of God in the academic community, and to demonstrate the relevance of the Bible to the needs of modern man."[27] Other important aspects of the program during Ward's ministry included discipleship groups, Sunday evening fellowship meals, retreats, and classes for credit from both Cincinnati Bible Seminary and Lincoln Christian Seminary. Counseling with students was always a major part of his ministry, and he became a part of the Residence Halls Resource Team, a group of professional counselors assigned to residence halls for counseling and other student services. He also taught in the speech department of the university as an associate instructor, which enhanced the visibility of the campus ministry in the university community. He initiated two football-related programs. One was a "Football Weekend," when high school students were invited to campus during an Indiana University football weekend and were hosted by the campus ministry. The other was the establishment of the regular Bible study, taught by Ward, for ten to twelve Indiana University football players.

A women's campus house was established in 1974, and Jeri Roesch, who came from the Michigan State campus ministry, was the women's coordinator from 1978 to 1980. A house for women students was purchased in 1983.

Missions were strongly emphasized during Ward's ministry, students taking work trips to Haiti and Mexico several times, and to Cookson Hills School every year. Two former students became missionaries in Zimbabwe and two in Thailand as well as one in Cairo, Egypt.

Steve Wesner was Ward's associate from 1972-1982. The breadth of the influence of this ministry under Ward Patterson's leadership can be measured by the following statistics. Ward writes: "Our students are serving in at least the following countries: Germany, Italy, Mexico, Thailand, Burma, Zimbabwe, Egypt, China, Nepal, Scotland, Finland, Holland, Australia, Taiwan, Japan, Pakistan, Malaysia and England."[28] In addition, Ward says:

> We number these professions among our graduates: journalists, bureaucrats, lawyers, patent attorneys, writers, artists, research chemists, doctors, surgeons, dentists, geologists, primary teachers, elementary teachers, junior high teachers, high school teachers, college professors, computer programmers, financial planners, insurance salesmen, entrepreneurs, manufacturers, sales representatives, accountants, comptrollers, nursing home administrators, missionaries, youth ministers, opera singers, symphony musicians, music teachers, coaches, physical therapists, bankers, Bible college professors, music ministers, military intelligence officers, telephone engineers, personnel managers, professional athletes, dramatists, drug counselors, homemakers, railroaders, airplane mechanics, transportation administrators, nurses, bakers, probation officers, political campaign managers, secretaries, preachers, campus ministers, editors, band directors, and linguists. I probably could list others if I gave a bit more time to it.[29]

In a brochure announcing the celebration of twenty years of campus ministry at Indiana University, Ward Patterson listed as one of the purposes of the ministry "to demonstrate and promote a Christian lifestyle with joy and enthusiasm."[30] This is a great summary of Ward Patterson's ministry at Indiana University. He left IU in July of 1991 to go to the Cincinnati Bible Seminary to teach campus ministry, where he is communicating his expertise and enthusiasm for campus ministry to scores of interested students.

When Ward Patterson left the Indiana University campus ministry in July of 1991 Ritchie Hoffman, who had been Ward's associate since 1982, became the campus minister. Ritchie's experience had also been good preparation for campus ministry. He began his college career as a physics major at the University of Illinois where he joined the Farmhouse Fraternity during his freshman year. Ritchie describes himself during this period of his life as a confirmed atheist. However, he was converted by the Christian lifestyle of a fraternity brother who was active in Campus Crusade for Christ. After graduation from the University of Illinois with a degree in Physics, he entered Lincoln Christian College, completed his degree, and went on to Lincoln Christian Seminary where he earned a graduate degree and came under the influence of Dr. James Strauss, who helped him sort out his faith in reference to his scientific background.[31]

Under Ritchie's leadership at IU the main features of the program have been continued, with some unique additions. Mid-week worship and fellowship, small group Bible studies, retreats and mission trips are the staples of the program, but special ministry to varsity football players, optometry students, business students and fraternities and sororities have been added.

Ritchie, at the request of the university, participated in a Residence Hall Resource Team and was assigned as chaplain to do crisis intervention, staff development and programming. This provided an unparalleled opportunity to reach new students. He also has been involved in special debates and panel discussions on campus on such subjects as "The Existence of God" with a philosophy professor, and "Science and Religion" with a science professor. There have been eight such debates and panel discussions in the past eight years in which Ritchie was involved.

There have been talented staff members to strengthen the ministry of the fellowship on campus during Ritchie's ministry. Linda Sarchet has been secretary since 1987, and Denise Buhr became the coordinator at the women's campus house in the spring of 1991. She had lived in the house while a student at IU, and she gave up a career in Library Science to serve as the women's coordinator. Denise recently began a Bible study with secretaries and clerical staff in an administration building that includes the offices of the Vice President of the university. Denise writes of this group:

> A group of women who work in various departments there formed a Bible study last fall and invited several of us who work with ministries on campus to join them. We meet over lunch each Thursday. It is still a small group and the topics right now are dealing more with personal growth issues than with outreach. However, the lessons learned each week are being taken into the homes and offices of these women and are changing the way they live and work. Others are seeing what God is doing and wondering about this thing called Christianity.[32]

Tim Scott and his wife Julie became Ritchie's associates in July of

1991. Tim is gifted in musical leadership, and has also taken over the Bible study with the varsity football players, a much overlooked group.[33]

The most unique aspect of the IU campus ministry under Ritchie Hoffman's leadership is a special ministry to homosexuals. In a culture — and particularly on a campus — where homosexuality is more and more open, Ritchie believes that one can show the compassion of Christ to these people without condoning their lifestyle. He is working with a young man who specializes in this ministry on the national level and he describes the ministry as follows:

> In recent years, I have spoken in nearly a dozen public panels or debates discussing homosexuality and the Biblical view toward it. However, this year marks the beginning of an even greater opportunity. I am participating in the birthing of a ministry to gays with someone healed of his homosexual brokenness. Scott left the gay lifestyle, married, and now has a vision to minister to gays in Bloomington. Some feel that Bloomington may have the highest per capita gay population of any place in the Mid-West. We finally have someone of Scott's background to help make Christ fully known at IU. Scott is receiving training through one of the national ministries to gays. He is leading a twenty week training seminar to equip others to minister to gays. In the spring, we plan to open this ministry to those who accept Jesus as Lord and want healing from their homosexual brokenness. I am helping Scott map out a strategy for this ministry. Pray for this ministry as we work together with area churches and campus ministries to expand its influence. In time, we hope to work into residence hall programming and the mainstream of student life at IU.[34]

If the purpose of campus ministry is to encounter all aspects of the university life with the gospel of Christ, the IU campus ministry certainly fulfills that purpose admirably. Gary Weedman and I, sitting in the Gables Restaurant in Bloomington in 1967, planning for and praying about a campus ministry at Indiana University, had no idea what God had in mind for this ministry!

# University of Wisconsin

Sam and Bonnie Fox, first campus ministers at the University of Wisconsin, left in 1972 and were succeeded by a series of campus ministers. Gary Edwards served from June 1972 to July 1974, Dan Johnston served from January 1975 to June 1980, Steve Odom served from August 1980 to June 1982, and Phil Laughlin served from August 1982 to May 1984.[35]

Bruce Jones became the campus minister in June of 1985. Bruce had graduated from the University of Wisconsin with a Bachelor of Science degree in mathematics, and had also received a Master of Divinity degree from Emmanuel School of Religion.[36] In 1975 the ministry at Wisconsin had purchased a house with room for seventeen students. This "Koinonia

House" has been the center of this ministry since. Bruce lived there with the students, and he testifies that it was truly a Koinonia "fellowship" House. In his newsletter of June 1989 he writes:

> Eighteen of us share K-House, so getting away from people is a tall order and treating them equally is out of the question. We get closer to certain people than others, laugh harder at their jokes, rejoice more at their successes and feel worse about their trials. Some are irked by an offense while others merely look the other way. We bend over backwards for some people and "just pray" for others. There is plenty of spiritual food for thought at K-House, too. A wide variety of backgrounds and beliefs has fed discussions on miracles, materialism, helping street people, Satan, legalism, how God guides, how to talk to agnostics, etc. We haven't always agreed but people don't change their minds when they are hurt or angry. So we strive to handle disagreements patiently and graciously, seeking God for truth and answers in confidence that we all will eventually understand better. I'm proud of K-House for its contribution to Christian unity. For us it may be only a matter of survival, but that is no small thing. The survival of the entire Church may depend on its ability to find such unity.[37]

The basic elements of the program at the University of Wisconsin under Bruce Jones' ministry were: Sunday worship in local churches (most students attended the Westwood Christian Church in Madison),[38] Soup Night Bible study on Wednesday nights, regular ministry at a local nursing home and retreats. During one memorable weekend retreat at Fort Wilderness in northern Wisconsin, the temperature fell to -20°F, but — "a great time was had by all."[39] The strength of Bruce Jones' ministry was his ability to dialogue with diverse groups on campus. He led a weekly "Agnostic-Christian Discussion," and he made a special effort to hold discussions with Muslim students and other non-Christian groups and individuals on campus. He encouraged his students to attend a series of lectures by Christian professors called "Dissenter's Forum." Some of the topics dealt with: humanism, economics, science, AIDS, ecology, and forgiveness.[40] The fellowship also sponsored a debate between Dan Barker of the Freedom From Religion Foundation, and Norm Geisler of the Liberty Center for Research and Scholarship on the topic, "Is There a God?" More than three hundred people attended this event.[41] Several times Bruce took classes at the University, and after taking a class titled "Anthropology 107 — Evolution of the Human Species" he wrote in his newsletter:

> Many evolutionists are able to look at large stones in a rough circle or a pattern of chips on the edge of a stone and confidently conclude that intelligent life had been there. Yet these same sleuths look at DNA molecules containing enough information to reproduce every variety of life on the planet and "reason" that no intelligence need be involved, that time and chance can reasonably account for this![42]

After five years of effective ministry at the University of Wisconsin Bruce Jones resigned to pursue a "tent-making" ministry as a mathematics teacher and athletic coach in public high school.[43]

Roger McMunn and his wife Jannette succeeded Bruce Jones at the University of Wisconsin in June 1990, and they continue as campus ministers there at this writing. Roger was involved with the campus ministry during his five years in college at Western Michigan University, after which he attended Great Lakes Bible College in Lansing, Michigan. The McMunns continue the basic program at the University of Wisconsin describing it as follows: "Our current weekly activities include evening house meals, resident meetings, prayer partners, weekly Bible studies with visitors, and various additional student activities and interaction in and through a house of sixteen students."[44] In addition, the McMunns also began a ministry with international students, with a special emphasis upon reaching Chinese students.[45]

This campus ministry, born in the turbulent 1960s, has continued the high standards set by Sam and Bonnie Fox, the first campus ministers at the University of Wisconsin.

## Ohio State University in Columbus

The first serious — and successful — attempt to work with college students among Christian Churches was made by W.R. Walker, minister of the Indianola Church of Christ in Columbus, Ohio, in the early 1920s. When W.R. Walker retired in 1948, Harold Scott, who succeeded him as senior minister, and Dean Jacoby, Harold's associate, continued to work with college students assisted by sponsors and student leaders.

In 1965, D.F. Miller, a member of the congregation, was called to work part-time with the now-named Student Christian Foundation at Ohio, now officially recognized by the university. In 1971, Ken Huff followed Mr. Miller as part-time campus minister with this group.[46] By 1973 the Indianola congregation began seriously to consider calling a full-time campus minister and to broaden the base of support by a appealing to other churches in the state of Ohio.[47]

In July 1973, James McPeak was called as full-time campus minister of the SCFO, the Student Christian Foundation of Ohio, Inc. Jim McPeak, a graduate of Ozark Bible College, had served for five years as minister of a congregation in Carmel, Indiana, before coming to Columbus. He served until 1988 at Ohio State, during which time he developed a program to include regular Bible study groups, recreation and fellowship activities, and participation in area retreats. Sunday worship for students was provided by the Indianola church, with bus service from the dormitories to the church each Sunday. During Jim's ministry at Ohio State there were thirty-five to forty students involved each year.

In 1988 Jim McPeak resigned and Steve Seevers succeeded him. Steve came from thirteen years of service as a successful campus minister at Ohio University. He had served one year in Vietnam, and had received an A.B. degree from Cincinnati Bible College and an M.A. in Apologetics from Cincinnati Bible Seminary. A campus house near the football stadium had been purchased in the 1970s, and it provided housing for four to five men students as well as a meeting place for the Thursday night Bible study and fellowship, the heart of the program. Mission trips were taken each year, alternating between Cookson Hills Christian School and out of the country mission trips in Mexico and Haiti. Steve said in 1992,

> We are trying to get ready for sixteen of us to build houses with AMOR out of El Paso and leaving on the 20th. These Spring Break trips are great for the students but sure are a lot of work. We'll be joining up with groups from Georgia, Georgia Tech, and Auburn. Excitement plus![48]

This group also participated in the retreats each year at Round Lake Christian Assembly which included all the campus ministries in Ohio. Steve Seevers considers the mission trips and small student led study groups as very important parts of the program in addition to the regular Tuesday night fellowship.[49] Steve and Lydia Seevers resigned in 1993 having served faithfully in two successful campus ministries for nearly twenty years.

Scott Thompson became campus minister at Ohio State in August of 1993. Scott had become involved in campus ministry while a student at Virginia Tech, where he worked with Leland Duncan. From there he went to Emmanuel School of Religion, graduating in 1993 before coming to Ohio State. There has been an active college student ministry at Ohio State University for seventy years — from W.R. Walker's in 1923 to the present. This is by far the longest history of campus ministry among any of our Christian churches.

## University of Minnesota and Mankato State University

In 1969, Dale Friddle, minister of the University Church of Christ in Minneapolis, began to work with students, building on the work which had been done by Jerry Gibson.[50] In 1975 Duane Stanley, a graduate of Minnesota Bible College, was called to become campus minister. A Board of Directors was formed and a house next door to the church was made available.

Duane Stanley, son of Lynn and Lucille Stanley, veteran missionaries in South Africa, also had received degrees from St. Cloud State University and the University of Minnesota. A student group began to gather into a community called Christian Student Fellowship under Duane's leadership. They worshiped with the University Church on Sunday mornings and during the week they had Wednesday evening Multi-Studies at the campus house. Leadership training and discipleship groups were formed in the group who soon grew into a fellowship of thirty-five to forty-five students by 1985. The students contributed to the support of the programs and also gave a considerable amount to missions.[51] In 1987 when Duane resigned, the campus ministry at the University of Minnesota was put under the sponsorship of the University Church, which by now had become Southeast Christian Church. The name of the group was changed to Campus Christian Fellowship and Jack Nicolay became the campus minister.[52] Jack, who was a member at Southeast Christian Church and a staff person at the university, continued the campus ministry at the University of Minnesota under the directorship of the elders of the church. Jack was a graduate of Minnesota Bible College and the University of Northern Iowa with a BA in psychology and religion, and he held a master's degree from Bethel Seminary in St. Paul, Minnesota, in theological studies. The main aspects of the program under Jack, in addition to the worship at Southeast Christian Church, included small group studies, service projects and social events. One of the special events was an annual seminar on "Faith and Reason" which was led by a Christian professor and which brought many people into contact with the reasonableness of the Christian faith.[53]

In 1987 when Southeast Christian Church took responsibility for this campus ministry at the University of Minnesota under the name Campus Christian Fellowship, the original Board of Directors for Christian Student Fellowship continued in existence, and in 1988 they were able to start a campus ministry at Mankato State University. They called Kevin Blanchard and his wife Samantha to be campus ministers at Mankato State.

The Blanchards had met while students at Lincoln Christian College, and they came to Mankato from four years of ministry with the church in Kasson, Minnesota. They did several innovative things to attract students during their ministry. On Tuesday noon they had a "Bag and Bible Study" and on Tuesday evenings they had a larger Bible study and fellowship time. On Wednesday mornings at 10:00 a.m. they met for one hour to study the claims of Christ. Ski retreats and studying a video series featuring Tony Campolo on "You Can Make A Difference" attracted new students and provided the basis of growth both in numbers and in maturity.[54] Taking advantage of Minnesota winters, they held several ski retreats which provided both recreation and intensive fellowship. In one of the newsletters, Keven Blanchard reminded his readers that the university itself is a ripe mission field.[55]

When the Blanchards resigned at Mankato State in June of 1992, the Campus Christian Fellowship, which had been the campus ministry at the University of Minnesota under the sponsorship of Southeast Christian Church with Jack Nicolay as campus minister, and the Christian Student Fellowship at Mankato State University, which had been under a separate Board of Directors, combined forces to concentrate on the campus ministry at the University of Minnesota. The original campus house next door to the Southeast Church was offered to the newly combined ministry. The Chairman of the CSF Board wrote in 1992:

We are going "back to Jerusalem!" The University of Minnesota was the birthplace of CSF. The U of M is the campus with the most active students (43,000). It is the one most of the young people from our churches will attend. It is a strategic campus with world-wide impact (7,000 international students attending). It is the place where CSF has committed to minister today and into the future.[56]

On December 1, 1992, Dave Burkum and his wife Cheri had accepted the campus ministry at the University of Minnesota under the new arrangement. Dave had graduated from Nebraska Christian College and had received two degrees in music from the University of Nebraska at Lincoln, where he was active in the campus ministry. Dave and Cheri came to the University of Minnesota from five years of ministry with the Howard Lake Christian Church in Minnesota. In his first letter to the students and supporters of this ministry, Dave wrote:

One walk across the U of M campus or through the student union building is all you need to get a sense of urgency and need for the ministry of CSF. It is a place where thousands of young people, tomorrow's professionals and leaders, are preparing for the future. It is a place where beliefs and attitudes are being shaped and influenced. It is a place where Christ needs to be made visible and known! I hope you will be a partner with me in this vital ministry of taking Christ to the U of M.[57]

One of the places where campus ministry originated among Christian Churches was at the University of Minnesota in 1955. More than thirty-five years later, it is still alive, and Christ is active on the campus at the University of Minnesota!

## NOTES

1. These figures do not take into account the campuses which were reached by Project Challenge in California. Since that movement was congregation-centered rather than campus-centered these figures are not available, but they would be impressive if known. Five campus ministries which were started in the 1970s were closed by the end of the decade. They were the campus ministries at:

The University of Idaho, Southeast Missouri State, Missouri Western, The Air Force Academy, and North Carolina State.

2. Charles Habib Malik, *A Christian Critique of the University*, p. 21.

3. Rick Rowland, *Campus Ministry*, p. 107.

4. Shockley, *Campus Ministry*, p. 100.

5. *Ibid.*, pp. 100, 101.

6. *Ibid.*, p. 101.

7. It was my experience at Purdue University in the 1970s in many meetings of the University Ministers Organization that "mainline" campus ministers were so concerned about the need for social change, and so angry that the students were not responding to these perceived needs, that they missed entirely the deeper spiritual hunger of students which, if attended to, would have motivated them to seek social change. Donald Shockley says in this connection: "Certainly we are correct in our understanding that the gospel is multifaceted and that the quest for social justice is prominent among its dimensions. But, if telling others that they ought to work in behalf of good causes is all that we have to say, we have lost the very thing which might motivate them to do so." Shockley, *Campus Ministry*, p. 113.

8. From a questionnaire completed in July, 1985.

9. *Christian Standard*, September 23, 1973, p. 16.

10. University of Kentucky Christian Student Fellowship, Newsletter, July 1990, p. 3.

11. Jerry's interest in Ghana, and in international students had been sparked by his experience in founding the campus ministry at the University of Minnesota in the late 1950s.

12. From a letter to the author August 31, 1989.

13. Among them are Mark Hollenbach who is on the staff from Central Christian Church in Mesa, Arizona, and Dan Beaver, an All-American field goal kicker who lived in the campus house, and is now a missionary in the Philippines. Source: letter from Jerry Gibson to author August 31, 1989.

14. I still use many of the penetrating essays Ron wrote while teaching at the University of Illinois in my Apologetics class at Pacific Christian College.

15. Shockley, *Campus Ministry*, p. 52.

16. Information on this campus ministry was obtained from various newsletters and from a phone conversation between the author and Dave Degler in June, 1993.

17. Brochure, 25th Anniversary program; other information on the Ball State ministry has been obtained from various newsletters and questionnaires.

18. Information on the continued campus ministry at Miami University in Ohio was obtained through several questionnaires and a phone conversation between the author and John Wineland in July of 1993.

19. A period of the "SCAMPS Scoop," newsletter of the group, from 1970 to 1977 reveals men such as: Dr. James Strauss, Dr. Wayne Shaw and Dr. Rondal Smith from Lincoln Christian College; Carl Ketcherside, of the Church of Christ; Dr. Richard Pierod, of the History Department of Indiana State. Several members of this group also attended a special showing of the film by Dr. Francis Schaeffer titled *How Should We Then Live?* in February, 1977.

20. The "SCAMPS Scoop," newsletter, February 1973, p. 2.

21. *Ibid.*, p. 1.

22. A five man *a cappella* singing group made up of SCAMPS and called JUSTi"FIVE"D was a by-product of the Singing Scamps. They were much in demand during their two years in college. "SCAMPS Scoop," October 1991.

23. *Ibid.*, June 1991, p. 1.

24. Summary of Mark Gallagher's thesis, p. 1.

25. SCAMPS Scoop, June 1989, p. 2.

26. Questionnaire, 1985, p. 3.

27. *Ibid.*, p. 1.

28. Letter to author, August 27, 1991.

29. *Ibid.*

30. Brochure "Twenty Years of Outreach to College Students," 1985, p. 2.

31. Information on Ritchie Hoffman came from several questionnaires he completed along several recent newsletters he supplied, and a telephone conversation with the author in June of 1993.

32. Newsletter, "On the Frontline at IU," Spring 1992, p. 4.

33. *Ibid.*, December 1991, p. 4.

34. *Ibid.*, Winter 1993, p. 5.

35. Unfortunately I do not have information on the campus ministry at the University of Wisconsin for the years 1972–1984.

36. I was fortunate to have Bruce Jones in my class on campus ministry at Emmanuel School of Religion in the summer of 1987. Bruce also was one of the people who took the clinical pastoral education course with Larry Brandon at the University of Kentucky.

37. Wisconsin Christian Student Fellowship, Koinonia House Newsletter, May-June 1989, p. 1.

38. Bruce was ordained in this congregation on Sunday, April 13, 1966. David Fulks, of Emmanuel School of Religion, was the preacher. Newsletter, April 1986.

39. Newsletter, February 1987, p. 2.

40. Newsletter, (no date).

41. Newsletter, April-June, 1990, p. 3.

42. Newsletter, March-April, 1988, p. 1.

43. Newsletter, April-June, 1990, p. 2.

44. Newsletter, Fall 1990, p. 1.

45. Newsletter, February-March, 1992.

46. Annual Reports of the Indianola Church, 1965–1972.

47. In July of 1973 I was invited to come to Columbus to share "the Purdue Story" with the elders of the Indianola congregation.

48. Letter from Steve Seevers to author, March 1992.

49. Questionnaire completed by Steve Seevers in 1989.

50. Information on this campus ministry between 1960 and 1974 is not available to me. I was able to meet with Dave Friddle and several interested people to

tell "The Purdue Story" in July of 1974.

51. Questionnaire completed by Duane Stanley, 1985.
52. Questionnaire completed by Jack Nicolay, 1989.
53. *Ibid.*
54. "CSF Newsletter," Spring 1990, p. 3.
55. *Ibid.*, Spring 1989, p. 4.
56. Report from CSF Board of Directors, 1992.
57. "CSF Newsletter," November 1992.

# CHAPTER SIX

# Campus Ministries
# Established in the Seventies

## Eastern Illinois University and Lakeland College

One of the first campus ministries of the Christian Churches to be established in the decade of the 1970s was at Eastern Illinois University in Charleston, Illinois. Bob Owens, a student at Lincoln Christian Seminary and a product of the campus ministry at the University of Illinois, made weekend visits to Charleston during 1969, encouraged by Ed Armstrong, minister at the Central Christian Church in Charleston. On September 1, 1970, a number of concerned Christians at Central Christian Church took steps to formalize the campus ministry at Eastern and Lakeland College at nearby Mattoon, Illinois. The formal name chosen was "Eastern-Lakeland Christian Campus Ministry."[1]

Soon after this meeting, Dr. J. Robert (Bob) Ross was called as full-time campus minister. Bob came to Charleston from Alabama A & M University where he was an instructor in philosophy and where he also served as a counselor in the office of student personnel. His degrees included a PhD in Theology from Emory University in Atlanta, Georgia, and a Bachelor of Divinity degree from Colombia Theological Seminary in Decatur, Georgia. He also had a Bachelor of Science degree in zoology from Southeastern Louisiana College — an awesome set of qualifications for campus ministry! Because of Bob's strong academic background, one of the main emphases of his ten year ministry at Eastern was on credit-level courses in Bible and religion. These classes were credited by Lincoln Christian College and students were able to receive credit for these courses at Eastern.[2]

There were many other aspects of the program, including a Wednesday fellowship night planned by students, small group Bible studies, a "Host Family" program, mission trips to Mississippi and Jamaica, outreach teams to churches, "Good News Weekends" (special music and guest speakers), and much more.[3]

The only property available in the beginning of this ministry was a small office rented from the Episcopal Campus Ministry, but in February of 1971 a house was leased which provided an office, a meeting room, lounge, kitchen and one room for student rental.[4] In August of 1977 a building which had been a fraternity house was purchased. This eight bedroom building, which came to be called "Covenant House," soon housed sixteen women students.[5] The growth of the fellowship during Bob Ross's ministry was so great that all facilities were outgrown, and by the time he resigned in 1980 plans were well under way to construct an adequate building.

Sunday worship services were begun on campus in January of 1972, utilizing the Booth Library Auditorium and forty-five students attended the first Sunday services. By spring this worship service had increased in attendance to eighty-six.[6] They participated in area retreats (French Lick and Little Galilee at first — later retreats for the campus ministries in Illinois were inaugurated). They also held special weekends for high school students and enlisted many for the campus ministry at Eastern in this way. Strong student leadership became a part of this ministry under Bob Ross and by the time he resigned in January of 1980 this was one of the strongest campus ministries in the country. Bob left to become director of the Christian Counseling Center at Mount Vernon, Illinois.[7] There were two associate ministers who worked with Bob at Eastern; Paul Bangert was the first, and Randy Evans succeeded him.

In January of 1980 Gary and Javonda Barnes became the campus ministers at Eastern Illinois University. They had been song evangelists in the churches in the Midwest, before which Gary had ministered with the Cornerstone Christian Church in Northridge, California. With the arrival of the Barnes a campaign was launched called "The Second Mile — the Second Decade Campaign," the purpose of which was to raise funds for a much-needed new building. Bill Stark, minister of the Broadway Christian Church in Mattoon, Illinois, and a strong supporter of this campus ministry from the beginning, chaired this campaign.[8] Gary Barnes, who had traveled extensively in Europe before coming to Charleston, led mission trips to England and Scotland during his four year ministry at Eastern. In November of 1982 Gary wrote an editorial in the newsletter entitled "Why Do We Need Campus Ministry?" in which he responded to the often heard question by well-meaning folks about the viability of campus ministry. Among other things, Gary pointed out:

> Students come to the state university for three basic reasons: 1) for a good education, 2) it is less expensive than private schools, 3) and they want to study further something the Bible College doesn't offer. The last of these three is a very important reason. Most Bible Colleges are unable to specialize in many areas because of expenses. At the state university they can offer many of these areas of specialization. We in the campus ministry can and do offer the Bible classes and fellowship that are needed and desired by many students. Last year alone we know that the campus ministries had 35% more in the number of students involved in our campus ministries than the number of full-time Bible College students in all our Bible

Colleges combined. Each year this number of students increases both in the Bible Colleges and campus ministries. We are not out to close down the Bible College as it provides a much needed service, but so do campus ministries. We in the campus ministry are here to help the student when they need it.[9]

The much-needed facility for this campus ministry was constructed in 1981 during Gary Barnes's tenure at Eastern. When he and his wife left in 1984, Roger and Sue Songer became campus ministers.

Roger and Sue Songer are natives of Illinois, both growing up on small farms near Newton. Roger first became interested in campus ministry while attending Rose Hulman Institute of Technology in Terre Haute (see the previous report on this campus ministry). He attended Saint Louis Christian College and Lincoln Christian College, receiving a degree from Lincoln and then went to Trinity Evangelical Divinity School in Deerfield, Illinois, where he received his Master of Arts in New Testament in 1979. He came to Eastern from a five year campus ministry at Oklahoma State University in Stillwater.

Roger and Sue Songer continued the diversified program that had been developed at Eastern by Bob Ross and Gary Barnes, adding some distinctive elements. Sunday morning worship services, Wednesday night Bible study, student-led small groups, short-term mission trips and a regular prison ministry are the main features of the program at Eastern under Roger's leadership. When asked to name the most important part of the program Roger pointed out that student "ownership" of the ministry and a disciplined program of discipleship are the strong points in his opinion. He had developed a ten-week discipleship curriculum which approximately four hundred students have taken and which included a printed manual of sixty-five pages.[10] Housing is provided at Eastern for twenty-five students — sixteen women and nine men — which strengthens the sense of community in this ministry. In October of 1985, the fifteenth year of the campus ministry at Eastern, Roger wrote the following:

> In the short history of the Christian Campus House over 225 young men and women have been baptized into Christ, and about 30 have given their lives to specialized Christian service in local church ministries or on the mission field. Many times this number are actively involved in leadership roles in their local churches, serving as elders, deacons, teachers, etc[11]

In September of 1988, Roger used the metaphor of explosion which we have previously suggested for campus ministry when he wrote:

> The new school year has begun and it has started off with a "BANG." We have prayed, planned, and prepared for our ministry to EIU students this fall and God has rewarded our efforts. We are only two weeks into the fall semester and we have already had about 150 different people at our various

activities and services. We have averaged about 75 students in attendance at all of our major functions. The beautiful thing about this is that most of these are people who are new to CCF. We are busting out at the seams with freshmen and transfer students. In addition we have a good core of leadership that has returned from last school year.[12]

Roger and Sue Songer continue as very effective campus ministers at Eastern and Lakeland College as this is being written.

## The University of Evansville and
## The University of Southern Indiana

There are two major universities in Evansville, Indiana. One is the University of Evansville, a private Methodist affiliated campus, and the other is the University of Southern Indiana, a four-year state university. Campus ministry on these two campuses was initiated by the Cullen Avenue Christian Church beginning in 1972. Ron Wernamont, minister at Cullen Avenue from 1972–1974, and Dennis Randall, minister there from 1974–1976 worked with these two campuses until Wendell Hose was called as full-time campus minister in 1976 at which time the ministry came under the direction of an area Board of Directors.

Wendell Hose and his wife labored on these two campuses for fourteen years. They conducted regular worship services at the University of Southern Indiana, and led Bible study and discussion groups for students, faculty and staff on both campuses. Wendell reported in 1989 that, in his opinion, the most successful activity during his ministry was the singing ministry to area churches made up of a group of students from the campus.[13]

In August of 1990, Mark Whited and his wife Becky came to Evansville to take over as campus ministers. Mark had been associate campus minister at Western Kentucky University in Bowling Green for several years, and he was able to bring some of his personal financial support and his experience with him to Evansville.

There has been dramatic growth of this campus ministry during the nearly four years of Mark Whited's leadership. There was no property when he arrived, since Wendell Hose had worked out of university facilities. In March of 1992, $25,000 was contributed by area churches and individuals toward the purchase of a campus house, and in addition to this a single congregation matched that amount with another $25,000. It was therefore possible to purchase the house with a minimum of debt.[14] The Whiteds lived in the downstairs part of the house and the upstairs was renovated to provide a large meeting room that is used for "discipleship groups, leadership meetings, prayer and a host of other activities."[15]

The larger part of this ministry is with students at the University of

Evansville, a smaller number participating from the University of Southern Indiana because it is a commuter college. During the school year of 1992–93 two hundred different students participated in the Christian Student Fellowship serving these two campuses and an evangelistic event was co-sponsored during that year with InterVarsity Christian Fellowship. Dr. James Sire, editor of InterVarsity Press, was the speaker and more than one hundred non-Christian students came to this event. In 1993–94, plans are being made to increase the impact of the ministry on the state campus, using a large building made available by the university for weekly meetings.[16] Two mission trips were taken in 1992: one to Dulac, Louisiana, to help rebuild houses which had been destroyed by Hurricane Andrew and another during the spring break of the same year to the inner-city of Fort Wayne, Indiana. Both of these mission trips involved several students. In the fall of 1993, eighteen graduates from these two campus ministries entered fourteen different professions in the "secular" world.[17] It looks like the beginning of a powerful, renewed campus ministry in Evansville, Indiana.

# Florida State University, Tallahassee

The campus ministry at Florida State University, Tallahassee, Florida, began in 1970 when First Christian Church in that city began a special effort to reach college students with the gospel. Soon a separate corporation was formed under the name Seminole Christian Campus House, and Thom and Mary Lou Miller were called as campus ministers. In 1979 a campus house was purchased at a cost of $90,000. This was a step of faith as little financial support was provided at this point.[18] The house became residence for the Millers and a base of operation for the ministry.

In 1985 in the Annual Report which marked the fifteenth year of this campus ministry, Thom Miller wrote:

> As we look back over the past decade and a half we can see the Lord's faithfulness. Who could foresee that over 1,500 students would become active at the Campus House and thousands more briefly touched by the ministry. Approximately 150 students have come to faith in Christ and experienced his death, burial and resurrection through baptism. 42 graduates have gone into some type of full-time Christian work, serving as missionaries, Bible College professors, music ministers, youth workers, campus workers and counselors. 68 couples have been married after being involved at the Campus House.[19]

During his ministry at Tallahassee, Thom took a degree from Florida State University with a major in Student Personnel and Home and Family. The program under Thom and Mary Lou's leadership has included Bible study groups, Sunday worship services at the Campus

House, one-on-one discipleship, fellowship meals and a special emphasis on retreats with outside guest speakers.[20]

In 1984, the original mortgage of $90,000 on the campus house was paid off, and the property was completely renovated at a cost of $67,000. This house, because the Millers lived there and provided a strong role model as a family, contributed greatly to the distinctiveness of this campus ministry. As we have noted before, campus ministries tend to take shape around the special gifts and personalities of the campus ministers. In this case, the Millers' home life created a special emphasis on healthy family life. In 1985 Thom had married sixty-nine couples out of the fellowship, and there was a "baby boom" as the couples began to raise families of their own.

The campus ministry at Tallahassee has kept in touch with its graduates through a "Has Been" organization, and "because we keep in touch we know a great majority of our former students become active somewhere in churches throughout America and the world."[21] A partial list of the various fields in which these Christian graduates work includes: ministers, camp directors, missionaries, doctors, elementary and high school teachers, magazine writers, lawyers, army chaplains, Christian counselors, Bible college teachers and administrators and many others.[22] Several interns received training under Thom Miller and are now acting campus ministers in other locations.[23]

Thom and Mary Lou left Tallahassee and the campus ministry at Florida State University in 1989 to accept a position as ministers of Marriage and Family with the Southwest Christian Church in East Point, Georgia.

Mike Waers succeeded the Millers as campus minister at Florida State University in 1989, and is carrying on this vigorous program of campus ministry. He considers the Sunday worship the most important aspect of the program and when he was asked what he considered the greatest opportunity in campus ministry in May of 1993 he said: "Reaching the lost who might never hear the gospel and watching them grow. Also seeing the enthusiasm of university students who often tackle what others might consider impossible tasks — their energy and enthusiasm is inspiring."[24]

# Pittsburg State University, Pittsburg, Kansas

Dr. Orville Brill, a physics professor at Pittsburg State and a member of the Countryside Christian Church in Pittsburg, Kansas, began holding Bible studies on campus of the university in the late 1960s, encouraged by his own congregation. In 1970 a board of directors from area churches was formed, and in 1972 the first campus minister, Leon Weece, was called. Leon served one year and was succeeded by John Steele (1973–1974), and Chuck Beaver (1975–1978).[25]

Don Smith became the campus minister in 1978, and has continued in that capacity to the present. Don had been youth minister at McAlester, Oklahoma, and he had attended Ozark Bible College and Lincoln Christian College. In 1971 a campus house was purchased, the debt was paid off in 1986, and it was remodeled in 1988. This original campus house serves as the meeting place for fellowship and a residence for seven male students. Later another house nearby was leased and it houses six women students. In 1992 all property and indebtedness had been paid and the ministry is now debt free.[26] The program at Pittsburg State consists of student-planned Wednesday fellowship and praise meetings, retreats, spring break mission trips, and work projects. Don Smith has attended classes at the university, and has done considerable pre-marital counseling.

A successful joint retreat has been held since the mid 1970s in combination with other campus ministries. Over 300 people have attended this retreat from three campuses for the past several years.[27] Don Smith has led a successful campus ministry for fifteen years at Pittsburg State University.

# Western Illinois State University, Macomb, Illinois

The campus ministry at Western Illinois State University at Macomb, Illinois, began in 1970 primarily as a result of the vision of two men — Roger Thomas, minister of the Maple Avenue Christian Church in Macomb, and Charles Syester, a professor in the college of education at the university. In that year the Western Illinois Campus Evangelism Association was established to support the new ministry, and Roger Thomas became the first President of the Board of Directors. Charles Syester served as campus minister, supported by Roger and the newly formed organization.

In January of 1973 John Derry was called as part-time campus minister, and in 1976 John moved to Macomb to minister full-time on this campus. Bible studies and activities were originally held in buildings on campus until the purchase of the campus house in 1976. In 1978 a huge facility which houses forty-six students in twelve apartments was purchased. On the lower level of this building there are three offices, a lounge, fellowship hall, kitchen, laundry room and a chapel. This building made possible the creation of a large community of Christian students which became the center of this campus ministry.

John Derry's talent for organization and teaching (degrees from both Lincoln Christian College and Seminary, and a Masters of Science degree in education from Western Illinois State University) created what amounted to a small Bible college on the campus at Western. He taught extension courses from Lincoln Christian College which could be transferred toward graduation from Western Illinois State University. In a typical school year John offered courses in: Life of Christ, Teachings of Christ, Old Testament Survey, Introduction to the Bible and Christian Faith in Our Society.[28]

In addition to the classes for credit, a special "Perfect in Christ Curriculum" was offered on Tuesday evenings. These courses were required of all campus house residents but were open to other interested individuals. This series of studies was repeated every two years and it included sections of study on Christian Character, Christian Doctrine, the Christian Mind and the Christian Church.[29] The rest of the program included Sunday worship in the campus chapel led by students, Sunday evening suppers, retreats, various fellowship activities, counseling and Christian service opportunities in children's homes and nursing homes.[30] Per Guldbeck, from Chicago, was in the Campus Ministry his freshman year at Western, then transferred to Lincoln Christian College. He returned to work as John Derry's associate and became the full-time campus minister when John left in 1985 to become Dean of Students at Milligan College in Tennessee.

After attending the French Lick Convocation for several years, students began in 1980 to attend a retreat organized by the campus ministers in the state of Illinois to replace French Lick when it moved to Tennessee, and in April they joined the Lake Ozark retreat which had been started by Roy Weece and the campus ministry at the University of Missouri.[31]

In February of 1983 the Western Illinois State University student newspaper featured a story on this remarkable campus ministry which pointed out that it had begun in 1970 with six or eight students, and by 1983 it was ministering to more than one hundred students each week.[32]

Per Guldbeck continued the program until 1989. When Per left, Charles Ferguson became campus minister and he carried on the leadership of this outstanding program. Charles lists study groups, worship services, retreats, social events, campus house community, outreach to the churches and camps, and a developing ministry to international students as the main strengths of the program. He quotes an article by Tom Plog, campus minister at Washington University in St. Louis, Missouri, "that Christian churches must begin to pay more attention to the eighty-five percent of their high school graduates who do not go to Bible college, and that the campus ministry is 'one of our movement's best kept secrets.' "[33]

## Murray State University, Murray, Kentucky

The campus ministry at Murray State University began in 1970. Christian students on the campus were responsible for initiating this ministry, which soon received the support of area churches. Jim King was the first campus minister serving from 1970–1972, and Dean Ross succeeded him in 1972.

A campus house near the university was purchased in 1973 and a worship room was added to the house that same year. A student led campaign paid off the final debt on this property in February of 1987.[34] The main emphasis of Dean Ross' ministry during the years has been on teaching. He has emphasized the credibility of the Christian faith, and its applicability to all areas of life through his teaching and preaching at Murray State. Results of this kind of ministry are reflected in the many testimonials from students and graduates who have gone from this campus ministry into many areas of the secular world with a strong faith.[35]

For several years a pregnancy testing and counseling service was sponsored and was housed in a building next to the campus house. Dean Ross has been chaplain in the dormitories and with the football team several times during his ministry.[36] In recent years an annual mission trip to Haiti has involved several students who have raised $750 each to pay their own way.[37]

In one of Dean Ross's editorials in the campus ministry newsletter, he quotes Dr. Garland Bare, long time medical missionary to Thailand, who said in his speech at the NACSF retreat in May of 1989, "Campus ministry is the most essential part of the church in helping to save the world." He went on to say that it is cheaper to send a Christian leader back to Thailand than to send an American missionary.[38] Dean Ross has recently summed up his twenty-one years of ministry at Murray State as follows:

> In the twenty-one years I have been here, there have been gigantic changes in our society. There are about thirty students who have gone on to Bible college or are in mission work. We have our property paid off. The Crisis Pregnancy Center in the house next to us is on its own, but we own the property. We have always been a teaching ministry, equipping the students to do ministry on their own. . . . It is an exciting ministry to see college students get turned on to the truth of the Christian faith.[39]

The campus ministry at Murray State is a relatively small campus ministry on a relatively small campus, but its influence on students over the years is out of all proportion to its size.

# University of Kansas at Lawrence, Kansas

In 1971, during the height of the so-called "Jesus Movement" on college campuses across the country, Ron Goodman, then minister at Antioch Church of Christ in Overland Park, Kansas, saw the need and opportunity for a campus ministry at the University of Kansas in Lawrence. In the fall of that year, with backing from Lawrence Heights Christian Church and North Lawrence Christian Church, Ron began working on campus one day a week, contacting students and leading a Bible study in the Kansas Union.

In the fall of 1972, Ron and his wife Barb moved to Lawrence to begin a full-time ministry on campus. The objectives of this ministry were: 1) to engage students from Christian Church and Church of Christ backgrounds in fellowship, study and outreach; 2) to evangelize on the campus; 3) to provide a campus house as a center of Christian activity and as a dormitory facility.

In 1973, a house was purchased to serve as the campus house (later called "Yeshua House"). In 1975, a second house, adjacent to the Yeshua House, was purchased to serve as a residential facility for female students. Ministry to the students was conducted through small and large group Bible studies, retreats, and one-on-one discipleship.

In 1976, Ron submitted his resignation, ending five years of service to Campus Christians. That summer, the board of directors hired Mark Baker, a KU graduate, to be the new campus minister. In 1977, Cyndy Clauss was hired to join Mark as associate campus minister. Cyndy was a graduate of Purdue University and had been involved with the campus ministry there. At this time approximately seventy students were involved in the campus ministry.

Upon the resignations of Mark and Cyndy in the spring of 1978, the board called Alan Rosenak, along with his wife Charlotte, to serve in the ministry of Campus Christians. Alan and Charlotte were graduates of Lincoln Christian College and Seminary.

A major decision was made in the Spring of 1980 to sell the Yeshua Houses and purchase a house two blocks north of the campus. Known as the "Campus Christian House," this facility could house up to twenty-nine students. Living arrangements were provided for both men and women. The house was operated on a cooperative living basis, with residents sharing the responsibilities for cooking and cleaning. To oversee the physical operation of the house, the board hired Steve and Sharon Batten from Lawrence in the summer of 1980.

Alan submitted his resignation in the spring of 1983, having served as campus minister for five years. In his place, the board hired Jim Musser in August of 1983. Jim graduated from Ball State University, where he was a student leader in the Christian Student Foundation, and from Emmanuel School of Religion. Melissa Penny was also hired to served as a part-time secretary.

Under Jim's leadership, a review of the purpose of Campus Christians was made in 1985 by the board and agreed upon: 1) discipleship — to prepare students for works of service that the body of Christ may be built up (Ephesians 4:12 and 2 Timothy 2:1); 2) evangelism — to present the claims of Jesus Christ to students and staff; and 3) fellowship — to provide opportunities for Christian students to get to know and encourage one another in the Faith.

In May of 1984, Steve and Sharon Batten resigned as house managers, having served in that position for four years. They were replaced by Richard White, a graduate of KU. Melissa Penny also resigned and Diane Wallace, a KU student, assumed her duties. In August, she submitted her resignation and Donna Bell was hired as the new secretary/bookkeeper.

As a result of financial problems and the recognition that the house was not fulfilling its original purposes, the Directors decided at a special meeting in May of 1985 to sell the facility. Within two weeks a buyer was found and the house was sold for nearly twice the amount it was purchased for five years earlier and the ministry re-located its offices four blocks from the campus.

"Campus Houses" which provide housing for students have been excellent tools for building Christian community on many campuses. However, the "housing business" has not always been a blessing. At the University of Kansas, the housing was becoming a burden to the ministry, and after the sale of the houses the ministry flourished. The First Christian Church in Lawrence (Ron Goodman, minister) provided rent free office space, and the meetings of the group were held in university facilities.

Pam Goodwin became associate minister to Jim Musser in July, 1986. Her ministry with women students at Lawrence and with nursing students at Kansas University Medical School in Kansas City added a new dimension to this campus ministry.[40]

The program carried on at Kansas University has centered around small group Bible studies (Koinonia groups), weekly large group meetings and mission trips. Jim Musser came to the ministry with a deep commitment to missions, having attended the Urbana missionary conference sponsored by Inter-Varsity in 1976. Slowly but surely over the years of Jim's ministry he has been able to get students involved in mission work trips to Haiti, the Idaho Christian Children's Home in Boise, and to Mexico. Jim himself spent the summer of 1986 on a mission trip to Africa.[41]

Larry Maddux became the associate campus minister at Lawrence in June of 1991. This campus ministry has grown slowly, but steadily, under Jim Musser's leadership. At one point in the early years he had only four students, but in the school year of 1992, more than sixty students were involved in this ministry.[42]

# Central Missouri State University, Warrensburg

The Parkview Christian Church in Sedalia, Missouri and the West Central Evangelistic Fellowship were instrumental in founding the campus ministry at Central Missouri State University in 1972. Dr. Dan Curtis, a professor at the university and an elder in the Northside Christian Church in Warrensburg, was an important influence in the organizing of this campus ministry. Up to now, we have said very little about the role of faculty sponsors of campus ministries. Contrary to popular opinion, there are many Christian faculty members at every university, and their acting as liaison between the university and campus ministries is a crucial factor in the establishment and growth of those ministries. Dr. Dan Curtis is such a person, and he continues at this writing as the campus coordinator of the campus ministry at Warrensburg.[43]

For two years local preachers served as acting campus ministers, but in 1974 Dennis Moss was called as campus minister, to be succeeded by R. Dean Hickerson in 1979. Dean, who was the founder of the campus ministry at Ball State University in Indiana in the 1950s, served at Warrensburg until 1986. Derry Gibson, while a student at Ozark Bible College, served as an intern with Dean Hickerson beginning in 1985, and when Dean left in 1986 Derry served as campus minister until 1988 when Paul Burhart, present campus minister, was called.

Paul Burhart became involved in the campus ministry at the University of Missouri while taking a degree in education there. Paul and his wife Daun have led this ministry in steady growth during the five years at Warrensburg. They have emphasized student leadership in all aspects of the program which include: Sunday night worship, Tuesday night Bible study, discipleship and "Family Groups." Paul meets for one hour each week with each student leader for guidance and encouragement.[44] Mission trips to Mexico, the inner-city in Memphis and St. Louis, and a regular ministry to Johnson County Criminal Justice Center in Warrensburg give students opportunities to be involved in outreach.

In November 1991, the campus house, which had served as a residence for male students and a center for activities for several years, was sold to the university and a smaller house a few blocks away was purchased. Paul Burhart, who is a skilled carpenter, did most of the remodeling and improvement on the new house, which has no student residents. As Paul says,

> This move — takes us out of the position of landlord. This has been a constant conflict of interest. This house can better be used by non-residents, and no one attends Bible study anymore because they 'have to' because they live in a campus house.[45]

Participation in the annual leadership conferences sponsored by NACCM, and attendance at area retreats have helped to strengthen the student leadership at Warrensburg. Paul Burhart describes an incident which took place in the spring semester of 1990 which illustrates how God works in unsuspected ways in campus ministry. Under the title "God Has a Plan," Paul writes:

> If I told you an atheist professor who teaches in the geology department at CMSU was giving his students extra credit to attend meetings this semester at the Christian Campus House, you might find it hard to believe. We are

showing a very educational and professionally done series of films called "Origins: How the World Came to Be." The series offers scientific evidence for the creation view of how the universe, our world and life itself, is created by God. We advertised these films via posters and flyers all over campus. The professor I mentioned before, who is a staunch evolutionist, saw the poster and made the offer of twenty extra credit points to his students to watch the films, take notes, and discuss it in class. So, unknowingly, the professor helped make the decision to show the series as well as promoting it for us in his classes. I call it God's plan. As a result, our Tuesday evening meetings which were growing in numbers already, swelled immediately to over fifty-five people.[46]

Thus God continues to work through campus ministry to establish the kingdom at Warrensburg and many other places during the decade of the 1970s.

# University of Missouri at Rolla

The University of Missouri at Rolla, part of the four campus University of Missouri system, was established in 1871 as the Missouri School of Mines. Today, in addition to offering degrees in a wide range of areas in the humanities and the social sciences, it is maintaining its reputation as one of the largest and most respected engineering schools in the nation. Several of the original promoters of campus ministry at Rolla were Christian professors who were themselves aware of the challenge of relating their scientific and academic life to the Christian faith.[47]

By the fall of 1972 interest in campus ministry at Rolla was high enough to call Roger Thomas as the first campus minister. When Roger resigned in 1977 to accept a call to work with the Christ on Campus ministry at the University of Oklahoma, a campus newspaper reported on his five year ministry at Rolla as follows:

> During the five years of Roger's leadership of the CCH ministry at UMR, hundreds of students have had a part in the outreach and growth of the ministry. Dozens have been baptized into Christ, scores of others have discovered a fuller life of faith through CCH."[48]

Roger Thomas also became one of the most prolific and widely read authors of articles about the campus ministry movement among Christian Churches. He was a valuable spokesman to the churches as an interpreter of campus ministry as a significant ministry worthy of serious attention.[49] Retreats at Roaring River, French Lick and Lake of the Ozarks, in addition to the organizing of a choral group called "Christian Campus House Singers" and participation by the campus house students in a program of intramural sports, were special features of the ministry at Rolla under Roger Thomas's leadership.

After Roger's resignation in 1977, Gayle Lucian was called as campus minister, serving from September 1977 to May 1984.[50] Bob Humphrey succeeded Gayle in June of 1984, and serves this ministry at present. Bob has carried on most of the programs initiated under Roger Thomas, and has added some new approaches. The intramural athletic program has been expanded and in 1993 the campus house basketball team became university champions.[51] In 1988 "Family Groups" of students were organized.[52]

In company with many other campus ministries, the campus house at Rolla has emphasized missions. In 1988 Bob Humphrey wrote: "The intense desire and concern for missions among CCF members has been exciting — Many of you don't know it but your support is not only helping to prepare young Christians to serve in the states, but also to send missionaries around the world."[53]

In April of 1992 Bob reported that three graduates from the campus house were working in mission-related fields. Jeff Wilhoit, a graduate in Computer Science, is working with Pioneer Bible Translators; Sonya Giesmann, a graduate in Engineering Management, is working with Wycliff Bible Translators, and Kevin Spengler, a graduate in Mechanical Engineering is working with New Tribes Mission.[54] So, the dream of the founders of the this campus ministry that even engineers can serve the Lord has come true.

Further confirmation of this exciting development is a project that took place on one of the mission trips to Mexico which was sponsored by the campus house. Bob Humphrey writes:

> One highlight that really stands out was a bridge we constructed a year and a half ago in Mexico. The missionary sent photos of the creek to be crossed and one of our civil engineering students designed a bridge. We took the plans with us and were able to construct the bridge with material native to the area. To date the bridge is still being used.[55]

Partly as a result of this experience, three graduates of the campus house have returned on their own to the same area in Mexico in order to help with special projects.[56]

The twenty year record of the campus ministry at the University of Missouri at Rolla is indeed an inspiring one.

# Central Michigan University at Mount Pleasant

The second campus ministry to be established in the state of Michigan under the direction of Gary Hawes was at Central Michigan University at Mount Pleasant in August of 1972 (see the story on the origin of the Michigan ministries in Chapter 4). Under Gary's direction this ministry continued to grow for three years as he devoted part of his time each week to the work at Central Michigan. Selected students and other staff members accompanied him to Central at least one day each week. They made dormitory calls, held counseling appointments, conducted regular leadership training sessions, and led student fellowship meetings each Tuesday evening. These meetings consisted primarily of singing, Bible teaching and prayer.[57]

In May of 1975 a large campus house was purchased located just one-half block from campus. In August of that year Michael Riness became the first full-time campus minister at Central Michigan. Michael had been active in the university as a student at Central Michigan. His ministry at Central continued for thirteen years. He resigned in May of 1988 to become the senior minister of the Grand Traverse Church of Christ in Traverse City, Michigan.

When Gary Hawes and his students began this ministry at Central there were no committed students to serve as a core group. After three years, however, when Mike Riness became full-time, there were twenty to twenty-five students involved, and by the time Michael left there were ninety to one hundred students active in this ministry.[58] All Central students are encouraged to give at least one year to volunteer mission work after graduation.[59]

In addition to regular Sunday evening fellowship meetings (Basic Christianity), Bible studies in the dormitories, and small family groups, Michael coordinated the weekly chapel meetings for the football team with an average of forty players and coaches in attendance, and he scheduled regular prayer times with the varsity basketball team.[60] Gary Hawes says this about Michael Riness' thirteen year ministry at Central Michigan:

> Tremendous growth has occurred at Central under Michael's leadership. Not only have several hundred students been ministered to, but many have matured greatly in their spiritual lives. Perhaps most important of all, are those who have been exposed to intensive leadership training to equip them to assume positions of responsibility in the body of Christ.[61]

In May of 1988, Michael O'Berski became the third campus minister to lead the fellowship at Central Michigan. Michael had been involved in the campus ministry as a student at Michigan State and then assisted in the new work on the campus of the University of Michigan. When that work became a full-time effort, Michael assumed the position of campus minister at Central where he served for over six years.

Michael continued the aggressive leadership at Central which had been started by Gary Hawes and Michael Riness, and in January of 1990 he left Central to become Administrative Director of the Michigan Christian Campus ministry under the direction of Gary Hawes at Michigan State University in Lansing.[62]

In August of 1991, Matt Schantz, who is a graduate of Great Lakes Bible College (1978) and Michigan State University (1990), became campus minister at Central. He had served a year as an intern at the University of Michigan under John Sowash, campus minister, before coming to Central.

Matt reports that the program at Central presently consists of two fellowship meetings, one on Thursdays which is a "seeker service" and includes drama and topical teaching, and another meeting on Sunday evenings which includes worship, communion, prayer and expository preaching. Students help plan all aspects of the program, and they participate in the calling and follow-up on new students.[63]

The campus ministry at Central Michigan University has been a strong and vital part of the "Michigan Miracle" for more than twenty years. We will take up the story of the other Michigan ministries later.

# Northeastern State University at Tahlequah, OK

Northeastern State University at Tahlequah, Oklahoma, is a small college which has increased in enrollment from six thousand to ten thousand in the past five years. The campus ministry there has more than kept pace with this growth. The Northeastern Campus Christian Fellowship, with Tom Tucker as campus minister, has been the largest Christian group on this campus for more than ten years.[64]

This campus ministry was established by a men's group from area churches in 1972. Tom and Barbara Tucker are the only campus ministers serving since its inception. The most unique aspect of this ministry is the fact that the university has set aside four dormitory areas in university housing which Tom Tucker supervises and which are made available exclusively to house students from the Campus Christian Fellowship. In 1990 these dormitories — two for women and two for men — housed one hundred and sixty students. Tom serves on the University Advisory Board for student housing and recruitment.[65] This is obviously a prime example of the kind of mutual cooperation that is possible between the university and a campus ministry when the purpose of the campus minister is to cooperate rather than to compete. In addition to this, Tom Tucker is a commercial pilot flight instructor, and he flies for and teaches flying at the university.[66]

Originally there were two houses owned by the ministry which were used for residences for Christian students. When the above mentioned arrangement with the university became possible one of the houses was sold. The other was expanded into a student center. This has become the location of weekly fellowship meetings attended by an average of one hundred students.

All aspects of the program at Tahlequah are geared toward developing responsible student leadership, not only for leading on campus, but for leadership in churches and careers after graduation. Students contribute $1,500 to $2,000 each year for mission projects, as well as participating in work projects at nearby Cookson Hills Christian School and other mission projects. Tom Tucker has been more than ably assisted by his wife Barb during the twenty years of their ministry at Northeastern. She has served officially as administrative assistant and unofficially as co-campus minister.

The Tuckers have developed an amazingly creative program at Tahlequah,[67] but the program is not the most powerful force at work at Tahlequah. The kind of life modeled by Tom and Barbara Tucker has been used by God to create this influential campus ministry. It is difficult to imagine how many strong Christian leaders have been produced by this campus ministry in its more than twenty year history, but the number would be impressive indeed if it were known.

## Iowa State University at Ames

In 1972 individuals from area churches became interested in establishing a campus ministry at Iowa State University at Ames, and in August of that year a board of directors was organized to fulfill their hopes. The first campus minister was Wayne Wolchuk (1972–1975) followed by Steve Tucker (1976–1979).[68]

In 1979 Dennis Hall was called to the Iowa State ministry from Northwest Missouri State; he served for six years. In 1972 a campus house for men had been purchased, and approximately a year later another house for women was obtained, each house providing housing for approximately thirty people. These houses also provided facilities for meetings. For various reasons both houses were sold in 1978, and during all of Dennis Hall's ministry university facilities provided office space and meeting places.[69] The program during these years featured Bible study and prayer groups, fellowship activities, mission trips and sports teams. The fellowship worshiped on Sundays with the North Grand Church of Christ in Ames. Dennis reports that the fellowship activities and sports teams were the most successful in drawing numbers of students during his ministry.[70]

John Woodward was called to Iowa State as campus minister in 1985. John is a graduate of Western Michigan University with a B.A. degree in English and Secondary education. In 1983 John and his wife Gwen went to Austria and worked from there with Christians behind the Iron Curtain in Eastern Europe. On returning from Europe John felt strongly that he should seek out a campus ministry. He expressed his conviction about the importance of campus ministry as follows:

> The University campus is one of the best training grounds for Christians to learn how to evangelize, use their gifts and to refine their Christian lives. The University is a mission field with students from over 100 countries, many who are lonely and hungry for friendship; this gives Christians a great opportunity to share Christ's love and reach-out to those in need.[71]

In addition to Wednesday night fellowship meetings, small group Bible studies and prayer meetings, the group at Iowa State makes yearly trips to St. Louis to work in an inner-city mission and bi-yearly trips overseas to Eastern Europe to work with Christians who formerly were behind the Iron Curtain. They hold an intensive learning retreat each year and make regular visits to supporting churches. John Woodward emphasizes active, involved student leadership at Iowa State. At this writing, forty-five students are significantly involved each semester, and they are seeking to employ a second staff person. Six ski trips tied in with a week of hard work at Cookson Hills School have been taken during John Woodward's ministry each year. The majority of the students worship on Sunday with the North Bend Church of Christ in Ames and the ministry has close ties with this congregation, which is very supportive of this growing campus ministry.[72]

# Washington University, St. Louis, Missouri and Southern Illinois University, Edwardsville, Illinois

There are several major university campuses in the St. Louis area, but there was no movement to establish campus ministries on any of them until 1973. In that year Paul Boatman, who was at that time Director of "His Place," an inner-city ministry in St. Louis, began to hold Bible studies with students at Washington University, University of Missouri at St. Louis, and St. Louis area community colleges.

The first *formal* campus ministry began in 1977 when His Place, under Paul Boatman's direction, took on an additional title of "Greater St. Louis Area Christian Student Fellowship." During the academic year of 1977-78 Paul Boatman spent about one-fourth of his time at Southern Illinois University at Edwardsville (about twenty-five miles from St. Louis). He began Bible studies there with about four students and by the end of the year seventy to eighty students were meeting for Bible study and/or prayer fellowships. During this same year, Paul also spent another one-fourth of his time leading Bible studies at the University of Missouri in St. Louis and area community colleges. About eight to ten students responded on each campus, but they never formed a reliable group.[73]

In 1978 Paul Boatman accepted a position on the faculty of Lincoln Christian College in Lincoln, Illinois, and by now a board of directors of area churches had taken responsibility for the various campus ministries in the St. Louis area. They called Mike Heston from the campus ministry at Southeast Missouri State University (Cape Girardeau). Mike served what had now become the Christian Student Fellowship for one year with Tom Plog serving as his assistant. In 1979 Tom became full-time campus minister with responsibility for four area campuses — Washington University, Saint Louis University, St. Louis area community colleges, and

Southern Illinois University at Edwardsville.[74] Tom had office space in a Church of Christ building, and used university facilities for meeting places for Bible study and fellowship. In 1982 Tom became the full-time campus minister at Washington University and John Garber became campus minister at SIU. Tom worked until 1986 using only university facilities for meetings. However, in October of 1985 he inaugurated Sunday morning worship services on the campus at Washington University — the first non-Catholic group to be accorded that privilege.

In 1985 Tom Plog's ministry was warmly endorsed by Russell E. Boatman, at that time president both of St. Louis Christian College and of the Board of Directors of the Christian Student Fellowship. In a letter written to the St. Louis area churches Russell Boatman not only recommended Tom Plog's ministry, but he also made a strong appeal for the importance of campus ministry in general. Russell wrote:

> What I am about to write may surprise you (coming from me) in view of the years I have devoted to Bible College promotion — including recruitment and fund raising. This is being written in behalf of the hundreds of young men and women who are attending secular colleges, and one who is laboring (sacrificially, it deserves to be said) to minister to their spiritual needs. There is a proverb which says: "The legs of the lame are not equal" (Prov. 26:7). That figures. Otherwise they (the lame) wouldn't be lame. For years we have in effect "crippled" the college youth of our churches who attend secular colleges by providing only for the spiritual needs of those who attend Bible colleges. Those attending secular schools not only face greater temptations but daily their minds are assaulted by ideas and ideologies which, left unchallenged, tend to destroy Christian faith. The Christian Student Fellowship under the leadership of Tom Plog is responding to that need and that challenge.[75]

A wonderful example of cooperation between a Bible college president and a campus ministry!

Partly, perhaps not wholly, as a result of Russell Boatman's letter the churches in the area gave enough financial support for the campus ministry to purchase a four-apartment complex which housed ten to twelve students and provided an excellent headquarters for the ministry, since it was located directly across from the Washington University campus. Tom Plog is carrying on a vigorous ministry to the thousands of students who come to Washington University from all over the world to study. Sunday morning worship services, Bible studies, service projects and mission trips are a part of the program. Tom also is given faculty privilege at the university, and he serves on an assembly series committee and on the panel for the Center for Inter-Religious Concerns. In 1989 the Christian Student Fellowship hosted the "Carols at Christmas" program which is a university function. The Washington University Symphony performed, and there were more than four hundred in attendance.[76]

More than seven hundred and fifty students have been significantly involved in the campus ministry, most of whom are now Christian leaders in the churches and various careers.[77] I agree with Tom Plog who said in April, 1992, "It is my opinion that longevity and Christ-centered programs have been the most advantageous to a successful campus ministry."[78] In 1991 John Garber left the campus ministry at SIU, and after Gary Barnes (former campus minister at Eastern Illinois) filled in as an intern, Tony Jackson was called as campus minister in 1992.

The entire St. Louis area has a much stronger Christian witness because of these effective campus ministries.

## Bowling Green University and the University of Toledo, Ohio

The campus ministry at Bowling Green University, Bowling Green, Ohio, and the University of Toledo, also in Ohio, are a joint operation with an organization called A.C.T., "Active Christians Today."

The groundwork for the Bowling Green ministry was laid by Darrel Fyffe, a faculty member at Bowling Green, along with a men's group in the area in the early 1970s.[79] Bruce Montgomery was called as the first full-time campus minister in 1973, and he served twelve years, leaving in 1985 to become senior minister of the Indianola Church of Christ in Columbus, Ohio. Steve Shertzinger joined Bruce in 1978, and these two men made an excellent team, building this campus ministry into one of the strongest in the nation. They put together a creative program with Bible study, worship, mission trips, and retreats. Each year they planned a fall and winter retreat for the group, including the students of the University of Toledo after that ministry began in 1980.

It is impossible to gather accurate statistics on the graduates from campus ministries across the nation, but the folks at Bowling Green made a special effort to keep in touch with their alumni. Each newsletter for several years carried a column of "Alumni News" and perusal of these lists gives one a glimpse into the amazing number of young people who carried their faith into the secular world from this ministry. In 1986 Steve Shertzinger wrote:

> The test of a campus ministry's effectiveness is what its graduates are doing five years after graduation! In some sense it's relatively easy to get a crowd of students together. Have a party, put on a concert, give some inducement that appeals to human desires and sure enough you'll have a crowd. But will that crowd by any different than it is today? We're gratified by how the alumni of Active Christians Today have expanded upon their faith since leaving campus. (Like your congregation, we cannot boast a 100% fidelity of our alums.) Nearly every week we receive a letter or call from an alum updating what they're doing. Some serve as missionaries. Others are

preaching in local congregations. Most are missionaries working on the "front lines" in "secular" jobs.[80]

When Bruce Montgomery left in 1985, Craig Herb, who had been volunteering for some time with this ministry, was added to the staff and continued for two years. Steve Shertzinger resigned in 1988 to become associate minister with the Greenwood Christian Church in Seattle, Washington.[81]

Dewey Thackston was called to be campus minister with A.C.T. in 1988, and he serves there at this writing. Sunday morning worship services have been discontinued, but Dewey reports they are emphasizing short-term mission projects and that students are taking more responsibility as leaders, even teaching some of the Bible study groups. Three retreats are held each year, one in the spring and one in the fall for Bowling Green and the University of Toledo groups, and one in the winter which includes all the campus ministries in the state of Ohio.

The campus ministry at the University of Toledo in Ohio began in 1976 with work done on that campus by Jim Nichols while he was minister at Central Christian Church in that city. By 1981 Active Christians Today at Bowling Green was strong enough to support a full-time campus minister at the University of Toledo. Bryan and Amber Rowoth were the first campus ministers in Toledo, and they served for three years until their tragic death in an automobile accident in the summer of 1984. This dedicated couple laid a solid foundation at Toledo, and after a search of several months, Steve and Leigh North were called to this ministry. Steve and Leigh were both graduates of Central Michigan University where they had both been active in the campus ministry under the direction of Michael Riness. They carried on the program which had been started by the Rowoths, in addition to which they led a group of students in a mission trip to Haiti in 1991.[82] The Norths served with distinction at Toledo until the summer of 1992 when they left to go to Lake Superior State University at Sault Ste. Marie. Until a new campus minister could be found for the University of Toledo Dewey Thackston served as campus minister. In October of 1992, Brian and Kendra Mizer were called as campus ministers at Toledo. They had been active in the campus ministry at Indiana State University after which Brian went to Lincoln Christian Seminary.

Writing in 1989, Steve North said: "Since 1985 we have had twenty-eight baptisms, twelve so far this year. I wonder how many baptisms campus ministries have as a total each year? During the past five years? We may be the prime evangelizers!"[83]

Perhaps an appropriate way to close this section on the campus ministry at Bowling Green and Toledo is to include the quotation from Ward Patterson's article, "The Good Life of a Campus Minister," which Steve North printed in the A.C.T.'s Newsletter in the spring of 1991,

I have been given time by dear brethren to read about issues that interest me. I have been permitted to give my attention to the warm, vital, and vibrant youth of this great university. I have been put in a place which abounds in concerts, lectures, and plays. I have been given the opportunity to be involved closely in the decision-making of wonderfully gifted people. I have been the recipient of the prayers of hundreds of people who value the campus work. I have been given a secretary who carries the office load with grace and who willingly sacrifices when the crunch of my plans and programs comes. I have been given student leaders who, without pay, give countless hours to the Lord's work here. I have been given a shepherding board of concerned men who journey halfway across the state to help us reach this campus for the Lord. I have been given the excitement of hugging a young Christian in the baptistery or leading him into a cold creek on a colorful fall day to bury him with the Lord. I have been able to pray with people who are standing alone in the frat houses and who teach me what it is to stand against the crowd for Jesus' sake. I have been allowed to serve my Lord in one of the most exciting arenas of the mind that exists in our nation. I guess I do have it pretty good![84]

# University of Tennessee at Knoxville

Several people from the Christian churches in the area of Knoxville, Tennessee, along with members of the faculty and students at Johnson Bible College, came together in 1972 to establish a campus ministry at the University of Tennessee in Knoxville.[85] In February of 1973, Sam Darden was called to be the first campus minister. Sam had an excellent background for campus ministry — he was a graduate of the University of Tennessee with a degree in Industrial Management and he also held an MBA degree from the University of Chattanooga and a BA from Johnson Bible College. Sam and his wife Kathy have led this ministry in an impressive numerical and spiritual growth over the past twenty years.

In September of 1981, Lynn Buckles, who was one of the original residents of the campus house at the University of Tennessee, began serving as part-time associate campus minister, and in January 1983, he became full-time. In 1974 a building near campus was obtained for a student center. The original building included a lounge area, an office, a residential area for four students and a kitchen. In 1978 a multi-purpose room was added, and in 1986 a baptistery and a counseling room were also added.[86]

The main emphasis of this campus ministry is the development of responsible leadership on the model of Ephesians 4. Sam Darden understands the role of the campus minister as that of an equipping minister, preparing leaders for the church. This purpose has been accomplished to a remarkable degree in Knoxville. Each issue of the "Tennessee Tabloid," the campus ministry's newsletter, has carried a testimonial from a student or students with the heading "What CSF Means to Me." Students majoring in engineering, chemistry, agriculture, veterinary medicine, education, and many others give moving testimony to the influence of the Christian Student Fellowship on their lives during their college years.

The program here includes Sunday worship services, small group Bible studies, prayer groups and special prayer services, mission trips and projects, counseling, and an annual homecoming for members of the fellowship. Sam Darden says that the most important and the most successful aspect of this program is the Sunday worship service held in the student center.[87]

In December of 1989, eleven people from this group went on a mission trip to Honduras. Karin Meade, a graduate of the fellowship, was serving in the Merendon Mountains of North Honduras as a nurse. They joined her there and spent several days in work projects. The trip was successful and one of the results of the trip was the organizing of the Spanish Bible Study at Johnson Bible College for students preparing for careers in Hispanic missions. Two young women who went on the Honduras trip are teaching these classes — Carrie Driver, from Johnson Bible College, and Terri Fitzpatrick, from the University of Tennessee Fellowship.[88] In 1992 a volunteer who works especially with Asian students was added to the staff also.

In October of 1987, Lynn Buckles and his wife Janene (whom he met and married at the University of Tennessee) accepted the call to become campus ministers at the University of Kentucky, where they now serve.[89] Mike Bliss served as part-time associate with Sam Darden for a year after Lynn Buckles left, and in August of 1988 Doug Shupe was called as full-time associate campus minister. Doug is a graduate of Johnson Bible College, and he came to the University of Tennessee from Florida State University where he received an MA in counseling. While at Florida State Doug served as an assistant campus minister with Thom Miller, campus minister there.[90] One of the frustrations of attempting to write the history of campus ministry is the inability to convey the true depth and power of these ministries in a few pages. For example, we have said very little about the place of humor in the campus ministry, but it is a definite factor. The "Tennessee Tabloid" carries a regular page of pictures captioned with the quotation from John 10:10, "I came that they might have life, and have it abundantly." These pictures show the exuberance, even the silliness, of Christian college students which is so much a part of campus ministry. It has been particularly difficult to convey the flavor of this particular ministry at the University of Tennessee. Sam Darden and his wife Kathy are truly remarkable people and they have touched thousands of lives during their time of service.

Sam taught a class session in the summer course on campus ministry at Emmanuel School of Religion in 1987. When he was asked by the students how campus ministers should relate to college students, Sam said: "1) love them, 2) treat them as adults, and 3) find a model of ministry that allows them to participate responsibly on the model of Ephesians 4."[91] Sam Darden and his co-workers have certainly exemplified these principles at the University of Tennessee.

# Northern Kentucky University, Highland Heights

The second campus ministry to be established by Challenge Unlimited (after the University of Cincinnati) was at Northern Kentucky University at Highland Heights, just across the Ohio River from Cincinnati. There have been only three campus ministers at Northern, and as is typical of campus ministry, each has built a ministry around his own talents and interests as they confronted the particular needs of this campus.

Bill Koontz, the first campus minister at Northern, spent two years at the University of Akron in Ohio before going to Kentucky Christian College where he graduated with honors in 1974. Bill says of his experience at Akron:

> Two factors have influenced me toward pursuing the campus ministry. The first stems from my background. While spending two years at Akron University without Christ, I searched for the answers to many of the dilemmas and problems that confront a student on campus. Now that Jesus Christ lives in my life, I feel prepared to once again meet the educational, social and spiritual challenges of the university.
>
> The second factor originates from my fellowship with Doug Dickey, whose ministry, guidance and encouragement I thank God for. Brother Doug was the first to direct my thoughts back to the needs of the campus. He spent a lot of time with me and showed a genuine concern that I be directed to the ministry that God had prepared me for.[92]

When Bill Koontz began his ministry, Northern was a small college on its way to becoming a university. It was also a commuter campus, the kind of campus which offers special kinds of problems to campus ministry. Bill did a serious study of the campus at Northern as he began his ministry, and the practical suggestion which resulted from that study are still viable for anyone involved in campus ministry on a commuter campus. Here is a brief summary of Bill's observations:

> 1. Know your gifts and the particular strengths you possess for this kind of ministry. 2. Become acquainted with as many administration, faculty and staff people as possible. Cooperate with them as much as possible. 3. Join any organization of campus ministers that might exist on campus. Such membership will provide ways to cooperate with other groups, and make you more visible to university officials. 4. Purchasing a building may not be necessary. During five years of successful ministry at Northern Kentucky, the campus ministry there never owned a building. University facilities are

numerous if you learn how to get access to them. 5. Programs should be *on-campus*, visible and available to students. 6. Offer your services as a speaker and/or a consultant to student government, dormitory government, resident hall counselors and assistants. 7. "Saturate yourself with prayer as you launch into one of the most challenging, crucial and thrilling missions of our time. The will of God will not lead you where the grace of God can not keep you."[93]

In an article on Bill's ministry in the campus newspaper, a reporter noted the unusual mixture of denominations represented in the group. Bill saw this as a practical application of Restoration principles, possible in campus ministry as in few other ministries.[94]

Bill was also able to initiate and teach, along with other campus ministers, two courses in religion at Northern — "some eighty students are enrolled in *Religion and Life* with approximately another thirty studying *Historical Survey of the Bible*. Both courses being new to Northern this semester." (from an article in "The Northerner," January 25, 1975).[95] After pioneering this ministry, Bill Koontz resigned at Northern Kentucky in 1977 to become director of Challenge Unlimited.

Tim Hudson came to the NKU ministry in 1977. He brought with him a wealth of experience which included service as a Bible college instructor and involvement in inner city and local church ministries. He received his undergraduate degree from Atlanta Christian College and a Master of Arts from Cincinnati Christian Seminary. Tim carried on an aggressive ministry for five years. Discipleship groups were the main emphasis during his tenure, but also emphasized were weekly worship, Bible studies, mission trips and quarterly retreats. Tim notes that a lack of trust between the program and supporting churches and the fact that Northern Kentucky University was seventy percent Catholic presented peculiar problems. In spite of that, sixty students became Christians during Tim's ministry, and they now serve as missionaries, elders, deacons, and youth workers in the church as well as ministering in their careers. This multiplication of influence is campus ministry's greatest opportunity, Tim says.[96]

Harold Orndorff has been campus minister at Northern Kentucky University since September of 1982. Harold's strength is in the academic area, although he gives attention to other areas of campus ministry as well. These areas include worship, Bible study, and regular retreats. Harold is a graduate of a state university and of Cincinnati Bible College and Seminary. In the state university he majored in science, secondary education and philosophy, and in seminary he specialized in theology and apologetics. Consequently, he has been recognized by the university as a faculty member, and has been able to teach courses for credit dealing with philosophy and worldviews from a Christian perspective.[97]

In 1981 a campus house was purchased located on more than one-half acre of land immediately adjacent to the campus. Three different campus ministers have served at Northern Kentucky University in the nineteen years of the ministry's existence — each with a distinctive emphasis, making for a diverse, but strong witness over the years.

# Oklahoma State University, Stillwater

Chuck Thomas, minister of the Ninth Avenue Christian Church in Stillwater, Oklahoma, and his congregation were responsible for originating the campus ministry at Oklahoma State University in the fall of 1970. After Chuck and his congregation had laid the groundwork, Bob Garringer was called as the first campus minister and he served from 1971–1973. Succeeding campus ministers were: Sam Collins, 1973–1975; Terry Hull, 1975–1976; John Lacey, 1977–1978.[98] Originally the name of the group was C.C.F., "Campus Christian Fellowship," but in 1974 the name was changed to F.O.C.U.S., "Fellowship of Christian University Students."[99] Roger Songer became campus minister in June of 1979 and during his five years of service as OSU, this ministry became solidly established. Roger came with excellent credentials and experience for campus ministry. He began his education at Rose Hulman Institute of Technology in Terre Haute, Indiana, then attended St. Louis Christian College for three years and Lincoln Christian College for one year, receiving his BA degree from Lincoln in 1976. After graduation from Lincoln, Roger attended Trinity Evangelical Divinity School in Deerfield, Illinois, receiving his MA in New Testament in 1979.

When Roger arrived at Stillwater, there were only three or four students active in the fellowship. During his five years of ministry, attendance at the Thursday night fellowship and Bible studies meetings reached a peak of fifty-five. There were twenty-five baptisms in those years and about ten people who entered various ministries and missions. Roger also developed a ten week Discipleship Curriculum which was presented on two levels — during a first semester it was taught to the group, and during a second semester it was taught on a second level to students on a one-on-one basis.

There was no building available at Stillwater, so the campus ministry leased space in a shopping center near campus which provided adequate space for offices and meeting rooms. Students attended worship services at the two local churches on Sunday mornings and Roger and several students visited churches on Sunday evenings to promote the program. Roger and his wife Sue left Oklahoma State in 1984 to become campus ministers at Eastern Illinois University in Charleston.[100]

Dave Rockey was called as campus minister at Oklahoma State University in 1984. He came from the campus ministry at Northwest Missouri State in Maryville where he had served for nine and one-half years. Dave is a graduate of Manhattan Christian College with an AB in ministry and at Northwest Missouri State with an MS in counseling and psychology. The program under Dave's ministry consisted of Bible study groups, fellowship meetings and church visitation teams, with a heavy emphasis on study groups which stretch and enrich personal relationships. Dave Rockey also emphasized small groups studying apologetics, especially using the works of Francis Schaeffer and C.S. Lewis. Dave says, "What I enjoy most is seeing graduates active and serving in local churches."[101] There are sixty to sixty-five students involved in the campus ministry at Oklahoma State as of 1993.

# Ohio University, Athens

The campus ministry at Ohio University at Athens began when Willard Love, minister of the East Athens Church of Christ and Tom Smith, director of Challenge Unlimited, began correspondence and conversation in 1974. At that time, Steve Seevers was a student at Cincinnati Bible Seminary working on a Master's degree in Apologetics after having earned an A.B. degree in Christian ministry at Cincinnati Bible College. During his time in Cincinnati, Steve had worked with Tom Smith in the campus ministry at the University of Cincinnati. The result of all of this was the beginning of the campus ministry at Athens in 1975 when Steve Seevers became the first campus minister.[102]

In the beginning, Tom Smith and Challenge Unlimited sponsored this ministry, and for six months handled the funds. However, after that time the ministry became independent. Tom was also a great help to Steve in making practical suggestions to get the ministry started. A board of directors made up of ministers and elders from the area churches was formed and the student group that was organized was originally called "Christ on Campus." In 1981 the name was changed to "Reach Out on Campus" and the organization was incorporated. Steve reports on his years as campus minister at Athens as follows:

> The peak attendance came in the 1979–1980 school year with three Bible studies averaging ninety in attendance (for the total of the three) on Tuesday, Wednesday and Thursday nights. Students led and taught these studies. Our Sunday worship averaged in the sixties. Throughout this time we used campus facilities and had an office adjacent to the campus. Through the mid-eighties we averaged thirty in the mid-week Bible studies, and we stopped the Sunday worship in 1981. Our small group Bible studies attracted the most attendance in 1984–1987. These were also student-led and averaged forty total. Around 1985 we rented a large room adjacent to the campus for Sunday evening services and office space. We averaged twenty-five in this service. In January 1988 Carolyn Davisson was hired to minister to the women. I resigned in July of 1988.[103]

When Steve Seevers resigned to become the campus minister at Ohio State University in Columbus, Carolyn Davisson became campus coordinator and served in that capacity for four years. Carolyn Davisson and her husband Donald got exposed to campus ministry when they worked with the campus ministry at Bowling Green, Ohio, before they moved to Athens in 1984. Carolyn is a "lay person" and a volunteer. She did a truly remarkable job, not only of holding this campus ministry together while there was no official campus minister, but also by helping it grow. Newsletters report participation of fifty to seventy-five students in some aspects of the program which included Tuesday night fellowship meetings for worship and study, small group Bible studies, "fun nights," and intramural sports. The East Athens Church of Christ was a strong supporter of this ministry, including students in leadership roles and carrying on an Adopt-a-Student program.[104]

Teaching and special programs were led during the four years of Carolyn's tenure by board members, graduate students, area ministers and former missionaries. The upbeat attitude of the students is reflected in the comments of a student who graduated in 1990:

> As a freshmen and a new Christian, ROC provided me with a cornerstone upon which to build my faith. I knew little about Christ's love and even less about the Bible itself. ROC gave me the ability to learn from people who were very knowledgeable about the scriptures. As a senior, I now know what it means to be a true Christian. I have personally benefitted from ROC and can't even begin to estimate the good it's doing for a growing number of students who are currently in the group. I pray that ROC is around for a long time to come.[105]

Richard and Connie Teske were called as full-time campus ministers beginning in July of 1992. Rich was raised in Truman, Minnesota, and attended the University of Minnesota majoring in music. While there, he became involved in the campus ministry and decided to become a campus minister. Toward this end, he entered Minnesota Bible College and obtained his B.A. He has served intern campus ministries at Southern Illinois University and East Tennessee State University and was the interim campus minister at the University of Minnesota in 1986.[106] He has an excellent background for campus ministry, and he and Connie inherited a strong program which had been built by Steve Seevers and Carolyn Davisson.

# Western Kentucky University, Bowling Green

The campus ministry at Western Kentucky University at Bowling Green provides an excellent example of campus ministry producing campus ministers. For several years during the late 1960s the Bowling

Green Christian Church provided bus transportation for students to all the services, including special classes in Bible school and the evening youth meetings.[107]

In the fall of 1974 Steve and Teresa Stovall began weekend trips to Western from Johnson Bible College where Steve was a student. Steve and Teresa had spent three years working in leadership positions in the campus ministry at Murray State in Kentucky. Steve had earned a degree in Math-Accounting at Murray and Teresa had received her Bachelor's degree from Murray before they went to Johnson Bible College to prepare for campus ministry. At Western Steve took graduate courses in philosophy and religion, and Teresa received a Master's degree in marriage and family therapy.[108]

In January of 1975 the Stovalls moved to an apartment in Bowling Green, and for three years they had Bible studies in their apartment and held meetings on campus in university facilities. In 1978 the campus ministry purchased an old fraternity house which had three rented apartments, three offices, vestibule, kitchen, lounge, and an assembly room with seating for seventy people.

In the spring of 1981 Mark and Becky Whited became associate campus ministers with the Stovalls at Western Kentucky. Mark was also a graduate of Murray State where he too had been active in the campus student fellowship. Mark and Becky met at Western where she was completing a Master's degree in Student Personnel.[109]

These two couples, with their deep roots in practical campus ministry at Murray State and their excellent academic preparation, along with their deep Christian commitment, led and built an outstanding campus ministry at Western Kentucky University. The basic elements of their program include: Sunday worship services in the campus house, "share groups" for Bible study and sharing, Tuesday night meetings for fellowship, teaching and worship, annual mission trips – they had sent mission interns to twelve countries by 1993 – and outreach ministry to the area churches.[110] The Whiteds' work at Western continued until 1989 when they became campus ministers at the University of Evansville in Indiana, where they are now leading an exciting campus ministry.

The original campus house served well, but required three renovations to keep up with the growth of the fellowship. However, by 1991 it was clear that new, larger facilities were needed, so land in the middle of campus was purchased in May of 1991 and on April 17, 1993 a new five hundred thousand dollar Ministry House was dedicated. The president of Western Kentucky University gave the dedicatory address, which indicates the kind of recognition and respect this campus ministry has gained on the part of the university.

The CSF is a member of the Western Kentucky University Campus Ministry Association, which makes possible co-sponsorship of all campus events such as praise gatherings, concerts of prayer, Easter sunrise services, and the placing of campus ministry brochures in every dorm room on campus each fall. The 1990 annual report summarizes a typical year at Western:

> Over 170 students have attended CSF this year; 40 on our fall retreat; 70 to our "Forever Friends" concert; 40-50 each Tuesday night at Focus with a high attendance of 65; 35 in our CARE groups; and 22 on our spring break mission work trip. There is, of course, a lot more to CSF than statistics. But we hope you can rejoice in the fact behind the figures, that CSF is growing and meeting needs here.[111]

But the above is only the beginning. Steve Stovall, in 1990, sketched the following "Dreams for the Future":

> An internship program for training campus ministers; programs on campus like "Adopt-a-Team," "Professor-care," and "Dorm Advance" to open avenues of ministry and witness; a "Week of Evangelism" each year; and an "International Ministry" for the hundreds of foreign students on our campus. We want to work in a more committed relationship with local churches hosting high school days, increasing our outreach team program, and working more closely with youth ministers across the state. The students have strong needs for programming through our campus ministry that would teach them biblical principles for choosing a vocation, dedicating their finances to the Lord, healing family relationship at home, preparing those the Lord is speaking to about missions, and developing the characteristics of responsibility and commitment that young people are struggling with in the 90s.[112]

Campus ministry is certainly alive and well at Western Kentucky University at Bowling Green!

# University of Nebraska, Lincoln

The Capital City Christian Church at Lincoln, Nebraska, was the seedbed of the campus ministry at the University of Nebraska. In 1965, A. Dale Crain, then the minister of the Capital City Church and a graduate student at the University of Nebraska, began meeting with students for Bible study in Selleck Hall on campus. From those meetings grew a large class of college/career people in the congregation. In 1968 when Dale Crain left to become campus minister at Indiana State University, Bob Chitwood was called as senior minister at the Capital City Church and he and his congregation, along with the Douglas Street Church of Christ in Lincoln, continued working with college/career young people, many of them students at the university. By 1975 the campus ministry was incorporated under the name "College/Career Christian Fellowship," and Bill

Weber was called as the first full-time campus minister.[113] (Bill had been working as an associate minister of the Capital City Church with special responsibilities for college/career people.)

Bill Weber led in getting this campus ministry established as he worked with them for three years, leaving in 1978 when he was succeeded by Bob Millikin. In that same year Dr. Garland Bare, former medical missionary in Thailand and a faculty member at the University of Nebraska in Lincoln, became aware of an old fraternity house on campus that was for sale. In May of 1978 the Board of Directors of the Fellowship purchased this house just three blocks from the university union. The house is university approved cooperative housing, is co-educational, and provides housing for as many as twenty-one college/career young people. By 1985 eighty-five young people had lived in this "Agape House," which has had house parents and a cook over the years.[114]

Bob Millikin served as campus minister until 1983 when he was succeeded by James Sennett. Bill Weber and Bob Millikin developed very effective programs for discipling and evangelizing college students during their ministries.[115] Jim Sennett carried on the extensive program which had been developed, including large Tuesday night Bible studies, small fellowship groups, social programs, mission trips, dormitory Bible studies, retreats, both local and area, service projects to the community, cooperative programs with other campus ministries and much more.[116]

Jim Sennett's unique contribution to the campus ministry at the University of Nebraska was a strong emphasis on what he called "a ministry of campus penetration." Jim was convinced that in addition to the good work done by campus ministries in converting and nurturing individual students, strategies must be developed to penetrate the university as a whole with the life-changing gospel of Christ. He thus agrees with Charles Malik.[117]

Jim Sennett offers the following practical suggestions for developing a strategy for penetration of the university, each of which he implemented to some degree while he worked at Nebraska as a campus minister.[118]

1. Maintain a high level of involvement in an association of campus ministers which exists on most campuses. Since the university administration looks to these organizations as "official" representatives of religion on campus, participation in them offers a viable way to influence policy and practice in the university. 2. The campus minister should enroll in classes at the university. Not only is this an opportunity to learn, but it also helps the campus minister experience what it is like to be a student. In addition it offers unprecedented opportunities to become known by professors and other students. Doing respectable academic work in class provides a model of an authentic Christian lifestyle often unlike that ever seen before by many faculty and students. 3. Volunteer to do writing for the student newspaper. (For three years Jim Sennett wrote an editorial column in the *Daily*

*Nebraskan* with his picture and personal by-line.) He was able to present alternative Christian views on many current issues, and in doing so he not only influenced the thinking of large numbers of people in the university community, but he also obtained wide name recognition for the campus ministry. 4. Move programs from the campus house to university facilities whenever possible. This campus ministry moved their Bible study to rooms in the student union during Jim's ministry and by being in the union they were more visible and accessible to a larger variety of students. 5. Hold social and fellowship programs in university facilities, away from the campus house as often as possible. This can offer an alternative to the destructive kinds of social life which often dominate a university campus.[119]

Jim Sennett does not mean to criticize the more traditional kinds of programs which are offered at campus ministries, which he agrees must continue, but he does challenge us to accept the notion of confronting the whole university with the gospel of Christ in imaginative ways.

In 1987 Dennis Durst became associate campus minister at Nebraska and in 1988 Jim Sennett left to pursue a PhD in philosophy full-time. Scott Pixler, a graduate of Ozark Bible College, and his wife Diana became campus ministers at Nebraska where they still serve as this is being written. Scott describes the ongoing programs of this campus ministry at the University of Nebraska in Lincoln as follows:

Our campus house is still located . . . in downtown Lincoln. Besides providing a discipleship-oriented housing opportunity for Christian young men, we also carry on a full slate of activities both on and off campus. Some of these ministries include: Bible studies, music, worship, prayer, small groups, evangelism, retreats, social events, conferences, counseling and evangelism. Besides being a recognized student organization at UNL on city campus, we also have Bible studies on the east campus of UNL and at Nebraska Wesleyan University where we have also become an official student group. . . . One of the greatest missionary opportunities in the history of Christianity is found in the large number of international students attending American universities and colleges. Out of the 24,000 students who attend UNL, more than 2,000 come from foreign countries. Half of those 2,000 come from the People's Republic of China. Many of these countries are closed to Christian missionaries altogether — our only opportunity to reach them is through their students who come here![120]

One has to be impressed with the variety and creativity that campus ministries display in their aggressive efforts to confront the university community with the gospel of Christ.

# University of North Carolina, Chapel Hill

Campus ministries are established on university and college campuses in many different ways. One of those ways is through the vision and dedication of an individual. Phil Laughlin was such an individual. Through his committed efforts he obtained the interest of several churches in the area in campus ministry, and in 1976 a campus ministry was organized at the University of North Carolina at Chapel Hill. It was formally organized and incorporated in September of 1977. A house near the heart of the campus was purchased in the same year.[121]

Frank and Debbie Dodson became the campus ministers at Chapel Hill in 1982. Frank had received his BA degree from Roanoke Bible College, and his Master of Divinity degree from Cincinnati Bible Seminary in 1981 with an emphasis on Theology and Apologetics. Unlike some campus ministries, Frank lists "campus house community" as one of the strengths of the program at UNC. In addition, Sunday worship services are held each Sunday morning in the student union and a sack lunch discussion group meets in the union every Wednesday noon. A fellowship meal at the campus house every Sunday evening, prayer breakfast on Friday, and regular social events round out the program on campus. The offerings from students support three mission projects monthly, and service projects are a regular part of the program. Frank says, "our mission trip to London in January (1992) and other mission programs have challenged many to be more evangelistic and to do mission or ministry work — both short and long-term."[122] Retreats are also a regular part of the program — in February 1993, students at UNC joined three hundred other students at the annual retreat at Gatlinburg, Tennessee.[123]

A unique program organized and sponsored by this campus ministry is the Carolina Christian Youth Conference for high school students. Six hundred and thirty-five attended this gathering in 1985 and one thousand fifty attended in 1989. In 1993 Bible studies were divided into men's and women's groups, and the annual parents day worship drew forty parents in 1993.[124]

In January of 1986 this campus ministry sponsored a full-time campus ministry at East Carolina University, and plans are being made to revive the campus ministry at North Carolina State and to begin a new campus ministry at Duke University. Frank became the first campus minister at East Carolina followed by Jim Poindexter (1986–1990). In 1990 a campus house was purchased and Tim Turner became the campus minister. Tim is carrying on a very successful campus ministry at the East Carolina University which includes no Sunday worship services because there are three churches in Greenville. The program does include mid-week meals for students, Bible studies in the dormitories and at the campus house. This campus ministry joins Chapel Hill in retreats in the fall at Gatlinburg, Tennessee.[125]

Here are campus ministries which carry a strong influence for Christ throughout the state of North Carolina and beyond!

# NOTES

1. Letter to author from Roger Songer, present campus minister, May 13, 1993.

2. A variety of credit courses were offered by Bob Ross at Eastern including: Christian Doctrine, Introduction to Theology, Bible Doctrine and so forth. In the fall of 1972 a course The Book of Revelation had such a large enrollment it had to be moved to a larger facility (Newsletter, August 1972). Bob wrote a classic article on "Apologetics and the University" carried by the *Christian Standard* in August 2, 1981, and this article has been much used by campus ministries across the country. (See *Christian Standard*, August 2, 1981.)

3. Information on this program came from a perusal of the newsletters from Bob Ross' ministry.

4. Letter from Songer.

5. Newsletter, August 1977.

6. Songer letter.

7. Newsletter, November 1979. Bob Ross had developed an extensive counseling ministry with students during his years at Eastern.

8. Newsletter, February 1980.

9. *Ibid.*, November 1982.

10. Questionnaire returned by Roger Songer, May 1992.

11. Newsletter, October 1985.

12. *Ibid.*, August-September 1988.

13. Questionnaire completed by Wendell Hose in 1989.

14. Letter to me from Mark Whited, May 4, 1992.

15. Newsletter, November 1992.

16. Letter to me in May of 1993.

17. *Ibid.*

18. 1985 Annual Report, p. 1.

19. *Ibid.*

20. *Ibid.*

21. *Ibid.*, p. 4.

22. 1985 and 1986 Annual Reports.

23. One of these is Rick Harper who is now campus minister at Georgia Tech in Atlanta, Georgia.

24. Questionnaire completed in May of 1993.

25. Questionnaire completed in 1985 by Don Smith, present campus minister. Detailed information about this campus ministry from 1972–1978 is not available to me.

26. Questionnaire completed by Don Smith, April 1992.

27. Letter to me from Dave Embree, campus minister at Southwest Missouri State, June 21, 1993.

28. Information packet, 1984, p. 6.

29. *Ibid.*

30. *Ibid.*, p. 9.

31. See footnote 125, p. 114 for a list of the various retreats held by campus ministers across the country.

32. *Western Courier*, Wednesday, February 16, 1983, p. 2.

33. Questionnaire completed by Charles Ferguson, April, 1992. The article by Tom Plog appeared in the *Christian Standard*, May 31, 1992, p. 9. In this same questionnaire Charles acknowledges that housing forty-six students in spite of its advantages requires a great deal of money and energy in maintenance. This is a problem which other campus ministries have encountered.

34. Newsletter, "Outreach," February 1987.

35. An example of this is the case of Kathy Zettler Finch who, after graduating from Murray, led a successful campaign among alumni of the fellowship to pay off the indebtedness on the campus house. Newsletter, Outreach, August 1986, p. 3.

36. Newsletter, Outreach, November 1985.

37. *Ibid.*, October 1988.

38. *Ibid.*, August 1989.

39. Questionnaire completed by Dean Ross, May 1993.

40. Campus Christians, Newsletter, January/February 1989, p. 4.

41. *Ibid.*, September/October 1986, p. 4.

42. Questionnaire completed May 1992.

43. Dr. Curtis is not only a dedicated Christian, but he is also a highly respected faculty member. In 1985 he received the Bylar Award, the highest honor given to CMSU faculty and administrators. "Newsletter from the Christian Campus House," Summer 1985, p. 2.

44. "Newsletter from the Christian Campus House," Fall 1992.

45. *Ibid.*

46. "Newsletter from the Christian Campus House," March/April 1990, p. 1.

47. Article in the *Christian Standard*, December 23, 1993, p. 5. The First Christian Church in Rolla, under the leadership of Henry Pratt, minister, also were promoters of the campus ministry at Rolla. I spoke at this church about "The Purdue Story" in the late 1960s.

48. "ONE," a newspaper published by all campus ministries on the campus at Rolla, August 1977, p. 3.

49. See a complete list of Roger's articles in the bibliography.

50. I have not been able to obtain information on this period of the campus ministry at Rolla.

51. Newsletter, March 1993, p. 3.

52. Newsletter, June 1988, p. 2.

53. Newsletter, September 1988.

54. Questionnaire completed by Bob Humphrey, April 1992.

55. *Ibid.*

56. *Ibid.*

57. "Fifteenth Annual Report of the Michigan Christian Campus Ministries," p. 3.

58. Questionnaire returned by Michael 1980 and 1985.

59. "Fifteenth Annual Report of the Michigan Christian Campus Ministries," p. 4.

60. Questionnaire, p. 1.

61. "Fifteenth Annual Report of the Michigan Christian Campus Ministries," p. 4.

62. "Campus Ministry Messenger," May-June 1991, p. 1.

63. Questionnaire completed by Matt Schantz, February 1992.

64. Questionnaire completed by Tom Tucker in 1990.

65. *Ibid.*

66. *Ibid.*

67. See Newsletter, April 4, 1987.

68. Information on the years 1972–1979 at Iowa State are not available to me.

69. The situation at Iowa State illustrates the ambiguous attitudes towards student housing held by different campus ministries. In some cases student housing strengthens the ministry, and in other cases, the care of the property becomes a burden. Apparently the Iowa State campus ministry took the latter attitude, for better or for worse.

70. Questionnaire completed by Dennis Hall in 1985.

71. Information folder on the ministry of the Christian Fellowship at Iowa State, 1986, p. 3.

72. Questionnaire completed by John Woodward, April 1992.

73. Information on Paul Boatman's ministry to the universities in the St. Louis area from 1973–78 came from a letter to the author in 1985.

74. From a letter to the author from Paul Boatman, 1977.

75. From a letter to St. Louis area churches written by Russell E. Boatman, President of St. Louis Christian College in December 1985.

76. Questionnaire completed by Tom Plog in 1989.

77. *Ibid.*

78. Questionnaire completed by Tom Plog April, 1992.

79. I was able to tell the "Purdue Story" to a meeting of this group in late 1969.

80. Newsletter, Summer 1986, p. 1.

81. Another example of "networking" among campus ministries is the fact that James L. Shields, Jr., who is senior minister at the Greenwood Church in Seattle is the son of James Shields who was one who worked with Jess Johnson to found the campus ministry at East Tennessee State University. Also, Donald and Carolynn Davisson, who worked as volunteers with this campus ministry, moved to Athens, Ohio in 1984 where they served as acting campus ministers at the campus ministry at Ohio University for several years while that ministry was searching for a full-time campus minister.

82. A.C.T.S. Newsletter, Spring 1991, p. 2.

83. Questionnaire completed by Steve North in 1989.

84. The article "The Good Life of a Campus Minister," by Ward Patterson, long-time campus minister at Indiana University, first appeared in the *Christian Standard*, May 1, 1977.

85. Among these was Gary Weedman, faculty member of Johnson Bible College. Gary was the first campus minister at Indiana University. I was able to meet with several of these people to tell the "Purdue story" in October of 1972 while I was speaking at Johnson Bible College.

86. Questionnaire completed by Sam Darden in 1990.

87. *Ibid.*

88. "Tennessee Tabloid," February 1991, p. 1. This is another excellent example of cooperation between Bible College and campus ministry.

89. "Tennessee Tabloid," September 1987, p. 1.

90. *Ibid.*, August 1988. In 1993 Doug Shupe married Debbie Smith — Debbie was one of the first members of the campus ministry at California State University in Fullerton in 1982 where I worked as a campus minister.

91. It was my privilege to teach the class at Emmanuel that summer. Sam's presentation was one of the highlights of the course.

92. From an article in the "Newsletter of Mission Services" by W. E. McGilvery, May 24, 1975, p. 7. Bill Koontz credits Kentucky Christian College as establishing his faith in Christ. He also spent a summer studying at Purdue University where he participated in the campus ministry, and he attended a class I taught at Emmanuel School of Religion in the summer of 1974.

93. From a chapter "Where to Begin?" in "The Gospel Goes to College: A Guidebook to Campus Ministry" — an unpublished collection of articles edited by Roger Thomas in 1977, pp. 81-89.

94. From an article in "The Northerner" by Marianne Osburg, Friday, April 23, 1976, p. 5. Tom Plog, campus minister at Washington University in St. Louis agrees with this point of view. He writes in the *Christian Standard*, May 31, 1992 on p. 9: "We have gained respect on campus because of our position based on restoration principles. We present Jesus as Lord through the teaching of scripture, not by adhering to denominational doctrines. We call people to Christ instead of gathering them to keep them in the denomination."

95. The teaching of these classes came under the critical scrutiny of *Americans United For Separation of Church and State* in January 1975. They failed to persuade the university to drop the course. "The Northerner," January 24, 1975.

96. From a questionnaire completed by Tim Hudson, May 1993.

97. From a questionnaire completed by Harold Orndorff, January 1989.

98. I do not have detailed information on the campus ministries at Oklahoma State from 1971-1979.

99. Questionnaire completed by Roger Songer in March 1980.

100. Questionnaire completed by Roger Songer, May 1992.

101. Questionnaires completed by Dave Rockey, 1990 and 1992.

102. Questionnaire completed by Carolyn Davisson in May 1993.

103. Letter to author from Steve Seevers, March 1992.

104. Questionnaire completed by Carolyn Davisson in 1992.

105. "ROC Report," Spring 1990, p. 3.

106. "ROC Report," Spring 1992, p. 1. Rich Teske was a student in the class in campus ministry which I taught at Emmanuel School of Religion in the summer of 1987.

107. The campus ministries section in the *Christian Standard*, August 31, 1968 and September 20, 1969.

108. Questionnaire completed by Steve Stovall, May 1990 and the "Annual Report of the Christian Student Fellowship," April 1990.

109. "Annual Report," April 1990, p. 3.

110. Questionnaire completed by Steve Stovall, May 1993.

111. "Annual Report," April 1990, p. 2.

112. *Ibid.*, p. 1.

113. From a letter written by Scott Pixler, September 1990. I was able to speak to the men and women in the Capital City congregation about "The Purdue Story" in November of 1971.

114. "Annual Report" written by James Sennett, April 1985.

115. Pixler letter, p. 1.

116. "Annual Report," April 1985.

117. Charles Habib Malik, *A Christian Critique of the University*, InterVarsity Press, 1982, p. 101.

118. These suggestions were made by Jim Sennett on an audio cassette which he sent to me in June 1987.

119. Jim Sennett entered a PhD program in philosophy while at Nebraska. He became first a teaching assistant and then a professor in the department, all of this with the full approval his board of directors.

120. Pixler letter, p. 2.

121. Information on the ministry of Phil Laughlin at Chapel Hill was limited, but he and his board of directors obviously established this campus ministry on a firm foundation. Phil wrote an excellent handbook containing practical suggestions for founding a campus ministry while he was at Chapel Hill. Unfortunately, it is undated and unpublished. I have a copy and I will be glad to send a copy to anyone who requests it.

122. Questionnaire completed by Frank Dodson, April 1992.

123. Newsletter, Winter 1993, p. 1.

124. *Ibid.*, p. 2.

125. Questionnaire completed by Frank Dodson, April 1993. Information on East Carolina came from a telephone conversation between the author and Frank Dodson in July of 1993.

CHAPTER SEVEN

# More Campus Ministries
# Established in the Seventies

## University of Nebraska at Kearney

When the campus ministry began at Kearney, Nebraska in 1975, it was on the campus of Kearney State College. In 1990 the college achieved university status and it became the University of Nebraska at Kearney. As the college grew, so did the campus ministry. It had been organized in the fall of 1975 as a result of the combined efforts of area leaders and a local church. There was a succession of short term ministers at Kearney until Greg Swinney arrived in 1984. The campus ministers were: Ed Smith, 1975–1976; Grady Sanders, 1976–1977; Rick Ferguson, 1978–1983; and Chris Laum, 1983–1984.[1]

A large house near campus was purchased by the newly-formed board of directors in 1975. The house was named "The Campus Lighthouse," and the ministry was called the "Campus Lighthouse Ministries." Greg Swinney came to Kearney with excellent preparation for campus ministry. He had graduated from Nebraska Christian College in Norfolk in 1978 and had received a Master's degree in New Testament Studies from Cincinnati Christian Seminary in 1981. While at Kearney he also received a Master's degree in Speech Communication from the university in 1992. Greg has put his academic background to excellent work in the campus ministry at this university. He has taught and supervised extension courses from Nebraska Christian College, credits transferable to the university, during most of his ministry. He also became a part-time instructor in the university in the Department of Fine Arts and Humanities beginning in 1987.[2] Greg's wife Laurie has not only been an excellent addition to the campus ministry, teaching Bible study groups and counseling students, but also teaches accounting classes at the university.[3]

As this campus ministry grew under Greg's leadership, there has also been accession of property. The original house, which provided office space, reading room and housing for women students, was renovated in 1989. In the same year another house near campus was leased to provide housing for male students, this one christened "Cornerstone."[4] Because of this development a name change was in order. "Campus Lighthouse Ministries" became "Christian Student Fellowship." In 1991, the original

177

house was sold and a new three-story brick building was purchased to provide more space for this growing ministry.[5]

This campus ministry has been notable for unusual and creative programming. The extension classes from Nebraska Christian College have been on such subjects as: marriage, preaching, history of the Restoration movement, and Biblical subjects. Dr. Lee Snyder, a faculty member at the university, has taught several of these classes along with Greg Swinney. In December of 1991, Dr. Snyder, who is the Christian Student Fellowship faculty sponsor, participated in a debate on the authority, accuracy and trustworthiness of the Bible with a liberal campus minister/theologian.[6]

Many campus ministries have begun to work with international students, but none have been more imaginative and practical in their approach than Greg Swinney and his students. They have purchased bicycles to loan to international students, most of whom cannot afford automobiles. This program has been hugely successful, as reported in a recent newsletter:

> Our bicycle loan program to international students continues to effectively reach out to our foreign friends. So successful is this outreach, in fact, that we have need of several more bicycles. Students from the Bahamas, Czechoslovakia, and Panama have visited the campus house in the last ten days and requested a bike. One of the students requesting our help is the President of the International Student Association for our entire campus! . . . Meeting this physical need of these foreign friends opens the doors for us to share with them concerning their spiritual needs. We follow up the bicycle contacts with Bibles and invitations to a variety of our activities.[7]

Mission trips have also been emphasized at Kearney. Students have gone to Cookson Hills School, Tijuana, Mexico, and Haiti. Student involvement with various service projects is described in a recent newsletter:

> As the academic year of 1992-1993 comes to an end, CSF reflects on this spring semester as one of mission, outreach and ministry. Students found themselves challenged to greater service in missions for the Kingdom. I wish you could see snapshots of this semester in our album. On one page you would find an eighteen year old coed leading worship at Nebraska State prison. Turn the page and see a young man normally behind a piano studying music at the college, only he is mixing cement by hand in a remote area of Juarez, Mexico. Next, you see another student leaning on a phone making calls raising support for the crisis pregnancy center. Obedience to the Lord through commitment in service might well be the theme of the 1993 spring semester.[8]

The importance of cordial relationships with the university on the part of the campus ministry is well illustrated here. Not only does Greg Swinney teach regular classes in communication and speech at the university, thus influencing hundreds of students outside of the fellowship, he also served a term as chair of the Cooperative Campus Ministers on the UNK campus. This involved his being the liaison between nine full-time university campus ministers and the university administration-faculty.[9] In one recent semester, as a result of his high visibility on campus, Greg spoke for: a freshman orientation session of one hundred fifty students, the Chi Omega sorority retreat, a Human Relations class dealing with religion and society, a dormitory lounge meeting, and a meeting of the Fellowship of Christian Athletes.[10]

Printed materials are important in any ministry, and Greg and his students have put out a consistently attractive newsletter with crisp news and interesting editorials. Greg also produced a *Spiritual Journey Notebook* which was published by College Press in Joplin, Missouri, and which went into a third edition in 1988. More than ten thousand of these notebooks were in use on both Bible college and secular campuses by 1993.[11]

Although Greg Swinney's leadership has been a definite factor in the diversity and growth of this campus ministry, he would be the first to say that he has had excellent support from board members, churches and students. In fact, in one early questionnaire when he was asked to list his biggest failure, he said, "trying to do it all on my own in the beginning — not expecting others to join me in the ministry and in making plans for the future."[12] In his column in the newsletter, "Lighting Up Our World" — he recently wrote:

> Seeing the Lord at work in the lives of students at Kearney State college is one of the highlights of my life. Nothing thrills me more than to see students grow in their faith and expand their spiritual horizons. It's happening here even in the midst of a pressure-filled world that says 'forget about God and party!'[13]

I can hear campus ministries across the country saying "Amen to that!"

## Northeast Missouri State, Kirksville

The *Campus Christian Fellowship* at Northeast Missouri State in Kirksville began in 1976 under the sponsorship of the Green Hills Area Men's Meeting. Dennis Hall was the first campus minister (1976-1979), Mike Hardee succeeded him (1979-1984), and Joe and Jennie Belzer, who now serve, became campus ministers at Kirksville in August of 1984. Jennie Belzer, Joe's wife, has served as part-time secretary as well as supporting him in the ministry in many other ways.

This ministry operates under a Board of Directors. They purchased a small house in August of 1976 which remained the headquarters for the ministry until August of 1984 when they purchased a three story house which was remodeled into a meeting place and a residence for ten men and women students. Joe Belzer is enthusiastic about the benefits of the house to the ministry. "What a great asset for fellowship and outreach," he says.[14]

Joe Belzer and his students and associates have a very diverse and active program on the campus. Wednesday night they have a large group Bible study and fellowship which is the heart of the program. In addition, small group relational Bible studies are held in the campus house. This campus ministry is very active in ministry teams to prisons, children's homes, and hospitals, and they take several mission trips each year. Retreats, both local and area, are also a source of fellowship and spiritual growth. Recently, several small groups studying topical issues have been especially successful. Relations with the university are very good. Joe says, "We are an official campus organization, and we have good relations with both faculty and administration. Occasionally, administrators will send students to us for counseling, and when the community is pressing the university to have a religious service, they will often refer them to us."[15]

In the 1989–1990 school year sixty to seventy students were significantly involved, and that number has increased since then because of new programs and projects that have been added to the ministry.

In studying this campus ministry one is impressed with the enthusiasm and optimism for ministry that is exhibited by both leaders and students.[16]

# University of Florida at Gainesville

The campus ministry at the University of Florida at Gainesville began in 1976 in the home of Bob and Pat Wade. They were supported in this move by the Westside Christian Church and members of the university faculty. They incorporated under a Board of Directors in 1977.

For several months Bible study and other meetings with students were held in the Wade home, but soon they were able to purchase a house just one block from the main gate of the university campus. The house is now debt free, and it provides "a home away from home" as well as a meeting place for the students of the fellowship.

No Sunday services are held on campus, but students worship with and serve in responsible positions in the Westside Christian Church. Many students have been influenced by this ministry over the years. Pat Wade has served as administrative assistant with her husband. Bob Wade wrote in 1980:

> Christian Campus House at UF in Gainesville, Florida has had the privilege of having three Jewish Christians as "regulars" while at U.F. All three have elected to go into full-time ministry in an effort the reach other Jewish people for Christ.[17]

After nearly seventeen years of faithful service on the campus at Gainesville, the Wades are now looking for a younger campus minister or a couple to take over the ministry.[18]

## Northeastern Oklahoma A & M at Miami

The campus ministry at Northeastern Oklahoma A & M (a junior college) at Miami began in 1976 when Mark Grigsby, now a professor at Ozark Christian College, and a group of interested men from the area churches caught the vision and organized a Board of Directors and initiated "Collegiates for Christ." After Mark Grigsby, campus ministers were Eddy Gibson, Chuck Beaver, and Terry Byrd.[19]

Lonnie Portenier, a student at Ozark Christian College, became part-time campus minister in 1989. He spent as much time as possible on campus, and when he was able to become full-time campus minister upon his graduation from Ozark in 1993, the ministry was well established. The campus house, located close to campus, has office space, meeting rooms and one apartment. No Sunday services are held on campus, but Tuesday night is Bible study night for the group, and on Monday noon, a free lunch open to all students is served by the ladies in the area churches. This is largely a time of fellowship with brief devotions. The group attends retreats in the spring and fall with other campus ministries and on Thursdays, the time is devoted to service projects. Lonnie says he is spending more time on campus since his graduation, especially in one-on-one meetings and nurturing relationships with students.[20] This is a small campus ministry on a small college — 2,500 enrolled — but it is reaching students for Christ.

## West Virginia University at Morgantown

The Christian Church campus ministry at West Virginia University in Morgantown grew out of the "Disciples Student Fellowship" and the First Christian Church in that city. Dr. David Nash and his wife Phyllis were volunteer campus ministers with the "Disciples Student Fellowship" for several years beginning in the early 1970s. Dr. Nash was chairman of the department of Pediatric Dentistry at the university, but he and his wife spent a great deal of time serving with the students.

In 1976 Dr. Nash and a few others, including Dan Omer, a graduate student at the university, and Mr. and Mrs. Elliot "Sandy" Bigelow, who had been associate minister with First Christian Church in Montecello, Kentucky, made an amicable separation from the Disciple Church and organized a "Community of Christians/a Christian Church." Dr. Nash, Dan Omer, and Sandy Bigelow and their wives became co-ministers of this new congregation which from the beginning was made up largely of students from the university. By 1979 the work with students had become so demanding that it required a full-time campus minister. After statewide solicitation of help from other churches for a full-time campus minister, in 1980 the church was absorbed into the Christian Student Fellowship, and Dennis Steckley was called as full-time campus minister.[21]

Dennis came to Morgantown from Ball State University in Indiana where he had been an associate campus minister with Williard Walls for three years. He was a graduate of Ball State and of Emmanuel School of Religion.[22] Working with a newly acquired house purchased in 1981 and with the strong support of the folks who had formed this campus ministry, Dennis built a strong ministry during his seven years at West Virginia University. Sunday worship services were held in the campus house, capable students were elected as officers; Bible study, fellowship, and two retreats each year were the staples of the program. Dennis resigned in 1987 to accept a position as Assistant Dean and Residence Hall Director at Tri-State University at Angola, Indiana. He also worked with the Tri-State Christian Fellowship in Angola, a young campus ministry organization.

Sandy Bigelow, who had moved with his family to Morgantown in 1976 to work with the newly formed church, was chairman of the Board of Directors of the campus ministry. Upon Dennis' resignation, Sandy was immediately called by his fellow Board members to accept the position of full-time campus minister. Sandy had graduated from Central Missouri State University with a BA in Speech and Public Relations and from Roanoke Bible College in Virginia. His heart has been with this campus ministry since he and his family moved to Morgantown, and he has served as an enthusiastic and committed leader. He describes the program as follows:

> Our largest attendance (35-70 flux) is Sunday A.M., but this is by no means our major thrust. We provide a contemporary-issues Bible study on Wednesday evening, two small growth groups on Monday and Tuesday and meals cooked by the students themselves on Friday nights, which includes a devotional and social outing. Some of our students meet for prayer and discussions in the morning and at noon at the student union. We also have a community service thrust, working with Habitat for Humanity and "In Touch and Concerned," a visitation program for the elderly shut-ins.[23]

In most of the reports on campus ministry which we have included in this book, we have mentioned the upbeat, optimistic side of work with college students. There is another side to this ministry, and Sandy Bigelow in his honest way reports on it. Since he spent four years in a state university where he saw and lived the other side of campus life, he knows and relates to the students who have come to college to "party." This is often a very destructive lifestyle, and most campuses, to be honest, have a large number of such students. Sandy is a campus minister who understands and knows how to relate to them.

There also is an increasing number of young people who come to college from single-parent, divorced or non-traditional homes. Many of them have been sexually and/or physically abused. The emotional needs of these students are immense, and they require a tremendous amount of time and energy from a caring campus minister, which Sandy Bigelow definitely is.

The campus ministry at West Virginia University, since its origin under Dave and Phyllis Nash in the early 1970s, has been a bright light of hope on that campus.

## University of Georgia in Athens

The campus ministry at the University of Georgia in Athens was also started by an individual. James Street was the founder of this ministry, which began in 1976.[24] Two buildings near the campus were purchased in 1977.

Tim Hudson succeeded James Street in 1982, coming from the campus ministry at Northern Kentucky. The program under Tim's leadership consists of Bible studies, fellowship meetings, discipleship and one-on-one sessions between the campus minister and the students. Tim says of the overall ministry at Athens:

> UGA is an old Southern Bible-belt school. Most students consider themselves Christians. Our challenge to them is to find a personal walk with Christ as Lord. Our model for doing that is to be a functioning family of God. Therefore, our house and residential program have become important as we have grown. Next year we will house seventeen students, have sixteen student leaders, take thirty students to a foreign mission field, and minister to over one hundred students on campus.[25]

There is also a growing ministry to international students on this campus, centered around "International Student Coffee House." Underlying many of the campus ministries surveyed in this book which we have not often explicitly mentioned, is the importance of a visible Christian community of caring persons. Tim Hudson has put most of his emphasis on this aspect of campus ministry and he sees his job as "equipping Christian students to live as the body of Christ."[26] Tim has clearly succeeded in reaching students through his ministry at the University of Georgia, as indicated by the growth of this campus ministry.

## Lake Superior State University at Sault Ste. Marie, Michigan

"His House Christian Fellowship" at Lake Superior State University in

Sault Ste. Marie, Michigan, began in 1977, the fourth campus ministry to be established in the state of Michigan by the "Michigan Christian Campus Ministries."

Tim Carpenter was the first campus minister, serving for five years, followed by Michael Riness, who served for two years. In 1983, Jane Nabor moved to Sault Ste. Marie to become campus coordinator, and Gary Hawes began making weekly trips to campus to serve as campus minister. Gary says that the key to the growth of this ministry beginning in 1983 was the personal attention to students, and the warm hospitality provided by Jane Nabor.[27] In 1987 Jane moved to the new campus ministry at Ferris State University in Big Rapids, Michigan, to become campus coordinator there.

In 1987 Dan Burton became campus minister at Lake Superior. Dan had graduated from Michigan State University in 1986 with a major in Materials and Logistic Management. He was baptized in his junior year while he was active in the campus house in East Lansing. Before coming to the ministry at Lake Superior, Dan had served as campus ministry intern at the University of Michigan in Ann Arbor, working with John Sowash. A house very close to campus was purchased in 1979, and by 1984 it was completely inadequate. One night during the spring of that year, five students came to the Tuesday night meeting at "His House" and were unable to get in. Gary Hawes described the situation in a letter he sent to his supporting churches:

> The house was literally jam packed with nearly sixty students crowded into a small living room, kitchen, and dining room. Most had difficulty hearing and many could not see each other because of the walls in the house. It was uncomfortably warm. We desperately need to provide a larger meeting area at Lake Superior State College.[28]

Because of the generous response to this letter an addition was built onto the campus house and dedicated in May of 1985. Using this expanded facility, and building on the results of Jane Nabor's hospitality ministry, Dan Burton led this fellowship in three years of continuing growth. The program consisted of Sunday and Thursday evening sessions for fellowship, teaching, music, prayer and praise time, Discipleship/Accountability groups, social events, and mission trips. Dan and his students also attended the fall, winter and spring retreats which brought all of the Michigan campus ministries together. In 1990 Dan Burton and his wife Sue moved to Cincinnati, Ohio, where Dan entered Cincinnati Christian Seminary to prepare for further ministry, possibly the mission field.

Dan Seitz and his wife Jennifer became campus ministers at Lake Superior State University when Dan Burton left. They had been involved in the campus ministry for several years while Jennifer was a student at

Lake Superior, and Dan had served a year as an intern in the campus ministry under John Sowash at Ann Arbor.[29] Dan Seitz describes the activities that took place during a typical school year during his ministry:

> Forty-five students were involved in student-led accountability groups. There was diligent prayer every morning at 7:00 a.m. Other students planned Friday night activities, visited a local nursing home, planned our annual Spring Retreat, and coordinated a fellowship-wide fasting program. Still other students were not satisfied with ministry only to LSSU and Sault Ste. Marie. One group dedicated their spring break to inner-city missions in Cincinnati, Ohio. Others gave their summer to missions work in Mexico and a camp for the handicapped in the upper peninsula. One student even spent the entire school year in Hungary sharing the gospel with hungry people![30]

In 1992 Dan Seitz and his wife left this campus ministry to move to Ohio and pursue a career in farming. Steve North and his wife Leigh came on as campus ministers at Lake Superior in August of 1992. Steve, a product of the campus ministry at Michigan State and a graduate of Great Lakes Bible College, came to this ministry from having served seven years as the campus minister at the University of Toledo in Ohio. When asked why he and his family left a metropolitan area to move to a rural town and a small university in Michigan — 3,500 students — he replied:

> God wants to do big things through this little university. God wants to do big things through our little ministry. God wants to do big things in the world through little MCCM. Most people will never know where Sault Ste. Marie is, but as committed Christian students continue to go from here into all the world, this place can make an eternal impact on thousands of lives. Who ever heard of Nazareth?[31]

# University of Oklahoma, Norman

Beginning in the early 1970s there was growing interest in campus ministry in the state of Oklahoma. The campus ministry at Oklahoma State had been organized in 1971, and in 1972 Tom and Barbara Tucker started the campus ministry at Northeastern State at Tahlequah. Because of this increased interest, an "umbrella" organization was formed in 1972 to promote and support existing campus ministries and to encourage the establishment of ministries on other campuses in the state.

Clark Waggoner was called to be the director of this organization, which was called "Campus Christian Fellowship," with headquarters in Sapulpa. Clark served in this capacity for five years, until 1977 when the Board of Directors of the organization voted to dissolve it. In the statement made at the time, it was pointed out that in many ways Clark and this group had worked themselves out of a job. These men gave three reasons for their decision to dissolve the organization: 1) the increasing response of the people throughout Oklahoma to the concept of ministering to university students; 2) the response of many mature Christian men to serve on the Board of Directors of the individual campus ministries; and 3) the increase in financial contributions made directly to each of the four campuses, making the umbrella organization superfluous.[32]

Before the CCF was disbanded, however, the organization had helped to start the campus ministry at University of Oklahoma. Mitch Simpson served as part-time campus minister while he was a student at the University, and when he left in 1973 to go to Cincinnati Bible Seminary, Jim Davis and his wife Sandi were called as the first full-time campus ministers at Norman. Jim had graduated from Mid-West Christian College in 1970, and when he was called he had nearly completed a graduate degree in Religion at Eastern New Mexico University, where Dean Overton was campus minister.

Jim and Sandi began holding Bible studies in their apartment and developed other aspects of the program using university facilities. In 1976 a two-story apartment house was purchased to serve as a campus house. This building, like all good campus houses, was located very close to the main campus at the University.

This new facility made possible new aspects of the program, including a "Friday Night Coffee House," for singing, special musical groups, and fellowship. A musical, "Light Shine," was organized in 1976. This production, which included ten songs incorporating the message of the beatitudes with some jazz, folk, rock, country, bluegrass, and gospel style numbers, was very well done.[33] It was presented in scores of churches over a two year period and it helped to publicize this campus ministry widely. In April of 1977, Jim and Sandi Davis resigned, and Roger Thomas was called as campus minister.

Roger Thomas came to the University of Oklahoma from five years of campus ministry at the University of Missouri at Rolla, and from having helped organize the campus ministry at Western Illinois University before that. Roger stayed until 1980, and this ministry was further strengthened by Roger's special talents. In 1972, Roger had developed a growing ministry in Christian journalism. His name has appeared often in the history of campus ministry, and he was a prolific writer during his service on several different campuses. He helped, through his writings, to clarify the philosophy and theology of this emerging ministry as it related to the overall ministry of the church. By 1977, when Roger began at the University of Oklahoma, he had written over seventy-five articles for nearly fifteen different national religious magazines including *Christianity Today, Eternity, Christian Standard, Lookout, Straight, Disciple, Campus Crusade World-Wide Challenge, His Nazarene Conquest, Wesleyan Encounter,*

186

and others. He had also authored various Bible school lesson material.[34]

During Roger's ministry at the University of Oklahoma he wrote an insightful article in which he pointed out that the campus ministries, which were emerging as a significant force were more than an extension of the youth programs at the local church. Roger claimed that campus ministry is "a valid form of higher Christian eduction." He went on to say,

> True Christian education is not limited to teaching Bible and religion but rather extends to every issue of life. Moreover, our approach must not be merely to teach the Bible alongside math, physics and history. Rather we must call disciples whom the Lord has led into those disciplines to fully integrate their faith with their academics.[35]

Ed Reynolds became Roger Thomas' associate at the University in 1979, and when Roger resigned in 1980, Ed became full-time campus minister until 1981. When Ed left in 1981, Randy Smothers assumed leadership of this campus ministry with Rusty Ferguson as his administrative assistant for one and a half years. Several Christian concerts were sponsored successfully.[36] Mike Nuthman succeeded Randy in 1985 and served as campus minister until 1991, when he left to become associate minister at Draper Park Christian Church in Oklahoma City.

Don Riepe became campus minister at Norman in August 1991. Don had studied aeronautical engineering at Wichita State in Kansas, and had also attended Ozark Bible College. He later served as minister at Paul's Valley, Oklahoma, as minister and at Antioch Christian Church in Oklahoma City as associate youth minister for nine years. Don reports that there are eight men living in the campus house, several from different denominational backgrounds. The Bible studies are enriched by the encounter of these students with New Testament Christianity. Several used computers have been installed in the campus house so that students who are majoring in computer science can get extra computer time, and the main library can be accessed through these computers as well. Don and his people have also offered a free washer and dryer service in the campus house to students — what practical ways to serve! A mid-semester retreat for the students is held, and in the spring they attend a joint retreat with students from Oklahoma State, Pittsburg, Kansas, Joplin, Missouri, and the other Oklahoma campus ministries.[37]

The dream of Clark Waggoner and his associates back in 1972 to promote strong campus ministries in Oklahoma has certainly been a success, even though the original organization had to disband.

# Southwest Missouri State, Springfield

In 1976, a group of interested people from area Christian churches formed a Board of Directors to establish a campus ministry at Southwest Missouri State University at Springfield. In 1977 they bought a house near campus and began holding Bible studies for students, led by local ministers. In 1978, Dave and Joyce Embree were called as full-time campus ministers. Dave is a graduate of Ozark Bible College, holds a degree in Antiquities at Southwest Missouri State University, and has also done graduate work in Religious Studies there, as well as taking some courses through Cincinnati Bible Seminary.

The heart of the program on campus is a Sunday night Praise and Fellowship Meeting held in the university union. A student writes of this meeting:

> Praising God! Lifting our voices in song! Prayer and thanksgiving! Every Sunday night at 8:30 p.m. the doors open up in room 102 of the SMSU campus union to be filled by 50 to 70 dedicated students. They lay their studies aside and come together to take time out and relieve their stress from hectic schedules.[38]

Other on-campus activities include Tuesday night Bible study, also held in the campus union and attended by seventy to ninety students each week. The relevancy of these Bible studies is indicated by titles given to some recent sessions: "Street Smart: Jesus Heart" based on Ecclesiastes; "Sex, Drugs, and Rock and Roll," based on the Song of Solomon, and "More Than a Fast Food Faith," based on Romans.[39] "Family Groups" are small groups of students who are committed to meeting together regularly for study, fellowship, mutual support, and recreation. On weekends a variety of social events are planned to provide an alternative to the party scene which is so much a part of the student life on most universities.

Activities off-campus include several areas of practical service, such as "Daybreak," a ministry to the elderly in a day care center, and "Victory Mission," where students work helping to feed the hungry on Friday nights.[40] Other off-campus events are recreational activities such as: rock climbing, canoeing, backpacking, and camping. The most important off-campus activities are mission trips. Dave Embree says these trips are not only of service to the missions, but they are life-changing experiences for the students. "When students speak of highlights, they speak of mission trips being most influential in their lives."[41] Regular service trips are taken to a St. Louis inner-city mission and in 1993 teams went to Honduras, where they laid block for a perimeter wall at the mission school, and to Matamoros, Mexico, where they built a house, dug a drainage ditch, and did painting and carpentry work for the mission there. One student said, "We even made the front page of several local papers! I guess folks around Brownsville, Texas, and Matamoros, Mexico are not used to seeing college students working over spring break."[42]

Lora Hobbs became associate campus minister at Springfield in 1986. She has been a very active campus minister with the group, not only working with counseling the women students, but also serving as Bible teacher, worship leader, retreat planner, and much more. Both Lora and Dave teach in the Department of Religious Studies at the university, and Dave teaches a campus ministry class at Ozark Christian College. Shannon McMurtrey, who joined the staff August, 1992, to serve as a part-time business manager, teaches continuing education classes for the university. All of these teaching responsibilities not only serve the university, but also give the campus ministry high visibility on campus and elsewhere.

Dave Embree wrote a major paper in 1978 entitled "A History of Campus Ministries at Southwest Missouri State University" for a class taught by Dr. James North at Cincinnati Christian Seminary. He has written a chapter for the book *Taking Education Higher*, a manual for campus ministries, edited by Greg Swinney.[43]

Student housing was a part of the program in the early days, but as in some other campus ministries, it proved to be more of a liability than an asset. However, the campus house remains the center of much activity. Retreats, here as well as elsewhere, are an important part of the ministry. 1993 marked the twenty-fifth year of the Annual Spring Retreat for area campus ministries sponsored by Roy Weece in the Christian Campus House at the University of Missouri. Dave Embree and his group, along with campus ministers from Missouri Southern and Pittsburg State in Kansas, also sponsor an annual fall retreat attended by more than three hundred students.[44]

Dave says of his relationship with other campus ministers on campus, "We have been very 'Restorationist' — virtually have been the 'official' campus minister here for Cumberland Presbyterian and Church of God, Anderson, Indiana. We have a specially close connection with other evangelical ministers. We held a banquet on the Restoration Movement with the Church of Christ and Disciple ministers recently."[45]

Dave Embree has said of campus ministry that "it offers the opportunity to produce servant-hearted disciples with a passion of ministry to the church and the world, and to be an advocate for Christ in a culturally critical setting." He and his people certainly have taken full advantage of these opportunities in the fifteen years of campus ministry at Southwest Missouri State University.

# Virginia Tech, Blacksburg

While Leland Duncan was a student at Bluefield College of Evangelism in Virginia in 1974, he began the groundwork for a campus ministry at Virginia Tech in Blacksburg. By the fall quarter of 1977 the ministry was well established and a Board of Directors representing churches in Virginia was organized. Terry Hodge worked with Leland from 1977 to 1979.

A house near campus was rented for seven years, and through generous support from the churches and an interest-free loan from the Virginia Evangelizing Fellowship the house was purchased in 1985. Many campus ministers have gone into this kind of ministry without any specific preparation. Leland says he received practical help from two sources as he began campus ministry — the Leadership Schools sponsored by NACCM, and a summer class on campus ministry at Emmanuel School of Religion taught by Willard Walls, campus minister at Ball State University in Indiana.[46] A listing of the program activities of this campus ministry looks very much like that of other campus ministries. What stands out about the way Leland Duncan has used these staples of campus ministry is that he has emphasized and modeled outreach ministry. He says outreach ministry to prisoners, elderly, children, and international students is vital "because it allows us to reach out, teach, model our teaching and fellowship all at once."[47]

There have been 145 baptisms through this ministry, which is remarkable in itself, but the amazing thing is that seventy of those have been baptisms of inmates of Bland Correctional Center! No campus ministry that we have surveyed has more nearly fulfilled Jesus' words when he said, "I was in prison and you visited me" (Matthew 25:36). One of the prisoners recently expressed his appreciation to Leland and his volunteers with the following poem:

> There's a man from outside who comes in each week
> And speaks kind works to the strong and weak.
> The glorious love of God he tells
> At the Bible studies we love so well.
> He takes his time from family and home
> To bring God's work to we who are alone.
> He doesn't have to come, he could stay away
> We're only prisoners with debts to pay.
> If he'd never been here he'd never be missed
> But by his visits we're filled with bliss,
> Because on his visits he tells the news
> Of God our Father and what He'll do
> For each of us who call on His name
> And repent of our sins, He'll forgive the same.
>
> So Brother Leland, we hope you know
> You have our love wherever you go,
> And many thanks for the things you share
> That prove to us you really care.
> And where, oh where, would we be today

If God hadn't sent you over this way![48]

In addition to the baptisms at the Correctional Center, five inmates are taking correspondence courses at Winston-Salem Bible College in North Carolina. This prison ministry has involved students who have been immeasurably strengthened by this hands-on kind of experience. Also outstanding is the outreach of the campus ministry at Virginia Tech to international students. Rick Swindell and his wife became associate campus ministers with Leland in 1988, specializing in reaching international students. Rick is deeply committed to this ministry, and has had an excellent background for it.[49] Rick reported on his ministry at Virginia Tech recently as follows:

> The work here has resulted in the conversion and baptism of a number of students from Mainland China, including at least one fairly high level communist party official, and in the baptism of students from Panama and Taiwan. The month of May has seen the baptism of a renowned visiting scholar from Mainland China and his wife to whom I have witnessed since 1989 here in Blacksburg. The Lord worked through several persons to reach these two, as was the case with my own conversion. Much of my work involves helping to solve problems for people like these, and I hope that my love shows them Jesus' love. I am focusing considerable attention these days on Muslim students, having armed myself with Arabic Bibles and the "Jesus" film in Arabic. Many are witnessing to the Chinese because they are converting, but no one else I know of is aiming at Muslims. These men will some day be leaders in their own countries, at least leaders in science and industry in places like Iran, Turkey, Saudi Arabia, and Kuwait.[50]

Six students have gone to Bible college from this ministry, and Scott Thompson, a recent alumnus of Emmanuel School of Religion, has just become the campus minister at Ohio State University in Columbus. Alumni from "Christ's Church" at Virginia Tech are serving the Lord in fifteen states and several foreign countries.[51] One can only marvel at what the Lord is doing through Leland Duncan and his colleagues at Virginia Tech!

# Western Michigan University, Kalamazoo

The third campus ministry to be established in Michigan under the sponsorship of Michigan Christian Campus Ministries was at Western Michigan University at Kalamazoo. In the fall of 1976 Gary Hawes and students from Michigan State spent one day each week on the campus of Western to contact and develop a core of committed students. By the fall of 1977 this ministry was sufficiently established to call Scot Jeffries as full-time campus minister. In 1981, during Scot's ministry, three houses across from the university campus were purchased to provide student housing, office and meeting space.[52] In August of 1982, John Sowash succeeded Scot Jeffries as campus minister at Western. John had been active as a student with the campus ministry at Central Michigan University where he received a Bachelor of Science degree in Biology. After graduating from Great Lakes Bible College he spent two years as assistant campus minister with Gary Hawes at Michigan State. John describes the highlights of the program at Western Michigan during his years there as follows:

> 1. Thursday night Bible study and prayer, emphasis is study and interaction. 2. Sunday night Bible study and prayer, emphasis is worship. 3. Sunday night meal, emphasis is fellowship. 4. Small group discipleship (3 men) meet weekly together informally. 5. Calling in dorms with each student, counseling, encouraging. 6. Yearly Mexico trip with missions emphasis.[53]

In 1988 John and Cheryl Sowash left Western Michigan to become the campus ministers at the University of Michigan at Ann Arbor. John Thybault became the campus minister at Western in July 1988 and serves there at this writing. John Thybault had also been active with the campus ministry at Central Michigan, and he graduated from there in 1980 with a degree in Social Science and Business. From 1983 to 1987 he was campus minister at the University of Cincinnati and was connected with Challenge Unlimited there. From 1987 to 1988 he was campus minister at Miami University in Oxford, Ohio. While John was in Cincinnati he worked on a degree in Christian Counseling at Cincinnati Bible Seminary. He describes the program at Western as consisting of: accountability/disciple groups (men and women separate), individual counseling and encouragement (a lot of hurting students are on campus), and he says, "We continue to have more and more students willing to do short-term missions and some are accepting a call to go for missions full-time."[54]

Rita Albertson has worked with John as a volunteer campus coordinator, Scott Schultz served an interim during the 1990–91 school year and Randy Dunning served an interim in 1991–92. John mentions one of the problems faced by campus ministry which we have not mentioned up to this point. He says, "I continue to struggle with the problem of integrating students from our campus ministry into our local Christian churches. Have campus ministries become a movement within a movement?"[55]

John says that campus ministry can be summed up in a sentence, "Bring 'Em In, Build 'Em Up, and Send 'Em Out." He goes on to say in his 1990–1991 Annual Report:

> "Sending 'em out" is the bittersweet of campus ministry. Judy went out to serve as an instructor at Grundy Mountain Mission School. David is serving an internship this fall at MSU. Tak returned to his home in Japan to be a

witness for Christ as a result of his decision at the Fall Retreat. Paul is in the planning stages of doing mission work in Honduras. Edward left on September 4 to do outreach in Hungary for the next nine months. David is now in Japan and on his way to the USSR to do mission work. Sue is serving the Lord through Occupational Therapy in Montgomery, Alabama. Tom and Brett are using their musical talents to glorify God. Tim is in grad school at Indiana University and involved in the campus ministry there. These and many other students were brought in, built up, and are now sent out; but they are not forgotten. They have gone so that others might "know Christ."[56]

So, the "Michigan Miracle" is reaching out far beyond the borders of the state "into all the world."

## Auburn University in Alabama

Dean Collins saw the need for campus ministry at Auburn University in Auburn, Alabama, in 1979. He recruited a board of directors from churches in the area, they purchased a house near the campus, and the first campus ministry of Christian Churches in the state of Alabama was under way. Dean had spent one year as a music major at Central Florida Community College in Ocala, and then transferred to Atlanta Christian College and graduated from there. When he moved to Auburn in 1979 he began work on a masters degree in Counseling and College Student Development, receiving the degree in 1982.

James Street, campus minister at the University of Georgia in Athens, and Thom Miller, campus minister at Florida State University in Tallahassee, were of great help to Dean Collins in the early days of his ministry at Auburn, providing encouragement and information. Working on a masters degree at Auburn gave Dean excellent insights into the lives of students. He says, "There is great value in studying on the campus where you serve. It provides individual contact with students, faculty, and administration."[57]

In 1982 a second house very near the campus was purchased, both houses serving as places of residence, one for women and the other for male students. Sunday morning worship services, Bible study and service groups, outreach to elderly, prisoners, and homeless are important parts of the program, but the activity Dean Collins lists as the "most successful" during his ministry was a Thursday night free dinner/fellowship. Dean says, "Through this dinner new people are introduced to the fellowship and from there they are recruited for worship, service, and study groups. Every year we make contact with hundreds of students through this program."[58]

Lisa Knight, a graduate of the University of Georgia where she became active in the campus ministry, moved to Auburn in 1983 and served as an intern with Dean Collins. While serving in this capacity, Lisa did an extensive survey of internships in campus ministry. At that point in the history of campus ministry, interns were not largely utilized, but since then, the practice has multiplied, and many campus ministries now have interns.[59] In 1985 Lisa became a full-time associate minister at Auburn, serving until 1987 when she took employment with Auburn University. In 1987 the two houses which had served primarily as student residences, since they had minimal space for meeting rooms, were sold to the university. The monies from that sale enabled Dean Collins and his co-workers to purchase a building just one block from the main campus of Auburn University, a building which had been a day care center and which had been the first building Dean and his people had tried to obtain ten years before.

Dean Collins was very successful in establishing the campus ministry at Auburn on a solid foundation, but he does admit that during the first seven years of his ministry, he did not use students in responsible positions of leadership. In 1986 he wrote as follows:

> One goal I have always had was for students to take more responsibility and leadership in planning and carrying out the mission of Auburn Christian Fellowship. But for nearly seven years, with a few exceptions, that had not happened. However, this year, partially because it was forced by my bout with hepatitis, students began to take some responsibility. The great news is that now even though I am fully recovered they have continued and even increased their leadership at A.C.F. The result has been a noticeable growth in the members of A.C.F. and I believe in the long run we will see numerical growth in our ministry.[60]

A study of the campus ministry at Auburn would indicate that the Lord used Dean Collins to achieve all of the goals he had set for himself in 1985 to some degree.[61] He left in 1988 to found "New Directions Counseling" in Atlanta, Georgia, but he continued to work with Scott Seagraves, the new campus minister at Auburn during the school year of 1988–89.

Scott Seagraves and his wife Karen came to Auburn from an interesting background. Scott had graduated from Georgia College in Milledgville with a degree in Accounting, after which he spent five years as the chief executive officer of his own small business. After getting his degree from Atlanta Christian College, a Bachelor of Theology, he became minister for singles at Southwest Christian Church in East Point, Georgia. Scott continued the aggressive and creative ministry started by Dean Collins at Auburn. The established features of the program were continued, and the Thursday evening free meal fellowship was the most successful part of the program. The campus house was located one block from the main campus of the university in a busy traffic pattern and was highly visible to students. Literally hundreds of students were recruited by this ministry during the combined leadership of Dean Collins, Scott Seagraves, and Lisa Knight. In August 1992, Scott left to become associate minister at Colonial Heights Christian Church in Kingsport, Tennessee, and to attend Emmanuel School of Religion for further preparation for ministry (the minister at the Colonial Heights Christian Church is Dick Carpenter, the first campus minister among Christian Churches at the University of Kentucky in Lexington in 1959!).[62]

Bruce Greco, who had been a student leader in the fellowship at Auburn during his student days there, became interim campus minister in August of 1992 and he served until September of 1993 when he returned to Emmanuel School of Religion to further his preparation for ministry. Bruce sustained the program at Auburn, and in September of 1993 Perry Rubin came on as full-time campus minister. Perry had graduated from West Georgia College in political science, and while there he became interested in campus ministry. He went on to Emmanuel School of Religion and then to Fuller Theological Seminary in Pasadena, California. While in California he met his wife Lara, who was a student at Pacific Christian College. After Fuller, Perry and Lara served as associate ministers at Southwest Christian Church in East Point, Georgia, where they worked with Thom Miller, former campus minister at Florida State.[63]

Prospects for a strong campus ministry at Auburn are very bright with this rich background of capable leaders and committed students. The way God continues to "network" and develop campus ministries is truly amazing!

# Michigan State University at East Lansing

By 1979 four campus ministries had grown out of the original campus ministry at Michigan State in East Lansing. Gary Hawes, the first campus minister at Michigan State, became Executive Director of the "umbrella" organization "Michigan Christian Campus Ministries" in 1979, and John Sowash became the campus minister at Michigan State in that year.

John served at MSU until 1984 when Dean Trune, the present campus minister, succeeded him. Dean holds two degrees from the University of Michigan, an undergraduate degree in business administration and economics, and a masters degree in industrial and operational engineering. Like all the other campus ministries in Michigan who are working as a part of MCCM, Dean says the most significant part of his preparation for campus ministry was the intensive one-on-one discipleship training he received under Gary Hawes and others.[64]

As the MCCM expanded to other campuses in the decade of the seventies, so did the founding campus ministry at Michigan State. Dean Trune began a Bible study at Olivet College in Olivet, Michigan, in 1991.

The campus ministry at Michigan State also grew and in 1989 Dean reported the development of a "family group" in one of the university residence halls that had grown to ten students. Increased outreach to international students also was a part of the campus ministry at Michigan State under Dean's leadership. In 1991 Dean reported as follows, "This last year overall was a fruitful year. At MSU, forty-five people were baptized and at Olivet, four students were baptized. God continues to do things beyond what we expect or deserve. We serve a powerful God!"[65]

The true extent and depth of campus ministry is beyond our capacity to report in any case, but especially so in the case of the state of Michigan. By the end of the 1970s there were five growing campus ministries in the state, and the end was not yet in sight. MCCM continued to expand in the state during the 1980s, and by 1990 its leaders were planning to establish campus ministries overseas in several places. The "Michigan Miracle" continues.

# University of Michigan at Ann Arbor

The fifth campus ministry established in Michigan by the Michigan Christian Campus Ministries was at the University of Michigan at Ann Arbor in September of 1979. This prestigious university is where the Disciples established the first Bible Chair in 1893, so this Christian church campus ministry has helped ministry to students by churches of the Restoration Movement to come full circle at the University of Michigan.

Gary Hawes, director of Michigan Christian Campus Ministries, served as the first campus minister at Ann Arbor. Each week for three years he and other staff members traveled to Ann Arbor to call on students, counsel, and teach. Three individuals had moved to Ann Arbor for the specific purpose of helping to establish this new ministry; each of them found employment with the university.[66]

One of the people who worked with Gary Hawes to found this ministry was Michael O'Berski. Michael had become a Christian through the campus ministry at Michigan State University while he worked on a degree in Industrial Arts Education. After graduation from MSU he went for two years to Great Lakes Bible College, which was very helpful because, he says, "I was very ignorant about the Bible."[67] Michael became the first full-time campus minister at the University of Michigan in 1981.

A campus house near the university was rented in November of 1982 with an option to buy. It was purchased in February, 1983, and its first full year of occupancy by students was the school year of 1983–84. "His House" became the center of activity including Sunday night dinner and fellowship, Thursday night Bible study and fellowship, discipleship groups, evangelistic outreach, nursing home visitation, Mexico mission trips, and retreats. Michael says the most important part of these activities was the discipleship groups, probably because his own growth in Christian faith was largely due to intensive discipleship by Gary Hawes and a few others.[68] In 1988, after seven years of fruitful leadership at the University of Michigan, Michael O'Berski became the campus minister at Central Michigan University in Mt. Pleasant. He was succeeded there by John Sowash in June of 1988.

Like most of the campus ministers in Michigan, John was active with a campus ministry while he was a student, in his case at Central Michigan. He went on for two years study at Great Lakes Bible College, after which he served as an intern under Gary Hawes at Michigan State. The programs which had been developed by Michael O'Berski were continued, with special emphasis upon accountability groups to encourage students in daily Bible study, prayer, witnessing, physical development, and service. There has been a growing outreach to international students during John Sowash's term at the University of Michigan. He says, "More students than ever are leaving the U.S.A. for mission work. Seven are currently preparing to leave for Russia, Japan, Africa, Mexico, and Bangladesh."[69] John recently summarized the current state of the campus ministry at the University of Michigan as follows:

> In one of the most highly educated and prosperous areas of the state of Michigan, there is a deep hunger for inner peace and fulfillment. Men and women, young and old, have come not only from the University of Michigan, but Eastern Michigan University, Lawrence Technological University, Washtenaw Community College, and several of the surrounding cities and towns to meet with us at His House Christian Fellowship for our weekly Bible studies. . . . The needs of our day are great — there is a tremendous moral and social breakdown going on in our states, cities, and families. The best of education is *not* addressing and meeting the needs of a hurting and empty nation . . . but Jesus can, and is, making a difference at the University of Michigan![70]

# Northwest Missouri State University, Maryville

In 1974 an Area Men's Fellowship decided to initiate the campus ministry at Northwest Missouri State University at Maryville. Bible studies were held on campus that fall, led by ministers from Countryside Christian Church in Maryville and the Christian Church in Ravenwood. That same year a campus house was purchased which was large enough to provide a home for a campus minister and also to house four male students and four female students.

In January 1975, Dave and Vicki Rockey became the first full-time campus ministers. By 1980, this campus ministry was one of the largest on campus at Northwest, and an effective ministry to international students had developed. Students from sixteen different countries were residents at the campus house during the 1980s.

In 1982, Dave and Vicki Rockey moved into their own home, and Dave and Alice Holland moved into the campus house as house parents. In the same year Dave Rockey became a counselor at the university counseling center, which opened up positive contacts with university staff and personnel. In 1984, after nine and a half years of faithful ministry at Northwest, Dave and Vicki Rockey moved to Stillwater, Oklahoma, to serve as campus ministers at Oklahoma State University. They left a ministry which had grown both in numbers and influence on the campus at Northwest.

Roger and Nancy Charley, former campus house students, became the campus ministers, moving into the campus house in the fall of 1984. Roger had graduated from Northwest Missouri State University with a BS in Business Management, and had also graduated from Iowa Christian College. Nancy had been baptized in 1977 while she was active in this ministry, so they both came with experience and enthusiasm for campus ministry. In the 1986-87 school year, after a few lean years, the ministry began to grow again. The Bible studies were moved from the campus house to the student union, and students who were not residents of the campus house began attending. In 1990, the campus house was sold to a fraternity, and a smaller house closer to campus was purchased. This new house, smaller and in a better location, became primarily a center for the activities of the fellowship rather than a residence for students.

In addition to a significant ministry with international students, in 1985 this campus ministry began regular mission trips during spring break. In the spring of 1993, Roger Charley and two alumni went on a trip to Haiti to serve with the Life Line Christian Mission in Goave. Roger Charley attributes the strength of this campus ministry to a strong emphasis on Bible study and the mission trips which are usually taken in conjunction with another campus ministry. Currently between eighty and one hundred students are involved in the main Bible study, special Bible studies with international students, dorm studies, or fellowship groups. Alumni from Northwest are serving as missionaries in Japan, ministering to the Navajo Indians, and teaching in Christian schools. One is serving as a youth minister and another as a campus minister in their local churches.[71]

# University of Oregon in Eugene

We have noted previously the early efforts by Eugene Sanderson to locate Bible colleges near state universities, an idea that was first advanced by Thomas Jefferson at the University of Virginia. Eugene Divinity School was founded in 1895 near the campus of the University of

Oregon so that, as Sanderson said: "The institution adjacent to the University of Oregon campus was so located that students might make use of the extensive resources of that state supported institution."[72]

Northwest Christian College, successor to Eugene Divinity School, has maintained that relationship to some degree over the years. However, it was not until 1978 when Richard Beswick founded the Restoration Campus Ministry at the University of Oregon that an aggressive movement was launched to carry the gospel to that historic institution. Dick Beswick had been converted to Christ through the influence of the Jesus Movement People. He earned a degree from the University of Oregon in Religious Studies with honors in 1974 and then went on to Yale University where he received a Master of Divinity degree in 1978. He and his wife Karen arrived in Eugene in the fall of 1978 and began appealing to the area ministers and churches to share his dream of taking the gospel to the University of Oregon. Slowly the churches responded, and a twelve-member board of trustees and a statewide board of associates were founded. Office space was rented in Koinonia Center, an ecumenical building housing several different campus ministers, and Dick began Bible studies and witnessing on the campus. A core of dedicated students responded, and by 1980 the unique programs which mark this ministry were taking shape.

"Bible Roundtables" became a staple of the program. These were described in a flyer as: "An hour of open discussion on basic issues, problems, and mysteries of life using the Bible as our source. If you are non-religious, religious, or Christian, you are welcome."[73] Dick says that in the beginning he tended to sermonize the whole hour in these sessions, then he learned to encourage a truly open discussion on some topic of general interest. Over the years this has been a source of very fruitful evangelism and Christian nurture touching and changing the lives of hundreds of students. In recent years, a special Roundtable for international students has been effectively instituted as well, especially successful in reaching Asian students. To get something of the flavor of these discussion, here are some of the topics, picked at random, which have aroused the interest and participation of students on this great university campus: "Biblical View of Pleasure," "Recreation and Ownership," "Is Jesus the Only Way to God?" "What About People who Never Hear the Gospel?" "Christianity and Psychology: Freud and Jung," "Salvation and Personal Identity," "Is the Bible Reliable?" "Perspectives on Creation vs. Evolution," "The Ethics of Euthanasia," "Jesus and Muhammad," "A Christian Response to the AIDS Epidemic," "Jesus and Buddha," "Is Christianity Anti-Intellectual?"[74]

From the beginning, Dick Beswick insisted on the close relationship between his ministry on campus and the local churches. After five years of renting space in the Koinonia Center, the campus ministry moved to

University Street Church of Christ, not just to have space in their building, but to minister along with that congregation. Dick taught classes for the University Street Church and in the Norvale Park congregation regularly. In 1984 a large house became available for rent. It was large enough to house several students and income from rent enabled the campus ministry to pay the rent on the house. It became "Cascade House," the geographical center of the ministry.

Not all events were held in the house, however; the Bible Roundtables were held at various locations on and near campus. The program that attracted the most attention and was probably the most effective in terms of confronting the university community with the gospel was the Mars Hill Forum, a serious of public debates and lectures on contemporary and controversial topics. Here is the stated purpose of these dialogues, which were modeled after Paul, the apostle's, experience on Mars Hill, and the C.S. Lewis Socratic Club at Oxford University:

> The Mars Hill Forum is committed to the exploration of concepts, worldviews and philosophies in search of ultimate truth through dialogue, critical analysis, and careful listening in an atmosphere of sensitivity and mutual respect. . . . From time to time points of view antithetical to biblical Christianity will be solicited within a flexible debate format. Our purpose is two-fold: 1) to demonstrate the adequacy of the Christian worldview in areas popularly thought to be outside the scope of religion; and 2) to express the love of the Christian community by careful listening and sharing of the truth, confident that a genuine search for truth leads ultimately to Christ.[75]

In one of these widely noted Forums Dick Beswick debated Swami Satya Vedant, a minister of the Church of Rajneesh on the subject "Jesus or Rajneesh? With Whom Does the Truth Lie?" This was at the time when the Rajneesh had collected a large commune of mostly young college-age people as his followers in Antelope, Oregon. Another topic for the Forum was a debate on Creation-Evolution between Dr. Duane Gish, of the Creation Research Seminars and Dr. David Wagner, a botany professor from the university. The New Age movement was very strong on the campus of the University of Oregon, so Dick and his people held several Forums dealing with this growing movement. Fortunately, Doug Groothuis, who is a best selling author with three books on the New Age movement, not only led in these Forums, but also became a full-time staff member with Dick Beswick.[76]

In addition to these rather more spectacular presentations, this campus ministry had a regular program of Bible studies, fellowship and praise gatherings, winter retreats on the Oregon coast, and regular Sunday worship services in the local churches.

Several interns served in this campus ministry over the years — Ken

Marsh, Steve Wilhite, Kari Rose, and Lisa and John Dellis, among others. Dick Beswick, in addition to teaching regularly in local congregations, also taught courses each year at Northwest Christian College on Comparative Religions and the New Age movement. Regular witnessing on campus is a low-key but effective ministry at Eugene which also won many college students to Christ during the fifteen years of its campus ministry.

Dick Beswick came to Oregon fifteen years ago very well trained academically, committed to college students and gifted with the kind of compassion which has made this campus ministry a truly effective one! This description, like all descriptions in this book, is inadequate to cover the real depth and power of this ministry in a few pages. Eugene Sanderson would be proud of what has happened at the University of Oregon almost one hundred years after he founded Eugene Divinity School!

# Conclusion

In late 1970, Lyle Schaller, a church growth specialist, predicted that campus ministry would be the most divisive ministry in the 1970s.[77] Viewing the situation from the point of view of traditional "mainline" denominations, Schaller listed several reasons for his prediction. Among them were: 1) a sharp difference of opinion about the nature of ministry between campus ministers and people in the supportive churches; 2) a demand on the part of students for more significant participation in planning and executing the programs of ministry on campus; and 3) a gradual decrease of giving to denominational treasuries which would cause campus ministry to be a low priority item as budgets would be carefully scrutinized.

Campus ministries among Christian Churches did not avoid all of these potentially divisive issues in the decade of the 70s. There were, and still are, different perceptions on the part of the campus ministers and the local churches as to what constitutes authentic ministry. Some of these differences are unavoidable since, although the gospel does not change, the way it is presented to different cultures must and does change. However, the animosity which sometimes existed between campus ministry and the churches in the beginning diminished considerably during the 70s as campus ministries gained recognition and respect, and as the relationship became more cooperative and less competitive.[78]

The other two potential problems mentioned by Schaller were almost totally overcome as campus ministries matured during the 1970s. Responsible and creative student participation in ministry became the hallmark of Christian church campus ministries across the country, as evidenced in the history recorded in the preceding chapters. Schaller said, in his prophetic article:

> The campus ministry must be seen as more than a ministry to students; it must also be seen as an opportunity for students to minister to the world — a great many of them (students) are not interested in being entertained, they want to serve. They are less interested in being ministered to than in being ministers to those in need of love, healing, and reconciliation.[79]

The enthusiastic response of students in Christian Church campus ministries during the 70s to the needs of hurting people, and to the challenge presented by missions and international students has certainly vindicated Schaller's prediction.[80]

The third potentially divisive issue mentioned by Schaller was solved as much by the traditional non-denominational and non-bureaucratic nature of churches in this branch of the Restoration Movement as by the unique character of campus ministry. Finances are a continuing problem for most campus ministries, but the money they do receive — and it is increasing — is not given through a bureaucratic denominational headquarters, but by churches and individuals who are in close contact with the campus ministries they support, and who are knowledgeable and enthusiastic supporters.[81] Not only that, but students and alumni of campus ministry are giving more and more, not only to finance the programs on campus, but also to support home and overseas missions.

Thus, a growing rapport between campus ministries and local ministers and churches, responsible involvement of students in planning and executing programs, and generous giving by people who know what is happening on the campus have combined to disprove Shaller's prediction that campus ministry would be a divisive force in the 1970s, at least among Christian Church campus ministries.

Another trend in campus ministries which has become more and more obvious during the 70s is the "networking" which has taken place. Campus ministries are producing campus ministers, as many who are converted on campus have gone on to Bible college and seminary to prepare themselves to return to campus ministry. This can be a negative factor if it causes campus ministries to become ingrown and self-satisfied, but a positive factor if it results in recruiting and training students to become leaders in the church and in the world. The latter was the case in the 70s as hundreds, indeed thousands, of students left the campuses to become ministers, missionaries, and dedicated Christian leaders in almost every sector of the "secular" world.

As Rick Rowland said, the 70s were the "golden age" of campus ministry, but the momentum generated in that decade carries over as the broadening continues in the 80s and 90s.

# NOTES

1. Information on this campus ministry from 1975 to 1984 is not available to me.

2. From Greg Swinney's resume, 1993.

3. Newsletter, "CSF Beacon," March 1991, p. 4.

4. Newsletter, December 1989, p. 2.

5. Newsletter, June 1990, p. 1.

6. Newsletter, December 1991, p. 4.

7. Newsletter, June 1990, p. 4.

8. Newsletter, April/May 1993, p. 1.

9. Newsletter, *Ibid.*, p. 3.

10. Newsletter, December 1988, p. 4.

11. Swinney resume, 1993.

12. Questionnaire completed by Greg Swinney, 1989.

13. Newsletter, December 1988, p. 4.

14. Questionnaires completed by Joe Belzer in 1985 and 1990.

15. Questionnaire, 1990.

16. From a telephone conversation with a student at Kirksville in July, 1993.

17. Questionnaire completed by Bob Wade in June 1980.

18. From a telephone conversation with Pat Wade, July 1993.

19. Questionnaire completed by Terry Byrd in 1982. Detailed information on this campus ministry from its beginning in 1976 up to 1989 is not available.

20. Telephone conversation with Lonnie Portenier, July 27, 1993.

21. A questionnaire completed by Sandy Bigelow, May 1993.

22. Dennis Steckley was a student in a class I taught in campus ministry at Emmanuel School of Religion in the summer of 1975.

23. A questionnaire completed by Sandy Bigelow, May 1993.

24. I do not have detailed information about this campus ministry from 1976 up to 1982.

25. Questionnaire completed by Tim Hudson, May 1993.

26. Questionnaire completed by Tim Hudson, 1989.

27. Jane Nabor is an example of the important role women have played in many campus ministries across the country.

28. Letter from Gary Hawes to supporting churches, September 10, 1984.

29. "Campus Ministry Messenger," May/June 1990, p. 1.

30. Michigan Christian Campus Ministries, "Annual Report," 1990–1991, p. 7.

31. "Campus Ministry Messenger," May/June 1993, p. 2.

32. CCF Report, Final Newsletter put out by Clark Wagoner in June 1977, pp. 1-2.

33. Newsletter, "Christ on Campus View," October 1976.

34. Newsletter, August 1977. See a more complete list of Roger Thomas' articles on campus ministry in the bibliography.

35. *Christian Standard,* March 26, 1978, p. 16.

36. Questionnaire completed by Randy Smothers in 1985.

37. Information about the ministry under Don Riepe came from a telephone conversation with the author in August, 1993.

38. "Annual Report," 1993, p. 8. Article by student Mary Robinson.

39. "Annual Report," p. 9.

40. *Ibid.,* p. 11.

41. Questionnaire completed by Dave Embree in May of 1993.

42. Annual Report, *ibid.,* p. 16.

43. Taking Education Higher: A Guide Book to Ministry on the University Campus, Ed. Greg Swinney (Lifechange Media: Kearney, NE), 1993.

44. Letter from Dave Embree to author, March 1993.

45. Questionnaire, 1993.

46. Questionnaire completed by Leland Duncan, April 1989.

47. *Ibid.*

48. Newsletter, 1984. This poem was signed as follows: From the Christian Brothers at Tuesday night Bible studies, Bland Correctional Center, Bland, Virginia, Clinton H. Spencer, December 2, 1984.

49. Newsletter, June 1988-May 1989, p. 1.

50. Newsletter, June 1990-July 1991.

51. Questionnaire completed by Leland Duncan, May 1993.

52. I do not have complete information on Scott Jeffries's four year ministry at Western Michigan.

53. Questionnaire completed by John Sowash in 1985.

54. Questionnaire completed by John Thybault in 1992.

55. *Ibid.*

56. 1990-91 Annual Report of Michigan Christian Campus Ministries, p. 8.

57. Questionnaire completed by Dean Collins, 1985.

58. *Ibid.*

59. The results of Lisa's survey, in which approximately twenty-eight campus ministries were surveyed, were not published, but I have a copy which I will be glad to send to anyone upon request.

60. Newsletter, 1986. Specific date not available.

61. Questionnaire completed by Dean Collins, 1985.

62. Information on the ministry on Scott Seagraves at Auburn came from a phone conversation with him in July 1993.

63. Information on Bruce Greco and Perry Rubin, came from the phone conversation with Scott Seagraves and another with Bruce Greco in July 1993.

64. Questionnaire completed by Dean Trune in 1985.

65. MCCM Annual Report, September 1990-August 1991.

66. Fifteenth Annual Report, MCCM, September 1983-August 31, 1984, p. 5.

67. Questionnaire completed by Michael O'Berski in 1985.

68. *Ibid.*

69. Questionnaire completed by John Sowash, March 1992.

70. Twenty-second Annual Report, MCCM, September 1, 1990-August 31, 1991, p. 8.

71. Information on this campus ministry at Northwest came from a questionnaire completed by Roger Charley in 1989 and from a letter to the author in July of 1993.

72. Leggett, Marshall J., MA thesis, "A Study of the Historical Factors in the Rise of the Bible College in the Restoration Movement," Butler University, IN, 1961, p. 20.

73. Flyer, 1980.

74. Copied from various undated flyers.

75. *Ibid.*

76. The books written by Doug Groothuis on the New Age which have been so popular are: *Unmasking the New Age, Confronting the New Age,* and *Revealing the New Age Jesus.* All of these have been published by InterVarsity Press in Downers Grove, Illinois.

77. *Your Church,* July/August 1970, article by Lyle Shaller, "The Campus Ministry: The Most Divisive Ministry of the 70s," pp. 14-ff.

78. The ideal is probably not a total lack of criticism between churches and campus ministries, but rather a continuing, constructive criticism by each of the other as different parts of the total body of Christ. See "College Students and the Church Can Get Together," *Christianity Today,* March 2, 1984, pp. 82-83.

79. Shaller, "The Campus Ministry," pp. 15 and 45.

80. See the article by Roy Weece, "Jesus Voted Yes," *Christian Standard,* July 26, 1987, pp. 1, 4-6, and the article by Willard Walls, "The University Student and World Evangelism," *Christian Standard,* February 14, 1982, pp. 12-13.

81. Lyle Shaller's prediction that there would be an increasing gap between local churches and denomination bureaucracies has been accurate, not just in mainline campus ministries, but in the mainline Protestant denominations as a whole. An article in *Newsweek,* August 9, 1993, pp. 46-48, says, "Many local congregations are rejecting control by denominational leaders and cutting back on the funds to support the national programs — if this break-away pattern persists, observes the Methodist Lyle Shaller, a consultant on church development, 'denominations will be left with what they do best — administering clerical pension funds.'" To see how this trend has affected the Disciples, see the article by Ronald Osborn, "The Irony of the 20th Century Christian Church (Disciples of Christ): Making it to the Main-Line Just at the Time of Its Disestablishment." *Midstream,* July 1989, pp. 293-312. Campus ministries among Christian Churches in the 70s were a trend in the opposite direction.

CHAPTER EIGHT

# Campus Ministries in
# Eighties and Early Nineties

College students of any age are too complex to be easily character-ized, but there is a general consensus among most social critics of the students of the 80s that there was a turning inward, and an emerging of the "Me Generation."[1] Arthur Levine encapsulates this attitude in the following much quoted interview:

> **Interviewer:** Will the United States be a better or worse place to live in the next ten years?
> **Student:** The U.S. will definitely be a worse place to live.
> **Interviewer:** Then you must be pessimistic about the future.
> **Student:** No, I'm optimistic.
> **Interviewer (with surprise):** Why?
> **Student:** Because I have a high grade point average and I'm going to get a good job, make a lot of money, and live in a nice house.[2]

Levine calls this attitude "going first class on the Titanic." By the beginning of the decade the idealism which had swept the college campuses in the 1960s was leeched out, and students in general were feel-ing apathetic and pessimistic about their ability to make any real differ-ence in the world. Levine says further:

> There is a sense among today's undergraduates that they are passengers on a sinking ship, a Titanic if you will, called the United States or the world. Perhaps this is part of the reason why suicide has become the second lead-ing cause of death among students in the 1970s exceeded only by accidents. Be that as it may, today's fatalism fuels a spirit of justified hedonism. There is a growing belief among college students that, if they are doomed to ride on the Titanic, they ought at least to make the trip as pleasant — make that as lavish — as possible and go first class, for they assume there is nothing better.[3]

Some of the reasons for this attitude can be seen in the nature of the university itself. Beginning with the Seventeenth Century Enlightenment, universities increasingly turned away from the ultimate questions about the meaning and significance of life, and became more and more objecti-fied and specialized. A freshman student entering the university in the 1980s faced a bewildering variety of choices, none of them helpful in his

207

search for wholeness and personal significance. Allan Bloom says:

> Each department or great division of the university makes a pitch for itself, and each offers a course of study that will make the student an initiate. But how to choose among them? How do they relate to one another? The fact is they do not address one another. They are competing and contradictory, without being aware of it. The problem of the whole is urgently indicated by the very existence of the specialties, but it is never systematically posed. The net effect of the student's encounter with the college catalogue is bewilderment and very often demoralization . . . This undecided student is an embarrassment to most universities, because he seems to be saying, "I am a whole human being. Help me to form myself in my wholeness and let me develop my real potential," and he is the one to whom they have nothing to say."[4]

One can understand how this situation virtually forced a student to choose a curriculum with some direction and purpose, even though that purpose might be materialistic and self-centered. *It is not too exaggerated to say that campus ministry may be the only place in the entire university where a student can find people who are dealing seriously with the ultimate questions of meaning and purpose.*

The consequence of this situation for campus ministries in the early 1980s was a period when students avoided commitment and threw all their energies into study during the week and partying on the weekends. In the early 80s this caused discouragement among campus ministers all over the country, and they commiserated with each other as they came together in retreats, especially in the annual retreat each spring.

By the middle of the decade, however, the situation turned around dramatically. Students began to do serious soul searching about their careers and their purpose in life, and they turned to campus ministries for help. They began to get involved in genuine service and mission projects, and hundreds made dramatic career changes, entering into service in the church, on the mission field, or in significant secular professions where they carried their Christian faith.

In the late 1980s and early 1990s the universities became pre-occupied with qualities of ethnic diversity and "political correctness." One can interpret this as an attempt to fill the vacuum which existed at the heart of the university with a strident concern for single issues — feminism, abortion, racism, and homosexuality, among others. Every one of these issues is of serious concern to any committed Christian, but in many cases the "political" became more important than the "correctness." Campus ministries by the end of the decade were experiencing pressure, and even incipient persecution, as they were being forced to choose among these often conflicting causes. Although it was more difficult in the 80s to do successful campus ministries, the difficulty only underscored the need for caring communities of Christians on the university campus. Campus ministries among Christian Churches met this challenge by establishing twenty new campus ministries and entering five additional states by the end of the decade.

The broadening of campus ministries continued into the early 1990s with four campus ministries being established by 1993.

## Campus Ministries in the State of Colorado

Campus ministry began in the state of Colorado in 1975 when John Schlieker began a part-time outreach to the University of Northern Colorado at Greeley, working through the Greeley Christian Church. John was a graduate of Lincoln Christian College, and while at Greeley he also received a Bachelor's degree from the University of Northern Colorado in communication and journalism. The arrangement with the Greeley congregation lasted until 1978 when it was terminated.[5]

By 1980, John Schlieker had married Janice Jones, who had graduated from Ozark Bible College and had worked with the campus ministry at Missouri Southern State College in Joplin during her college years. In 1980, with little visible support, John and Janice began a full-time campus ministry at the University of Northern Colorado. A house had been rented in 1977 for a campus house, rent being paid by student residents. Slowly John and Janice gained support from area churches, and in late 1980 they had formed a Board of Directors and an organization called "Colorado Christian Campus Ministries, Incorporated." The vision of the Schliekers, and the men on the board of directors, was to establish campus ministries on every college or university campus in the state of Colorado.

The first step toward that goal was the building of a strong campus ministry at Greeley. Through an intensive program which included Sunday evening fellowship meetings, small group daily Bible studies, one-on-one discipleship, and social events, this campus ministry was sufficiently established by September of 1984 to begin part-time campus ministries at Colorado State University at Fort Collins and at the University of Colorado at Boulder. The Schliekers divided their time by spending Monday, Wednesday, and Friday at UNC, Tuesdays at Boulder, and Thursdays at Fort Collins (being available on the latter two campuses for counseling, discipleship, Bible studies, and calling).[6]

Another accomplishment of the Schliekers was organizing in 1983 a winter retreat for area campus ministries. By 1984 the "area" had expanded and eighty-eight people from seven states gathered at Colorado Christian Service Camp in Como, Colorado, for study, inspiration, and fellowship.[7] This retreat has been an annual event since that time and has become a gathering for campus ministers from all over the Midwest, partly because it also included "some great skiing."[8]

By 1986 the campus ministry at Colorado State University had grown so much that the Schliekers moved to Fort Collins and ministered both there and at NCU until 1987, when George Dosher was called to become full-time campus minister at the University of Northern Colorado. During the seven years the Schliekers had been campus ministers at NCU, several students went to seminary, one became a campus minister, and twenty went as missionaries from one month to two years in Kenya, Zaire, Puerto Rico, and El Salvador.[9] The campus ministry at University of Northern Colorado continued to grow under George Dosher's leadership. Mission trips became a regular part of the program, especially trips to Cookson Hills Children's Home in Oberlin, Kansas. A preview of things to come in campus ministry took place at the University of Northern Colorado in the spring of 1993. An event called "Gay, Lesbian, and Bi-Sexual Awareness Week" was held; a Catholic priest and a Presbyterian minister led a discussion on "An Alternative Biblical View of Homosexuality." George and his students attended the sessions and tried to counter with a more Biblical view of the problem. George says, "I wish I could say that the above event was unique to the University of Northern Colorado. It is not; similar conferences have been held at Colorado State University and on campuses all over the country."[10]

While the ministry at UNC was growing under the leadership of George Dosher, the Schliekers were also enjoying steady growth in their ministry at Colorado State. In 1991 a much needed campus house was purchased. This large house, located directly across the street from two large university dormitories provided ample room for office space, meeting rooms, and a rentable apartment. The program on campus consisted of large and small Bible studies, short-term mission work trips, and larger trips to Scotland, the Ivory Coast, France, and Ecuador.[11] By 1992 more than two hundred students were involved in the ministry at CSU, and John Schlieker was making regular trips to the University of Wyoming at Laramie.

After John and Janice Schlieker spent one day a week at the University of Colorado in 1984 and 1985, John Mophew served on that campus part-time in 1987 and 1988. In 1988, Jerry Gibson, pioneer campus minister at the University of Minnesota and at the University of Illinois returned to campus ministry at the University of Colorado at Boulder. He is at present working primarily with international students for which he has special gifts, through Boulder Valley Christian Church. He also is working with the Fellowship of Christian Athletes at Boulder, and has baptized several of the varsity players. Jerry teaches an adult Bible class each Wednesday morning at 7:00 a.m. in the back of the university stadium which includes coaches, athletes, and other concerned Christians.[12] In all of Jerry Gibson's ministry he is more than adequately supported by his wife, Normadeene, who also teaches internationals in a special class at Boulder Valley Christian Church.

After the relatively small beginnings of campus ministry in 1975 when John Schlieker ministered to students at the University of Northern Colorado through the Greeley Christian Church campus ministries in Colorado are now strong on three campuses with a new one beginning in Wyoming. Many people have been used by God to create this growth, but as one who knows John and Janice Schlieker, I venture to say it would not have happened without them.

# Kent State University, Ohio

One of the best known universities in the country, if not the world, during the 1970s was Kent State University in Ohio. There, as is well known, four students were shot and killed by National Guardsmen as they led a protest on the campus against the Vietnam War.[13]

In 1969–1970 Richard Hostetter, a missionary to Ghana, was on furlough and was taking classes at Kent State. He and Ed Smith, director of NOAH, a church planting agency in Northeast Ohio, along with Dick Crabtree, then senior minister at First Christian Church in Canton, attempted to start a campus ministry at Kent State. They tried Sunday meetings on campus, and met with a few students in the music and speech building. With the shootings on campus on May 4, 1970 no one from outside the campus was allowed to conduct activities, and their efforts were not renewed in the next year.[14]

It was a decade later, in May 1980 when Andy and Debbie Wade launched a full-time campus ministry at Kent State. A meeting was held at First Christian Church in Canton that month to launch the new effort. Andy and Debbie Wade had talked to the people in the student life office at Kent State, and had learned that there were very few ministries active on campus, and only one with evangelical roots. Campus Crusade had been on campus but had pulled out, so there was a real need. Andy and Debbie "plunged in" to meet that need. Debbie received a graduate assistantship in music, and the area churches pledged $240 per month (rent on their apartment was $260 per month!). Seeing the courage and commitment of this couple, several churches made commitments, and a steering committee was established. In 1984 the committee formed the nucleus of the board of directors.

The Wades had the names of ten interested students, and they began meeting on Wednesday nights in the student center for Bible study and prayer. They also began holding Sunday morning worship services in a nearby classroom, but it was sporadic in attendance because so many of the students were commuters and were gone on Sunday. The Bible study groups, however, went from five to fifteen in three weeks, and as a result of a study of the book of Acts, two students with Roman Catholic backgrounds were baptized.[15]

After an attempt to transport students to nearby churches for Sunday morning worship for a while, the on-campus Sunday morning worship service was resumed, and this has been a successful part of the program since. Andy says, "We are the only group that meet on Sunday mornings on campus; some students have invited their friends to our service. We are helped by our informal manner, our attitude of worship, our convenience for students in that they go to eat together after the services!"[16]

The group attends regular retreats and the first Friday of every month Andy and Debbie Wade have a fellowship dinner in their home. When students are asked what is the most important part of the program in this campus ministry they invariably say the fellowship dinners in the home of the campus minister and his wife. "Family group" Bible studies were begun in 1992 in addition to regular Thursday night Bible studies and fellowship and afternoon Bible study and prayer groups which meet during the week. Residence hall staff are required at Kent State to present programs on the floors twice a semester. Andy and Debbie submit topics for discussion to the Resident Assistants, and as a result they are often called on to present panel discussions or dialogue with students on various issues. Andy is also a residence hall chaplain designated to assist and counsel with staff and students. Service projects are just beginning at Kent State, with plans to visit Grundy Mountain Mission School. Andy says, writing in August of 1993,

> It is exciting to be in campus ministry. Last year was one of the best, if not the best yet. Our weekly participation since our ministry began has been slowly growing. We have had as few as ten and as high as thirty-seven. We usually average two baptisms a year. Our graduates are active in churches, and they serve as artists, engineers, physicians, nurses, teachers, nutritionists, therapists, psychologists, accountants, computer specialists, and professors. We are proud of them.[17]

And we are proud of Andy and Debbie Wade and their exciting ministry at Kent State!

## The Campus Ministries in the State of Arkansas

The first campus ministry in the state of Arkansas began in the early 1980s when the Ozark Area Men's Fellowship began laying the groundwork for a campus ministry at the University of Arkansas at Fayetteville. In August of 1982, Mike Armstrong was called as full-time campus minister. Mike was a graduate of Ozark Christian College, and he came to Fayetteville from serving as youth minister with the Community Christian Church in Fort Scott, Kansas, where Leon Weece was the minister. (Mike attributes his interest in campus ministry to visits to Fort Scott by Roy Weece, brother of Leon and veteran campus minister at the University of Missouri.)

There was no campus house in Fayetteville when the ministry began, so meetings were held in Mike Armstrong's apartment and university facilities. This ministry grew slowly but steadily with the program consisting of one large gathering each week for Bible study and worship in the Arkansas Union, two other smaller Bible studies weekly, an evangelism program, six week "Seminars in Christian Living," weekly visits to the local nursing home and to the county jail, and one-on-one small discipleship groups.[18] Spring break mission trips to Mexico began early in this ministry and later mission trips were taken to the inner-city of Atlanta, Georgia, and overseas to Glasgow, Scotland.

In 1985, a house near campus was leased which provided office space, a small meeting area, and housing for four to six students. This house served the ministry until 1992 when a larger house was purchased. Mike Armstrong enlarged the outreach of this ministry when he was called to be assistant chaplain to the athletic department of the university, and through his work with the Fellowship of Christian Athletes. In 1991, two staff persons were called, Laurie Ostad as associate campus minister, and Don Crockett as minister to international students. Don was called with the understanding that he would raise his own support.

The mood of college students in the early 1980s was well described by Mike Armstrong in the 1985 newsletter:

> Though you don't find the overt rebellion and sharp counter-culture that used to be equated with the university campus, there is still a philosophy and mind-set that dominates campus. Though it is more acceptable to our American culture, it is just as wrong when compared to godly standards. The common attitude on campus today is one of apathy to anything other than grades, material success, and taking care of one's self. The "god" of American campuses is not Jehovah, but it is the almighty dollar and students will devote themselves totally to its pursuit. Allegiance and commitment to Christ has been replaced by commitment to "success" and a devotion to it that crowds out all else. Love, concern, and ministry to others become losers to the drive to take care of one's self and to do what is best for me. Treasures in heaven are exchanged for the promise of high salaries and materialistic security. And though our society applauds such "industry," the Bible calls it "greed, which is idolatry." Our Christian witness is needed on campus![19]

This apathetic attitude on the part of students in general is effectively overcome through this campus ministry. Mike wrote of the growing involvement of students in missions and service trips in 1988:

> Those of you who have been interested observers of the Christ on Campus program over the last six and a half years will have noticed a growing emphasis on our part on mission and outreach. In Fayetteville it takes the form of reaching our "Jerusalem" (the U of A campus), and of reaching our "Judea and Samaria" (the local and surrounding community through our

work with the incarcerated, the handicapped, the elderly, the young, and the local churches). But you have also seen a growing involvement by our students in reaching the "ends of the earth." This has been evidenced through our five years of Spring Break trips to Mexico, through our regular financial support of missions, through our work with the Haystack Missions Conference, through the regular missions speakers that we have, and through taking students overseas to work on mission fields first hand.[20]

If asked why campus ministries should challenge students to become actively involved in missions rather than leaving such an emphasis to the Bible colleges, Mike gives four reasons:

1. To stretch students and to help them learn to be content with less than the typical United States lifestyle, and to realize how most of the world lives.
2. To prepare them for a lifetime of mission involvement.
3. To realize the call of God on them to enter mission work.
4. To be of practical service to dedicated workers across the world.[21]

These goals have been accomplished to a remarkable degree at the University of Arkansas where students have gone from "Atheists to missionaries, from drugs to evangelists."[22]

In 1984 the second campus ministry in the state of Arkansas began when Max Goins, minister from Marianna, began leading Bible studies at Arkansas State University at Jonesboro. In September 1984, Rick Dunn became the new minister at the University Christian Church in Jonesboro, and at the same time he began working as part-time campus minister at Arkansas State. With support and encouragement from the campus minister and the board of directors at Fayetteville, Rick was able to get this campus ministry under way, but in 1985, University Church had grown to the point that Rick's ministry there began to require full-time attention.

In the fall of 1985, Tim Anderson was called as full-time campus minister at Arkansas State. Tim was a graduate of Mid-South Christian College in Memphis, Tennessee and Cincinnati Bible Seminary, and he came to Jonesboro from Crestview Christian Church in Memphis where he had served as youth minister. Tim served this campus ministry for one year, and in August of 1986, a team ministry made up of ministers in the area took over at Jonesboro. This team served as campus ministers with Eldon Richardson as the coordinator until 1988 when Eldon left the ministry at Christian Valley Christian Church in Jonesboro to become full-time campus minister at Arkansas State.

Two strong programs marked Eldon's ministry on this campus, a weekly noon lunch and study every Tuesday, and special work with international students. Typical of this ministry was the international night (held in 1989). Eldon describes this event as follows:

One of the highlights of the year for ASU, the community of Jonesboro, and the students from around the world (forty-two countries) is International Night. This even was held March 31 in the Carl Reng Center Ballroom. The program included songs, instrumental music, dances (very different from modern America), and a very colorful cultural costume exhibition called "A Parade of Countries." Christ on Campus played a large part at the event.[23]

International students were also served in a practical way through he gift of ten pounds of rice to any needy student. In 1990, Eldon and Fran Richardson served Thanksgiving dinner for thirty-five international students in their home.[24]

Financial support for the campus ministry at Arkansas State was not adequate, and in 1990, Eldon Richardson requested permission to seek employment outside of the campus ministry. In May of 1993, Eldon and Fran Richardson resigned this campus ministry.

In August of 1993 Don Crockett left his work with international students at the University of Arkansas and became the campus minister at Arkansas State at Jonesboro. A campus house was rented as a location for the ministry and as a residence for Don. A program of weekly Bible study in the house, one-on-one Bible studies, and mission trips to the inner-city of Memphis, Tennessee and to Mexico are the heart of the program.

At the time of the tenth anniversary of this campus ministry, the ten years could be summed up as follows:

We now have four full-time campus ministers serving on two campuses! We have witnessed one hundred forty-three people baptized into Christ from five different continents! Some of these have returned to their own countries and have introduced others to Jesus! We have had one hundred eleven students involved in life changing short-term mission opportunities! We have ministered to hundreds of students from dozens of nations on four different campuses! Christ on Campus alumni are serving Christ in many facets in churches across the country and around the world![25]

The eleven years of campus ministry in the state of Arkansas were summed up by Mike Armstrong in May of 1993 under the heading "What a Year!":

Some of the things that God has done this year are obvious things. Maybe the most obvious is the way He has supplied us with a new campus house for the ministry at the U of A and the funds to purchase and remodel it. How thrilling it has been to see God answer our prayers and God's people respond so generously! God has done other obvious things, as well. He has brought more students than ever through our doors and under the influence of the gospel through the Christ on Campus ministries at the U of A and ASU. Over the past year, almost three hundred students from at least thirteen countries have been exposed to Jesus through the Christ on

Campus ministry — plus those who have been taught from His Word by the over forty students who have taken part in ministries in jails, in nursing homes, in churches around the state, and other places around the world. Through our campus and jail ministries, over sixty people have been baptized into Christ this year. There were sixteen who went to serve in Mexico over Spring Break and there will be five from Christ on Campus serving the Lord in foreign missions this summer. God has also done some things that are not as obvious. Even though they are not as easily observed, they are still eternally significant. These are the changes in students' hearts, values, and commitments. These changes are seen through their sacrifice, witness, and vision. You observe these changes in hearing students talk of sharing Christ with their classmates, in seeing them meet the needs of their Christian brothers and sisters, and in watching as they come to grips with the implications of the gospel. In ways that are obvious and not so obvious, God has been working. What a thrill to be at a place where you can watch it happen![26]

# Wittenberg University, Springfield, Ohio

The campus ministry at Wittenberg University in Springfield, Ohio began in 1982. It grew out of the House Christian Fellowship, a renewal congregation in Springfield led by Grant Edwards and Mark Elliott.

Edward Korver is the campus minister, and most of the activities center around the two houses which are residences, one for men and one for women. The official name of the organization is Salt House, and it was founded to serve students at Wittenberg first as a lighthouse to reach out to students with the love of Jesus Christ and to develop people with hearts for God, and second, an off-campus haven or refuge where students can get away, relax, and hang out. A third purpose is to have fun and provide great social alternatives for students.

Salt House sponsors student-led small group Bible studies. These are activities in which students say they grow the most. In a personal and caring way, small groups focus on making the Bible come alive, seeing its relevance in all of life.

Every Sunday evening at 6:00 p.m. at the Salt House you will find a crowd of students enjoying a delicious cooked meal. This is a great time to catch up with friends or make new ones.

During the winter term, Salt House offers a nine week, intensive training class. Videos and live speakers challenge students to grow deeper in their Christian life. The school concludes with a Spring Break outreach to places like Mexico, England, and Canada.

Ed Korver summarizes the campus ministry at Wittenberg by emphasizing the importance of relationships. He points out that relationships are vitally important — "relationships with each other, relationships with God, and relationships with ourselves. To know that we are loved and accepted is our greatest need, and this campus ministry aims to reach out to the students of the university with that kind of love."

# Arizona State University, Tempe

The Arizona Evangelistic Association was the parent organization for the campus ministry at Arizona State University at Tempe. Mark Hollenbach, who had been converted by Jerry Gibson at the University of Illinois through Jerry's ministry with the University of Illinois football team, was called as the first campus minister in July 1983.

After careful preparations, and the formation of an advisory board to assist the work, the actual campus ministry began with meetings in the Memorial Union — one in the daytime for commuter students and one in the evening for residential students. By the spring semester of 1984 daytime meetings were discontinued, and the evening meetings were reaching twenty-five students.

In the fall semester of 1984 an International Student Host Family Program was initiated through the International Student Office at ASU, and in conjunction with Central Christian Church in Mesa, Arizona. Many international students were taken into homes in the area and befriended. In the spring semester of 1985 a campus house was leased in conjunction with First Christian Church in Tempe, and this house provided housing for female students as well as a convenient meeting place. Twenty students were involved during that semester.

In the summer of 1985 Mark Hollenbach was made a staff member at Central Christian Church in Mesa, Arizona, with responsibility for both the ASU ministry and the college-age ministry at Central Christian Church. In August of 1986 Mark became President of the Interfaith Council at ASU. He continued to minister to students on campus and to the college-age people at Central up until December of 1989. Slowly the group at Central became more the center of the ministry, and in May of 1990 the youth ministry department at Central incorporated all college ministries under their umbrella. Cal Jernigan took over the group at Central in 1990, and in January 1991, Dean Kuest became the college-age minister. At this writing an average of ninety meet every Sunday.

# Florida Atlantic University at Boca Raton

Florida Atlantic University in Boca Raton, Florida, which is about forty miles north of Miami on the "Gold Coast," had approximately 9,000 students in 1982. Paul Bledsoe and some visionary members of First Christian Church of Boca Raton saw the need for a campus ministry at FAU, and in 1982 they began to work toward that end. Paul Bledsoe had graduated from Florida Atlantic University with a Bachelor of Arts in Music in 1980, after which he entered Cincinnati Christian Seminary, receiving a Master of Ministry degree from there in 1982. He served as a ministerial intern in his own church, the First Christian Church in Boca Raton, in 1981, working with singles and college students. In the fall of 1982 Paul, now committed to campus ministry, spent five weeks working as an intern with Thom Miller at Florida State University.[27] In January of 1983 Paul was called to serve his home church as music minister, minister to singles, and part-time campus minister at Florida Atlantic University. From November 1982 until April 1983 Paul made an intensive study of the campus at Florida Atlantic University, his old alma mater. He also spoke in area churches in behalf of campus ministry, formed a board of directors made up of interested men from First Christian Church, and gathered a strong core group of committed students as a basis for launching the "on campus" phase of this ministry in the summer of 1983.

In the spring of 1983 this campus ministry was incorporated by the state of Florida, and was also accepted as an official student organization by the university. FAUND (Florida Atlantic University, New Disciples) was under way. Paul attended the annual campus ministers retreat at Spencer, Indiana, in May of 1983, where he met active campus ministers from all over the country. He writes of this crucial experience:

> This yearly gathering of campus ministers from across the United States was richly rewarding. There, for three days, with others having vast experience with student ministries, I was able to listen, learn, form opinions, and bounce ideas off of others wiser than myself. Lasting friendships, filled with brotherly council was formed with distinguished men in campus ministry — Larry Brandon, Roy Weece, Ward Patterson, Doug Dickey, and Tim Hudson. As I returned to Boca Raton from this "mountain top" experience, I had a clear vision and a resolute mind toward the mission God was leading me into.[28]

In May of 1983 a banquet was held at First Christian Church, which is located immediately adjacent to the FAU campus, to inform interested people and to solicit prayers and financial support for this emerging ministry. Forty-five people attended, and this encouraged Paul and his board to go ahead with their plans for this ministry.

The summer of 1983 was a time of careful preparation. Paul met administrators at the university, acquired information on alumni, and obtained permission to use university facilities for meetings. A Sunday night supper, with a free meal, was held at the church and the gathering was announced as "Sinners, Saints, and Skeptic-Student Suppers." Twelve to twenty students attended this supper throughout the summer, and those attending were encouraged to stay for the evening worship service at the church.

Contact was made that summer also with the United Campus Ministry on campus, and this "umbrella" organization included FAUND in their brochure and directed students to FAUND meetings.[29] The "break-through" in making FAUND known on campus, however, came in August of 1983. A "kick-off" introducing campus organizations to new students was held on campus. Paul and his leaders borrowed an idea from Thom Miller at Florida State, and they prepared a free "Student Survival Kit" for distribution. Each kit included notebooks, pens, cookies, toiletries, FAUND flyers, and calendars along with NIV New Testaments with the FAUND address stamped on the front. Paul writes of this distribution:

> While many other campus organizations were showcased, our group made a resounding impact because of our free give away. During the full two hours of exhibit time we were able to give away two hundred fifty of the kits and we signed up approximately twenty students for follow-up. This was considered a smashing success and a great way to kick-off our fall program.[30]

Through careful preparation, hard work, and prayer, Paul Bledsoe and his core students, with the support of First Christian Church, launched a well planned and effective campus ministry on the campus of Florida Atlantic University in the fall of 1984. The Sunday night suppers were continued, and "Bible Rap Sessions" were added on Tuesdays at 7:00 p.m. for study, fellowship, and recreation. "D" Groups, small groups committed to intensive discipleship training, were also added. A state-wide college-career retreat, sponsored jointly by FAUND and the campus ministry at Florida State, was held in the fall of 1984 at Camp Biblia in Cocoa, Florida, a central locale for the state. Thirty-seven people attended and twenty of them were from FAUND. At the close of the 1983–84 school year Paul Bledsoe was still part-time campus minister at FAU. He wore two other "hats" — music minister and minister to singles at First Christian Church. He expressed some frustration about this situation, since the campus ministry was growing into a full-time ministry but only had part-time leadership. He also faced a situation which other campus ministers have faced. Since the campus ministry at Florida Atlantic University was founded and led by a board of directors made up of members from First Christian Church, there was a tendency among the other churches in Florida to think of this campus ministry as a project of First Christian; therefore, many of them saw no need to support it.

In this connection we have noted before the opinion expressed by John McCaw, an early leader in Disciple campus ministries, that "no longer can any individual congregation be expected to take full responsibility for campus ministry on a college or university campus, partly because the responsibility of ministering to specialized university constituency which ebbs and flows with each academic year is extremely difficult and also because it is virtually impossible for one church to underwrite with its limited resources ministry to several hundred, sometimes several thousand, students through a single local congregation."[31]

Some of the frustrations felt by Paul Bledsoe were partially resolved when in 1985 he became full-time campus minister at FAU, and other churches began supporting this growing campus ministry. By 1988 when Paul left this ministry to accept a position as singles minister with the Chapel Rock Christian Church in Indianapolis, Indiana, the campus ministry at Florida Atlantic University was firmly established. More than fifty different people were attending at least one FAUND function each semester and they had a choice among the following events: on campus Bible lectures, prayer and praise services, study breaks with free food on campus for students during exam week, birthday parties for basketball players, two monthly fellowship dinners, and regular area retreats.[32]

After Paul Bledsoe departed, Amos Renner served as campus minister for two months, and Jim Greenwood, a long time supporter of this campus ministry, served as campus minister from January 1989 until August of that year when Tim Benham became campus minister. Tim serves in this capacity at Florida Atlantic University at this writing.

Tim Benham and his wife Cathy came to FAU from Indiana University in Bloomington, Indiana, where he received a Bachelor of Arts degree in the Classics. In May of 1989 he earned his Master's degree in Comparative Literature from Florida Atlantic University, and later received his Master of Divinity degree from Cincinnati Bible Seminary. By the fall of 1992, FAUND under Tim Benham's leadership had an extensive program on the campus. Since Florida Atlantic University is a commuter campus, and since religious groups are not permitted to do direct solicitation on campus or in the dorms, contacting students is a serious problem. FAUND solved this problem by "working the Breezeway":

> We are allowed to set up an exhibit in what is called the "breezeway" — a long, covered walkway through which most of the students pass between classes. We can display our materials here only twice a week, taking every third week off. It is here that FAUND meets most of the students who will participate in the Bible studies. These students will then pass the word along to their friends and neighbors.[33]

Through this contact with students, and through Tuesday and Wednesday Bible studies at the university center, Thursday evening fellowship hour, the university praise service at 5:00 p.m. on Sunday in the campus courtyard, and through intense work with international students, Tim Benham was able to report in the fall of 1992 as follows:

> FAUND Facts:
> *Over 2,000 different students have attended a FAUND function.
> *Over 40 different countries have been represented by FAUND students.
> *FAUND has held over 800 Bible studies during its past nine years of existence.[34]

From the very beginning days of the campus ministry, before Paul Beldsoe became full-time in 1985, Emily Nowselski became administrative director. Emily has served continuously from the beginning in this important capacity and has been a very vital part of this growing and significant campus ministry at Florida Atlantic University. The future looks bright for this campus ministry in Florida, and for other possible ministries in the state of Florida as the goal of FAUND is also to reach out to establish other campus ministries on other campuses.[35]

## Campus Ministries in the State of Pennsylvania

One of the ironies of the Restoration Movement is that the part of the country where it originated has in some ways been the area of its slowest growth. Christian churches are not numerous in the Northeastern United States, and campus ministry was slow to move into that part of the country.

The first full-time campus ministry in the state of Pennsylvania was established in 1983 at Penn State University at University Park.[36] In the spring of that year William "Buzz" Roberts and his wife Betty, who had been serving as ministers of youth in the Lycoming Christian Church at Linden, Pennsylvania for ten years, approached the elders of the State College Christian Church with a proposal to establish a Christian fellowship at Penn State. By 1984 a "parent" organization was formed, the Christian Student Foundation of Pennsylvania, CSFPA, with the purpose, not only of supporting campus ministry at Penn State, but also establishing campus ministries among as many of the 208 colleges and universities in the state as possible.

Buzz Roberts, along with working to establish the CSFPA, worked with university officials at the office of Religious Affairs at Penn State, and in September of 1983 the Christian Student Fellowship at Penn State was granted the status of a recognized student organization.[37] Along with the recognition of the group they were given rent free office space in the Eisenhower Chapel on the university campus.

The organization of the campus ministry was further refined with the establishment of a regional board of directors, made up of church leaders from the area, to oversee the ministry at Penn State while the board of governors of the foundation of the "parent" organization were committed to establishing campus ministries in other parts of the state as feasible.

The campus ministry at Penn State grew from six students at the beginning to more than seventy by 1987. By then the Penn State ministry was sufficiently established for the foundation to begin a second campus ministry in Pennsylvania.

Preparation for the Christian Student Fellowship at the University of Pittsburgh and Carnegie-Mellon University began in 1984. Noting the success of the campus ministry at Penn State, several students from the University of Pittsburgh along with the churches in the area made a request to the CSFPA board to consider establishing a fellowship at Pittsburgh and Carnegie-Mellon in 1985. After two years of careful preparation, the foundation board called Sam and Sherrie Brunsvold to be campus ministers there in the fall of 1987.[38]

Sam Brunsvold and his wife Sherrie were active in the campus ministry at Eastern Illinois University while they were students there. Sam majored in business at Eastern, then went to Lincoln Christian Seminary where he received a Master of Divinity degree in philosophy and theology. It was these two experiences to which Sam attributed his passion for campus ministry. At Eastern he had a broad liberal arts education, and practical emphasis on the "how-to" with campus ministry, and at Lincoln he studied under Dr. James Strauss, gaining an understanding of how great movements of thought impact the world.[39]

Office space for this campus ministry was provided by Central Christian Church in Pittsburgh, and the group worshiped with that congregation on Sunday mornings. The student union at the University of Pittsburgh and other locations on campus were used for other meetings. Friday fellowship meeting with singing, teaching, prayer, and recreation afterwards have been the heart of the program at Pittsburgh and Carnegie-Mellon. Prayer partners, regular recreation, and fall and winter retreats are also important parts of the program. Alternating nine week seminars are offered in the spring, one on "How to Study the Bible" and the other on "The Making of the Christian Mind." The intent of these seminars is to lay a foundation for students to integrate their faith, thought, and career. One of the innovative aspects of the program under Sam has been a ministry to graduate students. By the spring of 1993, twenty-four different people were meeting on a weeknight for supper, Bible study, and prayer. Also in 1993, a special study for international students was begun, including students from India, Germany, Korea, and South Africa. Sam says of these people, "Several are exploring Christianity seriously for the first time. They ask challenging questions that cut through some of the shallow views or inconsistent ways Americans live."[40]

The third campus ministry in Pennsylvania was established in 1989 at Bloomsburg University. A group of students attending Bloomsburg and Penn State Hazelton campus had friends attending the Christian Student Fellowship at Penn State, and they requested the foundation board of directors to help found a campus ministry at Bloomsburg. Much of the general work of organization was done by the students attending Bloomsburg, and in the summer of 1987 Jeff and Terri Jackson were called as full-time campus ministers.[41] Jeff Jackson attended Bowling Green State University in Ohio majoring in philosophy and computer science. He was active in the campus ministry there, and met his wife in that fellowship. After graduating from Bowling Green, Jeff earned a Masters degree in Old Testament from Emmanuel School of Religion. The center of the program at Bloomsburg is the Tuesday night Bible study/fellowship meetings. Small Bible studies for men and women were initiated in 1993, and group Bible studies covering all of the Old Testament books were also offered that same year. The group emphasized recreation along with serious worship and study.

All three of the campus ministries in Pennsylvania are led by campus ministers, students, and board members who are strongly motivated by a deep conviction about the importance of campus ministry. These convictions are summarized by a statement in a brochure published in 1989:

> College years are testing years for many students. More major decisions are made during these years than any other time. Tomorrow's leaders in business, education, government, science, and many other walks of life are trained today at the 208 different universities and colleges across the Commonwealth of Pennsylvania. It is imperative that the Gospel of Jesus Christ be proclaimed to those who will be the future leaders of our nation and the world. Therefore, the college campus is indeed a crucial mission field. Many students from different religious and non-religious backgrounds are searching for Biblically based Christian faith and fellowship. The fields are white unto harvest on the college campus. God desires that we tell His Good News there. From the campus His story can be taken to their hometowns, states, countries, and the world.[42]

By the summer of 1993, this aggressive campus ministry was making plans to establish a fourth campus ministry in Pennsylvania at Indiana University in Indiana, Pennsylvania, a campus of approximately 18,000 students.

The Restoration Movement is being strengthened in the "Campbell Country" of Pennsylvania as God uses these dedicated people to minister to the college and university campus in that state. Buzz Roberts deserves a great deal of credit for his vision and courageous action to initiate these campus ministries.

# University of Iowa at Iowa City

Dennis Hall, with the support of the University Christian Church in Coralville, Iowa, founded the campus ministry at the University of Iowa in June of 1985.

Dennis came to Iowa City as a veteran campus minister, having served at Northeast Missouri State University at Kirksville for three years, and as campus minister at Iowa State University at Ames for six years. He is a graduate of Ozark Bible College, and he served as a missionary intern in the Philippines while in college.

The University of Iowa, one of the most influential universities in the nation, was without a full-time campus ministry supported by Christian Churches until Dennis, with considerable courage and a lot of faith, moved his family to Iowa City in the summer of 1985 and with enthusiastic support from the leaders of University Christian Church, pioneered this campus ministry. There is no campus house for this group, named Active Christians Today (ACT, after the campus ministry at Bowling Green, Ohio). In the beginning space was rented in the Wesley Foundation Campus Ministry Center, which is less than one block from the main campus. Two other facilities were rented by this campus ministry until they arrived at their present location at 20 E. Market St. in "Old Brick."

The basic program at Iowa City has four facets: 1) Adoration, to provide experiences of worship, 2) Community, to provide Christ-centered activities, 3) Teaching, to provide Bible-based knowledge, and 4) Prayer, to seek, save, and teach. These objectives are met through a Sunday evening service of worship, regular recreational activities, along with regular Bible study groups and guest teachers. In the Spring semester of 1987 several guest speakers spoke for the group.

> Rodney Weline, in the doctoral program of the UI school of Religion, spoke on "In God's Image." Gene Harker, working on his Ph.D. in counseling, presented "Remedy For Worry." David Arbogast, graduate of Columbia University and an Architectural Conservator, covered "Churches and Cults."[43]

Dr. David McSpadden also spoke on "Single By Choice," and after his address he wrote to Dennis Hall as follows:

> I praise God for your continued faithfulness in your community. It was a privilege to fellowship with you during last weekend. You have a quality group. I believe your ministry at the campus to be on the cutting edge of our society and encourage you to "keep the Faith, Baby."[44]

Missions and ministry to international students are part of the program at ACT as well, including regular work trips being made to the children's home in Mexico City, for example.

The most unique aspect of Dennis Hall's ministry at the University of Iowa, however, is his ministry through athletics. In 1990, he began a program called AIM, Athletes Interest Ministry, through which the ministry sponsors athletic teams with Christ as the center. In the winter of 1993 over ninety students, faculty, and young adults were involved in several different athletic teams. Dennis wrote a rationale for this approach to campus ministry for a class at Lincoln Christian Seminary in 1991 in which he argues that Christ centered athletic teams provide a cultural bridge for the gospel to reach secular university students.[45]

Through prayer, hard work, and imaginative approach, Dennis Hall has established a viable campus ministry at the University of Iowa.

# Tri-State University in Angola, Indiana

The Disciples founded a Bible Chair at Tri-State University in Angola, Indiana, in the late 1920s. It was hugely successful in reaching students — at one point is was reported that "over two hundred young people went into full-time Christian service as a result of the Angola project."[46] Apparently this work languished over the years until 1985 when Gary Hawes and his people in Michigan, along with ministers from Christian churches in the Tri-State area and university administrators, "sought to meet the spiritual needs of students, by founding Tri-State Christian Fellowship."[47]

In January of 1986 Reggie Reed, minister at the Metz Christian Church in rural Angola, was called as part-time campus minister. Reggie served for two years, and in late 1987 the board of directors called Dennis Steckley from the University of West Virginia where he had served as campus minister for seven years. Dennis served as part-time campus minister for one year while also holding the position of Assistant Dean and Residence Hall Director at the university.

In early 1989 Howard Bloomquist, minister at Pleasant View Church of Christ in Angola, began serving as part-time campus minister. During Howard's two year term of service two campus houses were purchased, both within a block of the university library and across the street from the major campus. In August of 1990 Mike Hamm, youth minister with the Angola Christian Church, began as part-time campus minister with the TSCF, and he serves in that capacity at this writing.[48]

On Tuesday evenings twenty-five to thirty students meet in the campus house for a home-cooked meal and Bible study. Groups from the area Christian churches provide the meal on a rotating basis, which not only serves the students but keeps the area churches well informed of the excitement generated by the campus ministry on this campus. Some of the topics dealt with in these Tuesday night meetings have been: "Relationships: The Good, The Bad, and the Ugly," "The MATE Race — Dating Standards," and "Job Descriptions for Christians."

A recent testimony by a Tri-State student indicates the strength of this campus ministry. He wrote as follows:

> Tri-State Christian Fellowship has shown me more love and encouragement than I have ever felt. My fellow students show me that I am not alone in my belief in the Lord. They also show me that I do not have to give in to this world. The supporting churches show me that others care. Mike Hamm, the campus coordinator, brings out God's word. There is nothing as encouraging as hearing God's word and how it pertains to your life.[49]

It is good to know that a campus on which one of the original Bible Chairs was founded has now resumed an active and fruitful campus ministry.

# Ferris State University in Big Rapids, Michigan

The "Michigan Miracle" continued in the late 1980s as the sixth full-time campus ministry in the state of Michigan was established at Ferris State University in Big Rapids in September of 1987.

Following a familiar patter in Michigan, Gary Hawes, Executive Director of Michigan Christian Campus Ministries based in East Lansing, served as the first campus minister at Ferris State, assisted by other staff of MCCM who spent part of the day each week on the campus. Gary was more than ably assisted in this new ministry by Jane Nabor, who moved to Big Rapids in 1987 to serve as full-time campus coordinator. Jane had served in the same capacity for four years at Lake Superior State University in Sault Ste Marie, Michigan.[50]

This campus ministry grew more rapidly than was expected. Fifty-two people attended the first public meeting, and within six months, four students had been baptized and two urgent needs began to emerge: the need for the campus house, since every suitable room on campus was being outgrown, and the need for a full-time campus minister sooner than originally projected.[51]

By July of 1989 Gary Hawes was able to report as follows:

I am so excited as I consider what God is accomplishing through the Campus Ministry at Ferris State University. In less than two years, the ministry there has grown far beyond our expectations. Hundreds of students have been exposed to the Gospel message, and our meetings average more than fifty people each week on campus. We have had as many as a dozen international students in a single meeting. Twenty students have been baptized as a result of their involvement in the Campus Ministry at Ferris. Praise God![52]

An ideal house located one block from campus became available in the summer of 1989, and by the fall of that year enough money had been contributed toward the $59,000 purchase price so that it could be bought with only a $25,000 mortgage. The house at 526 South Michigan had room for student housing, office and study space for the campus minister, and meeting space for prayer and Bible study groups.[53]

The second imperative need, a full-time campus minister, was met in August of 1989 when Alan Bilinski was called as campus minister. Alan had been deeply involved in campus ministry while a student at Central Michigan University. He graduated from there in 1985 and worked as a district representative for the Boys Scouts of America from 1985 until

1988, when he began a year's internship with John Sowash, campus minister at the University of Michigan.[54] By the time of the MCCM annual report in August 1991, Alan could report as follows on the immediate past year at Ferris State:

> We are thrilled to have baptized eleven people into Jesus Christ. Eighteen people were involved with student accountability groups. Three FSU students served as student missionaries in Hungary for a year. Two FSU alumni served in campus ministry internships with MCCM. We established a walleyball ministry on Friday nights — a Christian alternative to the bars.[55]

In 1990 the Michigan Christian Campus Ministries was moving to establish campus ministries in China and the Philippines, an amazing expansion of the "Michigan Miracle."

# Georgia Tech, Atlanta

The Christian Campus Fellowship at Georgia Tech began in 1987 when Rick Harper and his wife Beth started the ministry "from scratch" with four students.

Rick is a graduate from the University of Georgia in management, and he was active in the campus ministry while he was a student there. He went on to Emmanuel School of Religion where he received the M.A. in religion in 1987. He credits his year of internship under Tom Miller, campus minister at Florida State, as "most helpful" in his preparation for campus ministry.

University facilities provided meeting places for this fellowship until 1989 when a house near campus was rented, later purchased in 1992. That same year another house was purchased next door to the original one, and was renovated to provide housing for six students. By 1993 this campus ministry had grown from four students in 1987 to 85 students in 1992, to 185 students in 1993, 100 of them being new students so that larger facilities were desperately needed. The board of directors, which had been formed from representatives of supporting churches during the first year of this campus ministry, in 1993 approved a two year campaign to raise $415,000 to build a *Matthew C. Farmer Fellowship Hall*. The building will include six bedrooms, office space, kitchen and kitchenette, and meeting rooms for 200 people.[56]

What has generated such phenomenal growth in this campus ministry? How have Rick Harper and his wife and their associates made themselves available to God's purpose to reach college students is such a remarkable way? A careful study of the program at Georgia Tech indicates that the key to growth is the development of active, responsible student leadership.

Rick says, "CCF is a firm believer that the purpose of campus ministry is to develop leaders for the church and society in the years to come. In order to accomplish this objective, CCF has four leadership teams."[57] The results of this emphasis upon leadership has not only produced strong leaders in the campus ministry at Georgia Tech, it has also sent out leaders into the world. "Currently five CCF graduates are in seminary planning to enter some form of ministry in the future, with many others having such plans for after graduation. CCF believes that the world needs leaders in every realm of society. Over one hundred alumni are serving the Lord in thirteen different states, in churches, business, and homes. All CCF have chosen to be involved in full-time Christian work ranging from campus ministers to missionaries. CCF is making a worldwide impact."[58]

Rick Harper is assisted at Georgia Tech by Paul Zook, associate campus minister, hired in 1992. Paul is a graduate of Georgia Tech and is presently attending Emmanuel School of Religion. Three interns, all former Georgia Tech students, will be working with the fellowship in 1993. They are Jonathan Powell, Greg Coley, and David Tulley.

Weekly activities begin with Sunday morning worship at Southeast Christian Church in East Point, Georgia, a congregation which has been a strong supporter of this campus ministry, and a worship and prayer time at the CCF house on Sundays at 6:00 p.m. On Monday from 11:00-1:00 a devotional lunch is provided at the campus house. This is a key part of the program in reaching new students. Rich says of these luncheons:

> I believe the key to growth is to provide activities that encourage new student involvement. At the University of Georgia where I attended (1979-1983) I noticed that a large number of students slipped through the cracks because Bible study was intimidating to first time students. I use luncheons as a type of Minor League system which feeds Bible study. For these fellowship opportunities give them a chance to feel part of the group then they enjoy Bible study and become involved as part of my core group.[59]

Every other Tuesday at 5:30 p.m. a "Roundtable" is held. A light dinner is provided free of charge, and a guest speaker is invited to speak on a relevant topic (recent topics — career choice and decision making). Prayer time is scheduled on Monday at 3:30 p.m., and the "Two-for-Two" are dorm Bible studies led by students. In 1993, fifty students have been involved in this program. The name "Two-for-Two" comes from Acts 2:42.[60] Mentorships, one-on-one meetings between staff and student leaders, "jam sessions," three person groups that meet each week to discuss various scriptures, and leadership group meetings with staff members are all held at various times. Special activities include "Feeding Frenzy," the first Thursday of each month, a theme party once each quarter, four retreats a year, two leadership retreats a year, and attendance at the National Leadership Conference every summer, plus intramural sports during the year. The strength of the alumni of this campus ministry is indicated by the "Alumni One Percent Club," a plan for 50% of the total budget of this campus ministry to be provided by alumni in ten years, and total support in twenty years. This plan would mean that this campus ministry would not be dependent upon the churches for any financial support in twenty years.

In studying this campus ministry one is impressed with the way God has used Rick Harper's commitment and enthusiasm for campus ministry to build this remarkable ministry at Georgia Tech. Rick says:

> Each week I am invigorated and challenged as I spend time with the young people of CCF. Hearing their struggles and heartaches along with their victories takes up most of my days. I remember the words of the late Matt Farmer who served as Chairman of the Board, "Relationships Mean Everything." And so they do.[61]

# Northern Illinois University at DeKalb

After Darrell Malcom left DeKalb in 1983, the campus ministry at Northern Illinois University languished somewhat. Rob Gray, a former student at Northern, became part-time campus minister in 1982, and during his tenure, the Christian Campus Ministry was incorporated, received university recognition, and came under the oversight of a board of directors. In 1988, Rob Gray became the full-time campus minister and served for one year.

Scott Stocking became the full-time campus minister in 1989 and serves in that capacity at this writing. Scott graduated from the University of Nebraska in Omaha, with a degree in psychology and religion, and completed seventy hours of work towards a master of divinity degree at Lincoln Christian Seminary. He also was active in the campus ministry at the University of Nebraska in Lincoln while Bob Milliken and James Sennett were campus ministers there. He counts this latter experience as his best preparation for campus ministry.[62]

This campus ministry had functioned without a campus house from its inception in 1963, but in 1990 a house with high visibility across from the university student center was leased. The house served well as head-quarters for ministry until February of 1993 when failure to enlist enough residents to pay the lease caused the board of directors to cancel the lease for the 1993–94 school year. Moving meetings to facilities on campus, Scott says, "will give us larger areas to meet in. This will help foster more student involvement and growth in numbers. We are excited about the new opportunities for ministry and outreach this change will bring."[63]

Each year this campus ministry sponsors a Bible Reading Marathon. Scott wrote about this event, which he says has been "a boom for recruitment."[64]

A spring break trip to Mexico to work with AMOR Ministries in building houses is a regular event. It has not only served the Mexican people, but it has been a growing experience for the students who participated.[65]

In a letter written to supporters of the ministry in February of 1993, Scott Stocking called attention to two kinds of warfare the ministry was engaged in on campus. One was the increasing pressure on Christian groups from the homosexual community accusing Christians of hate and bigotry, in spite of their efforts to demonstrate love and the truth of Christ.[66]

In February 1993 Scott Stocking compared the growing pressure on Christian groups on the university campuses with the situation the church faced in ancient Rome:

> In ancient Rome, Christians were not persecuted because they believed in God — Rome was very tolerant of a vast number of religions and cults. Christians were persecuted because they worshipped God only. They refused to acknowledge the Caesar as "Lord God Almighty" and paid for it with their lives. . . . Today, we have a new Caesar, *Caesar Politicus Correctus*. On campuses across the nation, as well as in the political arena, Political Correctness has become the litmus test for social righteousness and acceptance. Those who proclaim *Caesar Politicus Correctus* as Lord are readily accepted and considered "normal" or "moral." Those who refuse to bow down to this new Caesar are automatically branded as bigots, racists, sexists, and ignorant. . . . CCM is reaching out to those who persecute us, showing them the love and compassion of Christ. Pray for a softening of their hearts that they might receive Christ. Pray that we might declare the Word of God fearlessly.[67]

The external warfare faced by this campus ministry at Northern Illinois is compounded by the internal battle — lack of financial support. This courageous and committed campus ministry, having struggled for several years, was finally closed down in the summer of 1994 because of lack of financial support from the churches. There are other campus ministries reported in this book which are handicapped by lack of financial support, but the campus ministry at Northern Illinois seems to typify the situation in a particularly tragic way. *One of the primary questions facing the campus ministry in the 1990s and beyond is the question of financial support.* Will churches in the brotherhood recognize the importance of campus ministry in the Kingdom of God, and support it so that it might do its exciting and unusual work? We will take this matter up in the next chapter.

# Vincennes University, Indiana

Vincennes University at Vincennes, Indiana is a two-year school which enrolls about 8,000 students. The campus ministry began there in 1989 as an outgrowth of the college Sunday School class at the Franklin Heights

Christian Church. The first meetings were held in the home of Frank and Leasa Frye. Cliff Healy was the first campus minister. Cliff was part-time campus minister from August 1991 to July 1992, and Alan Scott was part-time campus minister from August 1992 to May 1993.

Scott Shipman, minister of the Calhoun Christian Church in Calhoun, Illinois, became part-time campus minister at Vincennes in June of 1993. The headquarters of the ministry is a campus house which houses male students and is the location of a Tuesday night Bible study attended by about twenty-five students. A larger group of about fifty attend a Thursday night worship service which is held in the chapel on the campus of the university.

Mission trips include service in the Midwest flood area in the summer of 1993, and regular visits to the Christian Children's Home in Oblong, Illinois. Eight students have gone to Bible college from this campus ministry at both Cincinnati Bible Seminary and Lincoln Christian College during 1993. This is an effective and growing campus ministry at this small college in Indiana.

## Montana State University, Bozeman

The campus ministry at Montana State University at Bozeman began in 1989. Mark Feasline is the campus minister. The program includes Monday night meetings dealing with topics that are designed to attract non-Christians. Recent topics have been creation and evolution, history, politics, and Biblical topics.

On Friday evenings the group meets together for Bible study, singing, and prayer. Small group Bible studies are also organized in as many areas of the campus as possible.[68]

## Eastern Kentucky University at Richmond

The campus ministry at Eastern Kentucky University began in 1968, with Larry Brandon as the first campus minister and the Big Hill Avenue Christian Church as the sponsoring group. Joe Whitaker became campus minister early on and he served part-time until 1989.

Rob Newman was a student at Eastern in 1975 when he came in contact with the Christian Student Fellowship. When Joe Whitaker left the leadership of the group in 1989 Rob became the part-time campus minister. He is an insurance agent full-time, but serves as campus minister as an outreach of Big Hill Avenue Christian Church in Richmond where he serves as an elder.

Considering the part-time nature of the leadership of this campus ministry, it has a very active program, reaching 100–150 students each semester. On Sunday a Bible study is held in Burnham Hall on campus at

9:30 a.m. and transportation is then provided to Big Hill Avenue Christian Church for morning worship. On Wednesday evening at 7:00 p.m. the students gather at the Daniel Boone statue on campus where the church van picks them up and takes them to Christian homes in the community for "CSF Meeting" in which they share fellowship, devotions, and refreshments. Regular visits are made by the students to Willis Manor, a retirement home, and on Friday evening they "meet at the statue" for various social activities. The CSF sponsors concerts by contemporary Christian artists each semester, a hayride, and fall and spring retreats are regular parts of the program.[69]

# SPECIALIZED MINISTRIES TO COLLEGE-AGE YOUNG PEOPLE WHICH BEGAN IN THE 1980'S

There were some atypical ministries to college-age students which began in the 1980s which do not fit the traditional pattern. Three of them were: the college-career ministry at Eastview Christian Church in Bloomington, Illinois; the college-career ministry at Eastside Christian Church in Fullerton, California; and the academic classes at the University of California at Los Angeles sponsored by Westwood Foundation.

## The College-Career Ministry at Eastview Christian Church in Bloomington, Illinois

The Eastview Christian Church in Bloomington, Illinois, has had a strong ministry to college-age students throughout its history. (see Chapter Four, pp. 88-90) In May of 1988 it took a definite surge forward in this aspect of its ministry.

Ken Osness, a student at Pacific Christian College, was called as Young Adult Minister in May of 1988, succeeding Darrell Sloniger, who had been minister to fifty to seventy-five of this age group for several years. After Ken Osness arrived he spent a few months in study and preparation, and in the fall of 1988 separate worship services were begun for the college-career people, and this age group was "targeted" to be ministered to in specialized ways. Gary York, Senior Minister at Eastview, preached for the Sunday worship services for the "New Community," as this group had come to be known, until August of 1991 when Ken Osness began to preach to the Sunday worship services. By this time, 350 people were attending the Sunday worship services and were participating in leading small groups and service projects. By May of 1993, New Community had grown to 550 and it became necessary to move to University High School just a few blocks from the campus of Illinois State University.

This phenomenal growth Ken Osness attributes to several specialized approaches in ministry to these "Busters," young adults born in 1965 and later.[70] One factor is the emphasis upon participation and relationships. Many of these young people have not been adequately parented, and they are hungry for relationships with their peers. New Community recognized this need, and developed dozens of small groups, each led by people out of the fellowship (thirty of them in the fall of 1993).

Deriving leadership out of the groups satisfies a need of the Busters — a need to participate significantly. Ken says in his opinion a spectator role, which is the role often assigned to these young people by traditional churches, will fail totally to engage them in serious consideration of the Christian faith.

Music is another specialized area of this ministry. A full-time associate music minister has developed two contemporary bands out of the group, and careful and prayerful thought is given to the music used in the service each Sunday.

Much use is made of dramatic skits, audio-visual presentations, and sports leagues, all with a strong evangelistic emphasis aimed at this specialized age group.

There is a vast Biblical illiteracy among them, and Ken Osness aims his preaching to meet this need. His sermons are largely topical in form with many contemporary illustrations but they are Biblical in content. The Eastview Church in Bloomington and the Eastside Church in Fullerton (see below) have developed a format for reaching college-age young adults which is hugely successful. Any church which is located near a college campus and which is willing to take seriously evangelizing this age group can learn a great deal from these two ministries.[71]

## California State University at Fullerton and Eastside Christian Church, Fullerton

In July 1982 a campus ministry was established at California State University in Fullerton, California. This campus ministry is unique in that its base of operation is Eastside Christian Church, which is located a few blocks from the CSUF campus.

Roger Worsham, who had been youth minister with the Eastside congregation for many years, was named College Career Minister in 1982, and charged by the congregation with reaching Cal State students with the gospel. Ben Merold, minister at Eastside, asked me to work with Roger as co-campus minister supported part-time by Eastside. Pacific Christian College also supported this venture by providing an attractive meeting place for the Campus Christian Fellowship just across the street from the university campus.

The program in the beginning consisted of weekly meetings on campus called "Dialogue and Discussion," a Wednesday night Bible study in the meeting room at Pacific Christian College, and a Sunday morning Bible study at the Eastside church taught by Roger Worsham.

One of the strong features of this ministry consisted of well-planned winter and summer recreation events which were designed to attract non-Christian students, and to build a strong fellowship among the Christian students. Roger Worsham is especially gifted in planning summer water ski trips, winter snow ski trips, and well planned retreats which attract hundreds of students.

The "Dialogue and Discussion" meetings on the Cal State campus were promoted by an information table located in a well traveled location on campus operated by students and with posters liberally distributed on campus. These meetings were planned to be honest, open discussion of issues that are often controversial, but that can be addressed in ways to capture the interest of Christians, critics, or simply those who are curious. Topics such as the following attracted fifty to seventy-five students each week, both Christian and non-Christian:

> Emotional and Spiritual Survival in College
> Sex and the Single Student
> A Good Word for Atheists
> Does Christianity Make Sense?
> Is Christianity a Crutch?
> Putting the Steam in Your Self-Esteem
> Evolution-Creation
> Understanding the Abortion Issue
> Was Jesus a Wimp?
> Homosexuality and Christianity

This program proved to be hugely successful in reaching students who might not otherwise have paid any attention to a traditional Bible study.

In 1986 Roger Worsham and the Campus Christian Fellowship at Fullerton made a move that may be a sign of things to come in reaching college-career young people for Christ. A worship service called "University Praise Service" specially tailored to reach the "Busters" — the generation of people younger than the "Boomers," began, and from the beginning 275–300 college-age young people attended the services. Using music, drama, emphasizing relationships and Biblical preaching, this service became immediately attractive to hundreds of college-age young people.

Because it offers a non-threatening atmosphere for non-Christians, it has succeeded in reaching hundreds of "seekers" since 1986, and people are baptized nearly every week. The worship service serves as a "feeder" for students to get involved in other aspects of the program such as: Bible studies, small groups, mission and service trips. The people involved in this unique ministry consist of approximately sixty percent college students and forty percent "career" young people.

By the early 1990s it had become necessary to have two services in order to accommodate the crowds of college-age young people who were attending.

The program on the campus at Cal State Fullerton continued with Troy Dean, Roger's associate campus minister, leading Bible study groups on the campus each week. Troy also has led two groups of students to the Ukraine to witness and to reach young people for Christ there. This unique campus ministry is reaching the "Busters" in truly exciting ways and it provides a model for other churches across the country to reach college-career students.

# Westwood Foundation and Academic Classes at The University of California at Los Angeles

In 1975 a new institution among Christian churches was founded near the UCLA campus in Westwood. Westwood Christian Foundation, a dream of Dr. Myron Taylor, minister of the Westwood Hills Christian Church, and Dr. Robert O. Fife of Milligan College, was conceived as a "consortium of church related colleges, seminaries, and institutions cooperating in the advancement of Christian teaching and inquiry."[72] Among the goals of the Foundation were: an educational program to offer accredited courses at the college in graduate level Bible and other subjects, ministry to students on the UCLA campus and the endowment of a series of lectureships which would bring outstanding Christian scholars from around the world to West Los Angeles.[73]

Two of these goals were reached in truly remarkable ways during the eighteen years of the existence of the Foundation. Hundreds of ministers, missionaries, and other Christian leaders took classes through this unique school in Westwood near the University of California in Los Angeles. The Foundation-sponsored lectureships featured several world-famous Christian scholars, among them Malcolm Muggeridge, Dr. Hans Kung, and Dr. Thomas F. Torrance. Two lectureships each year brought outstanding leaders to Westwood from all branches of the Restoration Movement. Dr. Fife wrote of the Foundation as follows in 1990:

> Instead of starting another free-standing Christian college or seminary (which would have been very costly), the Foundation was established to fund and administer quality academic work which our existing schools would offer. Thus, the Foundation is not a school in the usual sense of the word, but a helping institution, enabling our accredited schools to focus a portion of their academic strength in this strategic center. Millions of dollars would have been required to establish a new and accredited school. But the Foundation, through the cooperation of our already established schools, has enabled several hundred ministers, missionaries, lay leaders, and enquirers to study here.[74]

The goal of ministering to UCLA students was not accomplished as originally planned, that is by having a full-time campus minister on the UCLA campus, but in the providence of God hundreds of UCLA students have been significantly impacted in a program which exceeded all expectations of the leaders of the Foundation in the beginning. Dr. Fife describes this development as follows:

> When we commenced our work in 1975, Dr. Myron Taylor and I ventured the hope that within a decade UCLA would take notice of our presence. Neither of us dreamed that almost immediately I would find warm acceptance and welcome among scholars, some of whom are now fast friends. Nor could we possibly have predicted the utterly unique and unprecedented relationship which was to develop between the Foundation and the University. This relationship began when professors at UCLA expressed a desire for New Testament and other courses concerning Christian history. In response to this need we called Dr. Scott Bartchy to become the Foundation's Resident New Testament Scholar, and made him available at the University's request to teach an experimental course in new Testament, entitled, "Early Christian History." Little did we anticipate that fifty students would enroll for that first class, which we funded. Other classes which followed were so highly appreciated that a year ago, Dr. Bartchy was honored as one of three outstanding teachers in UCLA.[75]

Dr. Bartchy had taught an experimental class at UCLA in 1980 which was so well attended that an arrangement was made with the university for Dr. Bartchy to teach two courses in 1981–1982 school year; courses which would be supported by Westwood Christian Foundation. This arrangement between the university and Foundation continued until 1990. During that ten year period the Westwood Christian Foundation contributed more than $1.25 million to support the UCLA curriculum in New Testament which was taught by Dr. Bartchy. In 1982 Dr. Bartchy was appointed adjunct professor and was given an ongoing appointment, with the understanding that the funds for his support would continue to come from the Foundation.

In 1990, the Westwood Foundation discontinued its financial support of Dr. Bartchy's teaching at UCLA, and the university began to pay him as a part-time professor. By 1993 Dr. Bartchy had been given a full-time appointment at the university and received a full salary.

Hundreds of students have been reached at this great university with scholarly biblical teaching by Dr. Scott Bartchy. Since 1980 he has taught 3,000 students in the junior/senior level and the upper-division graduate level at the university. In the same period of time he has taught 1,500 students who are freshmen/sophomores. The courses in the upper-division have been a series as follows: History of Early Christianity, Religious Environment of the Early Church, and Jesus of Nazareth in Historical Perspective. The undergraduate course which he has continued to teach is a course in the History of Western Civilization with a special emphasis on the period of the New Testament church. During these years Dr. Bartchy has also been a mentor and counselor for several scores of students who have gone on to receive their PhDs in the general field of the early history of Christianity.

This program at Westwood Foundation and UCLA is not a typical campus ministry, but it has obviously been a strikingly successful program in reaching students at a great university who might not otherwise every have been exposed to a scholarly presentation of New Testament Christianity.

# CAMPUS MINISTRIES IN THE EARLY 1990s

The broadening of the campus ministries which began in 1970 and continued into the 1980s was still happening in the early part of the 1990s. The following campus ministies were organized or continued in the early part of the decade.

## Northern Michigan University at Marquette

In 1991 the seventh campus ministry in the state of Michigan was founded at Northern Michigan University at Marquette. The usual pattern was followed, Gary Hawes, executive director of MCCM and a student, Doug DeLiefde from Ferris State Campus Ministry, made regular trips to Marquette together to gather a core of students.

In August of 1992, John Robenault became the full-time campus minister at Marquette. During the 1992–93 school year a house was purchased two blocks from campus. The house is the headquarters for His House Fellowship, and it also houses four girl students.

A vigorous program of witness for Christ is carried on in this northernmost outpost of campus ministry in the state of Michigan. John Robenault reported on the activities of this campus ministry as follows in February 1993:

> Six months ago (August 1992) I began my role as full-time minister at Northern Michigan University. I praise God that He has placed me in such a wonderful location! Not only has God been glorified through the lives of some sixty students involved with the fellowship, but He also continues to teach and lead us in exciting new ways each week. Now that the first semester is over, it is good to look back on how God has worked on the campus of NMU. My greatest thrill was to witness six students accept Christ and be baptized due to their involvement with His House Christian Fellowship. It is very important that we not only win students to Christ, but also help them develop a deep and intimate relationship with God. Through accountability groups and small group Bible studies, these students encourage one

another to grow closer to God. Bible studies in the dorms also provide a unique opportunity of outreach. Our goal is to have at least one Bible study in each of the nine dorms. Not only do the students know how to have fun, but they also know how to worship and serve the Lord with intensity. Last term I was amazed at how the students encouraged me through their commitment to Christ. When two students voiced an interest in a short-term mission trip to Haiti over their Christmas break, the other students pulled together to offer their support. Through car washes, pop can drives, bowl-a-thons, and donations, they came up with $1,600 for the trip. That's intense! We now meet Wednesday evenings on campus in the university center, and Sunday evenings at my home two blocks from campus. At this time, I am working on forming a core group of students. These students are faithfully dedicated to God through His House Christian Fellowship. They help me minister more effectively on campus, especially in the area of outreach.[76]

The "Michigan Miracle" has resulted, not only in seven strong campus ministries in the state of Michigan, but in the early years of the 90s Gary Hawes and his people at Michigan Christian Campus Ministries were making plans to establish campus ministries in both China and the Philippines.

## West Georgia College, Carrollton

The campus ministry at West Georgia College in Carrollton, Georgia began in the fall of 1992 in a small rented home which was donated to the group for one year.

Tony Crumbley, a 1987 graduate of Atlanta Christian College, is the campus minister and he reports an exciting beginning for this ministry. Twelve students met in a Bible study in fall of 1992, by the end of the spring quarter in 1993 the group had grown to twenty-five students. The program of the Campus Christian Fellowship consists of a weekly Bible study on Tuesdays at 8:00 p.m., a free dinner on the first and third Thursday nights, and a Friday luncheon each week. Leadership training classes are held twice a month, four retreats are held each year, and many weekend activities such as cook-outs, football games, and theme parties are held regularly.

Partners support the program with prayer, and regular service trips are taken to work with the homeless in Atlanta.

Tony Crumbley reports that the most exciting feature of the group is the atmosphere of family that characterizes this fellowship.

## University of Cincinnati, Ohio

The campus ministry at the University of Cincinnati began in 1969 under the sponsorship of Challenge Unlimited, the "umbrella" organization for campus ministry which was located in Cincinnati. (See Chapter Four, pp. 104–106)

From 1969 to 1990 there was a succession of campus ministers at the University of Cincinnati. Roger Callahan was the first, and he was succeeded by Roger Swango, Tom Smith, Dave McPherson, John Thybault, and Dave Wilmore. In 1990 Challenge Unlimited left the campus of the University of Cincinnati to focus their work on the campus ministries at Northern Kentucky and Miami of Ohio.

The University of Cincinnati was "uncovered," so to speak, so a church called University Christian Church was organized near the campus to minister to the students and the university community. Leaders in this venture were Dave Faust, Rick Rusaw, Tony Gore, and Steve Price. At this time UCC was meeting on Sunday mornings at Kruick Community Center, which is located two blocks from the UC campus. While the focus of the church was on the students from UC and on the university community, it was hard to do much of a ministry to the students without a full-time campus minister. The search continued for a campus minister, but it took until 1992 before that person was located. Several other people helped out during this interim.[77]

In January of 1992 Dan Burton was hired as the first full-time campus minister working out of the University Christian Church. Dan was a product of the campus ministry at Michigan State University. He and his wife Sue were trained by Dean Trune while they were at MSU. Dan was first a student at MSU, then an intern at the University of Michigan, where he learned from Michael O'Berski. Dan then began a three year ministry at Lake Superior State University while he was mentored by Gary Hawes. After studying at Cincinnati Bible Seminary for two years, Dan and Sue Burton decided to accept UCC's challenge to work as campus ministers. There was an understanding at the time of Dan and Sue's coming that they were probably only going to be at UCC for two years, as they felt a call to the foreign mission field. University Christian Fellowship became an established group on the campus at UC in 1992.[78]

In September 1992 University Church began meeting on Sunday mornings at the University YMCA on the edge of the campus which allowed them to minister more effectively to students at the university, and to have greater influence on campus.

In January 1994 David Foster and his wife Jan, both converted at the campus ministry at Western Michigan University, became worship leaders, which allowed Dan Burton to focus on the fellowship groups on campus. In February 1994 eight fellowship groups, which meet together weekly for Bible study, fellowship, and prayer, were reaching over fifty students and community people. The attendance in the combined Christian Church and University Christian Fellowship grew from thirty-six in 1990 to one hundred twenty as of March 1994. Dan Burton says of this group, "We are a growing body that is culturally mixed and racially diverse. We are unique in that we balance a Campus Ministry with a Community Church. We have young families and many students who come together to worship and join together in our weekly small groups."[79]

In June 1994 Dan and Sue Burton will be leaving to begin their foreign mission work in Ethiopia with Christian Missionary Fellowship and the University Christian Church will be hiring a full-time campus minister as a replacement.

## Mesa State College in Grand Junction, Colorado

Typical of the vision some people are catching for the spread of campus ministries in the 1990s is the work of Western Colorado Campus Ministries, organized in 1993 by a group of churches on the western slope. A newsletter announcing the organization of this group includes the following description:

> Not since the days of the Intermountain Bible College have the Christian Churches on the Western Slope had the opportunity to join together in a mission project. The Western Colorado Christian Campus Ministries (WCCCM) affords us just such an opportunity! We are all aware of the difficulties faced by our young people after graduation from high school. Campus ministries are proving to be an extremely viable answer to some of these problems — namely, reaching young people for the Lord and giving our Christian youth on the secular campus a "lifeline" to the church as they begin making life choices. Our research has shown that the campus ministries do, in fact, work and that Mesa State is ripe for this program. The vision for WCCCM is to "plant" a campus ministry at Mesa State College with a full-time minister.[80]

In March of 1993 the churches of the area contributed five thousand dollars toward the establishment of a campus ministry on the campus of Mesa State College at Grand Junction. In late 1993, Leland Griffin, former minister at Northeast Christian Church in Grand Junction, was called as part-time campus minister. Most of the meetings of the group, called Christian Student Fellowship, are held in the facilities provided by the Northeast congregation. By early 1994, forty students were involved in this campus ministry at Mesa State and the board members and supporting churches of the WCCCM are looking forward to the possible establishment of campus ministries at Western State College in Gunnison College and Fort Lewis College in Durango.

This work in Western Colorado is significant in at least two ways: it is an example of how campus ministry can "fill the gap," at least partially, when a Bible college has to close its doors, and it is evidence of the continuing spread of campus ministries into new territory in the early years of 1990. (Other suggestions regarding the relationship between campus ministries and Bible colleges will be made in the next chapter.)

## NOTES

1. Two of the widely read and much quoted studies of the students of the 80s were Arthur Levine's *When Dreams and Heroes Died* (San Francisco: Jossey-Bass, 1983), and the late Allan Bloom's *The Closing of the American Mind*, (New York: Simon & Schuster, 1987).

2. Levine, *When Dreams and Heroes Died*, p. 103.

3. *Ibid.*, pp. 104-105.

4. Bloom, *The Closing of the American Mind*, p. 339.

5. Questionnaire completed by John Schlieker in 1985. Information on this campus ministry between 1978 and 1980 is not available to me.

6. "Colorado Connection," Newsletter, September 1984, p. 1.

7. "Colorado Connection," March 1984, p. 1.

8. "Colorado Connection," October 1992.

9. Questionnaire completed by John Schlieker, May 1992.

10. "Colorado Connection," July 1993.

11. Questionnaire completed by John Schlieker in 1992.

12. Newsletter, "World Wide Mission Outreach," 1989, p. 3.

13. In addition to the four students who were killed, another nine were wounded. This shocking affair is given thorough coverage in *The Kent Affair*, Ed. Casale, Ottavio M., and Paskoff, Louis (Boston: Houghton Mifflin Co., 1971).

14. From a letter to the author from Andy Wade, August 1993.

15. *Ibid.*, p. 2.

16. *Ibid.*, p. 3.

17. *Ibid.*

18. From a questionnaire completed by Mike Armstrong, 1985.

19. Newsletter, "Christ on Campus," November 1985.

20. Newsletter, December 1988, p. 1.

21. *Ibid.*, p. 2.

22. Questionnaire completed by Mike Armstrong, May 1992.

23. Newsletter, "Christ on Campus," May 1989.

24. *Ibid.*

25. Letter to supporters, 1992.

26. Newsletter, "Christ on Campus," May 1993, p. 1.

27. Thom and Mary Ann Miller often appear in this history of campus ministry as a positive and encouraging influence to many campus ministers and campus ministries. They continue this influence as they serve as associates at Southeast Christian Church in East Point, Georgia.

28. From a rough draft of a project submitted to Cincinnati Christian Seminary as part of a requirement for Masters of Ministry. Information on Paul Bledsoe's

early ministry at FAU also came from this document.

29. *Ibid.*, p. 16.

30. *Ibid.*, pp. 18, 19.

31. Quote from McCormick, pp. 37, 38.

32. Questionnaire completed by Paul Bledsoe in 1989.

33. "New Disciple News," Fall 1992, p. 2.

34. *Ibid.*, p. 2.

35. Most of the information on this campus ministry came from a letter and a packet of materials sent to me by Emily Nowselski in September of 1992.

36. Calvin Ross and Central Christian Church, Pittsburgh, had worked with students at the University of Pittsburgh before 1983, but the details of that ministry are not available to me.

37. "1993 Annual Report," CSFPA.

38. *Ibid.*, pgs 1, 2.

39. Questionnaire completed by Sam Brunsvold in 1989.

40. "1993 Annual Report," p. 21.

41. *Ibid.*, p. 2.

42. Promotion flyer, CSFPA 1989.

43. Newsletter, April 1987.

44. *Ibid.*

45. Unpublished paper, "Athletic Interest Ministry: A Culturally Viable Approach to Campus Ministry," Lincoln Christian Seminary, 1991.

46. McCormick, *Campus Ministry*, p. 15. McCormick is quoting here from a Ph.D. dissertation by Ronald B. Flowers, "The Bible Chair Movement in the Disciples of Christ Tradition: Attempts to Teach Religion at the State Universities," School of Religion, University of Iowa, 1967, p. 156.

47. Letter to the Author from Mike Hamm, September 1993.

48. Information on this campus ministry came from letters to the author from Dennis Steckley, December 1987 and from Mike Hamm, September 1993.

49. Brochure, TSCF, 1993.

50. In August of 1989, Jane Nabor left for Hong Kong to join a team of three other missionaries. Jane acquired a position in teaching English in Beijing at the Middle School attached to the University of Beijing. Jane's twofold goal is to initiate a ministry in Beijing with university students and to open a channel for American university students to go to China to serve. The "Michigan Miracle" moved to China! "Campus Ministry Messenger," September-October, 1989, p. 4.

51. "Campus Ministry Messenger," March-April, 1988.

52. "Campus Ministry Messenger," July 1989.

53. "Campus Ministry Messenger," July 1989 and September-October 1989.

54. "Campus Ministry Messenger," 1989.

55. "MCCM Annual Report," September 1, 1990 – August 31, 1991.

56. From brochure, "Exalting Christ," 1993, p. 4.

57. From brochure, "Destiny of Excellence," 1993, p. 6.

58. Letter to author from Rick Harper, September 1993.

59. Questionnaire completed by Rick Harper in 1989.

60. From brochure, "Destiny of Excellence," p. 5.

61. From brochure, "Exalting Christ," p. 2.

62. Questionnaire completed by Scott Stocking in 1989.

63. Newsletter, "Pressing On," February 1993, p. 1.

64. Newsletter, Fall 1990, p. 2.

65. Newsletter, Spring 1991, p. 1.

66. Newsletter, March 1993, p. 2.

67. Newsletter, February 1993, p. 4.

68. Letter to author from Mark Feasline, October 1993.

69. Information on this campus ministry came from a letter and a brochure sent to the author by Rob Newman in the Spring of 1994.

70. An excellent study of the "Busters" is the book by George Barna titled *The Invisible Generation: Baby Busters* published by Barna Research Group, 647 W. Broadway, Glendale, CA 1992.

71. Ken Osness and Roger Worsham made an excellent presentation of their ministries to the North American Christian Convention held in St. Louis in July of 1993. A tape recording of their presentation may be obtained from Christian Audio Tapes, 888 Corporation, Bridgeport, IL 62417.

72. *Christian Standard*, May 25, 1980, p. 4.

73. *Ibid.*, p. 4.

74. "The Lamp," Newsletter of Westwood Christian Foundation, October 1990, p. 4.

75. Open letter to friends of the Westwood Christian Foundation, 1975-1990, pp. 1, 2.

76. "Campus Ministry Messenger," February 1993, p. 2.

77. Information from this campus ministry was obtained from a FAX sent to the author by Dan Burton in March 1994.

78. *Ibid.*

79. *Ibid.*

80. Support letter sent out by Clifton Christian Church, Clifton, Colorado, in 1993.

# CHAPTER NINE
# The Future of Campus Ministry

The year 1993 marked the 100th anniversary of the establishment of a Bible Chair by the Disciples at the University of Michigan at Ann Arbor. In the succeeding years all three branches of the churches of the Restoration Movement have, in different degrees, initiated programs to take the gospel of Christ to the college campus.

I have tried here to give an accurate account of the more than thirty years of campus ministry among Christian Churches. I think readers will agree that it is an amazing and exciting story. It is my fervent hope that the "best kept secret" is now out in the open for all to read and evaluate. The question now, however, is whether campus ministry among Christian Churches has a future.

There is often a crisis in a well-played game of tennis called the "breakpoint." At that juncture the game can go either way, depending upon the comparative skill, aggressive play and perhaps the will to win of the participants. I suggest that, as we enter the final decade of the 20th century, campus ministry among Christian Churches is at the breakpoint in its history. If its tremendous potential for continued spreading of the gospel in the modern world is acknowledged and adequately supported by the churches, then the future of campus ministry will be assured. If, on the other hand, campus ministry continues to be looked upon as a *para-church* movement of negligible importance to the church as a whole, then one of the most significant movements within the contemporary church will have been effectively neutralized. Donald Shockley states the issue clearly:

> When campus ministries tell their story today it is not merely in order to justify an appeal for continued financial support. Rather, it is out of genuine concern for the welfare of the church and society that the story is told. Campus ministry is not a distant cousin; it is member of the immediate family, and the status of its health therefore affects the well-being of the church as a whole.[1]

It is true that campus ministries do not always take the organizational shape of existing local churches. That does not mean, however, that they are not a genuine part of the church of Christ, following His command to

"Go into all the world and preach the Gospel to the whole creation" (Mark 16:15 RSV). They are an outpost of the church adapting themselves to become the cutting edge of the gospel's penetration of the university campus.

When a tennis player arrives at the breakpoint in a game, it is no time for defensive measures aimed at self-preservation. Nor is this a time in history for the church to be preoccupied only with defending itself against the forces of evil. Again Donald Shockley is on the mark when he says:

> History teaches us that when an institution — political, religious, or otherwise — becomes obsessed with the details of self-preservation, it has entered a period of decline . . . now is not the time for those who care about campus ministry to go into a survival mode. Now is the time for the church to determine what its mission in higher education is and fulfill it with renewed vigor.[2]

In the preceding chapters I have tried to make the case for this renewed vigor on the part of campus ministry as a vital part of the church as a whole. Let us recapitulate.

## Campus Ministry & The University

Alexander Campbell's prophetic insight that the Bible and moral values must be at the heart of every institution of higher learning has been fulfilled on scores of campuses through campus ministry. Bible study — life-changing encounters with the Word of God — is at the heart of every campus ministry whose story has been told here. Granted, the greater life of the university has been largely unaffected by this biblical emphasis, but nevertheless thousands of students who would otherwise have been left vulnerable to the destructive forces operating on the modern multiversity have found meaning and purpose for their lives through exposure to the biblical message. Campus ministry, with its biblical core, has created for these students a centering magnet amid the otherwise fragmentary forces of university life.

Campbell's contention that the Bible *and* moral values must be at the center of higher education sounds absurdly quaint when "diversity" and "political correctness" are the burning issues in the contemporary university. Campbell pleaded eloquently for his position:

> I give my vote for learning and science and for high attainment in all branches of useful knowledge, but I would not give morality for them all; and therefore I have resolved never to speak in favor of any literary institution, from a common school to a university, however superior their literary eminence, that does not first of all, and above all, exercise a sovereign and supreme guardianship over the morals of its students and wards, and endeavor to make good rather than great men.[3]

If by morals Campbell meant a set of pietistic rules superimposed upon the university and its students arbitrarily, then he has nothing to say to the modern university. If, however, by moral values he meant to refer to the question of the essential nature of human beings, their origin, nature and ultimate purpose (and I contend that this is indeed what he meant), then he is absolutely right. Tragically it is this very question — namely the question of the ultimate meaning and purpose of human life — which the university, for whatever reason, cannot or will not address. The irony here is that the value-vacuum which has been created by this failure on the part of the university has led to an attempt to impose new rules, rules of "diversity" and "political correctness," which in practice have become more coercive and authoritarian than any set of pietistic rules which "moralists" have attempted to superimpose upon the university in the past.[4]

I have suggested previously (Chapter 8, p. 208) that the gatherings of campus ministries may be the only place on many campuses where the ultimate questions are confronted. Indeed whether addressed elsewhere on campus or not, we have noted hundreds of cases in the preceding pages in which students have found sanctuary and succor in campus ministry as they struggle with the ultimate questions.

As important as it is for the individual students to find Christ through campus ministry, it is probably more important that campus ministry be an aggressive witness for Christ to the whole university. This, as Charles Malik has insisted, is the larger purpose of campus ministry — that is, to challenge the most influential institution in the modern world with the claims of Christ.

If this seems too grandiose a purpose for campus ministry, my response is if not campus ministry, then who? If not now, when?

## Campus Ministry & Students

In the previous chapters I have pointed out that, from the point of view of campus ministry, the approximately 13 million students now on university and college campuses can be roughly divided into three categories. The first of these is made up of "our" students — that is students from Christian Churches which we estimate number at least 80,000. The second and largest category is the millions of unreached and unevangelized students.[5] The third category is the international students who number in the hundreds of thousands. I have mentioned above the stresses and strains which are endemic to life on the contemporary campus — sexual, emotional, academic, and career pressures which all students face. It is in this environment that campus ministries may do their best work. The provision of a loving community of peers in which one may be accepted and cared for is probably the most powerful aspect of these ministries. That this kind of loving community is a perennial need of college students is a given, but the deeply flawed nature of much of modern society has intensified the importance of this aspect of ministry on campus.

When I entered campus ministry in the mid-sixties the students were actively opposed to the university assuming the role of *in loco parentis* — that is of attempting to be a substitute for their parents. I was as vocally opposed to the universities assuming this role as were the students. They were young adults needing to learn how to be responsible for themselves, and any continued dependency on *either* parents or a parenting university could only keep them immature. Now, however, in the 1990s, I and many others have done a radical about-face on this issue. William H. Willamon, Dean of the Chapel at Duke University, has recently written on this issue. He argues that in the 50s there was a legitimate need for students to search for freedom and self-expression. Now, however, in the 1990s when so many students have come from dysfunctional homes in which they have been wounded and emotionally incapacitated, they seem much more interested in the search for roots, stability, order, and identity. Willamon says:

> A person who has spent many years counseling students on our campus noted that a better case could be made for supporting *in loco parentis* during the 1990s than during the 1950s. Increasing numbers of our students have been inadequately parented. They arrive on campus having missed important aspects of human development — interaction and conflict with their parents over values. They were left to their own devices. They are not people yearning to be left alone by adults.[6]

Willamon is not arguing for the restoration of *in loco parentis*, nor am I, but he is arguing that college students are not yet mature adults, capable of thinking for themselves or of making their own decisions and left to themselves they become "willing victims of the most totalitarian form of government — namely submission to their peers, obeisance to people just like them. This is not freedom."[7]

Neither the university nor the campus ministry can or should be parents to these young people, but the campus ministry can be, and has been, a supportive community for thousands of them during the past thirty years. One cannot read the account of campus ministries in this book without being struck by the constantly recurring testimony of students who say, "I've found a caring community on campus." There is a vast difference between a "caring community" and a cultic community. The former provides the supportive environment in which a student can grow into maturity; the other creates an oppressive environment in which a student becomes dependent on some authority figure and thus remains immature. I have not detected any "cultic" tendencies in my examination of campus ministries in this book.[8] Having found acceptance in a loving community, students are then open to the possibility that they might also be accepted by a loving God.

Before leaving this section on campus ministry and students, I must acknowledge a recurring problem with students who come to campus from Christian Churches. It is a common experience with campus ministers that students who come from Christian Churches are notoriously difficult to recruit for campus ministry.[9] There are undoubtedly numerous reasons for this situation, one being that it is part of the college experience to throw off what are perceived as restraints from "back home." Participation in a Christian fellowship may be seen as one of these restraints. However, the problem is so widespread that it might be prudent to re-examine how churches prepare their students for college. Mark Gallagher, campus minister at Indiana State University, has written a thesis on this subject, and he has several practical suggestions to make for churches to consider as they prepare their students for college (see Appendix D).

# Campus Ministry & Christian Leaders

Those of us who entered campus ministry in the 1960s were convinced that the job of the Bible college was to recruit and train ministers and missionaries, while the job of campus ministry would be to recruit and train "lay" leaders for the church. It has come as a pleasant surprise that campus ministry has been amazingly successful in recruiting Christian leaders both for the ministry of the church and for Christian leadership in the world. Again, a careful reading of the history presented here will show that large numbers of university and college students, especially in the past ten years, have been converted on campus and proceeded through Bible college and seminary to full-time service in the churches and on the mission field.

One of the frustrations in this area is the inability to arrive at specific numbers, this because most campus ministries have not kept accurate records. However, a recent survey of two of our Christian Church seminaries may help us to see the trend toward the production of Christian leaders which has developed in campus ministry in recent years. Ward Patterson, veteran campus minister at Indiana University, now teaching campus ministry classes at Cincinnati Bible College and Seminary, recently wrote as follows:

> As to the Seminary here, I haven't been very successful at getting information on totals over the years, but I think you might be interested to know that in 1992, 35% of our seminary students came from state schools. That is 61 out of 173. So far in 1993, 14 of the 45 new students in the seminary are

from state colleges, 31%. So I think that it would be safe to say that as far as we are concerned, about ⅓ of our students are coming from state universities and ⅔ from Bible Colleges.[10]

A similar phenomenon has surfaced at Emmanuel School of Religion in Johnson City, Tennessee. The April, 1992 "ENVOY," newsletter of Emmanuel, featured 26 students out of a student body of 141 attending the school in the spring semester who had come from state universities and secular colleges. The article commented as follows:

A growing number of Emmanuel students come to the seminary to pursue graduate ministerial preparation from state universities and secular colleges. Often they are the product of very effective campus ministries around the country. While Emmanuel is pleased and proud to have students who have completed their undergraduate studies at various Bible colleges, university students have brought a diversity extremely representative of the typical church. These university students in their undergraduate years have been preparing for numerous non-church vocations in law, business, education, medicine, science, engineering. They come to Emmanuel School of Religion to redirect or solidify their preparation for service in the church for the cause of Christ.[11]

David Fulks, Director of Admissions at Emmanuel School of Religion, has for several years observed the movement of students from college and university campuses into seminary to prepare for Christian service. He recently wrote an article, "The Campus Minister — One Man's Opinion" in which he said:

Of course, there are many exciting forms of ministry. Among the most exciting aspects of Campus Ministry are the following:
1) Campus Ministry offers the church a very effective vehicle for reaching and involving young adults . . . college students are making lifestyle choices, moral choices, and choices of a mate. It is apparent to me that the influence of the church is desperately needed in all of these matters. . . . The church must be present and effective in serving college students. The Campus Ministry affords such an opportunity.
2) Campus Ministry provides the context in which the call to ministry can be extended to the many talented, compassionate, committed young people whose initial vocational choice has taken them to the university rather than to a Christian College.
3) Campus Ministry provides the opportunity for the church to counter the secular-humanistic influence to which many of our college and university students are exposed. . . . For some, it provides the lifeline which alone prevents them from being swept away by those who hide their ignorance of the gospel in a cloak of quasi-intellectualism.
As long as there is a college or university campus anywhere without the benefit of campus ministry there are too few campus ministries. There are many campus ministries which are sorely underfunded. Perhaps we agree that no mission budget can be considered comprehensive unless there is at

least one campus ministry included.
But then it is only one man's opinion.[12]

In addition to recruiting ministers, missionaries and full-time Christian leaders in significant numbers, campus ministry is also producing thousands of mature Christian leaders who are carrying their witness into every stratum of contemporary culture. Almost twenty years ago, Knofel Staton, then a member of the faculty at Ozark Bible College, in his characteristically insightful way, began to ask who would produce the Christian leaders so desperately needed in all sectors of society.

> Our society needs a flood of Christians to permeate education, medicine, law, business, journalism, politics, theater, etc. Who hasn't seen the need for the Christian world-view to be beamed into the news media, our government leaders, the workings of law, sports activities, and all levels of education? Don't we need people with a Christian perspective to decide on television programming, to produce movies, and to author books (have you glanced over the paperback book racks lately?)? Don't we need psychologists and counselors who know the Bible and believe in it?
>
> Who determines what will be included in the curricula for our schools that in turn can influence our society? Specialists in education, that's who. Why should we leave these positions primarily to non-believers? Now our elementary schools are being infiltrated because non-believers have poured their philosophies into their area of work. Currently, important areas of education are in a state of flux and conflict. Let us not leave these decisions to non-believers.[13]

Campus ministry has been answering Knofel's urgent questions by producing these leaders for more than thirty years.

## Campus Ministry & International Students

Another surprising and exciting development is the growing interest in missions which has been generated through campus ministry. One phase of this interest is the participation of large numbers of students in missionary and service trips, both at home and abroad. Stimulated by these experiences, hundreds of students have gone into short-term and long-term missions service from campus ministry. (Again actual figures are hard to come by, but a careful reading of the preceding pages will show the strength of this trend.)

The other aspect of missions which has become a part of many if not most of our campus ministries is work with international students. Hundreds of thousands of international students have come to study in American universities and colleges in the past thirty years. Nearly every campus ministry we have studied has some type of ministry to these students, many of them impressively effective.[14]

The incredible potential for reaching the whole world with the gospel of Christ which exist in campus ministry was sharply underlined by Ziden Nutt, director of Good News Productions, International in Joplin, Missouri, when he addressed the campus ministers' retreat at McCormick's Creek State Park in Spencer, Indiana, in May of 1993. Here is a summary of Ziden's impassioned plea to the assembled campus ministers:

> Certainly, one of the greatest factors in the total saturation of the world with the gospel of Christ is found within campus ministries on universities across the Americas and around the world. I do not believe there is a greater asset that the church has than in the resource people and potential for outreach that we find in the campus ministries.
>
> Many international students have been hand picked by governments to meet specific academic goals and return to government and community responsibilities. Not only are they extremely valuable during their time on campus to work together and give guidance in strategies for reaching their people group but also to assist in the many aspects of productions that they can use and distribute upon their return to their homeland.
>
> We have found them to be key factors in evangelistic and leadership efforts in various countries. A coordinated effort to identify these people, their talents and expertise, and to maintain a constant contact with them, could well mean the difference between fulfilling the great commission or leaving the task undone.[15]

## Campus Ministry & The Bible Colleges

Although in the early days there was considerable misunderstanding and unnecessary feelings of competition between campus ministries and Bible colleges, that situation has improved remarkably so that now there is generally a strong sense of cooperation between these two institutions. That is not to say, however, that there is no room for legitimate contrast and comparison.

One important difference is in the kind and number of students who are targeted. By and large those who are attracted to the Bible college are already committed Christians. (Though not all, by any means, as those of us who teach in Bible colleges can testify!) Most of these are from Christian Churches, but again not all of them. According to the ratio we have suggested — 10 students from Christian Churches on the college and university campuses for every 1 from Christian Churches who go to Bible college — there are approximately 80,000 of "our" students in the state and private universities and colleges. These students are of primary concern to campus ministries, although as I have pointed out, they are often unaccountably difficult to reach. Until the advent of campus ministry more than thirty years ago, these students were virtually ignored by both the Bible college and the churches, although there were a few happy exceptions to this rule.

The largest number of students targeted by campus ministries are the millions of secular, non-Christian types. These students are often surprisingly open to the gospel, and thousands of them have been converted by campus ministries over the years.

The difference in kinds and numbers of students who are ministered to does not mean that there is no mutual ministry between Bible colleges and campus ministries. In the early days most, not all, campus ministers were graduates of Bible colleges. Increasingly, students who are converted on campuses go to Bible college to become more biblically literate, and many of these become campus ministers. (Note especially the campus ministers who came from campus ministries in the state of Michigan.) Several campus ministries also continue to offer Bible college courses for credit with special arrangements between the campus ministry and the Bible college. In these and other ways Bible colleges and campus ministries are now working together to spread the gospel, which is as it should be.

Another significant difference between campus ministry and Bible colleges is in the area of cost-effectiveness. Bible colleges, unlike campus ministries, are burdened with very costly capital expenditures which keep many of them in a precarious financial state continually. (The president of one of our Christian colleges recently told me that the major portion of his time and energy is spent in raising money to build or repair buildings.) As a result of this situation the cost per-student per-year in Bible colleges is relatively high. In the 1993–94 school year, according to figures reported in the *Christian Standard*, the cost ranged from $15,306, the highest, to $2,039, the lowest.[16] Campus ministries have a tremendous advantage here in that they do not need to build classrooms, administration buildings, libraries, dormitories or gymnasiums because these buildings are provided by the state — or private sources in the case of private colleges.

On most, if not all campuses, campus ministries have free access to university property as needed. This results in a tremendous savings in operational costs and means that the cost per-student per-year is radically lower than for Bible colleges. This cost is difficult to compute accurately in the case of campus ministry. Budgets vary greatly and student participation is not easy to record accurately. However, it is possible to arrive at some fairly accurate figures in this area. For example, Purdue Christian Campus House had a total budget of $270,680 in the 1993–94 school year. The number of students who were reached in a significant manner during that year was, conservatively, 600. (A total of 1,200 students participated in some manner.) This means that the cost per-student per-year was approximately $450 compared to the $2,039 — lowest cost per-student per-year for the Bible College.[17]

Of course, one can argue that the students in the Bible college are more intensely involved in biblical education than those in campus ministry. People in the seminaries our campus ministry "grads" are attending report that these students compare favorably in Bible knowledge and commitment to Bible college graduates.[18]

I refer to the financial plight of the Bible colleges with a great deal of sadness, although I have not been the first to do so. Several different suggestions have been made to solve the problem — merger, increased contributions from churches, more aggressive recruiting of ministerial prospects, more frugal budgeting and so forth.[19]

In a very real sense the Bible colleges have kept alive the biblical core of the Restoration Movement. (See "The Bible Road From Bethany," Chapter Two, pp. 36–43) If it becomes necessary for some of these valuable institutions to close down, it is not beyond imagining that many of their remaining resources — professors, libraries, finances from sale of buildings, for example — might be channeled into campus ministry. Such a move would be in the spirit of the Bible Chair movement which began 100 years ago, as well as the educational philosophy of Alexander Campbell embodied in Bethany College and the dream of Eugene Sanderson to unite the Bible college and the state university. Such a move could be of immense value in evangelizing the university and the world.

## Campus Ministry & The Restoration Movement

To many of us who were brought up in churches of the Restoration Movement, and who thought we understood and appreciated the genius of that movement, it was a surprise to discover how amazingly relevant the essential elements of the movement are in campus ministry.[20]

The movement which arose on the American frontier in the early 1800s, led by Alexander Campbell, Barton W. Stone and others, has been rather generically called the Restoration Movement. It was a movement that looked both ways. It looked back at the early church when it was in its vigorous prime, and it looked ahead toward an ideal church in which the essential elements which God had planned to exist would be embodied.

There have been some serious misunderstandings of the movement, perhaps especially among those of us who have been a part of it all of our lives. It is not intended to look back at some static "golden age" of the church which is to be anachronistically reconstituted in the contemporary world. It is rather the recognition that essential living principles in the church which was founded by Christ and put into practice by the Apostles can and must be "restored" if the church is to function as God intended it to.[21]

The "Restoration Movement" is not an end in itself, but a movement to find and implement the essential characteristics of the church as God intended it so that the world may be won. Providentially, conditions came together in campus ministries which have called forth these essential elements in a remarkable way.

Contemporary college students, for the most part, have very little interest in bureaucratic ecclesiastical organizations. Our emphasis upon the church as a fellowship, an organism rather than an organization, is powerfully attractive to them. I have made this point in these pages, perhaps to the point of being boringly repetitive, but I risk this repetition because this is so vital a part of campus ministry. I am convinced that the deepest hunger in every college student, indeed in every human being, is for love and acceptance. Scores of students at Purdue University were first attracted by the quality of the fellowship — not the doctrine, not the teaching, not even the Bible, in the beginning, but by the powerful magnetism of people who deeply care for each other and who are accepting and non-judgmental toward the "stranger" in their midst. Long before the Restoration Movement Jesus said, as we all know, "By this all men will know that you are my disciples, if you have love for one another" (John 13:35 RSV).

Impatience with ecclesiastical organization is matched in most college students' minds with a rejection of secular divisions. In many ways an inclusive unity based only on the Bible is easier to practice in the atmosphere of the campus than it is in many local churches. When there is no concern for membership rolls and rigid organization, there is a freedom and an openness which is powerfully attractive to college students. I have often preached in university worship services which included students from many different ethnic groups as well as students from Catholic, Jewish and several denominational backgrounds. Often students have approached me and said, "I think I want to be baptized, but I don't want to join your church." I was overjoyed to be able to point out to them that I didn't "have a church," and that their baptism would be into the universal church of Christ rather than into some secular expression of the church. John Derry, veteran Campus Minister at Western Illinois University, wrote as follows while he was ministering there:

> We welcome those from denominational backgrounds because, for many of them, it is their first exposure to a concept of New Testament Christianity. I am impressed by their eagerness to learn and willingness to search the Scripture to determine exactly what is God's will for His disciples. It is this very attitude that leads many of them to desire to be immersed into Christ. Never before have they been challenged to test their viewpoints in light of the Word. But such opportunities as this would not exist without the spirit of Christian unity. It has been an attractive quality through the years which we seek to preserve.[22]

"No creed but Christ, no book but the Bible" is also a powerfully attractive position to promote on the campus. Creeds and doctrines are not of interest to most college students, at least in the beginning. An appeal to a personal relationship with the living Christ as against the rational arguments of a dogmatic creed is winsomely attractive to them. They find almost childlike pleasure in serious study of the Bible. This is not to say that students are not interested in doctrine and theology; they are, and often intensely so, but the appeal of a personal commitment comes first.

The non-clergy nature of the Restoration Movement and the emphasis on the priesthood of all believers is also refreshingly attractive to many college students. The campus minister as a mentor, an older brother/sister in the faith, a fellow seeker is a model never before encountered by students who come from churches where the clergy-laity distinction is sharply drawn. Since ordination is not required in order to participate in the planning and leadership of worship services, students are allowed, indeed encouraged, to become responsible leaders and participants — not only in the worship services, but in the planning and leadership of campus ministry as a whole.[23]

The church as a united fellowship, based on the Bible, non-creedal and non-clergy, with an emphasis upon the priesthood of all believers is indeed alive and well in campus ministry.

# Women In Campus Ministry

No history of campus ministry among Christian Churches would be complete without recognizing the important role of women in that history. It is impossible to give credit to all the women who have contributed to the phenomenal growth of campus ministry among Christian Churches, but the following names are typical of scores of others.

Shirley Felix has been a vital part of the campus ministry at Purdue University for more than twenty-six years. She has been much more than a secretary. She has been the chief financial officer, official correspondent, counselor and "den mother" to hundreds of students, and much more. She has been as important to the campus ministry at Purdue as any of the designated leaders.

Peggy Clark Brandon was an administrative assistant on the staff at Purdue campus ministries for six years. She not only did administrative work, planned programs and retreats, but she also taught classes and did extensive counseling with students, ministering to students who might not otherwise have been reached.

Sally Keisling has been Gary Hawes' administrative assistant since the early days of "the Michigan miracle." Gary would be the first to say that Sally has contributed as significantly to the phenomenal growth of campus ministry in Michigan as any of the other talented leaders. Gary Hawes also credits Jane Nabor with being the key person in establishing two of the campus ministries in Michigan. She served as Campus Coordinator and was one of the key persons in founding the campus ministries at both Lake Superior State University at Sault Sainte Marie and at Ferris State University in Big Rapids. Her "gift of hospitality," Gary said, was crucial in the establishment of both of these campus ministries.[24]

Janice Schlieker served as co-campus minister along with her husband John as they established the three campus ministries in the state of Colorado. Janice also contributed greatly to the growth of the National Association of Christian Campus Ministries in her role as secretary/treasurer from 1987 through 1993.

Sue Gallagher has also been a co-campus minister along with her husband Mark at Indiana State University since they began there in 1978. She has been the director of the popular "Singing Scamps" during all those years, and has also done teaching and counseling with students.

Emily Nowselski has been a consistent contributor to the campus ministry at Florida Atlantic University at Boca Raton since its inception in 1982. She has been administrative director of this campus ministry from the beginning, and has provided continuity between campus ministers during transitional periods.

Carolyn Davisson became Campus Coordinator at Ohio University when Steve Seevers resigned, and she was actually acting campus minister for four years, not only holding things together until Rich Teske was called as campus minister in 1992, but also initiating programs and leading the ministry in growth during this transitional period.

"Women in ministry" is a controversial issue in some Christian Churches, but there is no question that the women here are only a few of the many women who have contributed significantly to the thirty year history of campus ministry among Christian Churches.

# Conclusion

This history of campus ministry among Christian Churches is the product of twenty years' experience as a campus minister and ten years of study and research. The project has been much more difficult than I had anticipated, but I take deep satisfaction in being able to record, however inadequately, this remarkable story. Obviously, it has indeed been a "movement" which could not ever have been manipulated by human means and that God intends for this ministry to be an important part of the church as a whole. My fervent hope is that the churches will recognize this fact and that campus ministry will continue to be one of the major movements of the church as it seeks to evangelize the world in the coming 21st century.

# NOTES

1. Shockley. *Campus Ministry*, p. 2.

2. *Ibid.*, p. 5.

3. Quoted by McCormick, *Campus Ministry*, p. 2, from *Millennial Harbinger*, 1837, "Bacon College" pp. 570-571. John Henry Cardinal Newman, writing in 1852 agrees with Campbell. "In a word, religious truth is not only a portion, but a condition of general knowledge. To blot it out is nothing short, if I may so speak, of unraveling the web of university teaching." *The Idea of a University* (San Francisco: Rinehart Press, Ed. Martin J. Svoglic, 1960), pp. 52-53. See also *American Academy of Religion News*, 1993, the letter from Dr. Barbara De Concini, Executive Director of AAR, and professor of Religion and Culture at Emory University, to Thomas B. Day, President of San Diego State University, regarding the elimination of the Religion Department at San Diego State University. She writes, "By selecting religion for elimination, you remove one of the few programs capable of overcoming fragmentation and isolation which (too frequently) characterize the large urban university. No department in the contemporary university has a longer history of thinking through how best to bring a variety of disciplines to bear on central human questions. At the very time when the call for interdisciplinary reflection has assumed prominence in all fields, San Diego State has taken a step backward by eliminating the one department in the university that specializes in interdisciplinary inquiry."

4. For cogent discussions of this issue of diversity and political correctness, see the editorial by George Will "Curdled Politics on Campus" (*Newsweek*, May 6, 1991, p. 72), the article "Taking Offense," (*Newsweek*, December 24, 1990, pp. 48-54), and the longer essay "Illiberal Education" by Dinesh D'Souza in the *Atlantic Monthly*, March, 1991, pp. 51-79.

5. I am not suggesting here that all who do not come from Christian Churches are unevangelized. There are thousands of Christians on campus from other churches.

6. From the article, "Reaching and Teaching the Abandoned Generation," by William H. Willamon, *Christian Century*, October 20, 1993, pp. 1016-1019.

7. *Ibid.*, p. 1018.

8. Unfortunately, Churches of Christ have not been so fortunate in this regard. Rick Rowland gives an extensive account of the divisive effect of "The Boston Church of Christ" cultic movement among their campus ministries. Their healthy campus ministries are still trying to recover from this movement. Rowland, *Campus Ministry*, pp. 144-190.

9. Typical of many campus ministers Dick Beswick, Campus Minister at Oregon State, expresses his frustration over this matter, "It seems to me that one continual weakness in our campus work has been our inability to attract and retain freshmen who come from high school groups in our own church tradition. It is like being yanked out of the wading pool and thrown in the deep end of the big pool for many of them. Years when I have had good interns we have been more successful in this regard." Campus ministries must take responsibility in this matter, but they cannot reach these students without the cooperation of both their parents and their home churches. See also Pam Painter, "Help College Students in Battle," *Christian Standard*, October 2, 1988, pp. 1, 4-5; Jean Cunningham, "A New Look at an Old Problem," *Christian Standard*, January 30, 1965.

10. Letter to author from Ward Patterson, January 23, 1993. Interestingly enough, Dr. Lewis Foster, long time honored professor at Cincinnati Bible Seminary, predicted in a private conversation with me in about 1973 that in his opinion campus ministry would become the most fruitful recruiting ground for ministers and missionaries.

11. "ENVOY," Emmanuel School of Religion, April, 1992, pp. 1, 3. I sent a questionnaire to all twenty-six of these students asking them what had influenced them to go to seminary. Eight replied, all of them had strong Christian influence while at college, and four of them were specifically influenced by campus ministries of the Christian Church.

12. Letter to author from David Fulks, October, 1992.

13. Knofel Staton, "Needed: A Christian Multipurpose Education," *Christian Standard*, January 5, 1975, p. 15.

14. Typical of the commitment many campus ministers and campus ministries have made to reaching international students for Christ is the work of Don and Jennifer Follis at the University of Illinois in Urbana. This story is recounted in chapter five, p. 120. A letter from Don Follis dated January, 1993, includes the following exciting paragraph: "I do think, however, that working with international students from our home here in the States is a tremendously cost-effective way to do missions. Having Chinese students hear the Gospel for the first time in my living room is quite exciting. Who would have thought, say even twenty years ago, that China would send so many students to the U.S. to study? There are now nearly 40,000 mainland Chinese students here in the U.S. They are the cream of the crop, naturally."

15. Letter to the author from Ziden Nutt, June 23, 1993.

16. *Christian Standard*, February 20, 1994, pp. 4-7.

17. Annual Report, Purdue Christian Campus House, 1993-94, pp. 2 and 8. Other campus ministries report the following costs per year: Georgia Tech — $650; University of Nebraska — $400; University of Western Kentucky — $400; all eight campus ministries in the state of Michigan — $1,000.

18. I have had a unique opportunity to compare students in campus ministry — sixteen years at Purdue University during which I taught Milligan College extension courses for nine years, and Bible college students — twelve years of teaching at Pacific Christian College. My judgment is that Bible college students do indeed spend more time in serious study of the Bible, but that students in campus ministry make up for this comparative lack of extended Bible study by their strong motivation and commitment.

19. See "Christian Colleges — A Suggested Solution to Inadequate Funding and Declining Enrollment" by Bill D. Claycomb, *Christian Standard*, January 22, 1989, pp. 8-10; and "Christian Colleges — Another Suggestion" by W. Ray Kelley, *Christian Standard*, March 26, 1989, pp. 11-12 for discussion of the problem in Christian Church colleges; and see "Will Bible Colleges Survive the 1990s?" in *Christianity Today*, September 16, 1991, pp. 22-28 for discussion of the problem in evangelical Bible colleges.

20. Several writers have called attention to this phenomenon. Among them Charles Garrison in *Forgotten Christians*, pp. 109-112; and John Derry writing in the *Christian Standard*, November 29, 1981, p. 7. I am indebted to both of these men as I write these sections.

21. Dr. William Richardson, retired professor from Emmanuel School of

Religion, has called to my attention that the church does not have to be perfect in order to be restored. In a letter to me dated April 9, 1994, Dr. Richardson writes:

Even short of being the "ideal church" a church may be said to possess the essential marks of the church as given by Christ. Note that Eph 4:1-6 describes a status already enjoyed by the church. (The restoration movement does not have a unique conception of the marks of the church; it simply appeals to the NT as the norm by which such matters should be measured.)

The restoration program, as I see it, is that the church be a fellowship possessing these marks — faith, sacrament, teaching, ministry, mission — as the *means* of growing toward the maturity Christ wills it to have ("the ideal" Eph 4:13-16). And the NT is the norm for measuring its obedience to the will of Christ. You will note that Paul appealed to this basic order in seeking to correct their misconduct.

22. "Restoration Movement on the Secular Campus" by John Derry in *Christian Standard*, November 29, 1981, p. 7.

23. Again the wisdom of this restoration principle was confirmed by my experience at Purdue. An ecumenical campus ministry on the campus, which had at least 10,000 potential student constituency in the combined denominations represented, hardly ever attracted more than 150 people to Sunday worship services, which were largely clergy dominated. Our Sunday worship services at the Christian campus house, in which music and worship were planned and presented by student teachers with the campus minister as advisor/consultant, and with about 1,000 student constituents on campus, routinely averaged 350–400 each Sunday.

24. "Campus Ministry Messenger," MCCM, September/October, 1989, p. 4.

# Appendix A
## Officers of the NACSF (NACCM) From 1963 to 1995

(Note: The following information has been compiled from several different sources. Information about the early days of the organization comes from minutes of the meetings and a brief history of the founding of the organization. From June 1967 to June 1971 a quarterly newsletter of the NACSF called "The Exchange" was published. Not all issues are available, but much of the following information from 1967 to 1971 came from the issues that are available. Other sources are: the files and memory of Dennis Steckley, Secretary-Treasurer of the NACSF from 1981-1984; the files and memory of Janice Schlieker, Secretary-Treasurer of the organization from 1987 to the present; and various issues of *The Directory of the Ministry*. Whatever inconsistency there may be is the author's responsibility.)

The Association developed from a series of meetings held during the summers of 1963, 1964, 1965, and 1966 at the Southport Heights Christian Church in Southport, Indiana. These meetings were initiated by Mr. Charles Garrison, campus minister at the University of Kentucky, for the purpose of an "exchange of ideas for an effective campus work." Those invited were "all persons who have in the past or hope in the future to work with college students, also any officers of college groups who would enter well into the spirit of the meeting. . . ."

1963-1964   Mr. Garrison served as Chairman of the informal sessions in 1963, and was selected as Chairman of the organization when it was formally organized in 1964.

1965   Chairman, Mr. Ed Bernard, Minister at Corbin, Kentucky
Secretary-Treasurer, Richard Drees, Ohio State University
(Charles Garrison was appointed Chairman of the Bylaws Committee at this meeting)

1966   Chairman, Stan Smith, Campus Minister at the University of Illinois
Vice-Chairman, David Lemons, University of Illinois
Secretary-Treasurer, Richard Drees, Ohio State University
(By-laws adopted at this meeting)

1967 ("The Exchange")
Chairman, Stan Smith, University of Illinois
Treasurer, Richard Drees, Ohio State University
Editor, Ed Bernard, "The Exchange"

1968 ("The Exchange")
President, Doug Dickey, Purdue University
Vice-President, Elwyn Miller, Michigan State University
Secretary-Treasurer, Charles Garrison, University of Kentucky
Editor, Ed Bernard, "The Exchange"

1969 ("The Exchange")
President, J. David Lang, Illinois State University
Vice-President, Roger Callahan, Challenge Unlimited, Cincinnati, OH
Secretary-Treasurer, Charles Garrison, University of Kentucky
Editor, J. David Lang, "The Exchange"

1970 ("The Exchange")
President, A. Dale Crain, Indiana State University
Vice-President, Gary Edwards, Ball State University, Muncie, IN
Secretary-Treasurer, Charles Garrison, University of Kentucky
Editor, J. David Lang, "The Exchange"

1971 ("The Exchange")
    President, Gary Edwards, Ball State University
    Vice-President, James Saunders, East Tennessee State University
    Secretary-Treasurer, A. Dale Crain, Indiana State University
    Editor, Jack Haun, "The Exchange"
1972 (Directory)
    President, Jack Haun, Indiana University
    Vice-President, Tom Smith, Challenge Unlimited, Cincinnati, OH
    Secretary-Treasurer, J. David Lang, Illinois State University
1972-1973 (Directory)
    The same officers are listed as in 1972. Either the information was not
    updated, or the same officers served for two years.
1973-1974    No information available
1974-1975    President, Jack Haun, Indiana University
    Vice-President, Roy Weece, University of Missouri
    Secretary-Treasurer, Judy Trotter, Standard Publishing, Cincinnati
1975-1976    President, Roger Thomas, University of Missouri, Rolla, MO
    Vice-President, Roy Weece, University of Missouri
    Secretary-Treasurer, Judy Trotter, Standard Publishing
1976-1977    President, Roy Weece, University of Missouri
    Vice-President, Tom Smith, Challenge Unlimited, Cincinnati, OH
    Second Vice-President, Clark Waggoner, Sapulpa, OK
1977-1978    President, Will Walls, Ball State University, Muncie, IN
    Vice-President, Clark Waggoner, Sapulpa, OK
    Second Vice-President, Roger Thomas, University of Missouri
    Secretary-Treasurer, Roger Callahan, Purdue University
1978-1979    President, Larry Brandon, University of Kentucky
    Vice-President, Bruce Montgomery, Bowling Green State University
    Secretary-Treasurer, Gary Hawes, Michigan Christian Campus Ministries, East
    Lansing, MI
1979-1980    President, Dave Walker, Miami University, Oxford, OH
    Vice-President, Dennis Steckley, West Virginia University
    Secretary-Treasurer, Gary Hawes, Michigan Christian Campus Ministries
1980-1981    President, Ron Simkins, University of Illinois
    Vice-President, Jim Bilbro, University of Missouri
    Secretary-Treasurer, Gary Hawes, Michigan Campus Ministries
1981-1982    President, Jim Bilbro, University of Missouri
    Vice-President, Gary Hawes, Michigan Campus Ministries
    Secretary-Treasurer, Dennis Steckley, West Virginia University
1982-1983    President, Don Follis, University of Illinois
    Vice-President, Peggy Clark, Purdue University
    Secretary-Treasurer, Dennis Steckley, West Virginia University
1983-1984    President, Peggy Clark, Purdue University
    Vice-President, Dave Embree, Southwest Missouri State University
    Secretary-Treasurer, Dennis Steckley, West Virginia University
1984-1985    President, Dave Embree, Southwest Missouri State University
    Vice-President, Tim Hudson, University of Georgia, Athens, GA
    Secretary-Treasurer, Roger Songer, Eastern Illinois University was appointed
    after the elected Secretary-Treasurer, Bryan Rowoth, University of Toledo was
    killed before taking office.
1985-1986    President, Tim Hudson, University of Georgia
    Vice-President, Tom Tucker, Northeastern Oklahoma State University
    Secretary-Treasurer, Roger Songer, Eastern Illinois University
1986-1987    President, Tom Tucker, Northeastern Oklahoma State University
    Vice-President, Mark Gallagher, Indiana State University & Rose Hulman
    Secretary-Treasurer, Roger Songer, Eastern Illinois University

1987-1988    President, Mark Gallagher, Indiana State University & Rose Hulman
Vice-President, John Thybault, Miami University, Oxford, OH
Secretary-Treasurer, Janice Schlieker, Colorado State University, Fort Collins

1988-1989    President, John Thybault, Miami University, Ohio
Vice-President, Mike Armstrong, University of Arkansas, Fayetteville
Secretary-Treasurer, Janice Schlieker, Colorado State University

1989-1990    President, Mike Armstrong, University of Arkansas
Vice-President, Steve Stovall, Western Kentucky University
Secretary-Treasurer, Janice Schlieker, Colorado State University

1990-1991    President, Steve Stovall, Western Kentucky University
Vice-President, Leland Duncan, Virginia Tech University
Secretary-Treasurer, Janice Schlieker, Colorado State University

1991-1992    President, Leland Duncan, Virginia Tech University
Vice-President, Andy Wade, Kent State University
Secretary-Treasurer, Janice Schlieker, Colorado State University

1992-1993    (Name of organization changed to National Association of Christian Campus Ministries)
President, Andy Wade, Kent State University
Vice-President, Scott Pixler, University of Nebraska, Lincoln
Secretary-Treasurer, Janice Schlieker, Colorado State University

1993-1994    President, Scott Pixler, University of Nebraska
Vice-President, Roger Songer, Eastern Illinois University
Secretary-Treasurer, Dave Rockey, Oklahoma State University

1994-1995    President, Roger Songer, Eastern Illinois University, Charleston
Vice-President, Roger Charley, Northwest Missouri State University, Maryville
Secretary-Treasurer, Dave Rockey, Oklahoma State University, Stillwater

# Appendix B
## Campus Minister's Retreats
## Sponsored by NACSF and NACCM 1968–1995

(Note: This information on campus minster's retreats which were sponsored by NACSF-NACCM has been compiled by reference to "The Exchange" (NACSF Quarterly Newsletter published from 1967 to 1971), and with information supplied by Dennis Steckly, NACSF Secretary-Treasurer from 1981 to 1984, and Janice Schlieker, NACSF-NACCM Secretary-Treasurer from 1987 to the present. Any inconsistencies are the responsibility of the author.)

| Date | Year | Location |
|------|------|----------|
| | 1968 | Lake Region Christian Assembly, Cedar Lake, IN<br>Guest Speaker: Dr. Elwyn Brown, Faculty, Indiana University |
| July 6-8 | 1969 | Met at North American Christian Convention, Cobo Hall, Detroit, MI<br>Guest Speakers: Pete Gillquist, Former Regional Director for Campus Crusade; Dr. Dudley Dennison, Cardiologist, Milligan College, TN |
| May 13-16 | 1970 | Turkey Run State Park, IN<br>Program: A. Dale Crain, and campus ministers |
| July 6-9 | 1971 | Met at NACC, Dallas<br>Guest Speakers: W.F. Lown, President, Manhattan Christian College; Jim Bevis, Campus Minister, Nashville, TN Church of Christ; Ed Erskine, Minister, Granger, IN |
| March 14-15 | 1972 | Pokagon State Park, Angola, IN<br>Program: Various campus ministers |
| March | 1973 | Merom Institute, Merom, IN<br>Program: Various campus ministers |
| Spring | 1974 | Shakertown, KY<br>Program: Various campus ministries |
| Spring | 1975 | Thompson House, Ladue Woods, St. Louis, MO<br>Guest Speaker: Fred P. Thompson Jr., President |
| March 25-27 | 1976 | Merom Institute, Merom, IN<br>Guest Speaker: John Alexander, President, InterVarsity, various workshops. Idea for student leadership conference began here. |
| March | 1977 | Lake Williamson Christian Center, Centralia, IL<br>Theme: Christian Community/ Alternative Lifestyles |
| May 18-20 | 1978 | St. Louis Christian College<br>Theme: Nature of Scripture<br>Speakers: J. Barton Payne; Roger Thomas, campus minister at Rolla, MO, editor of *The Gospel Goes to College*, a compilation of articles by twenty campus ministers. |
| May 17-19 | 1979 | Adrian College, Adrian, MI<br>Guest Speaker: Tom Mullen, Dean, Earlham College, Richmond, IN |
| May 8-10 | 1980 | Emmanuel School of Religion, Johnson City, TN<br>Guest Speaker: Beauford Bryant, Emmanuel School of Religion, Various workshops |
| May 11-16 | 1981 | Lincoln Christian Seminary, Lincoln, IL<br>Theme: A Challenge to Deeper Life<br>Speakers: Wayne Shaw, Bruce Shields, James Strauss |

| | | |
|---|---|---|
| May 19-21 | 1982 | Ozark Bible College<br>Theme: Campus Ministry and the Restoration Plea<br>Speakers: Paul Butler, Jim Girdwood, Doug Dickey, Seth Wilson;<br>Various workshops |
| May 18-20 | 1983 | McCormick's Creek State Park, Spencer, IN<br>Theme: Renewed in His Image: Redemption & Healing<br>Speakers: Ron Simkins, Elder, New Covenant Fellowship,<br>Urbana, IL |
| May 16-18 | 1984 | McCormick's Creek State Park<br>Theme: I Bless the Lord: A Practice of Worship<br>Speaker: Tom Smith, Elder, Fellowship Christian Church,<br>Cincinnati, OH |
| May 22-24 | 1985 | McCormick's Creek State Park<br>Theme: Sharpen Our Focus<br>Speakers: Roy Weece and various campus ministers |
| May 21-23 | 1986 | McCormick's Creek State Park<br>Theme: Encouraging One Another<br>Speaker: Boyce Mouton, Minister of First Christian Church, Carl<br>Junction, MO |
| May 20-23 | 1987 | McCormick's Creek State Park<br>Theme: Seasons of Refreshing<br>Speaker: Bob Yawberg, Minister, Broadway Christian Church,<br>Forth Wayne, TX<br>Worship Leader: John Elliott, Nashville, TN |
| May 18-20 | 1988 | McCormick's Creek State Park<br>Theme: Charged and Recharged<br>Speaker: Lee Turner, Former missionary to Pakistan<br>Worship Leader: John Elliott, Nashville, TN |
| May 17-19 | 1989 | McCormick's Creek State Park<br>Theme: Standing Before the Lord<br>Speaker: Dr. Garland Bare, M.D., Lincoln, NE |
| May 16-18 | 1990 | McCormick's Creek State Park<br>Theme: He Restores My Soul<br>Speaker: Don Finto, Belmont Church of Christ, Nashville<br>Worship Leader: John Elliott, Nashville, TN |
| May 15-17 | 1991 | McCormick's Creek State Park<br>Speaker: Roy Weece |
| May 20-22 | 1992 | McCormick's Creek State Park<br>Theme: Come Unto Me<br>Speaker: Larry Brandon, Former campus minister at the<br>University of Kentucky. Now hospital chaplain at Kokomo, IN. |
| May 26-27 | 1993 | McCormick's Creek State Park<br>Theme: "Grace is Sufficient"<br>Speaker: Dick Beswick, Campus minister, University of Oregon,<br>Eugene, OR |
| May 25-27 | 1994 | McCormick's Creek State Park<br>Theme: "Measuring Success"<br>Speaker: Doug Dickey, Pacific Christian College, Fullerton, CA |
| May 23-25 | 1995 | McCormick's Creek State Park<br>Theme and speaker to be announced |

# Appendix C
## Student Leadership Conferences
## Sponsored by NACSF-NACCM 1976–Present

The Leadership Conferences were the result of a discussion held among campus ministers at the retreat in the spring of 1976 at Merom Institute in Indiana. Realizing that the "central nervous system" of a healthy campus ministry is well-equipped student leaders, a week of student leadership training "for Restoration Movement campus ministry leaders from all over the United States" was planned for the Fall of 1976 at Washington University in St. Louis. Sixty students and campus ministers gathered for the first conference, and it was such a success it has been an annual event since.

| | |
|---|---|
| Fall, 1976 | Washington University, St. Louis, MO |
| | Program not available |
| August 7-12, 1977 | Washington University, St. Louis, MO |
| | Theme: The Character of a Christian Leader |
| | Worship leaders: Campus ministers from across the country |
| August 13-18, 1978 | St. Louis Christian College |
| | Program: Workshops led by campus ministers |
| August 12-17, 1979 | Cincinnati Bible Seminary |
| | Program: workshops, worship, classes |
| | Leaders: Roy Weece, Jack Cottrell, Doug Dickey, Marshall Hayden, and others |
| August 17-22, 1980 | Cincinnati Bible Seminary |
| | Program: workshops, worship, classes |
| | Leaders: various campus ministers |
| August 15-20, 1981 | Cincinnati Bible Seminary |
| | Theme: Grace: In Experience and Expression |
| | Program: workshops, worship, classes |
| | Leaders: various campus ministers |
| August, 1982 | St. Louis Christian College |
| | Program information not available |
| August 13-18, 1983 | Cincinnati Bible Seminary |
| | Theme: Reflecting His Image |
| | Program information not available |
| August 11-16, 1984 | Cincinnati Bible Seminary |
| | Theme: Seek First the Kingdom |
| | Program: workshops, worship, classes |
| | Leaders: Will Walls and other campus ministers |
| August 10-15, 1985 | Cincinnati Bible Seminary |
| | Theme: Missions: Not an Option |
| | Program: Workshops, worship, classes |
| | Leaders: Roy Weece and other campus ministers |
| August 9-14, 1986 | Cincinnati Bible Seminary |
| | Theme: Spiritual Discipline |
| | Program: workshops, worship, classes |
| | Leaders: Tom Smith, Bill Koontz, and other campus ministers |
| August 8-13, 1987 | Cincinnati Bible Seminary |
| | Theme: Pure Religion |
| | Program: workshops, worship, classes |
| | Guest Speaker: Knofel Staton, President, Pacific Christian College |

| | |
|---|---|
| August 6-11, 1988 | Cincinnati Bible Seminary |
| | Theme: Equipping the Saints |
| | Program: workshops, worship, classes |
| | Guest Speakers: John Caldwell, Minister, Kingsway Christian Church, Indiana; David Roadcup, Professor, Cincinnati Bible Seminary |
| August 5-10, 1989 | Cincinnati Bible Seminary |
| | Theme: Be Prepared: I Peter 3:15 |
| | Program: workshops, worship, classes |
| | Guest Speaker: Boyce Mouton, Minister, First Christian Church, Carl Junction, MO |
| August 4-9, 1990 | Washington University, St. Louis, MO |
| | Theme: Not by Might, Not by Power, But by God's Spirit: Zech. 4:6 |
| | Program: workshops, worship, classes |
| | Guest Speaker: Knofel Staton, President, Pacific Christian College |
| August 3-8, 1991 | St. Louis Christian College |
| | Theme: Complete Leadership: Called, Compassionate, Creative |
| | Program: workshops, worship, classes |
| | Guest Speaker: Allan Dunbar, Calgary, Alberta, Canada |
| August 8-13, 1992 | Cincinnati Bible College |
| | Theme: Called by God's Glory, Participating in His Holiness, Escaping the Delusion (2 Peter 1:3-4) |
| | Program: workshops, worship, classes |
| | Guest Speaker: Don Hinkle, San Jose, CA |
| August 7-12, 1993 | William Jewell College, Liberty, MO |
| | Theme: Treasures in Jars of Clay (2 Corinthians 4:7) |
| | Program: workshops, worship, classes |
| | Guest Speaker: Tommy Oaks, Knoxville, TN |
| August 6-10, 1994 | William Jewell College, Liberty, MO |
| | Theme: Truth or Trial |
| | Program: workshops, classes |
| 1st week, August, 1995 | William Jewell College |
| | Theme and speaker to be announced |

# Appendix D
## Suggestions to Help Churches Prepare Young People for College

In 1983, Mark Gallagher, campus minister at Indiana State University at Terre Haute, did some research to determine some of the reasons for the non-participation of students from Christian Churches in campus ministries. (Unpublished thesis at Lincoln Christian College, "Why Don't Our Kids Come to SCAMPS?" by Mark Gallagher, 1983).

In 1983 there were one hundred students at Indiana State University from Christian Churches, but only twenty of them became active in any way in campus ministry. Mark included the following suggestions to churches to help prepare the students for college. He recognizes that the campus ministry and the families of the students also have responsibilities in this area, but he suggests that the churches consider the following matters.

Those students who enjoy the strong support of their home congregations are more likely to become involved in the campus ministry. College students need to know that someone at home cares about them. Campus ministry begins long before the student enters college. Preparation begins as early as junior high school. College is a dangerous place for the under-prepared, and many young people simply become overwhelmed by their environment.

Churches have the responsibility, along with the campus ministries and parents, of getting their students involved in the campus houses and keeping them involved. Many churches have failed to take this responsibility seriously.

Students, whether they attend Bible college or the university, are in need of a ministry of encouragement. Care packages from the women's fellowship, visits and letters from Sunday School teachers and youth sponsors, opportunities to serve when visiting at home, as well as genuine concern of the home minister are effective expressions of caring to these students. Here are some further suggestions:

1. Actively support campus ministry. Include campus ministries in your area in your missions budget and make sure that your young people and their parents are informed about this matter.
2. Educate your people about campus ministry. Schedule outreach groups from the campus ministries to visit your church. Feature the campus houses on your mission bulletin board. Take your high school students to visit campus ministries. Use the campus ministries as resource people for revivals, retreats, seminars, and supply preaching.
3. Stress responsible discipleship with your young people, but don't wait until their senior year. From the earliest ages, stress the importance of faithfulness to Christ and remind them that college will be a time of testing for them.
4. Take an interest in the educational plans of all your young people, not just those who are going to Bible college. Determine where they are going to college, what their major will be, where they will live, and how you can help.
5. Help your students make connections with the campus houses where they plan to attend college. Take them to visit the ministry, introduce them to the campus minister, and make sure that the campus minister gets their name and addresses.
6. Continue to minister to your students after they go to college. Visit them, take them out to dinner with the campus minister, telephone them, write to them and send care packages. When they come home make it a point to notice them, see how they are doing, and give them opportunities to serve. Let them know that you care.

# Appendix E
## Currently Existing Campus Ministries

Several of the campus ministries listed could not be included in this book for several reasons. I regret the exclusion of these stories. The primary reason was that a deadline, already long delayed, had to be met, and there was no time to collect the necessary information to give these ministries adequate treatment. Perhaps some future edition of the history of campus ministry will be able to include them, along with others which will no doubt come into existence between now and then. The omitted campus ministries are marked here with an asterisk, with my personal apologies.

### ALABAMA

AUBURN UNIVERSITY
Auburn Christian Fellowship
Perry Rubin, CM
315 S. Gay Street
Auburn, AL 36830-7432
O   205-821-3963

### ARIZONA

ARIZONA STATE UNIVERSITY
Christian Campus Ministry
Dean Duest, CM
933 N. Lindsay Rd.
Mesa, AZ 85213
O   602-924-4946

UNIVERSITY OF ARIZONA*
John & Marcia Puckett, CM
1990 E. Prince Rd.
Tuscon, AZ 85719

### ARKANSAS

ARKANSAS STATE UNIVERSITY
Christ on Campus
Don Crockett, CM
P.O. Box 2133 SUA
Jonesboro, AR 72467
O   501-972-5428

UNIVERSITY OF ARKANSAS
Christ on Campus
Mike Armstrong, CM
520 N. Lindell
Fayetteville, AR 72701
O   501-521-8358
H   501-521-5310
Laurie Ostad Sims, Assoc. CM
H   501-442-3601

### CALIFORNIA

CAL STATE, FULLERTON
Campus Christian Fellowship
Doug Dickey, CM
2500 E. Nutwood Ave.
Fullerton, CA 92631
O   714-879-3901
H   714-774-5487

Roger Worsham, CM
EastSide Christian Church
2505 Yorba Linda Blvd.
Fullerton, CA 92634
O   714-871-6844

Don Hinkle
San Jose Christian College
790 S. 12th (Box 1090)
San Jose, CA 95108

### COLORADO

COLORADO STATE UNIVERSITY
Christian Student Fellowship
Janice & John Schlieker, CMs
1501 S. Whitcomb
Ft. Collins, CO 80521
O   303-482-0024
H   303-221-0024

MESA STATE COLLEGE
Christian Student Fellowship
Leland Griffin
621 1/2 Pioneer Rd.
Grand Junction, CO 80504
O   303-243-0702

UNIVERSITY OF COLORADO
Christian Student Fellowship
Jerry Gibson
270 W. Sutton Cir.
Lafayette, CO 80026
O & H   303-665-9640

UNIVERSITY OF NORTHERN COLORADO
Christian Student Fellowship
George Dosher, CM
924 20th Street
Greeley, CO 80631
O 303-351-0024
H 303-356-2356

**FLORIDA**

FLORIDA STATE UNIVERSITY
Christian Campus Fellowship
Mike Waers, CM
524 W. College Ave.
Tallahassee, FL 32301
O 904-224-1958
H 904-422-1100

FLORIDA ATLANTIC UNIVERSITY
FAUND Campus Ministries
1st Christian Church
Tim Benham, CM
700 NE 29th Place
Boca Raton, FL 33431
O 407-367-3510
H 407-395-1665

UNIVERSITY OF SOUTH FLORIDA*
Steve Trinkle
4100 S. Manhattan Ave.
Tampa, FL 33611

UNIVERSITY OF FLORIDA
Christian Campus House
CM
20 NW 12th Terrace
Gainesville, FL 32605
O 904-376-1682
H 904-378-5174

UNIVERSITY OF NORTH FLORIDA,
JACKSONVILLE U., FLORIDA COMMU-
NITY COLLEGE, JACKSONVILLE
Christian Campus Ministry
Tim Jones, CM
4316 Barnes Road
Jacksonville, FL 32201
O 904-733-2356
H 904-399-8870

**GEORGIA**

UNIVERSITY OF GEORGIA
Georgia Christian Campus Fellowship
Tim Hudson, CM
1080 S. Milledge Ave. (P.O. Box 609)
Athens, GA 30605
O 706-548-9625

H 706-546-5085
Angela Denton, Assoc. CM
H 706-549-9450

GEORGIA TECH
Georgia Tech Christian Campus Fellowship
Rick Harper, CM
767 Techwood Drive NW
Atlanta, GA 30313
O 404-872-3856
H 404-969-6243
Paul Zook, Assoc. CM
H 404-875-8794

WEST GEORGIA COLLEGE
West Georgia Christian Fellowship
Tony Crumbley, CM
PO Box 10041-WGC
Carrollton, GA 30118
O 706-834-0277
H 706-459-0143

**ILLINOIS**

LINCOLN CHRISTIAN SEMINARY
Dr. Paul Boatman
Box 178
Lincoln, IL 62656
O 217-732-3168
Steve Barmes
O 217-732-1302
H 217-732-7344

EASTERN ILLINOIS UNIVERSITY
Christian Campus House
Roger & Sue Songer, CM
PO Box 172
Charleston, IL 61920
O 217-345-6990
H 217-345-6776

ILLINOIS STATE UNIVERSITY
Jim Simkins, CM
300 Normal Ave.
Normal, IL 61761
O 309-452-2466
H 309-452-9536
Dan DeVilder, CM
H 309-452-2466

NORTHERN ILLINOIS UNIVERSITY
NIU Christian Campus Ministry
Scott & Shannon Stocking, CM
901 Lucinda
Dekalb, IL 60115
O 815-758-5941
H 815-758-4315

OLNEY CENTRAL COLLEGE*
Christian Campus House
400 Sam St.
Olney, IL 62450

SANGAMON STATE UNIVERSITY*
Christian Student Fellowship
Todd Magruder
2438 Ardmore
Springfield, IL 62702
O&H   217-753-4621

SOUTHERN ILLINOIS UNIVERSITY
Christian Campus Ministry
Donald Wooters, Director
302 N. Robinson Circle
Carbondale, IL 62901
O   618-457-7501
H   618-457-8796

SOUTHERN ILLINOIS UNIVERSITY-
EDWARDSVILLIE
Christian Student Fellowship
Tony Jackson, CM
4618 Wood Road
Bethalto, IL 62010
O   314-721-7178
H   314-327-8885

WESTERN ILLINOIS UNIVERSITY
Campus Students For Christ
Charles Ferguson, CM
1545 Riverview Dr.
Macomb, IL 61455
O   309-873-4787
H   217-357-6611
Shane Taylor, Assoc. Cm

UNIVERSITY OF ILLINOIS
Christian Campus Foundation
Dennis Durst, CM
810 W. Oregon St.
Urbana, IL 61801
O   217-344-5711
H   217-367-9334

Internal Outreach
Don Follis
1312 Philo Road
Urbana, IL 61801
H&O   217-367-8616

Ron Simkins
507 W Nevada
Urbana, IL 61801

**INDIANA**
BALL STATE UNIVERSITY
Christian Student Foundation
Willard J. Walls, CM

1411 W. Riverside Ave.
Muncie, IN 47303
O   317-289-7133
H   317-747-9711
Charles Gerber
H   317-289-1631
Matt & Joy Stafford
H   317-644-2670

INDIANA STATE UNIVERSITY
Christian Campus Ministry
Mark & Sue Gallagher, CM
601 N. 8th St.
Terre Haute, IN 47807
O   812-232-6853
H   812-466-4472

INDIANA UNIVERSITY
IU Campus Christian Ministry
Ritchie Hoffman, CM
707 E. 8th Street (Box 1456)
Bloomington, IN 47408
O   812-332-8972
H   812-876-7219
Tim Scott, CM
H   812-335-1327

PURDUE UNIVERSITY
Purdue Christian Campus House
Roger Callahan, CM
1000 State St.
West Lafayette, IN 47906
O   317-743-3612
H   317-423-1432
Rob Schrumpf, Assoc. CM
H   317-743-0304
Shirley Felix
H   317-589-3231

Peggy & Larry Brandon
214 N. Lincoln (PO Box 429)
Galveston, IN 46932
H   219-699-6119

TRI-STATE UNIVERSITY
Mike Hamm, CM
Tri-State Christian Fellowship
400 S. College St.
Angola, IN 46703
O   219-665-6771
H   219-665-3366

UNIVERSITY OF EVANSVILLE
UNIV. OF SOUTHERN INDIANA
Student Christian Fellowship
Mark & Beckey Whited, CM
PO Box 5163
Evansville, IN 47716
O   812-471-5927
H   812-477-7829

**VINCENNES UNIVERSITY**
Christian Campus Fellowship
Scott Shipman, CM
406 Harrison (PO Box 448)
Vincennes, IN 47591
O  812-882-1261
H  618-863-2796

**LIFELINE CHRISTIAN MISSION**
Ralph Lemmon
4425 W. 59th St.
Indianapolis, IN 46254
O  317-291-0872
H  317-291-4561

**NEW BRUNSWICK CHURCH OF CHRIST**
Ed Roark, Youth Minister
6480 S. St. Rd. 39
Lebanon, IN 46052

## IOWA

**UNIVERSITY OF IOWA**
Active Christians Today
Dennis Hall, CM
PO Box 70
Iowa City, IA 52244
O  319-354-6444
H  319-626-6454

**IOWA STATE UNIVERSITY**
ISU-Christian Fellowship
John Woodward, CM
Box 1038 ISU Station
Ames, IA 50010
O  515-294-5325 &  515-232-8617
H  515-232-1901
Dan Toney, Assoc. CM

## KANSAS

**KANSAS STATE UNIVERSITY\***
Christian Student Fellowhsip
OraLee Nischan, Coordinator
2109 Prairie Lea Pl.
Manhattan, KS 66502

**PITTSBURG STATE UNIVERSITY**
Campus Christian
Don Smith, CM
212 E. Williams
Pittsburg, KS 66762
O  316-232-9280
H  316-232-2543

**UNIVERSITY OF KANSAS**
Campus Christians

Jim Musser, CM
PO Box 1795
Lawrence, KS 66044
O  913-842-6592
H  913-749-0455
Lanny Maddux, CM to Internationals
402 E. 15th Place
913-749-2543

## KENTUCKY

**EASTERN KENTUCKY UNIVERSITY**
Christian Student Fellowship
Rob & Wanda Newman
1237 Poosey Ridge Road
Richmond, KY 40475
O  606-623-1592
H  606-328-3725

**MURRAY STATE UNIVERSITY**
Murray Christian Fellowship
Dean Ross, CM
1508 Chestnut St.
Murray, KY 42071
O  502-753-7356
H  502-753-6424

**NORTHERN KENTUCKY UNIVERSITY**
Christian Student Fellowship
Harold & Cindy Orndorff, CM
311 Johns Hill Road
Highland Heights, KY 41076
O&H  606-781-7134

**UNIVERSITY OF LOUISVILLE\***
Southeast Christian Church
Dave Stone, CM
2840 Hikes Lane
Louisville, KY 40218

**UNIVERSITY OF KENTUCKY**
Christian Student Fellowship
Lynn Buckles, CM
502 Columbia Avenue
Lexington, KY 40508
O  606-233-0313
H  606-272-9556
Rex Graham
H  606-271-2396

**WESTERN KENTUCKY UNIVERSITY**
Western Christian Student Fellowship
Steve & Teresa Stovall, CM
1654 Normal St.
Bowling Green, KY 42101
O  502-781-2188
H  502-781-7079

## MICHIGAN

CENTRAL MICHIGAN UNIVERSITY
His House Christian Fellowship
Matt Schantz, CM
1028 S. Main St.
Mt. Pleasant, MI 48858
O   517-772-0013
H   517-772-1917

FERRIS STATE COLLEGE
His House Christian Fellowship
Alan Bilinski, CM
526 S. Michigan
Big Rapids, MI 49307

LAKE SUPERIOR ST UNIV
His House Christian Fellowship
Steve North, CM
511 W. Easterday
Sault Ste. Marie, MI 498783
O   906-632-0126

MICHIGAN CHRISTIAN CAMPUS
MINISTRIES
Gary Hawes, Exec. Director
Sally Seisling, Admin. Asst.
917 Sever Drive
East Lansing, MI 48823
O   517-351-7844

MICHIGAN STATE UNIVERSITY
His House Christian Fellowship
Dean Trune, CM
4920 S. Hagadorn
East Lansing, MI 48823
O   517-351-8910

UNIVERSITY OF MICHIGAN
His House Christian Fellowship
John Sowash, CM
925 E. Ann St.
Ann Arbor, MI 48104
O   313-663-0483
H   313-231-9278

NORTHERN MICHIGAN UNIV
John Robernault, CM

WESTERN MICHIGAN UNIVERSITY
His House Christian Fellowship
John Thybault, CM
1010 Knollwood
Kalamazoo, MI 49007
O   616-382-6224
H   616-349-1497

Louis MM. Detro Memorial Library
Great Lakes Bible College
6211 W. Willow Hwy.
Lansing, MI 48917

## MINNESOTA

UNIVERSITY OF MINNESOTA
Christian Student Fellowship
David Burkum, CM
1515 Brook Ave., SE
Minneapolis, MN 55414
O   612-378-2657
H   612-789-5808

MANKATO STATE
Christian Student Fellowship
CM
PO Box 3361
Mankato, MN 56002-3361

## MISSOURI

CENTRAL MISSOURI STATE U.
Christian Campus House
Paul Burhart, CM
221 Broad St.
Warrensburg, MO 64093
O   816-747-8723
H   816-429-1170

MISSOURI SO. STATE COLLEGE
Koinonia Christian Campus Ministry
David Weaver, CM
Rt. 7 Box 947
Joplin, MO 64801
O   417-781-5683
H   417-623-3205
Phil Mehrens, Assoc. CM
H   417-782-5352

S.W. MISSOURI STATE U.
Christian Campus House
Dave & Joyce Embree, CM
622 E. Monroe
Springfield, MO 65806
O   417-862-8080
H   417-869-5004
Lora Hobbs, Assoc. CM
H   417-887-3473
Shannon McMurtrey
Tammy Melchien, Intern
H   417-886-2240

N.E. MISSOURI STATE U.
Campus Christian Fellowship
Joe Belzer, CM
1010 S. Halliburton
Kirksville, MO 63501
O   816-665-5772
H   816-665-7033

N.W. MISSOURI STATE U.
Christian Campus House
Roger Charley, CM
904 College Ave.
Maryville, MO 64468
O  816-582-7170
H  816-582-3789

UNIVERSITY OF MISSOURI, COLUMBIA
Christian Campus House
700 S. College Ave.
Columbia, MO 65201
O  314-442-6443
Roy Weece, CM
H  314-442-2900
Craig Thompson, CM
H  314-875-8968
Glenn Russel, CM
Randy Dolan
H  314-875-3823

UNIVERSITY OF MISSOURI, ROLLA
Christian Campus Ministry
Bob Humphrey, CM
607 State St.
Rolla, MO 65401
O  314-341-3567
H  314-341-2794

WASHINGTON UNIVERSITY
Christian Student Fellowship
Paul Patterson, CM
6649 University Dr. (PO Box 2940)
University City, MO 63130
O  314-721-7178

CENTRAL CHRISTIAN CHURCH
Rick Cole
1503 N. Leonrard Rd.
St. Joseph, MO 64506

**MONTANA**

MONTANA STATE UNIVERSITY
Campus Ministry
Mark Feasline, Steve Vick, CMS
362 W. Hulbert Rd.
Bozeman, MT 59715
O  406-388-6146

**NEBRASKA**

UNIVERSITY OF NEBRASKA, KEARNEY
Christian Student Fellwoship
Greg Swinney, CM

2310 14th Ave (PO Box 2424)
Kearney, NE 68848-2424
O  308-234-3922
H  308-234-1444
Lynette Thompson, Assoc. CM

UNIVERSITY OF NEBRASKA, LINCOLN
Christian Student Fellowship
Scott & Diana Pixler, CM
Capital City Christian Church
7800 Holdredge
Lincoln, NE 68508
O  402-464-0398
H  402-435-8796

Will Weber
621 Gercke
Norfolk, NE 68701

**NEW MEXICO**

EASTERN N.M. UNIVERSITY
Christian Campus House
Dean Overton, CM
223 South Avenue K
Portales, NM 88130
O  505-356-6292
H  505-359-0608
David Dale, Assoc. CM

**NEW YORK**

COLUMBIA UNIVERSITY*
Campus Christian Fellowship
Joe O'Neal, CM
PO Box 1971
New York, NY 10025

**NORTH CAROLINA**

EAST CAROLINA UNIVERSITY
Campus Christian Fellowship
Tim Turner, CM
PO Box 2613
Greenville, NC 27836
O  919-752-7199
H  919-830-5285

UNIVERSITY NORTH CAROLINA,
CHAPEL HILL
Campus Christian Fellowship
Frank Dodson, CM
PO Box 758
Chapel Hill, NC 27514
O  919-942-8952
H  919-968-1050

APPALACHIAN STATE UNIVERSITY
Campus Christian Fellowship
Rt. 3 Box 403
Boone, NC 28607

## OHIO

BOWLING GREEN STATE UNIV.
Active Christians Today
Dewey & Barbara Thackston
612 E. Wooster St.
Bowling Green, OH 43402
O  419-352-6486
H  419-893-2822

Challenge Unlimited
PO Box 19097
Cincinnati, OH 45219
O  513-281-2605

UNIVERSITY OF CINCINNATI
University Christian Fellowship
Dan Burton, CM
270 Calhoun M.L. #39
Cincinnati, OH 45221-0039
O  513-281-2640
H  513-281-2877

CINCINNATI CHRISTIAN SEMINARY
2700 Glenway Ave. (PO Box 043200)
Cincinnati, OH 45204
O  513-244-8120
Ward Patterson

KENT STATE UNIVERSITY
Christian Student Foundation
Andy & Debbie Wade, CM
PO Box 3221
Kent, OH 44240
O  216-673-9274
H  216-673-9261

MIAMI UNIVERSITY
Christian Student Fellowship
John Wineland, CM
16 E. Walnut
Oxford, OH 45056
O  513-523-3394

OHIO STATE UNIVERSITY
Student Christian Foundation
Scott Thompson, CM
82 E. Lane Ave.
Columbus, OH 43201
O  614-294-0347
H  614-888-5872

OHIO UNIVERSITY
Reach Out on Campus
Rich Teske, CM
PO Box 2613
Athens, OH 45701
O  614-592-1086
H  614-594-7728

Carolyn Davisson
48 E. Franklin
Nelsonville, OH 45764
H  614-753-1738

TEAM EXPANSION
Chris Bushnell,
Mobilization Coord.
PO Box 4100
Cincinnati, OH 45204-4100

UNIVERSITY OF TOLEDO
Active Christians Today
Brian & Kendra Mizer, CM
2018 Bretton Place
Toledo, OH 43606
O  419-537-1580
H  419-471-9638

WITTENBURG UNIVERSITY
Christopher DeTombe
914 N. Foundation
Springfield, OH 45504

FELLOWSHIP CHRISTIAN CHURCH
Tom Smith
10029 Spiritridge
Cincinnati, OH 45247

NORTH AMERICAN CHRISTIAN
CONVENTION
Rod Huron, Conv. Director
Box 11326
(4210 Bridgetown Rd.)
Cincinnati, OH 45211-0326

David McPherson
7915 Maple Leaf Dr.
Cincinnati, OH 45243-1938

## OKLAHOMA

NORTHEASTERN OK A&M
Collegiates for Christ
Lonnie Portenier, CM
PO Box 501
Miami, OK 74355
O  918-540-1474
H  918-540-1774

NORTHEASTERN STATE UNIVERSITY
Campus Christian Fellowship
Tom & Barbara Tucker, CM
Box 886
Tahlequah, OK 74465
O 918-456-1234
H 918-456-8230
Trish McAlpine-Whitney
H 918-458-0658

OKLAHOMA STATE UNIVERSITY
THE FELLOWSHIP OF CHRISTIAN
UNIVERSITY STUDENTS (FOCUS)
Dave & Vicki Rockey, CM
PO Box 682 (316 N. Husband)
Stillwater, OK 74076
O 405-624-9902
H 405-372-5942

UNIVERSITY OF OKLAHOMA
Christ on Campus
Don Riepe, CM
824 Elm
Norman, OK 73069
O 405-364-2703
H 405-794-2112

**OREGON**

UNIVERSITY OF OREGON
Restoration Campus Ministry
Dick Beswick
2880 University
Eugene, OR 97405
O 503-344-1523
H 503-726-5480

**PENNSYLVANIA**

Christian Student Foundation
PO Box 11082 (Parent Org.)
State College, PA 16805

BLOOMSBURG UNIVERSITY
Christian Student Fellowship
Jeff Jackson, CM
583 W. Main Street
Bloomsburg, PA 17815
O&H 717-387-0143

PENN STATE UNIVERSITY
Christian Student Fellowship
William "Buzz" Roberts, CM
205 Eisenhower Chapel
University Park, PA 16802
O 814-865-1562
H 814-359-2879

UNIVERSITY OF PITTSBURGH/
CARNEGIE-MELLON
Christian Student Fellowship
Sam Brunsvold
134 N. Dithridge Street
Pittsburgh, PA 15213
O 412-621-6760
H 412-362-2831

**SOUTH CAROLINA**

UNIVERSITY OF SOUTH CAROLINA*
Dutch Fork Christian Church
Box 97
Irmo, SC 29063

**TENNESSEE**

EAST TENNESSEE STATE UNIVERSITY
ETS Christian Student Fellowship
David Degler, CM
829 W. Pine St.
Johnson City, TN 37604
O 615-928-2870
H 615-743-9642

MILLIGAN COLLEGE
Tommy Oaks, CM
Rt. 8 Box 2680
Elizabethton, TN 37643
H 615-688-0708

UNIVERSITY OF TENNESSEE
Christian Student Fellowship
Sam Darden, CM
2001 Lake Ave.
Knoxville, TN 37916
O 615-523-7261
Doug Shupe
H 615-970-2158

EMMANUEL SCHOOL OF RELIGION
One Walker Drive
Johnson City, TN 37601
David J. Fulks
O 615-461-1535
H 615-929-0031
Dan Lawson
O 615-461-1531

John Elliott
PO Box 121474
Nashville, TN 37212
615-331-1322

**TEXAS**

DALLAS CHRISTIAN COLLEGE
David Morgan, Dean of Students
2700 Christian Parkway
Dallas, TX 75234

Campus Ministry
Fredereick L. Black
2125 S. Monroe
Amarillo, TX 79109

TEXAS WOMEN'S UNIVERSITY*
Denton Christian Church
PO Box 548
Denton, TX 76201

**VIRGINIA**

VIRGINIA TECH
Christ's Church at VA Tech
Leland Duncan, CM
PO Box 352
Blacksburg, VA 24063-0352
O   703-552-8292
H   703-951-3866

MOUNTAIN EMPIRE COLLEGE*
First Christian Church
Campus Minsitry
PO Box 645
Big Stone Gap, VA 24219

**WASHINGTON**

Steve & Annabelle Schertzinger
833 N.E. 170th
Seattle, WA 98155

**WEST VIRGINIA**

MARSHALL UNIVERSITY*
Campus Lite
Don Williams, CM
Norway Ave. Church of Christ
PO Box 5703
Huntington, WV 25703
O   304-696-3057
H   304-525-6922

WEST VIRGINIA UNIVERSITY
Christian Student Fellowship
Sandy Bigelow, CM
2903 University Ave.
Morgantown, WV 26505
O   304-599-4445
H   304-599-3113

**WISCONSIN**

UNIVERSITY OF WISCONSIN
Wisc. Christian Student Fellowship
Roger McMunn, CM
Koinonia House
111 N. Orchard St.
Madison, WI 53715
O   608-251-4151
H   608-274-1089

**CANADA**

UNIVERSITY OF CALGARY*
Warren Horricks
Bow Valley Christian Church
2816 11 St. NE
Calgary, Alberta, Canada T2E7S7
403-291-2221

**PHILIPPINES**

Philippines Campus Ministry
Scott McKinney
Baguio City, Philippines

# Bibliography

## BOOKS

Aeschilman, Michael D. *The Restitution Of Man: C.S. Lewis And The Case Against Scientism*. Grand Rapids: Eerdmans, 1983.

Allen, Diogenes. *Christian Belief In A Post-Modern World*. Louisville: Westminster/John Knox Press, 1989.

Beach, Waldo. *Conscience On Campus*. New York: Association Press, 1958.

Bloom, Allan. *The Closing Of The American Mind*. New York: Simon and Schuster, 1985.

Butler, Richard. *God On The Secular Campus*. Garden City, NY: Doubleday and Company, 1963.

Campolo, Tony and Bart. *Things We Wish We Had Said: Reflections Of A Father And His Grown Son*. Dallas: Word Publishing, 1989.

Clebsch, William A. *From Sacred To Profane In America: The Role Of Religion In American History*. New York: Harper and Row, 1968.

Davis, M. M. *How Disciples Began And Grew*. Cincinnati: Standard Publishing Co., 1915. (Revised, 1947)

Dickey, Douglas A. *What Else? Alternative To Christianity*. Cincinnati: Standard Publishing Co., 1978.

Dyrness, William A. *How Does America Hear The Gospel?* Grand Rapids: Eerdmans, 1989.

Earnshaw, George E. (Ed.) *The Campus Ministry*. Valley Forge, PA: Judson Press, 1964.

Ellwood, Robert S. Jr. *One Way: The Jesus Movement And Its Meaning*. NJ: Prentice-Hall, 1973.

Garrett, Leroy. *The Stone-Campbell Movement*. Joplin: College Press, 1985.

Garrison, Charles. *Forgotten Christians: A Guidebook For College-Career Work*. Joplin: College Press, 1967.

Garrison, W. E. and DeGroot, Alfred T. *The Disciples Of Christ: A History*. St. Louis: Bethany Press, 1948.

Gonzales, Justo L. *The Story Of Christianity, Vol. I*. San Francisco: Harper and Row, 1984.

Gresham, Perry Epler. *Campbell And The Colleges*. Nashville: Disciples of Christ Historical Society, 1973.

Groothuis, Douglas R. *Confronting The New Age*. Downers Grove, IL: InterVarsity Press, 1988.

Groothuis, Douglas R. *Unmasking The New Age*. Downers Grove, IL: InterVarsity Press, 1986.

Hammond, Phillip E. *The Campus Clergyman*. New York: Basic Books, 1966.

Kemp, Charles F. *Counseling With College Students*. Philadelphia: Fortress Press, 1964.

Latourette, Kenneth Scott. *A History of Christianity*. New York: Harper and Row, 1953.

Leggett, Marshall. *Introduction To The Restoration Ideal*. Cincinnati: Standard Publishing, 1986.

Malik, Charles Habib. *A Christian Critique Of The University*. Downers Grove, IL: InterVarsity Press, 1982.

McCormick, Thomas R. *Campus Ministry In the Coming Age*. St. Louis: CPB Press, 1987.

McCoy, Charles S. and McCarter, Neely D. *The Gospel On Campus*. Richmond, VA: John Knox Press, 1964.

McKenna, David L. *The Coming Great Awakening*. Downers Grove, IL: InterVarsity Press, 1990.

Moser, Charles A. (Ed.) *Continuity In Crisis: The University At Bay*. Washington, DC: University Professors For Academic Order, Inc., 1974.

Newbigin, Leslie. *Foolishness To The Greeks: The Gospel And Western Culture*. Grand Rapids: Eerdmans, 1968.

_____ . *The Gospel In A Pluralist Society*. Grand Rapids: Eerdmans, 1989.

Newman, John Henry Cardinal and Svoglic, Martin J. (Ed.) *The Idea Of A University*. San Francisco: Rinhart Press, 1960.

Rosenthal, M. L. (Ed.) *Selected Poems And Two Plays Of William Butler Yeats*. MacMillian Paperbacks, 1962.

Rowland, Rick. *Campus Ministries: A Historical Study Of Churches Of Christ Campus Ministries From 1706–1990*. Forth Worth: Star Bible Publications, 1991.

Schaeffer, Francis. *The New Super Spirituality*. Downers Grove, IL: InterVarsity Press, 1972.

Schumacher, E. F. *A Guide To The Perplexed*. New York: Harper and Row, 1977.

Shedd, Clarence P. *Two Centuries Of Student Christian Movements: Their Origin And Inter-Collegiate Life*. New York: Association Press, 1934.

Shockley, Donald G. *Campus Ministry: The Church Beyond Itself*. Louisville: Westminster/John Knox Press, 1989.

Smith, Huston. *Beyond The Post-Modern Mind*. New York: Crossroads, 1982.

Swinney, Greg (Ed.) *Taking Education Higher: A Guide Book To Ministry On The University Campus*. Kearney, NE: Lifechange Media, 1993.

Walsh, Brian J. and Middleton, J. Richard. *The Transforming Vision: Sharing A Christian World View*. Downers Grove, IL: InterVarsity Press, 1984.

Walsh, Chad. *Campus Gods On Trial*. New York: MacMillian Co., 1962.

Weedman, Gary. *Higher Education And The Restoration Movement*. Lincoln, IL: Lincoln Christian College Press, 1983.

Witmer, S. A. *The Bible College Story: Education With Dimension*. Manhasset, NY: Channel Press, 1959.

Young, Norvel M. *A History Of Colleges Established And Controlled By Members Of The Churches Of Christ*. Kansas City, MO: The Old Paths Book Club, 1949.

## UNPUBLISHED SOURCES

Baird, Harry R. "The Life Of E.C. Sanderson" (M.A. Thesis). IN: Butler University, 1957.

Bode, Erwin R. "The Future And Campus Ministry" (Article). IN: Indiana Office of Campus Ministry, 1981.

Clark, Robert Stanley. "Church, Student Movements, And Campus: An Overview Of Their Relationship During The Past Twenty-Five Years" (M.A. Thesis). Johnson City, TN: Emmanuel School of Religion, 1990.

_____ . "The University As A Forum For Faith: The Historical Context Of Campus Ministries And Student Movements" (paper submitted for a summer session in campus ministry). Johnson City, TN: Emmanuel School of Religion, 1987.

Degler, Dave. "Shaping The Future Of The Appalachian Christian Student Fellowship At East Tennessee State University" (M.Div. dissertation). Johnson City, TN: Emmanuel School of Religion, 1993.

Dickey, Douglas A. "Opportunities In Campus Ministry" (Workshop). Louisville: North American Christian Convention, July 13, 1989.

Embree, Dave. "A History Of Campus Ministry At Southwest Missouri State University" (paper written for a class by James North). Cincinnati: Cincinnati Bible Seminary, 1978.

Hall, Dennis. "Athletic Interest Ministry: A Culturally Viable Approach To Campus Ministry" (Paper). Lincoln, IL: Lincoln Christian College, 1991.

Leggett, Marshall J. "A Study Of The Historical Factors In The Rise Of The Bible College In The Restoration Movement" (M.A. Thesis). Indianapolis: Butler University, 1961.

Musser, James A. "Campus Ministry: Equipping Students For Leadership Among Christian Churches/Churches Of Christ" (M.Div. thesis). Johnson City, TN: Emmanuel School of Religion, 1983.

Phillips, Richard. "Enlightenment Impacts On The Nature Of The Church And Ministerial Education: A Mixed Blessing" (Address). Malibu, CA: Pepperdine University, July 1989.

Saunders, James Donovan. "Bridging The Church-University Gap: A Study Of The Potential Contribution Of Campus Ministry" (M.A. thesis). Johnson City, TN: Emmanuel School of Religion, 1969.

Smith, G. Stanley. "Campus Ministry: A Summary Of Statements Regarding The Christian Ministry At Secular Campuses." Champaign, IL: University of Illinois, 1967.

Thomas, Roger (Ed.) *The Gospel Goes To College: A Guide Book To Campus Ministry.* 1978.

Tiffin, Gerald C. "The Interaction Of The Bible College Movement And The Independent Disciples Of Christ Denomination." CA: Stanford University, 1969.

# PERIODICALS

Allison, B. G. "The American Campus As A Spiritual Force," *Christianity Today.* May 10, 1968.

Barrett, J. Edward. "Things Change In Thirty Years," *Theology Today.* July, 1984, pp. 183-187. (Focus on religious courses in the university)

Brown, Robert McAfee. "The Boundary Between Biblical Perspectives And Religious Studies," *NICM Journal.* Summer, 1981, pp. 69-82.

Chitwood, Bob. "For Campus Ministries And Christian Liberal Arts Schools: An Encouraging Word," *Christian Standard.* August 24, 1986, pp. 5-6.

Clark, Marybelle. "Will Pancakes Keep A Student Faithful?" *Christian Standard.* July 30, 1967.

Claycomb, Bill D. "Christian Colleges — A Suggested Solution To Inadequate Funding And Declining Enrollment," *Christian Standard.* January 22, 1989, pp. 8-10.

Cunningham, Jean. "A New Look At An Old Problem," *Christian Standard.* January 30, 1965, pp. 3-4.

Curtis, Dan B. and Curtis, Gary. "Guidelines For A Successful Campus Ministry," *Christian Standard.* September 24, 1989, pp. 1, 5-6.

Derry, John. "Restoration Movement On The Secular Campus," *Christian Standard.* November 29, 1981, p. 7.

Dickey, Douglas A. "Campus Ministry: Third Force In Christian Education," *Christian Standard.* June 8, 1975, pp. 7-8.

_____ . "Campus Ministry At Purdue: A Growing Ministry For Growing Christians," *Christian Standard.* September 23, 1973, p. 9.

_____ . "Telling It At Purdue," *Christian Standard.* April 30, 1972, pp. 7-8.

D'Souza, Dineah. "Illiberal Education," *The Atlantic Monthly.* March 1991, pp. 51-79.

Ferm, Dean William. "Reflections Of A College Chaplain," *Theology Today.* April 1976, pp. 53-60.

Follis, Don. "I'm Graduating From College — What Now?" and "I'm Heading To College — What Now?" *The Lookout.* June 4, 1989, pp. 6-7.

_____ . "Reaching International Students For Christ," *Christian Standard.* August 23, 1992, pp. 8-9.

Fuller, Elmer. "Let's Stop Losing The Youth," *Christian Standard.* April 28, 1991, pp. 12-14.

Gardner, Barbara M. "I Am Thankful For Campus Ministries," *Christian Standard.* September 2, 1990, pp. 5-6.

Gardner, Kara D. "Campus House — A Satisfied Customer," *Christian Standard.* September 2, 1990, p. 6.

Gardner, Lynn. "Campus Ministries Are Worthy Of Support," *Christian Standard.* September 2, 1990, pp. 4-5.

Garrison, Charles. "The Church Goes To College," *Christian Standard*. July 6, 1963, pp. 7-8.

Gordon, Ernest. "The Word And The Campus," *Christianity Today*. May 8, 1964.

Grant, Fern Babcock. "Seeking A Dynamic Student Christian Movement" (Interview by Parker Rossman), *Christian Century*. April 20, 1983, pp. 373-375.

Hauerwas, Stanley. "How Christian Universities Contribute To The Corruption of Youth: Church And University In A Confused Age," *Katallagete*. Summer, 1986.

Hawkins, Scott. "College Students And The Church *Can* Get Together," *Christianity Today*. March 2, 1984.

Huber, George. "The Church Faces A Never-Again Opportunity And Obligation To Serve On *The University Campus*," *Christian Standard*. August 18, 1962, pp. 3, 4, and 16.

_____ . "Need For A Campus Ministry," *Christian Standard*. January 14, 1964.

Hudson, Tim and Sheila. "Campus Ministry: The Challenge Ahead," *The Lookout*. June 4, 1989.

Johnson, Robert L. "What Is Campus Ministry?" *NICM Journal*. Fall, 1979, pp. 5-11.

Kelley, W. Ray. "Christian Colleges — Another Suggestion," *Christian Standard*. March 26, 1989.

Landry, Sabin P. Jr. "Christian Ministry To The Campus In Historical Perspective," *Review And Expositor*. Summer, 1973, pp. 30-32.

Lang, J. David. "Good News On The Campus Scene," *Christian Standard*. November 1, 1970, pp. 17-22.

_____ . "It Was Wow!" *The Lookout*. April 30, 1967.

Lawson, Dan R. "College Ministry In The Local Church," *Christian Standard*. July 4, 1982.

Marsden, George M. "Christian Schooling: Beyond The Multiversity." A review of *The Idea Of The University: A Reexamination*, by Jaroslav Pelikan, Yale University Press. *Christian Century*. October 7, 1992.

Nischan, Rich. "The University Campus Is White For Harvest," *Christian Standard*. August 24, 1986, pp. 1, 5.

Osborn, Ronald E. "The Irony Of The Twentieth-Century Christian Churches (Disciples of Christ): Making It To The Mainline Just At The Time Of Its Disestablishment," *Mid-Stream*. July, 1989.

Painter, Pam. "Help College Students In Battle," *Christian Standard*. October 2, 1988.

Patterson, Ward. "The Good Life Of A Campus Minister," *Christian Standard*. May 1, 1977.

Plog, Tom. "Respect For Campus Ministry," *Christian Standard*. May 31, 1992.

Puckett, Walter. "Why The Campus Ministry?" *Christian Standard*. September 19, 1971.

Ratzlaff, Paul. "Ecumenism, Restoration, And Campus Ministry," *Christian Standard*. August 17, 1975.

Ross, James Robert. "The Cross And The Gown: Christian Witness In The Secular University," *Mission*. April, 1972.

Ross, Robert. "Apologetics And The University," *Christian Standard*. August 2, 1981.

Root, David. "College-Career Convocation," *Christian Standard*. May 16, 1964.

Scanzoni, John. "No Faith To Lose," *Eternity*. December, 1965.

Schantz, Matt. "Campus Ministries Are Bringing: A Light In A Dark Place," *Christian Standard*. December 13, 1992.

Shaller, Lyle. "Campus Ministry: The Most Divisive Ministry Of The 70s," *Your Church*. July/August, 1970.

Shie, Kathy and Bob White. "Christians Do Attend Secular Colleges," *Christian Standard*. September 2, 1973, p. 10.

_____ . "The Christian Student On The Secular Campus," *Christian Standard*. September 9, 1973, pp. 8-9.

_____ . "The Home Church And Its College Students," *Christian Standard*. September 16, 1973, p. 4.

Shockley, Donald G. "Campus Ministry: A Contrarian Investment Strategy," *Christian Century*. October 23, 1985, pp. 951-953.

Snyder, J. W. "Presenting Christian Truth At The University Level," *Christianity Today*. February 16, 1968, pp. 9-12.

_____ . "Why Not A Christian College On A University Campus?" *Christianity Today*. February 17, 1967.

Staton, Knofel. "Christian Colleges — Which Kind?" *Christian Standard*. June, 1991.

_____ . "Needed: A Christian Multi-Purpose Education," *Christian Standard*. January 5, 1975.

Steckley, Dennis. "Effective Ministry On Campus," *Christian Standard*. March 18, 1984.

Stone, Sam. "Campus Ministries Fill Unique Place," *Christian Standard*. September 2, 1990.

Terry, Darrell. "Advance Into The Twentieth Century," *Christian Standard*. April 30, 1967.

_____ . "A Local Church College-Career Action Plan — For Such A Time As This," *Key Magazine*. Standard Publishing Co., October/November/December, 1967.

Thomas, Roger W. (Articles arranged chronologically by periodicals)
"Young Saints Look At The Church" (3 parts), *Christian Standard*. January 21, 28, and February 4, 1973.
"Fishing In Deep Water," *Christian Standard*. March 18, 1973, pp. 6-9.
"The Cross And The Slide Rule," *Christian Standard*. September 23, 1973, p. 5.
"How To Live With Your Spiritual Family," *Christian Standard*. October 28, 1973, pp. 9-10, and November 4, 1973, pp. 22-23.
"A Ministry Of Friendship," *Christian Standard*. November 11, 1973, pp. 13-14.

"Christian Education: Past and Present," *Christian Standard*. September 29, 1976, p. 4.

"An Idea Spreads," *Christian Standard*. January 19, 1977, pp. 9-10.

"Fellowship 77: No Longer Strangers," *Christian Standard*. April 24, 1977, pp. 5-6.

"Chicken Little Goes To College," *Christian Standard*. May 22, 1977, pp. 7-8.

"Remembering The Forgotten Christians," *Christian Standard*. September 18, 1977, pp. 9-10.

"The Whole Gospel For The Whole Man," *Christian Standard*. March 26, 1978.

"The God Question," *Christian Standard*. May 21, 1978, pp. 8-9.

"The Bible Question," *Christian Standard*. May 6, 1979, p. 13.

"Reflection: The Campus Still Needs Christ," *Christian Standard*. March 16, 1979, pp. 15-16.

"The New Revolution," *Lookout*. July 13, 1975, p. 2.

"A People Ministry," *Lookout*. April 11, 1976, pp. 3, 16.

"News of CCH," *Lookout*. May 16, 1976, p. 13.

"They Came To Learn ... And Left To Lead," *Lookout*. October 24, 1976, pp. 8-9.

"Future Unlimited," *Lookout*. June 5, 1977, pp. 5-6.

"The Campus For Christ Now!" *Lookout*. August 21, 1977, pp. 8-9.

"Satan Proofing Our Youth," *Lookout*. April 16, 1978, p. 16.

"Changing Tomorrow's World Today," *Lookout*. April 1, 1979, pp. 3-4.

"Your Youth Ministry," *Lookout*. April 27, 1980, pp. 6-7.

"Taking A Land Of Promise," *Restoration Herald*. January, 1973, pp. 6-8, 17.

"A Blueprint For Action," *Restoration Herald*. September, 1978, pp. 8-10.

"Caution: College Ahead," *Straight*. June 3, 1973, pp. 6-7.

"Caution: College Ahead," *Key To Christian Education*. Summer, 1977, pp. 37-38.

"Summer Survival Guide," *His*. June, 1984, p. 26.

Toland, Lewis. "Share Christ On The State Campus," *Christian Standard*. January 23, 1977.

Troutman, Charles H. "What's Wrong With Campus Ministries?" *Christianity Today*. February 16, 1968, pp. 12-14.

Walls, Willard. "The University Student And The World Evangelism," *Christian Standard*. February 14, 1982.

Weece, Roy. (Articles arranged chronologically)

"If A House Could Talk," *Christian Standard*. September 10, 1972.

"Developing Christians," *Christian Standard*. September 23, 1973.

"Packing For College," *Christian Standard*. December 19, 26, 1976.

"Personal Evangelism," *Christian Standard*. December 3, 1978.

"Conversation Openers," *Christian Standard*. December 10, 1979.

"The Strangers," *Christian Standard*. March 4, 1984.

"A Busy Body," *Christian Standard*. June 10, 1984.

"A Healthy Body," *Christian Standard*. September 9, 1984.

"Manna And Money," *Christian Standard*. December 9, 1984.

"Jesus Voted Yes!" *Christian Standard*. July 26, 1987.

"The Devil Can't Make Me Do It," *Christian Standard*. November 6, 1988.

"Gifts and Gifted," *Christian Standard*. March 31, 1991.

"What Are You Doing With *His* Money?" *Christian Standard*. June 30, 1991.

"God's Grace Family," *Christian Standard*. September 29, 1991.

"Planned Poverty," *Christian Standard*. December 29, 1991.

Will, George. "Curdled Politics On Campus," *Newsweek*. May, 1991.

Willamon, William. "Reaching And Teaching The Abandoned Generation," *Christian Century*. October 20, 1993.

Wilson, John F. "A Biblical Basis For The Campus Ministry" (Reprint, no date), *Campus Journal*.

Wooters, Donald J. "I'll Come If..," *Christian Standard*. March 22, 1987.

## MISCELLANEOUS SOURCES

Campbell, Alexander. "Baccalaureate Address," *Millennial Harbinger*. 1852.

_____. "Bacon College," *Millennial Harbinger*. 1837.

_____. "Education," *Millennial Harbinger*. 1837.

_____. *Millennial Harbinger*. 1850.

_____. "Knowledge Indispensable To Religion," *Millennial Harbinger*. 1841.

Gallup, George Jr. "The Search For Faith On Campus" (Interview by Robert L. Johnson), *National Institute For Campus Ministries, Associates Newsletter*. Winter, 1981.

Hargrove, Earl C "Bible-Centered Education A Must" (Address before 14th annual meeting of the Accrediting Association of Bible Colleges), Chicago: October 27, 1960.

Hawthorne, John W., Roberts, Michael K., and Davidson, James D. "Campus Ministry in Indiana: 1980" (A report of the Indiana Office of Campus Ministry — 10th), May, 1981.

Hordern, William. "The College Students And Religion: The Seeking Generation," *The Episcopalian*. (Date not available)

_____. "When A Christian Goes To College," *The Episcopalian*. (Date not available)

Marty, Martin E. "The Milieu Of Campus Ministry: Higher Education Center For The Study Of Campus Ministry," *Yearbook IV*. Valparaiso, IN: 1981, pp. 55-64.

Wycliff, Don. "A Critic Of Academia Wins Applause On Campus" (Education Section), *New York Times*. September 12, 1990.

_____. "Crisis On Campus: Why Does Spiritual Unrest Haunt The Universities?" *Christianity Today*. September 2, 1966.

_____. "Will Bible Colleges Survive The 90s?" *Christianity Today*. September 16, 1991.

## FUND RAISING SOURCES

Emswiler, Tom Neufer. *Money: For Your Campus Ministry, Church, Or Other Non-Profit Organization – How To Get It*. Normal, IL: The Wesley Foundation, 1981.

Piguet, Leo A. (Ed.) *Fund Raising: A Primer For Campus Ministries*. National Institute For Campus Ministries, Inc., 1976.